Handbook on the Working of Ministry of Parliamentary Affairs

About the Editor

V.K. Agnihotri, an IAS officer of 1968 batch, belong to the Andhra Pradesh Cadre of the service. Born on 25 August, 1945, he obtained his Masters degrees in English Literature and Political Science from the University of Allahabad, Allahabad. He has obtained his Ph.D. in Public Policy Analysis and Design from the Indian Institute of Technology, Delhi. He has been a Visiting Fellow at the Queen Elizabeth House, University of Oxford, in 1991-92.

Among several responsible positions with the State and Central Governments, Dr. Agnihotri has held posts of Collector of Visakhapatnam District, Director of Handlooms and Textiles, Government of Andhra Pradesh and Development Commissioner for Handlooms (Ministry of Textiles), Government of India. He has been the Joint Director at the Lal Bahadur Shastri National Academy of Administration, Mussoorie, and Additional Secretary to Government of India in the Department of Administrative Reforms and Public Grievances. Currently he is Secretary to Government of India in the Ministry of Parliamentary Affairs.

His areas of specialisation are Public Policy, Good Governance, Administrative Reforms, e-Governance, Rural and Cottage Industries, Panchayati Raj, Primary Education and Parliamentary Systems and Procedures.

He has several publications to his credit including books entitled *Environment and Development, Skills for Effective Administrators, Public Policy Analysis and Design, Dimensions of the New Economic Policy, Socio-Economic Profile of Rural India, Effective and Responsive Administration, Department of Administrative Reforms and Public Grievances: Through the Ages, Manual of the Department of Administrative Reforms and Public Grievances*, and *Quality Management in Government: Theory and Practice.*

Handbook on the Working
of
Ministry of Parliamentary Affairs

Conceptualised and Edited by
Dr. V.K. Agnihotri
Secretary
Ministry of Parliamentary Affairs

CONCEPT PUBLISHING COMPANY, NEW DELHI-110059
July 2004

Cataloging in Publication Data—DK
Courtesy: D.K. Agencies (P) Ltd. <docinfo@dkagencies.com>

Handbook on the working of Ministry of Parliamentary Affairs / conceptualised and edited by V.K. Agnihotri.
p. cm.
Includes bibliographical references (p. 177-178)
Includes index.
ISBN 8180691942

1. India. Ministry of Parliamentary Affairs.—Rules and practice—Handbooks, manuals, etc. 2. Parliamentary practice—India—Handbooks, manuals, etc. I. Agnihotri, V. K. (Vivek Kumar), 1945-

328.54 21

ISBN 81-8069-194-2 (HB)
ISBN 81-8069-195-0 (PB)

First Published 2004

Published and Printed by
Ashok Kumar Mittal
Concept Publishing Company
A/15-16, Commercial Block, Mohan Garden
New Delhi-110059 (India)
Phones: 25351460, 25351794
Fax: 091-11-25357103
E-mail: publishing@conceptpub.com

संसदीय कार्य तथा
शहरी विकास मंत्री
भारत सरकार
नई दिल्ली-110 001

सत्यमेव जयते

Minister of
Parliamentary Affairs and
Urban Development
Government of India
New Delhi-110 001

गुलाम नबी आज़ाद

Ghulam Nabi Azad

Message

I am happy to learn that the Ministry of Parliamentary Affairs is bringing out, for the first time, a Handbook containing, in detail, the procedure followed for transaction of various functions allotted to it, important decisions/precedents relevant thereto, sample of various communications used, etc. This Handbook is meant to guide the officials of the Ministry in discharging their duties and responsibilities effciently and effectively.

The Ministry has already brought out, in March 2004, a Statistical Handbook containing, in analytical form, certain significant statistical data and information relating to important business transacted by the Parliament. The Statistical Handbook, which has also been placed on the website of the Ministry, has been widely appreciated and has proved of immense usefulness to all concerned as a reference material in regard to the parliamentary work. I understand that the proposed Handbook will compliment the Statistical Handbook and will be of great help to the officials of the Ministry, particularly the new entrants.

I am sure this publication will inspire other Ministries/Departments of Government of India to bring out similar handbooks to demystify their procedures and systems.

(GHULAM NABI AZAD)

New Delhi: June 23, 2004.

सुरेश पचौरी
Suresh Pachouri

सत्यमेव जयते

राज्य मंत्री
संसदीय कार्य मंत्रालय
भारत सरकार
नई दिल्ली-110 011
Minister of State for
Parliamentary Affairs
Government of India
New Delhi-110 011

Dated: 24th June, 04

Message

Procedures and Practices play an important role in the functioning of the Parliamentary system of governance. I am happy to learn that the Ministry of Parliamentary Affairs is bringing out a Handbook containing the procedures and practices followed for transacting the business allotted to this Ministry for the first time. I hope the Handbook will prove immensely useful to the officials in efficient discharge of their duties. I wish the venture a success.

(Suresh Pachouri)

सत्यमेव जयते

बिजय कृष्णा हांडिक
Bijoy Krishna Handique

राज्य मंत्री
रक्षा एवं संसदीय कार्य
भारत सरकार
नई दिल्ली-110 011
Minister of State for
Defence & Parliamentary
Affairs
Government of India
New Delhi-110 011

Message

It is heartening to know that the Ministry of Parliamentary Affairs is bringing out a Handbook on the functions allotted to the Ministry. I hope that this publication, which the Ministry is bringing out for the first time, will be of great use to the officials of the Ministry in transacting their business speedily and effectively. I compliment the Ministry for this laudable initiative and extend my sincere wishes for the success of this new venture.

(B.K. Handique)

New Delhi. July 3, 2004

श्रीमती सूर्यकांता पाटील

Smt. Suryakanta Patil

सत्यमेव जयते

Minister of State for
Rural Development and
Parliamentary Affairs,
Government of India,
Krishi Bhavan, New Delhi-110 001
Krishi Bhavan
Tel.: 23782211, 23782063
Fax: 23782328
Parliament House
Telefax: 23010895, 23011824,
23034638

Message

I am pleased to learn that the Ministry of Parliamentary Affairs is bringing out the second part of the Handbook of the Ministry containing, in detail, the procedures to be followed for transaction of various functions allotted to the Ministry. Bringing out a publication of this nature is a commendable achievement on the part of the Ministry and I compliment them for the efforts put in for this purpose. There is no doubt that this new publication will prove a valuable source of information for all the officials of the Ministry, particularly the new entrants. I wish the endeavour all success.

(Smt. Suryakanta Patil)

New Delhi. July 3, 2004

PREFACE

Life is an unending journey of discovery, but it need not necessarily be so while handling one's official business. A carefully documented procedural manual of all the main processes managed by an organisation could eliminate the element of surprise and uncertainty which one encounters when inducted into a new organisation or when there is a change of assignment in the same organisation.

All organisations, particularly government organisations, are understandably very busy managing the work allocated to them. In the course of this daily grind it is difficult to find time to look at the administration of various processes from the outside or to reflect internally on them. However, if certain critical processes have to be managed well and their quality has to be guaranteed in all situations, irrespective of the personnel entrusted with the tasks, a modicum of documentation is absolutely essential. As a matter of fact, process documentation is the first step in the journey of quality assurance leading to ISO quality certification.

The Ministry of Parliamentary Affairs handles several key processes relating to the management of government business in Parliament and issues pertaining to the welfare of Members of Parliament, among others. In the nature of things, these processes entail a zero-defect approach. The Handbook of the Ministry of Parliamentary Affairs has been designed with this end in view. The chapters in this book were identified in the context of the work allocated to the Ministry in the Government of India (Allocation of Business) Rules, 1961 (as amended up to 12/1/2004). The broad framework of each chapter comprises explaining the concerned task through a background note, listing out various components of the process and documenting the policy decisions taken from time to time with regard to that process. At the core of these chapters is a set of samples provided as annexes, which will facilitate speedy and efficient implementation of the processes. In most cases, a check list too has been included in order to achieve the objective of zero-defect.

The preparation of this Handbook, spread over several months on account of pressure of routine work during the Parliament sessions, has been a journey of introspection and self-discovery for all of us involved in this unique and exciting project. All the officials and staff members associated with the preparation of this Handbook have really looked within and taken time off to look at the processes from the outside in order to document, in the minutest of details, different aspects and dimensions of every process. I would, in particular, like to put on record my deep and abiding appreciation of the wholehearted commitment of Shri K.K. Thakur, Deputy Secretary to the project. Without his faith in the outcome of the project, it would have been a non-starter. He has been by far the key contributor to the text of the Handbook. My thanks are also due to all the other main contributors to the Handbook, namely, Shri Dhani Ram, Deputy Secretary; Smt. Santosh Prabha, Under Secretary; Shri Bhoj Raj, Under Secretary; Shri M. S. Chopra, Under Secretary; Smt. Rewa Rani, Under Secretary; Shri Joseph Zacharias, Section Officer; Smt. Suman Bara, Section Officer; Smt. Manorama Bhardwaj, Hindi Officer; and Shri P. Bepari, UDC. They all did an excellent job of developing the material and providing the inputs, beyond the call of normal duty. In the fitness of things, Shri P. Gopalakrishnan, Joint Secretary, a recent entrant to the family of the Ministry of Parliamentary Affairs, put together the chapter on 'Ushering in a New Lok Sabha', which was not part of the original scheme of the Handbook. I am also grateful to all other officers and staff members of the Ministry of Parliamentary Affairs, who contributed to the preparation of this Handbook in different ways.

I am also grateful to the Minister of Parliamentary Affairs and the Ministers of State in our Ministry, who have greatly appreciated and encouraged the preparation of this document. I am sure, this Handbook will serve as a beacon light for all those organisations in government which have to manage critical and specific processes within an inviolable time frame. I look forward to receiving valuable suggestions for further improvement of this pioneering initiative.

New Delhi
June 20, 2004

V.K. Agnihotri
Secretary
Ministry of Parliamentary Affairs

CONTENTS

ABBREVIATIONS

A&P	:	Accounts and Purchase
ATR	:	Action Taken Report
AC	:	Air Conditioning
AIWC	:	All Indian Whips' Conference
BAC	:	Business Advisory Committee
CGEIS	:	Central Government Employees Insurance Scheme
CCPA	:	Cabinet Committee on Parliamentary Affairs
CGHS	:	Central Government Health Scheme
CEA	:	Children's Educational Allowance
CC	:	Consultative Committee
CGA	:	Committee on Government Assurances
DA	:	Dearness Allowance
DCRG	:	Death-*cum*-Retirement Gratuity
DTC	:	Delhi Transport Corporation
D.O.	:	Demi Official
Deptt.	:	Department
GPF	:	General Provident Fund
GSR	:	General Statutory Rule
HMPA	:	Hon'ble Minister of Parliamentary Affairs
ISO	:	International Organisation for Standardisation
IFA	:	Internal Financial Adviser
IFD	:	Internal Finance Division
ICPS	:	Institute of Constitutional and Parliamentary Studies
JC	:	Joint Committee
JPC	:	Joint Parliamentary Committee
JE	:	Junior Engineer
LTC	:	Leave Travel Concession
LDC	:	Lower Division Clerk
LS	:	Lok Sabha
LSR	:	Rules of Procedure and Conduct of Business in Lok Sabha
LS Sectt.	:	Lok Sabha Secretariat
ME	:	Members' Emolument
MP	:	Member of Parliament

MPA	:	Ministry of Parliamentary Affairs
MOS	:	Minister of State
MOS(BH)	:	Minister of State for Defence and Parliamentary Affairs (Shri B.K. Handique)
MOS(SK)	:	Minister of State for Rural Development and Parliamentary Affairs (Smt. Suryakanta Patil)
MOS(SP)	:	Minister of State for Personnel, Public Grievances & Pensions and Parliamentary Affairs (Shri Suresh Pachouri)
NCT	:	National Capital Territory
NDMC	:	New Delhi Municipal Committee
OM	:	Office Memorandum
O&M	:	Organisation and Methods
OBC	:	Other Backward Classes
OTA	:	Over Time Allowance
OSD	:	Officer on Special Duty
PMO	:	Prime Minister's Office
PSU	:	Public Sector Undertaking
PSI	:	Permanent Special Invitee
RS	:	Rajya Sabha
RSR	:	Rules of Procedure and Conduct of Business in the Council of States
RS Sectt.	:	Rajya Sabha Secretariat
SC	:	Select Committee
SCs	:	Scheduled Castes
SD	:	Directions by Lok Sabha Speaker
STs	:	Scheduled Tribes
SO	:	Statutory Order
SOR	:	Statement of Objects and Reasons
TA	:	Travelling Allowance
UO	:	Unofficial
UDC	:	Upper Division Clerk
UT	:	Union Territory

1

THE GENESIS, EVOLUTION AND STRUCTURE OF THE MINISTRY

Coordinating Agency in Parliamentary Democracy

In a parliamentary democracy, parliamentary work constitutes one of the important preoccupations of the government. The day-to-day working of the system makes large claims on the time and resources of the various administrative departments of the government. Though, at any given time, the Houses of Parliament may be concerned with a single legislative proposal or an issue of Government policy or the performance of a department in charge of an individual minister, the total parliamentary programme, over a period of time, covers numerous intricate issues (financial, legislative and non-legislative) concerning various Ministries/Departments of the Government. In order that this enormous and diverse parliamentary work may be handled efficiently on behalf of the Government in the Houses of Parliament, it is necessary to have a coordinating agency between Parliament and the Government as a whole. In India, this task is presently assigned to a full-fledged Ministry, known as the Ministry of Parliamentary Affairs in charge of a Cabinet Minister.

Genesis of the Ministry of Parliamentary Affairs

Before the Indian Independence Act, 1947 came into operation, the Secretary of the Ministry of Law, who used to be a nominated member of the Legislative Assembly, assisted the Leader of the House in the Central Legislative Assembly. The Legislative Department of the Government of India, *inter alia*, served as the coordinating agency between the Central Legislative Assembly and the entire Executive Wing of the Government.

With the establishment of a popular and responsible Government on the passing of the Indian Independence Act, 1947, the Law Secretary ceased to be a member of the Assembly and functions of coordination devolved on the Government Chief Whip, who was, on the analogy of the practice obtaining in the House of Commons, appointed Secretary to the Leader of the Assembly. The functions assigned to him were:

(1) to arrange Government Business before the House;
(2) to maintain liaison between the Hon'ble Ministers and the other Members of the House in relation to official and non-official business before the Legislature;
(3) to maintain contact with the Hon'ble Speaker and the Legislative Assembly Department in relation to Government Business;
(4) to arrange priority for Government Business in consultation with the Hon'ble Ministers concerned and the Ministry of Law;
(5) during the non-session period, to attend to arrangements connected with the holding of meetings of the various Select Committees in consultation with the Legislative Assembly Department and the Ministries concerned; and
(6) generally, to act under the directions of the Hon'ble Leader.

On a realistic appraisal of the importance of the office of the Government Chief Whip, he was given the rank of a Minister of State from 14 December, 1948. Keeping in view the onerous functions assigned to the Government Chief Whip, and taking note of the fact that his counterpart in the U.K. had been provided with a separate staff and organisation to assist him, a small organisation, with a nucleus staff was created on 26 January, 1949 in the Ministry of Law to assist the Government Chief Whip in discharge of his functions. This office was designed to serve as a Secretariat to the Government Chief Whip. This arrangement was intended to be purely temporary till a separate full-fledged Department of Parliamentary Affairs, with the Government Chief Whip (designated as Minister of Parliamentary Affairs) as the administrative head of the Department, was formed on 16 May, 1949 by a Government Notification **(Annex I-A).**

Functions

When the Department of Parliamentary Affairs was created in the year 1949, its functions mainly consisted of:

(i) efficient and smooth running of the parliamentary machinery;
(ii) mapping out the time of the session and providing details of the Government's programme of business;
(iii) to extract from the proceedings of the House, assurances, promises and undertakings given by Ministers on the floor of the House and to watch and report to the House the progress of action taken on these assurances from time to time;
(iv) co-ordination of the activities of the Standing Committees attached to various Ministries; and
(v) to act as an instrument of co-ordination effecting liaison between the various sections which come in contact with Parliament, such as between Ministers and the House, between the Speaker and the Members, and between the individual Members of the House.

On 3 April, 1952, when the Upper House (Rajya Sabha) was constituted, the Department of Parliamentary Affairs was made responsible for all the above functions in respect of that House as well.

With the passage of time, the functions of the Department of Parliamentary Affairs went on expanding. These functions in the year 1950 consisted mainly of the following:

(i) providing secretarial assistance to the Parliamentary and Legal Affairs Committee of the Cabinet;
(ii) liaison with the Speaker/Chairman and Parliament Secretariats;
(iii) liaison with Ministries/Departments of the Government of India;
(iv) discharge of responsibilities towards the Prime Minister as the Leader of the House; and
(v) liaison with the Members of Parliament.

The functions of the Ministry expanded in 1954 when, on recommendations of the Ministry of Law, the work relating to subjects under entry 73 of the Union List, namely "Salaries and Allowances of MPs and Officers of Parliament", was transferred to the Ministry. Informal Consultative Committees consisting of Members of Parliament attached to various Ministries/ Departments were formed in the same year and the functions regarding the constitution and working of these Informal Consultative Committees devolved on the Ministry of Parliamentary Affairs. Later, in 1959, Informal Consultative Committees for the various Zonal Railways were also constituted and work relating to the constitution and working of these too was assigned to this Ministry. The nomenclature of Informal Consultative Committees was changed on 20 June, 1969 and these Committees were designated as Consultative Committees which provided a forum for Members of Parliament to have free and frank discussion with the Minister in charge as well as officials of the concerned Ministries regarding their policies, programmes and activities.

In 1956, the Ministry was allotted the following functions:

(i) fixation of dates of summoning and prorogation of the two Houses of Parliament;

(ii) timely preparation of the programme and business for the session through co-ordination of legislative proposals emanating from various Ministries;

(iii) laying down priorities and order of Government Business for each House from day to day;

(iv) determination of the House in which Bills, other than Money Bills, should originate and the timing and stages of their consideration (including reference of Bills to Select/Joint Committees);

(v) broad allocation of time between Legislative and non-Legislative Business;

(vi) implementation of assurances given by Ministers in Parliament;

(vii) determination of Government stand on recommendations made by Parliamentary Committees in their reports;

(viii) to advise Ministries on procedural matters and on state of business in the House; and

(ix) to maintain informal contact with Leaders of Opposition/groups and to ascertain their views on allocation of time for various discussions and to render assistance to individual Members interested in discussions on specific problems of public importance.

As on 1 March, 1973, the functions of the Ministry, allocated by the President under article 77(3) of the Constitution, were as follows:

(1) Dates of summoning and prorogation of the two Houses of Parliament, dissolution of Lok Sabha, President's address to Parliament.
(2) Planning and co-ordination of Legislative and other official business in both Houses.
(3) Allocation of Government time in Parliament for discussion on motions given notice of by Members.
(4) Liaison with Leaders of groups and Deputy Chief Whips.
(5) Lists of Members of Parliament on committees and other bodies set up by the Government.
(6) Appointment of Members of Parliament on committees and other bodies set up by the Government.
(7) Functioning of Consultative Committees of Members of Parliament for various Ministries.
(8) Implementation of assurances given by Ministers in Parliament.
(9) Government's stand on Private Members' Bills and Resolutions.
(10) Secretarial assistance to the Cabinet Committee on Parliamentary Affairs.
(11) The Salaries and Allowances of Members of Parliament Act.
(12) The Salaries and Allowances of the Officers of Parliament Act.
(13) Advice to Ministries on procedural and other parliamentary matters.
(14) Coordination of action by Ministries on the recommendations of general application made by Parliamentary Committees.
(15) Officially sponsored visits of Members of Parliament to places of interest.

(16) Matters connected with powers, privileges and immunities of Members of Parliament.

In 1976, the Ministry was made responsible for the work relating to the Manual for Handling Parliamentary Work in Ministries/Departments. This work was transferred from the Department of Personnel and Administrative Reforms.

For the first time, the offices of the Leader of Opposition in the Lok Sabha and the Rajya Sabha were created on 1 November, 1977 by an Act of Parliament and the work relating to the salary and allowances of the Leaders of the Opposition in Parliament was assigned to this Ministry.

In December, 1985, the following two Items were added to the list of functions allotted to this Ministry, after entry 16 thereof:

(17) The Salary and Allowances of Leaders of Opposition in Parliament Act, 1977 (33 of 1977).
(18) Parliamentary Secretaries - functions.

In 1990, a scheme comprising a National Youth Parliament Competition for Kendriya Vidyalayas and the Nehru Parliamentary Quiz Contest was launched by the Ministry.

On 23 September, 1992, determination of policy and follow-up action in regard to matters relating to Zero Hour became part of the functions allotted to this Ministry.

Training courses in Parliamentary procedure and practices for officers of State Governments were initiated by the Ministry in 1994.

Thus in January, 1997, the following items of work were allocated to the Ministry by adding them after entry 18 as under:

(19) Organisation of Youth Parliament Competitions in Schools/Colleges throughout the country.
(20) Organisation of All India Whips' Conference.
(21) Determination of policy and follow-up action in regard to matters raised under Rule 377 of the Rules of Procedure and Conduct of Business in Lok Sabha and by way of Special Mentions in the Rajya Sabha.
(22) Manual for Handling Parliamentary Work in Ministries/Departments.

In 1997, a scheme for National Youth Parliament Competition for Jawahar Navodaya Vidyalayas as well as Universities/ Colleges was launched by the Ministry. In 1999, the Leaders and Chief Whips of Recognised Parties and Groups in Parliament (Facilities) Act, 1998 was passed. The functions of the Ministry at present, as per the Government of India (Allocation of Business) Rules, 1961 (Notification dated 6 January, 2004) are as at **Annex I-B.**

Nomenclature of the Department

The Department of Parliamentary Affairs was re-designated as the Ministry of Parliamentary Affairs in 1985 by a notification dated 4 January, 1985 amending the Government of India (Allocation of Business) Rules, 1961.

On reorganisation of the various Ministries/Departments on 25 September, 1985, the Ministry of Parliamentary Affairs was redesignated as the Ministry of Parliamentary Affairs and Tourism with two Departments (i) Department of Parliamentary Affairs; and (ii) Department of Tourism.

On 12 May, 1986, the Ministry of Parliamentary Affairs and Tourism was bifurcated into two separate Ministries under the Presidential Motification to the Government of India (Allocation of Business) Rules, 1961, namely, Ministry of Parliamentary Affairs and Ministry of Tourism. Since 12 May, 1986, it has been a separate Ministry of the Government of India.

Cabinet Committee on Parliamentary Affairs (CCPA)

With the creation of a bicameral Parliament consisting of several representatives of the people, it was deemed desirable that the Cabinet should delegate the overall responsibility regarding detailed parliamentary matters to a small standing committee of the Cabinet, specialising in this task. A Parliamentary and Legal Affairs Committee was accordingly constituted in 1949. This committee was subsequently named as the Cabinet Committee on Parliamentary Affairs (CCPA). The Department of Parliamentary Affairs has been providing the Secretarial assistance to this committee since 1954, before which it was provided by the Ministry of Law. (Even during the period 1949 to 1954, the Department of Parliamentary Affairs used to render secretarial assistance to the committee in regard to planning of Government Business in both Houses of Parliament.)

As on 1 March, 1973, this committee consisted of the following members:

(i) Minister of Defence (Chairman),
(ii) Minister of Law, Justice and Company Affairs,
(iii) Minister of Parliamentary Affairs,
(iv) Minister of State for Parliamentary Affairs,

Ministers other than those mentioned above, who are concerned with the subject matter under discussion with the committee, are also invited to attend meetings when necessary. Functions allocated to the Committee and its present composition can be seen at **Annex I-C.**

Administrative Structure

In the year 1950, the Department consisted of a Secretary of the rank of Under Secretary to the Government of India, 16 other officers and staff. The budget estimate for the Department for the year 1950-51 was Rs. 90,000 only. The Department grew steadily and in the year 1956, the administrative machinery consisted of one Secretary of the rank of Deputy Secretary to the Government of India and 42 other officers and staff and the budget estimate for 1956-57 was Rs. 1,48,000. In the year 1972-73, the Department consisted of a Secretary of the rank of Joint Secretary to the Government of India, two Deputy Secretaries, three Under Secretaries and 137 other officers and staff. The budget estimate for 1972-73 was Rs. 12,18,000, the revised estimate being Rs. 12,34,000.

In the year 2004-05, the Ministry of Parliamentary Affairs consists of a Secretary of the rank of Secretary to Government of India, a Joint Secretary, three Deputy Secretaries and six Under Secretaries, with a total sanctioned staff strength of 129 (August, 2004). The budget (non-plan) for the Ministry stood at Rs. 5.89 crore (BE 2004-05). The Organisational Structure of Ministry is at **Annex I-D.** The details of sections along with their staff strength and the work allocated to them is at **Annex I-E.** The details of decentralisation of powers in respect of cases in each section of the Ministry of Parliamentary Affairs are provided in **Annex I-F.**

Thus, from a small cell with a nucleus staff to help the

Government Chief Whip in Parliament, the Department of Parliamentary Affairs has gradually grown into a full-fledged Ministry of the Government of India, under the charge of a Cabinet Minister, assisted by two to five Ministers of State serving as a vital link between Parliament and the Government as a whole.

Status of the Secretary

The post of Secretary, Ministry of Parliamentary Affairs, was equivalent to that of an Under Secretary to the Government of India up to 26 November, 1952. It was made equivalent to the status of a Deputy Secretary to the Government of India up to 28, November, 1963 and upgraded to the status of a Joint Secretary to the Government of India with effect from 29 Novermber, 1963. It was upgraded to the status of an Additional Secretary to the Government of India with effect from 3 June, 1980. It was again upgraded to the status of a Secretary to the Government of India with effect from 18 February, 1984, but as personal to the then incumbent Shri Ishwari Prasad (a member of the Indian Administrative Service) up to 29 February, 1988 and Shri B.N. Dhoundiyal (a member of the Indian Administrative Service) up to 12 July, 1990. With effect from 13 July, 1990, the post of Secretary of the Ministry was upgraded to the status of a Secretary to the Government of India on a regular basis. The list of Secretaries of this Ministry is at **Annex I-G.**

Status of the Minister of Parliamentary Affairs

In the year 1948, the Government Chief Whip was given the rank of a Minister of State in the Council of Ministers and designated as the Minister of Parliamentary Affairs. In 1962, the Minister of Parliamentary Affairs was given the rank of a Cabinet Minister. In the year 1966, the Minister of Parliamentary Affairs was appointed the Leader of the House in the Lok Sabha and the Minister of State, in-charge of Parliamentary Affairs, was made the Government Chief Whip. (At that time, the Prime Minister was a Member of the Rajya Sabha). In March, 1967, however, the Prime Minister on her election to the Lok Sabha became the Leaders of the House and the Minister of Parliamentary Affairs was made the Government Chief Whip. (During a brief interval from February 1969 to June 1970, the

Minister of Parliamentary Affairs had the status of a Minister of State. From June 1970 onwards, he has held the rank of a Cabinet Minister.)

In the year 1952, as a result of enlargement of duties of the Minister of Parliamentary Affairs with the emergence of the two Houses of Parliament, two Government Deputy Chief Whips were appointed to assist him in the performance of his parliamentary duties, one for the Lok Sabha and the other for the Rajya Sabha. The Government Deputy Chief Whips enjoyed the privileges and the amenities available to Parliamentary Secretaries from 1954 to 1968, when they were given the status of Deputy Ministers. In 1962, the strength of the Government Deputy Chief Whips was raised to three, two in the Lok Sabha and one in the Rajya Sabha. In addition, a Member of the Rajya Sabha was appointed as Government Whip in charge of the Informal Consultative Committees. In April, 1966, the Government Whip in charge of the Informal Consultative Committees was also designated as the Government Deputy Chief Whip. After the fourth general election in 1967, the Department had one Cabinet Minister, one Minister of State and two Deputy Ministers. In addition, there was one Government Deputy Chief Whip in charge of the Informal Consultative Committees. Subsequently, in the place of Deputy Ministers, three Government Deputy Chief Whips were appointed, two for the Lok Sabha and one for the Rajya Sabha, in addition to one Government Deputy Chief Whip in charge of the Informal Consultative Committees. One more Government Deputy Chief Whip was later appointed in April, 1969 to look after the work relating to implementation of Government Assurances given by Ministers on the floors of the Houses. With effect from 1 April, 1968, the status of the Government Deputy Chief Whips was raised to that of a Deputy Minister in the Government of India (with a marginal difference in pay).

At present, the Minister of Parliamentary Affairs is assisted by a Minister of State in the Rajya Sabha and two Ministers of State in the Lok Sabha. A list of Ministers, Ministers of State and Deputy Ministers, who have held charge of the Ministry of Parliamentary Affairs is at **Annex I-H.** The allocation of work among the Ministers is at **Annex I-I.**

2

Ushering in a New Lok Sabha

On the constitution of a new Lok Sabha, there are certain actions which are required to be taken by the Ministry of Parliamentary Affairs. These are discussed below.

Appointment and Swearing in of Speaker *pro tem*

As per the second proviso to article 94 of the Constitution, the office of the Speaker becomes vacant immediately before the first meeting of the new Lok Sabha. In that case, the duties of the Speaker are to be performed by a Member of the House appointed for this purpose by the President as Speaker *pro tem.* Similarly, as per article 99 of the Constitution, every Member of the House shall, before taking his seat, make and subscribe before the President or some person appointed in that behalf by him, an oath or affirmation according to the form set out for the purpose in the Third Schedule of the Constitution. For this purpose, normally three other elected Members of the Lok Sabha, before whom the other Members may make or subscribe the oath/ affirmation, are also appointed by the President. Normally, the seniormost Members (in terms of number of years of membership of the House) are generally chosen for the purpose, even though there have been exceptions to this practice.

As soon as the new Government is formed, the Legislative I Section prepares a list of the seniormost Lok Sabha Members. The list will indicate their seniority in terms of their tenure in the Lok Sabha as well as in the Rajya Sabha. The list prepared after the constitution of the XIV Lok Sabha is at **Annex II-A.** The list is then submitted to the Minister of Parliamentary Affairs/ Prime Minister for identifying a Member as Speaker *pro tem* and another three members as persons before any of whom the other Members may make or subscribe the oath/affirmation

(Annex II-B). After the approval of the Prime Minister, the consent of these Members is obtained by the Minister of Parliamentary Affairs, generally over the telephone. Thereafter, the Minister submits a note to the President **(Annex II-C)** seeking his approval to the appointment of the Speaker *pro tem* and the other three Members and also seeking the convenience of the President to the date and time of the swearing in ceremony. During the XIV Lok Sabha, the Member of Parliament proposed to be appointed as the Speaker *pro tem* was also to be subsequently proposed for election as Speaker. Under the circumstances, a question arose as to whether two Speakers *pro tem* are to be appointed in order to have a different Speaker *pro tem* in the Chair at the time of election of the Speaker. This was examined in consultation with the Department of Legal Affairs **(Annex II-D)** and it was decided to have two *pro tem* Speakers. The draft order, duly vetted by the Legislative Department, regarding appointment of two *pro tem* Speakers to be issued by the President is at **Annex II-E.**

After approval of the President, the Ministry informs the Speaker *pro tem* and other Members regarding their appointment **(Annex II-F).** The Lok Sabha Secretariat is also informed through a UO Note forwarding the original orders signed by the President **(Annex II-G).**

The President administers the oath to the Speaker *pro tem* in the Rashtrapati Bhawan. The other three Members appointed by the President to assist him in administering the oath/ affirmation are administered the oath/affirmation by the Speaker *pro tem* in the Lok Sabha. The Speaker *pro tem* then administers the oath / affirmation to the newly elected Members with the help of the three persons so appointed by the President. Since the session of the Lok Sabha starts at 11.00 a.m., the time generally fixed for swearing in of the Speaker *pro tem* is in the morning of the same day at 9.30 a.m, subject to the convenience of the President. A copy of the minute to minute programme of the swearing in of the Speaker *pro tem* of the XIV Lok Sabha is at **Annex II-H.**

The arrangements for the swearing in of the Speaker *pro tem* are made by the President's Secretariat and invitations are also issued by that Secretariat. By convention, they have been inviting the Vice President, the Prime Minister, the Minister of

Parliamentary Affairs, and the Ministers of State of the Ministry of Parliamentary Affairs, the Secretary-Generals of the Lok Sabha and Rajya Sabha and Secretary of the Ministry of Parliamentary Affairs. If any other senior officer of the Ministry of Parliamentary Affairs is required to be present in the function, prior intimation has to be given to the office of the Military Secretary to the President.

By convention, the Minister of Parliamentary Affairs accompanied by the Secretary, Ministry of Parliamentary Affairs, assembles at the residence of the Speaker *pro tem* designate half an hour before the time fixed for the swearing in and accompanies the Speaker *pro tem* designate to the Rashtrapati Bhavan. The Minister also presents a bouquet to the Speaker *pro tem* designate. (This has to be arranged in advance by the P&W Section.) The car for the Speaker *pro tem* designate is arranged by the Lok Sabha Secretariat. The Minister also calls on the Speaker *pro tem* in his chamber after the swearing in and, if he so desires, he and the other Ministers of State for Parliamentary Affairs too may present bouquets to the Speaker *pro tem* in his chamber. (The Minister's office has to check this and arrange the bouquets, if required.)

Date and Time for Commencement of the First Session, President's Address and Election of the Speaker

Immediately after the formation of the Council of Ministers, a Note for the Cabinet is required to be prepared, seeking approval of the Cabinet on the following points:

- date of commencement of the First Session of the Lok Sabha and its duration;
- date of commencement of the next Session of the Rajya Sabha and its duration;
- date of holding of election of the Speaker; and
- date and time of delivery of the President's address to both Houses assembled together in the Central Hall of Parliament.

In case the new Lok Sabha is constituted in the early months of a financial year and the Parliament had earlier only approved a Vote on Account, then the question of having a Budget Session along with the First Session of the Lok Sabha will also have to be examined. Normally, only a short session is first convened to administer the oath/affirmation, election of the Speaker, President's address, etc. and the Budget Session is summoned subsequently.

After obtaining the approval of the Cabinet to the above proposals, the Minister of Parliamentary Affairs submits a note to the President for obtaining his approval to the Cabinet decisions on points at Sr. Nos. (i), (ii) and (iv) **(Annex II-I).** After the President's approval, the decisions with regard to the above are communicated to the two Secretariats of Parliament, which issue summons to the Members.

Consideration of the Confidence Motion

If the President directs the Prime Minister to obtain the Vote of Confidence, a draft motion proposed to be moved by the Prime Minister in the Lower House is sent to the Prime Minister's Office to enable him to sign the same and send it to the Secretary General, Lok Sabha. (During the XIV Lok Sabha, Government had the majority and a Confidence Motion was not required.) However, the communication sent to the Prime Minister's Office during 1998 along with the format of Confidence Motion are at **Annexes II-J & II-K.**

Appointment of the Leader of the Lok Sabha

In case the Prime Minister is not a Member of either House or is a Member of the Upper House, the Minister of Parliamentary Affairs requests the Prime Minister to nominate a Minister who is a Member of the Lok Sabha to function as Leader of that House. After obtaining approval of the Prime Minister, the Minister of Parliamentary Affairs informs the Speaker accordingly. Communication sent to the Lok Sabha in this regard is at **Annex II-L.**

Appointment of the Leader of the Rajya Sabha

In case the Prime Minister is not a Member of either House or is a Member of the Lok Sabha, the Minister of Parliamentary Affairs requests the Prime Minister to nominate a Minister who is a Member of the Rajya Sabha to function as Leader of that House. After obtaining approval of the Prime Minister, the

Minister of Parliamentary Affairs informs the Chairman, Rajya Sabha accordingly. Communication sent to the Rajya Sabha in this regard is at **Annex II-M.**

President's Address to Parliament

Once the decision of the Cabinet and President is obtained regarding the date and time of the President's address to Parliament and communicated to the Lok Sabha Secretariat, the Ministry of Parliamentary Affairs does not have any specific role to play regarding the President's address. However, when the President arrives in Parliament House, he is received by the Minister of Parliamentary Affairs also. The President is received at Gate No. 5 by the following VIPs in the order mentioned below:

1. Chairman, Rajya Sabha,
2. Prime Minister,
3. Speaker, Lok Sabha,
4. Minister of Parliamentary Affairs,
5. Secretary-General, Rajya Sabha, and
6. Secretary-General, Lok Sabha.

These VIPs have to reach the Gate in the reverse order of priority. Thus, the Secretary-Generals of the Lok Sabha and the Rajya Sabha have to reach first and others thereafter. The Minister of Parliamentary Affairs presents bouquets to the President and the VIPs at Sl. Nos. 1 to 3.

A procession is formed to take the President from Gate No.5 to the Central Hall. The procession comprises those who have received the President at Gate No. 5 as well as the Secretary to the President and certain other members of the staff from the President's Office.

Once the President's address is delivered, a copy thereof is laid on the Table of both Houses by the Secretary-Generals concerned. Thereafter, the ruling party moves a Motion of Thanks to the President's address in the Lok Sabha as well as in the Rajya Sabha, which has to be proposed and seconded by two Members of the ruling alliance. Copies of the formats for the Motion of Thanks are at **Annexes II-N & II-O.**

Election of the Speaker

Once the date for the election of the Speaker has been approved by the President and notified by the Lok Sabha Secretariat, any member may give notice in writing, addressed to the Secretary-General, of a motion that another Member be chosen as the Speaker of the House. This has to seconded by a third Member and has to be submitted before noon on the day preceding the date of election. The format of motion for election of the Speaker, Lok Sabha is at **Annex II-P.** The motion for the ruling party alliance is generally arranged by the Office of the Minister of Parliamentary Affairs, as per his directions.

Appointment of Leaders of the Opposition in the Lok Sabha and Rajya Sabha and allotment of Rooms in Parliament House

The Chairman of the Rajya Sabha and the Speaker of the Lok Sabha recognise the Leaders of the Opposition in the Rajya Sabha and in the Lok Sabha respectively as per provisions made in Section 2 of the Salary and Allowances of Leaders of Opposition in Parliament Act, 1977. Pursuant to this, the Ministry of Parliamentary Affairs notifies in the Gazette of India about the recognition of the Leaders of the Opposition in the Lok Sabha and the Rajya Sabha. Similarly, the Ministry also issues another Notification regarding the derecognition of the Leader of Opposition in either House of Parliament, whenever the Leader of Opposition demits the office. (Specimen copies of the Notifications issued in this regard are at **Annexes II-Q to T).**

The Ministry of Parliamentary Affairs also allocates rooms for the Leaders of the Opposition in the Parliament House. By convention, room numbers 43 and 44 on the Ground Floor of the Parliament House are allotted to the Leaders of the Opposition by the Ministry of Parliamentary Affairs **(Annex II-U).**

Allotment of Seats to MPs in Lok Sabha / Rajya Sabha

The allotment of seats in the Lok Sabha/Rajya Sabha to the Members of Parliament is a function of the concerned Secretariat. Normally, no seating arrangement is made in the Lok Sabha till the election of the Speaker. Blocks of seats are allotted to each party and the Minister of Parliamentary Affairs can make suggestions to the Lok Sabha/Rajya Sabha Secretariats in respect of the block to be allotted to the ruling party alliance.

3

SUMMONING AND PROROGATION OF BOTH HOUSES OF PARLIAMENT AND DISSOLUTION OF LOK SABHA

BACKGROUND

Summoning

Article 85(1) of the Constitution empowers the President to summon each House of Parliament to meet at such time and place as he thinks fit, but six months shall not intervene between its last sitting in one Session and the date appointed for its first sitting in the next Session. [Notwithstanding outer limit laid down in article 85, the Parliament may have to be called before 31 March in order to pass at least a Vote on Account to carry on the administration as no money can be withdrawn from the Consolidated Fund of India except under appropriation made by law passed in accordance with article 114(3). Besides, articles 352(4 &8), article 356(3) and article 360(2)(c) lay down certain time limits for summoning the Houses of Parliament.] The President exercises the power to summon the Houses on the recommendation of the Prime Minister or the Cabinet.

Normally, three Sessions, namely the Budget, Monsoon and Winter Sessions, are held in a calendar year. The question of having more or less fixed dates for the commencement of the three Sessions was considered by the General Purpose Committee of the Lok Sabha at their sitting held on 22 April, 1955, and they recommended the following time-table for the three Sessions:

Session	Date of Commencement	Date of Termination
Budget Session	1 February	7 May
Autumn Session	15 July	15 September
Winter Session	5 Novembr or the fourth day after Diwali, whichever is later	22 December

The Cabinet agreed with these recommendations. The above time-table has not, however, been observed in practice. Sessions have commenced on different dates though more or less in the specified months, and the duration has varied according to the volume of business conducted by the Houses*.

Rule 33 of the Rules of Procedure and Conduct of Business in Lok Sabha provides that 'unless the Speaker otherwise directs, not less than ten and not more than twenty-one clear days' notice of a question shall be given.' Rule 39 of the Rules of Procedure and Conduct of Business in the Rajya Sabha provides that 'unless the Chairman otherwise directs, not less than fifteen clear days' notice of a question shall be given. 'There is no maximum limit, in terms of days, for tabling notice of a question in the Rajya Sabha. Therefore, in order to provide 21 clear days for tabling the questions by the Members of Lok Sabha, it is, as far as possible, ensured that all procedural formalities for convening the Sessions are completed and summons are issued to the members at least 21 clear days before the proposed date of commencement of the Session. This is, however, not always possible and there are several instances when the summons to members have been issued at an interval of less than 21 clear days **(Annex III-A).** After general election, owing to paucity of time the two Houses are normally convened at an interval of two to seven days. (The VI Lok Sabha was constituted on 23 March, 1977. The summons regarding the first session of the XIII Lok Sabha scheduled to commence on 20 October, 1999 were issued on 16 October, 1999; refer **Annex III-A**).

It is not necessary that the Lok Sabha and Rajya Sabha should be summoned simultaneously or on the same date. (First Session of two Houses convened after constitution of new Lok Sabha are normally summoned on different dates.)

**Practice and Procedure of Parliament (Fifth Edition)* (pp. 173-74).

Summoning of Houses for Joint Sitting

Under article 108 of the Constitution, the President may call a joint sitting of both Houses if a Bill passed by one House and transmitted to the other House:

(a) is rejected by the other House; or
(b) the Houses have finally disagreed to the amendments to be made in the Bill; or
(c) more than six months elapse from the date of the reception of the Bill by the other House without the Bill being passed by it.

In the past, joint sittings of the Houses have been convened on three occasions under this provision (**Annex III- B**).

PROCESS

The process for summoning the Houses *inter alia* involves the following steps:

(a) To obtain the approval of the Cabinet to the date of commencement and duration of the Session. In case of first Session after general election and first Session of the year, approval is obtained for the time, date of the President's address to the two Houses assembled together;
(b) To obtain a copy of the minutes of the meeting of the Cabinet in which approval was accorded to the above proposals; where, however, there is urgency, may be deputed necessary authority from the Cabinet Secretariat in this regard;
(c) To obtain the approval of the President to the date of commencement of the Session and where necessary, the venue, date and time of the President's address;
(d) To inform the Secretary-Generals of the Lok Sabha and Rajya Sabha Secretariats about the date(s) of commencement of the Session and its duration and where necessary, venue, date and time of the President's address and also that the President has accorded his approval thereto. The Cabinet Secretary and Secretary to the President to be endorsed copies of such communications for information.

About 45 days before the probable date of the Session, a Note for consideration of the Cabinet *inter aila* indicating the proposed date of the commencement and duration of the Session and, where necessary, proposed time and date of the President's Address is prepared and, after obtaining the approval of the Minister of Parliamentary Affairs, the requisite number of copies thereof (at present 55 copies) are sent to the Cabinet Secretariat. The following points are taken into consideration in preparation of the 'Note for the Cabinet':

(a) Bills pending in two Houses on the conclusion of the last Session of Parliament and Ordinances promulgated, if any, during the inter-session period, which may have to be passed by the two Houses during the ensuing Session.
(b) Financial Business to be taken up during the Session, if any.
(c) Time bound essential non-legislative business, if any, e.g. Confidence Motion, consideration and adoption of Resolution regarding President's Rule in any State etc.
(d) Number of sittings of corresponding Sessions of Parliament held during the last five years and average number of sittings of a Session. (For a proposal to convene the Budget Session, the number of sittings of Budget Sessions held during the last five years and the number of sittings of a Budget Session, on an average, are kept in view.)
(e) Date and time of the President's Address, in case of first Session after general election or/and first Session of every calendar year.
(f) Need to set apart some time for discussion on matters of urgent public importance likely to be moved by members.
(g) Election for State Legislative Assemblies, if any, during or before the proposed dates of the Session.

After the Cabinet has approved the proposal of the Ministry with or without amendment, the Ministry waits for the receipt of the minutes of the meeting of the Cabinet in the normal course. In case of urgency, the Cabinet Secretariat is formally requested, immediately after the meeting, to give an authority as soon as possible to the effect that the proposal of the Ministry has been approved by the Cabinet, with or without any change in the dates etc., to enable it to take further necessary action in the matter immediately.

On receipt of the minutes of the meeting or requisite authority from the Cabinet Secretariat, a note from the Minister of Parliamentary Affairs to the Hon'ble President containing the proposal approved by the Cabinet is submitted for approval and signature of the Minister **(Annex III-C)**. The Note, as duly signed by the Minister, is sent in a sealed cover to the President's Secretariat along with a copy each of the "Note for the Cabinet" as considered in the meeting and 'minutes/authority' received from the Cabinet Secretariat. After delivery of the note in the President's Secretariat, the Ministry keeps in touch with the concerned branch/officers in the Secretariat, and in case of delay, efforts, preferably at Secretary level, are made to expedite the approval. After receipt of President's approval to the proposal, Secretary-Generals of the Lok Sabha and Rajya Sabha are informed of the Government's decision in the matter through a letter from the Secretary, Ministry of Parliamentary Affairs **(Annexes III-D & E)**. Further necessary action in the matter including notifying the dates of the Session and issue of summons to Members of the two Houses is taken by the respective Parliament Secretariat after obtaining approval of the Hon'ble President.

Summoning of Joint Sitting of two Houses

The administrative Ministry concerned with the Bill, after obtaining the approval of the Prime Minister, requests the Ministry of Parliamentary Affairs to take necessary action for convening the joint sitting of the Houses for the purpose of deliberation on the Bill. In case the administrative Ministry approaches the Ministry in the matter without obtaining the approval of the Prime Minister, the Ministry takes the approval of the Prime Minister for the purpose. Thereafter, a note from the Minister of Parliamentary Affairs *inter alia* indicating the purpose and date on which the two Houses are proposed to be summoned for joint sitting is submitted to the President for taking his approval to the proposal **(Annex III-F)**. Along with the note, draft Messages to be sent by him to the two Houses in this regard are also enclosed for his approval and signature. The Order of the President, when received, is sent by the Minister of Parliamentary Affairs to the Presiding Officers of the two Houses for summoning the two Houses for a joint sitting on the date(s) as approved by the President **(Annexes III-G & H).** The presidential Message sent to the Presiding Officers of the Houses only mentions the date of joint sitting leaving the duration of the joint sitting to the discretion of the Speaker, Lok Sabha, who presides over the joint sitting of the two Houses.

DECISIONS

Earlier, the approval of the Cabinet Committee on Parliamentary Affairs (CCPA), except when it had not been constituted, used to be obtained to the proposals regarding the commencement and duration of the Sessions. However, at such times, when the Cabinet Committee on Parliamentary Affairs had not been constituted, the approval of the Cabinet was obtained to the proposal. Such occasions were, however, very few and far between. Normally, occasions of this nature arose in respect of Sessions convened immediately after constitution of new Lok Sabha/formation of new Ministry as by that time the Cabinet Committee on Parliamentary Affairs is normally not constituted.

However, since the Budget Session, 1999 of Parliament, such proposals are sent to the Cabinet for approval.

PROROGATION OF THE HOUSES

BACKGROUND

Under Article 85(2) of the Constitution, the President may from time to time prorogue Houses or either House of Parliament. Termination of a session of the House by an Order by the President under the above constitutional provision is called 'prorogation'. Prorogation normally follows the adjournment of the sitting of the House *sine die.* The time-lag between the adjournment of the House *sine die* and its prorogation is generally two to four days, although there are instances when the House was prorogued on the same day on which it was adjourned *sine die.* It is also not necessary that the two Houses are prorogued on the same day. There have been instances when one House was prorogued on its adjournment *sine die* while the other House was not prorogued on its adjournment *sine die.* (141st Session of Rajya Sabha which commenced on 23 February, 1987 was adjourned *sine die* on 20 March, 1987 and was prorogued on 24 March, 1987. However, the Eighth Session of the VIII Lok Sabha which commenced on 23 February, 1987 was adjourned *sine die* on 12 May, 1987. The Speaker, exercising his powers under proviso to Rule 15, reconvened the sittings of the Lok Sabha from 27 July to 28 August, 1987, with the result that its Eighth Session which commenced on 23 February, 1987 continued till 3 September, 1987 and the House was not prorogued during the period of adjournment. The Lok Sabha was prorogued on 3 September, 1987.)

PROCEDURE

Either a day before or on the day when the Houses are scheduled to adjourn *sine die* on the conclusion of their Session, a Note for the Cabinet Committee on Parliamentary Affairs *inter alia* proposing that the Houses which are scheduled to adjourn *sine die* on the following day/same day, may be prorogued on their adjournment *sine die,* is submitted for the approval of the Minister of Parliamentary Affairs. After the approval of the Minister, the approval of the CCPA to the proposal contained in the Note is normally obtained through circulation of papers. In case the CCPA has not been constituted by that time, a Note containing the proposal on the above lines, after it has been approved by the Minister, is submitted to the Prime Minister soliciting his approval to the proposal **(Annex III-I)**. After the CCPA/Prime Minister, as the case may be, has accorded his approval to the proposal, the Secretary, Ministry of Parliamentary Affairs, through a letter, communicates the decision of the Government in the matter to the Secretary-Generals of the two Houses. **(Annexes III-J & K).** The two Parliament Secretariats then separately obtain the approval of the President to the proposed date of prorogation of their respective Houses. After the President has accorded his approval, it is notified in the Gazette Extraordinary and simultaneously a paragraph in the regard is also inserted in the Parliamentary Bulletin Part II of the respective Houses informing the members of the prorogation of the Houses.

DISSOLUTION OF LOK SABHA

In terms of Article 83(2) of the Constitution, the House of the People, unless sooner dissolved, shall continue for five years from the date appointed for its first meeting and no longer and the expiration of the said period of five years shall operate as a dissolution of the House. As per the Government of India (Allocation of Business) Rules, 1961, the function regarding dissolution of the House of the People has been allocated to the Ministry of Parliamentary Affairs.

Despite the fact that this function has been assigned to the Ministry, it, however, rarely initiates proposal regarding dissolution of the Lok Sabha. It was only on two occasions, viz., at the time of dissolution of VII and X Lok Sabha, when the Ministry really performed this function. Otherwise, the Cabinet, without any formal note submitted to it for its consideration, takes *suo motu* decision regarding the date of dissolution of the House of the People whether it is on the eve of completion of its normal term or when it is proposed to dissolve the House prematurely. Further, necessary action in regard to obtaining the approval of the President to the Cabinet's recommendation and, sometimes, even communicating the President's Order regarding approval of the proposal to the Lok Sabha Secretariat, under intimation to this Ministry, is also taken by the Prime Minister's Office.

Whenever, the Ministry has to take action in this regard, either on its own or when directed by the Minister of Parliamentary Affairs/Prime Minister's Office, it submits, about a week before the completion of the prescribed term of the Lok Sabha, a 'Note for the Cabinet' soliciting its approval to the proposed date of dissolution of the House of the People. When the Cabinet has accorded its approval to the proposal, the Minister, through a note addressed to the President, seeks the President's approval to the proposed date of dissolution as recommended by the Cabinet. Before according his approval to the proposal, the President may ask for formal confirmation from the Secretary, Ministry of Parliamentary Affairs, as provided in the letter at **Annex III-L**, whether proposed essential Legislative and Financial Business has been transacted by the Lok Sabha before it was adjourned *sine die*. The President's approval, when received, is communicated by the Secretary, Ministry of Parliamentary Affairs, to the Secretary-General, Lok Sabha, who after obtaining necessary approval, gets it gazetted.

DECISIONS

Requirement of Placing Proposal Regarding Prorogation of Rajya Sabha before Cabinet Relaxed

The ninth Session of the VI Lok Sabha and 111th Session of the Rajya Sabha were adjourned *sine die* on 20 August, 1979. Subsequently, the Lok Sabha was dissolved by the President on 22 August, 1979 and it was felt necessary to prorogue the Rajya Sabha. The Lok Sabha and Rajya Sabha Secretariats were informed of the Government's decision to prorogue the Rajya Sabha which was prorogued on 24 August, 1979 itself. Proposals to prorogue the Rajya Sabha following the dissolution of the IX Lok Sabha on 13 March, 1991, the XI Lok Sabha on 4 December, 1997 and XII Lok Sabha on 26 April, 1999 in similar situations were, however, placed before the Cabinet Committee on Parliamentary Affairs for its approval and after the Committee approved the proposals, the two Secretariats were requested to take further necessary action in the matter.

Houses Prorogued with the Approval of Prime Minister

First Sessions of the XI, XII and XIII Lok Sabhas and corresponding Sessions of the Rajya Sabha were prorogued after obtaining the approval of the Prime Minister as the Cabinet Committee on Parliamentary Affairs had not been constituted by then. (Rule 12 of the Government of India (Transaction of Business) Rules - Departure from Rules:- The Prime Minister may, in any case or classes of cases permit or condone a departure from these Rules, to the extent he deems necessary.)

Lok Sabha Prorogued during Recess Period of Budget Session to enable the Government to Promulgate Ordinances

Ninth Sesion of X Lok Sabha and 170th Session of the Rajya Sabha were adjourned for recess on 13 May, 1994 to meet on

13 June, 1994. In order to enable the Government to promulgate Ordinances, the Lok Sabha which was adjourned on 13 May, 1994 was prorogued on 23 May, 1994. (The Rajya Sabha which was also adjourned on 13 May, 1994 was not prorogued.) After prorogation of the Lok Sabha, the following three Ordinances were promulgated:

1. The Manipur Municipalities Ordinance, 1994 (promulgated on 24 May, 1994);
2. The Punjab Municipal Corporation Law (Extension to Chandigarh) Ordinance, 1994 (promulgated on 24 May, 1994); and
3. The New Delhi Municipal Council Ordinance, 1994 (promulgated on 25 May, 1994).

The Bills relating to the above Ordinances were passed during the next Session of the Lok Sabha and in the second part of the same Session of the Rajya Sabha held after the recess.

CHECK LIST

A check list of steps to be taken at various stages in regard to summoning, prorogation of the Houses and dissolution of the House of the People is at **Annex III-M.**

4

LEGISLATIVE AND FINANCIAL BUSINESS OF THE GOVERNMENT

In a parliamentary democracy, the main task of the Parliament relates to Government Business. Planning of Government Business, therefore, assumes great significance. The function of planning and coordination of Legislative and other official business in both the Houses of Parliament has been allocated to the Ministry of Parliamentary Affairs under the Government of India (Allocation of Business) Rules, 1961.

Any business initiated or moved by a member of the Council of Ministers in either House of the Parliament is known as the Official or Government Business. Government Business comprises the Legislative, Non-legislative, Financial and Non-financial business introduced or moved/piloted by the Ministers in either House. The Rules of the two Houses provide that on the days allotted for transaction of Government Business, the business sponsored by the Government shall be given precedence and that it shall be arranged in such order as the Presiding Officers of the two Houses may determine in consultation with the Leaders of the respective Houses. Barring the Question Hour and two and a half hours during the Private Members' days (in the Rajya Sabha, no Government Business is normally provided on the Private Members' days), the entire time of the two Houses is at the disposal of the Government for transaction of Government Business. However, the Government normally agrees to provide for discussion on topics of urgent public importance, as demanded by Members from time to time and recommended by the Business Advisory Committees of the Houses, during the time available for Government Business. In this chapter, the official Legislative and Financial business taken up in the two Houses of Parliament alone has been dealt with. In so far as the other official business taken up in the two Houses is concerned, it has been dealt with separately in chapter 5 of this Handbook.

Government Legislative Business

Any Bill(s) introduced or moved for consideration and passing/piloted by the Minister(s), constitute the Government legislative business. [Bills introduced or moved for consideration and passing by any Member (other than a Minister) in the two Houses, whether he/she belongs to the ruling party/parties or opposition parties/groups, constitute the Private Member's Legislative Business. This can be taken up only during the time set apart for Private Members Business in the two Houses, i.e. two and half hours on the last working day of the alternative week or any other day in a week as may be specified by the Presiding Officer in each House.]

Financial Business

The Financial business brought before the Houses by the Government consists of the following items:

- (i) Presentation of the Railway and the General Budgets and Statements of Supplementary/Excess Demands for Grants;
- (ii) Presentation of the Budgets and Statements of Supplementary/Excess Demands for Grants in respect of State(s) under President's Rule;
- (iii) General discussion on the General and Railway Budgets; discussion and voting on the Demands for Grants on Account, Demands for Grants, Supplementary and Excess Demands for Grants in respect of the General and Railway Budgets;
- (iv) Introduction, consideration and passing of the Appropriation Bills in respect of various Demands voted by the Lok Sabha;
- (v) Introduction, consideration and passing of the Finance Bill; and
- (vi) General discussion on the Budgets, discussion and voting on Supplementary Demands and Excess Grants of States and Union Territories which are under President's Rule, and introduction, consideration and passing of the connected Appropriation Bills.

PROCESS

In discharge of this function, the Ministry of Parliamentary Affairs plans the Government Business in the following three stages:

(i) Likely business for the entire session, i.e. Tentative List of Government Legislative and other Business for the session;

(ii) Planning of business on a weekly basis, i.e. statements made by the Ministers of Parliamentary Affairs in each House every week regarding the Government Business likely to be taken in the respective Houses during the following week; and

(iii) Planning of business in the two Houses on a day to day basis, i.e. furnishing lists of government business to the Lok Sabha and Rajya Sabha Secretariats daily for inclusion in the Lists of Business of the respective Houses for the following day and the day thereafter.

Government Business for the Entire Session - Tentative Lists

In order to chalk out a tentative plan of the Government Legislative, Financial and other business for a session, it is essential that the Ministry of Parliamentary Affairs should have with it, in advance, information regarding various items of business which Ministries/Departments intend to bring before the Houses during the ensuing session. Though the information regarding the Bills which remain pending in the two Houses on the conclusion of the previous session of the Parliament and the Ministries administratively concerned with these Bills is available with the Ministry, it, however, is not aware whether the administrative Ministry would move its pending Bills for consideration and passing during the next session. It is only the administrative Ministry which can authoritatively state whether it proposes or does not propose to bring a particular pending Bill during the ensuing session. Not only the pending Bills, a Ministry may also bring fresh Legislative proposals or any item of Non-legislative and/or, Financial business during the forthcoming session. It is, therefore, imperative for the Ministry of Parliamentary Affairs to approach all the Ministries/

Departments of the Government of India sufficiently in advance of each session of Parliament to obtain the details regarding the Legislative and other business proposed to be brought by them in Parliament during the ensuing session.

For this purpose, as soon as the two Houses are prorogued on the conclusion of their preceding session or as soon as the new Government is formed after the general election or otherwise, the Secretary, Ministry of Parliamentary Affairs, addresses a D.O. letter **(Annex IV-A)** to his counterparts in all the Ministries/ Departments of the Government of India, requesting them to furnish, by a prescribed date [normally four weeks before the commencement of the session (this may vary, depending upon the time available before a session)], information regarding the Legislative (pending as well as new Bills) and other business likely to be introduced/moved by them during the forthcoming session, in the prescribed proforma **(Annex IV-B)**. In this communication, an indication about the probable date on which the next session is likely to start is also given.

The position of receipt of replies from the Ministries/ Departments is monitored and the Ministries from whom the replies are awaited, are telephonically requested at various levels to expedite them. On the expiry of the date prescribed for furnishing the information, the Parliament Units of the defaulting Ministries are formally reminded at the level of the Under Secretary. Thereafter, whenever necessary, the Secretary and other senior officers in the Ministry also telephonically request their counterparts/concerned senior officers to expedite the information. The information received from various Ministries/ Departments is compiled in the format as at **Annex IV-C.**

With a view to finalising the Tentative List of Government and other business for the session, the information received from various Ministries/Departments is processed in two stages. In the first stage, the list, particularly the Bills included in the List, are individually scrutinized in consultation with the Legislative Department of the Ministry of Law & Justice with reference to the stage of drafting of the 'Note for Cabinet', preparation of the Bill and whether the Cabinet has accorded its approval/fresh approval, where necessary, to the Bill or not. This gives a broad idea to the Ministry about the state of preparedness of each Bill and also whether with this preparedness, it will be feasible for the administrative Ministry to complete all the procedural formalities to bring the Bill before Parliament during its ensuing session, in time. For this purpose, a meeting of the Secretary, Ministry of Parliamentary Affairs, with the Legislative Secretary is arranged, in the latter's office, about eight to ten days in advance of the session, which is also attended by the senior officers of the two Ministries. In this connection, a D.O. letter **(Annex IV-D)**, forwarding the consolidated list of business furnished by various Ministries/Departments (in format at **Annex IV-C**), is addressed by the Secretary, Ministry of Parliamentary Affairs, to the Legislative Secretary, about ten to twelve days before the session, requesting him to fix a meeting for the purpose. In actual practice, the Secretary normally first fixes up the meeting in informal consultation with the Secretary, Legislative Department, and thereafter addresses the D.O. letter to him, forwarding therewith a copy of the consolidated list.

In the second stage, after the Bills included in the list have been scrutinized in consultation with the Legislative Department, the Minister of Parliamentary Affairs takes a meeting, about a week in advance of the session, with the Secretaries/senior officers of the concerned Ministries to review and finalise the Government Business for the next session. For this purpose, a note, about a month in advance of the session, is submitted to the Minister seeking his/her convenience regarding the time and date, preferably about a week in advance of the session, for the meeting. Sometimes, when it is not convenient to the Minister, one of the Ministers of State for Parliamentary Affairs indicated by the Minister, presides over the meeting. After the Minister/ Minister of State has indicated his/her convenience regarding the date and time for the meeting, the Lok Sabha or the Rajya Sabha Secretariat, as the case may be, is requested to reserve, for a specified date, one of the larger Committee Rooms in the Parliament House or Parliament House Annexe for the purpose. After the reservation of the Committee Room has been confirmed by the Secretariat, the Secretary addresses a D.O. letter **(Annex IV-E)** to the Secretaries of the Ministries/Departments concerned requesting them to attend or depute the concerned senior officer(s) of the Ministry to the meeting. A list of items of business concerning each Ministry, which is to be reviewed in the meeting, is also forwarded to the Ministry with the D.O. letter.

Simultaneously, a Note from the Secretary, MPA, to the Minister/ Ministers of State for Parliamentary Affairs, requesting them to attend the meeting, is also sent, along with a copy of the consolidated scrutinized list of the items of business to be reviewed in the meeting. Arrangements for tea/refreshment, security at the venue of the meeting, entry passes for the officers of various Ministries/Departments, attendance sheet for obtaining the signatures of the officers attending the meeting, etc. are made after taking necessary approval from senior officers or IFD, wherever necessary.

Each item included in the scrutinized list is taken up one by one in the meeting (either in the ascending or the descending order, or from the middle, as may be decided by the Minister, keeping in view the order followed in the earlier meeting) and is accorded priority after discussion, if necessary, with the officers of the Ministries/Departments concerned. Depending upon their importance and urgency, they are accorded, category A or B or C (Minister sometimes may also accord A+, B+, A -, B - categories.) Bills to replace Ordinances, all items of Financial business and any item of Legislative or other business which is required to be passed by Parliament within stipulated period/date, viz., adoption of resolution regarding Proclamation issued under Article 356 in respect of a State, are always accorded the highest priority. Items of business accorded categories A+, A-, B+ are those which are to be necessarily taken up during the session. Items accorded categories B and B- are those which may be taken up either for introduction only or for introduction and also for consideration and passing during the second/later part of the session. While items accorded category C are those which are of lowest priority and are not expected to be taken up during the session. Minutes of the meeting are prepared and, after their approval by the Minister, are circulated to the concerned Ministries/Departments, etc. for information and necessary action.

On the basis of the decisions taken in the Minister's meeting, Tentative Lists of Government Legislative and other Business likely to be taken during the forthcoming session are prepared in respect of each House separately. (Items accorded C category in the meeting are not included in the Tentative Lists, while items accorded the remaining categories are included, if necessary, with remarks, viz., for introduction only, etc.) After their approval by the Secretary/Minister, the Tentative Lists as in the format as at **Annex IV-F,** are sent to the Lok Sabha and the Rajya Sabha Secretariats, about three to four days in advance of the session, for publication in their Parliamentary Bulletins Part II for the information of the Members of their respective Houses and the Ministries/Departments. (During the session which commences with the President's Address in terms of article 87(2) of the Constitution, the copies of the Tentative Lists are sent to the two Secretariats after the President has addressed the Houses.)

Though all the items of business included in the Lists may not necessarily be taken up during the session, the lists, however, give a broad idea to the Members about the Legislative and other business likely to be brought by the Government during a session and also affords them an opportunity to prepare themselves in advance for participation in discussion on such items in the Houses. Besides, the lists also apprise, and, thereby, enable the Ministry/Department concerned to plan/take necessary action in advance for introduction/consideration and passing of their Bills by the Houses during the ensuing session. It also enables the Ministry of Parliamentary Affairs to plan and prioritise the business for the session.

Planning of Business on Weekly Basis

During the session periods, the Ministry reviews and plans the Government business on a weekly basis. On the basis of such reviews, the Ministers of Parliamentary Affairs also make statements in the two Houses every week, normally on the last sitting of the House in the week, about the Government business likely to be brought during the following week. In the Lok Sabha, it is included in the List of Business while in the Rajya Sabha, it is not included in the List of Business of that House for the day on which the statement is proposed to be made. As the statements are made almost simultaneously in the two Houses - after Question Hour and laying of Papers - the Minister of Parliamentary Affairs makes the statement in the Lok Sabha and the Minister of State for Parliamentary Affairs from the Rajya Sabha, makes the statement in the Rajya Sabha. At the time of making of these statements, Secretary is expected to remain present in the Official Gallery, Lok Sabha and the Joint Secretary is expected to remain present in the Official Gallery, Rajya Sabha to assist, if necessary, the Ministers, as also to attend to any exigencies that may arise in relation to the statements.

The Ministry prepares these statements, keeping in view the importance and urgency of various items of Official business which are ready or are likely to be ready for listing in a couple of days/in the following week and also the time likely to be available for transaction of Government Business during the following week. As these statements are prepared during the session periods, they also take into account the Government Business likely to be disposed of by the Houses on the day the lists are prepared as also on the following day. Thus, for the statement prepared on Thursday, the business likely to be disposed of by the Houses on Thursday and Friday is also taken note of. Such statements, prepared for each House separately, are submitted every Thursday or on the penultimate sitting of the Houses every week, for the approval of the Minister. The statements are approved by the Minister on the same day. After their approval, the Secretary informs the Secretary-Generals of the two Secretariats **(Annexes IV-G & IV-H),** along with the requisite number of copies of the statement, about the statements to be made by the Minister of Parliamentary Affairs in the Lok Sabha and by the Minister of State for Parliamentary Affairs in the Rajya Sabha on the next day. After the Ministers have made statements in the two Houses, the Members, with the permission of the Presiding Officers, may make submissions/suggestions, if any. Normally, Ministers do not resbond to these submissions, however, if necessary, or if directed by the Chair, the Minister may react to the suggestions/submissions made by the Members. The weekly statements give advance information to the Members about the impeding business during the following week and also an opportunity to the Government to sense the mood of the House on its proposed business and, if necessary, to recast it accordingly.

Planning of Government Business on Day to Day Basis

During the session periods, the Ministry of Parliamentary Affairs reviews, plans and provides the Government Business for consideration in the two Houses on day-to-day basis. The Ministry is responsible for providing Government Business, in the order of priority which it deems appropriate, in the two Houses. The responsibility of bringing out the printed Lists of

Business, containing the Private as well as the Government Business, is that of the respective Parliament Secretariats. For inclusion of any items of the Government Business in the Lists of Business of the Houses for any date, the Ministry has to request the two Parliament Secretariats through the List of Government Business sent to them daily during the session period. Initially, the Ministry furnishes the Lists of Government Business for the first two or three sittings of the two Houses to two Secretariats separately, about two to three days in advance of the Session. After the commencement of the session, the Lists of Government Business are provided to the two Secretariats daily. Normally, the List of Government Business in respect of each House is provided to the Secretariat concerned two days in advance of the date to which it relates. However, when if it becomes necessary to take up any business on the same day, a Supplementary List of Government Business is sent to the Parliament Secretariat concerned on the same day *inter alia* requesting that such business may be included in the List of Business for that day as per the priority indicated in the Ministry's communication. The matter can be taken up in the House concerned only after its Secretariat issues the Revised Supplementary List of Business. All the proposals regarding the Lists of Government Business are issued after approval of the Minister of Parliamentary Affairs. (These proposals are not normally routed through the Minister(s) of State for Parliamentary Affairs.) At any time before the item included in the List of Business is taken up by the House, the Government can withdraw that item or change its order of priority or issue the revised List of Government Business, as the case may be, for that day.

Points to be Kept in View While Submitting the List of Government Business

While submitting the proposals for Lists of Government Business to the Minister, the Ministry has to ensure that the items being suggested for inclusion therein fulfil the following criteria:

(i) All the procedural requirements for listing of the item(s) for introduction or consideration and passing, as the case may be, have been fulfilled. The Ministry/ Department may also be consulted on phone, as far as possible.

(ii) BAC of the House concerned has allotted time for its consideration/discussion (However, for introduction, no time allocation by the Committee is necessary). (Items of business which have not been allotted time can also be proposed in exceptional circumstances, viz., when no Government Business with time allotment is available, etc. The allocation of time, in such cases, is to be done by the Speaker/Chairman with the approval of the House.)

(iii) Note being submitted indicates against each item the time allotted, if any, by the BAC as also whether the Bill, if being included in the proposal, has already been examined by the Standing Committee.

(iv) Total time allotted to items being suggested for a particular day is not less than time available for transaction of Government Business on that day (Normally, four hours in the Lok Sabha - from 2.00 p.m. to 6.00 p.m. and three hours in the Rajya Sabha - from 2.00 p.m. to 5.00 p.m., are available for transaction of Government Business. However, on Fridays or on the last sitting of the Houses in a week, i.e. Private Members' day, only one and a half hours - from 2.00 p.m. to 3.30 p.m. - are available in the Lok Sabha for transaction of the Government Business; while in the Rajya Sabha normally no Government Business is provided on such days unless recommended by the BAC, Rajya Sabha or decided otherwise by the Government, keeping in view the urgency of the business.

(v) Whether the items being suggested have been included in the weekly statement of Government Business for that week (Although, it is not necessary as per the Rules of the Houses, care should, however, be taken to obviate any objections being raised by Members on the floor of the Houses).

(vi) In case of Constitution Amendment Bills, whether the BAC has recommended the date, etc. for its introduction or consideration and passing. (As the Constitution Amendment Bills require special majority for their introduction or consideration and passing, they are normally included in the List of Business if BAC of the House concerned has recommended the date on which they may be taken up as also the time when they will be put to the vote of the House.

Time Allocation to Government Business by the BACs

Meetings of the Business Advisory Committees of the two Houses are held normally once a week during the session periods. Before the commencement of each session of Parliament, the Ministry reviews the Bills remaining pending in the two Houses on the conclusion of the last session of Parliament as also the new Bills (particularly relating to Ordinances) or other items of business for which all procedural formalities have been completed and which can be taken up during the first week and thereafter in the two Houses. In case, allotment of time to any of these items has not already been made by the Business Advisory Committees of the respective Houses, efforts are made to seek allotment of time thereto from the committees as soon as possible. Thereafter, the position in respect of time allotment for Government Business in each House is reviewed from time to time, particularly after the weekly statements regarding Government Business are made by the Ministers in the two Houses and time allotment for such items of Business - new as well as old - which have not already been allotted time, is sought from the committees. All proposals seeking allotment of time from the committees are sent with the approval of the Minister.

There is a slight difference in the procedure followed in this regard by the two Secretariats. The meetings of the BAC, Lok Sabha, are normally convened when the Ministry makes a request to the Lok Sabha Secretariat to move the BAC for allotment of time to certain items of Government Business. In case of the BAC, Rajya Sabha, the Chairman, Rajya Sabha, fixes the date and time of its meeting and, thereafter, a request is sent by the Rajya Sabha Secretariat to the Ministry to furnish items of Government Business to which allocation of time is to be sought from the committee in its scheduled meeting. In exceptional cases, the Ministry may, however, request the Rajya Sabha Secretariat to move the committee for allocation of time to urgent items of Government Business. Further, the time allotted by the BAC, Lok Sabha, to any business which is not taken up, lapses on the conclusion of the term of that Lok Sabha and not on conclusion of the Session during which that business had been allotted time by the committee. Time allotted by the BAC, Rajya Sabha, lapses, if the business to which it had allotted time is not taken up in that session and it has to be sought afresh from the committee, during the next session or during that session in which that business is proposed to be taken up. Therefore, in obtaining allocation of time for items of Government Business from BAC, Rajya Sabha, total time available in the session should be kept in view.

Time Table of Likely Government Business

During every session of Parliament, particularly after the first meeting of the Business Advisory Committees of the Lok Sabha and the Rajya Sabha, a time-table of the likely Government Business in the days to come may be prepared and updated in the following proforma:

DATE	SUBJECT	NATURE OF BUSINESS	DURATION (in hours)	CUMULATIVE TOTAL (in hours)
1	2	3	4	5

One assumption implicit in the time-table is that the working time for Government Business available in the Lok Sabha is 4 hours and it is 3 hours in the Rajya Sabha. A sample of the time-table for the Lok Sabha and the Rajya Sabha is at **Annexes-IV-I & J.** The last column of the time-table relating to cumulative total is filled up in respect of subjects for which time has been specifically allotted by the Business Advisory Committee of the concerned House. Time-table may be updated every working day, highlighting (or bold typing) the current day's business.

Procedural Requirements for Listing of Government Business

Various procedural formalities which are required to be fulfilled by administrative Ministries/Departments concerned in respect of various items of Government Business are indicated in the following sections.

Introduction of Bills

A Bill can be listed for introduction only after the following procedural formalities have been completed:

(i) For introduction of a Bill in the Lok Sabha, notice of Motion (English and Hindi versions), duly signed by the Minister has been sent to the Lok Sabha Secretariat seven days before the date on which the Bill is sought to be introduced, unless the Speaker allows the Motion to be made at a shorter notice (Direction 19A of the Directions by the Speaker).
In the Rajya Sabha, notice of the Motion has to be given in advance but there is no requirement of sending it seven days in advance.

(ii) Printed copies of the Bill (English and Hindi versions), duly scrutinised by the Legislative Department, have been circulated to the Members two days in advance of the date on which the Bill is sought to be introduced (Direction 19B), except in the case of Appropriation, Finance and Secret Bills.
In the Rajya Sabha, Bills can be introduced even if copies of the Bill are circulated only a day in advance or sometime, even on the day of its proposed introduction.

(iii) Where the Bill attracts the provisions of the articles 3, 117(1), 274 and 348 of the Constitution, the President's recommendation/sanction for its introduction has been obtained and communicated to the Parliament Secretariat.

(iv) Where, however, the requirement as mentioned at (ii) above has not been fulfilled and the Ministry desires to introduce a Bill in the Lok Sabha at a shorter notice than the period prescribed therein, the Minister concerned may address a letter to the Speaker, Lok Sabha, seeking relaxation of the Direction 19B for introduction of the Bill. The Minister concerned may also consult the Leaders of major opposition parties in the Lok Sabha in this regard and inform the Speaker that they have no objection to the introduction of the Bill. Such requests should be accompanied by 550 copies of the Memorandum (English and Hindi versions), including one copy in each version duly authenticated by the Minister, explaining the reasons as to why the Bill is sought to be introduced at a shorter notice than the period prescribed in Direction 19B.

(v) In case of Bills proposed to be introduced, one copy of the Bill (English and Hindi versions), duly authenticated by the Minister concerned, may also be supplied by the Ministry to the Parliament Secretariat concerned before introduction of the Bill.

Bills for Consideration and Passing

A Bill can be listed for consideration and passing in the House only after the following procedural formalities have been completed:

(i) The Bill has already been introduced in the House in which it is proposed to be listed for consideration and passing.

(ii) Notice of Motion (English and Hindi versions) for consideration and passing of the Bill, duly signed by the Minister concerned, has been received in the Parliament Secretariat.

(iii) Where, however, the Bill attracts the provisions of article 117(3) or 274(1) of the Constitution, the President's recommendation for its consideration has been obtained and communicated to the Parliament Secretariat concerned. The President's recommendation has to be obtained separately in respect of each House.

(iv) In case of Bills passed by one House and proposed to be listed for consideration and passing in the other House, (a) a message regarding its passing by the former House has been reported in the House in which the Bill is proposed to be listed. (For expediting the message, the administrative Ministry has to ensure that copies of the Bill (other than Appropriation Bills), in both English and Hindi versions, are scrutinised by the Legislative Department as soon as possible and are sent to the Parliament Secretariat concerned to enable it to send the message to the other House); (b) copies of the Bill (English and Hindi versions) as passed by one House, have been printed and circulated to the Members of the House in which the Bill is proposed to be listed for consideration and passing; and (c) where the Bill is proposed to be listed for consideration and passing, at a notice shorter than two days, the Minister concerned has addressed a letter to the Presiding Officer of the Lok Sabha or the Rajya Sabha, as the case may be, for relaxation of the requirements of Rule 116 of the Lok Sabha Rules or Rule 123 of the Rajya Sabha Rules, as the case may be.

(v) Where the Bill proposed to be introduced is also proposed to be taken up for consideration and passing on the same day, the Minister concerned, citing reasons underlying its urgency, may address a letter to the Presiding Officer for grant of permission to list the Bill for consideration and passing on the same day. Consensus in the BAC of the concerned House, obtained by the Minister of Parliamentary Affairs, facilitates this process.

Coordinating Government Legislative Business

Management of Government Legislative business in Parliament requires coordinating the efforts of several agencies such as, the Ministry concerned with the Legislative business, President's Secretariat, Cabinet Secretariat, Lok Sabha and Rajya Sabha Secretariats, Ministry of Law and Justice (Legislative Department), Government Printing Press, etc. In some of these organisations, further coordination among these different units is also required such as, in the case of Lok Sabha Secretariat, coordination among Legislative Branch, Printing Branch and Distribution Branch is needed.

Introduction, Consideration and Passing of Bills Seeking to Replace Ordinances

In terms of article 123(1) of the Constitution, the President may promulgate such Ordinance as the circumstances appear to him to require. An Ordinance has the same force and effect as an Act of Parliament. Every Ordinance is required to be laid before both Houses of Parliament and it ceases to operate at the expiration of six weeks from the assembly of Parliament unless it is replaced by an Act of Parliament before the expiration of the above period (Where the Houses of Parliament are summoned to reassemble on different dates, the period of six weeks shall be reckoned from the later of those dates). An Ordinance can be withdrawn any time by the President.

The Ministry of Parliamentary Affairs is responsible for laying of copies of the Ordinances in both Houses of Parliament. Besides, it also coordinates with administrative Ministries for introduction, consideration and passing of the Bills seeking to replace Ordinances by both Houses of Parliament within the stipulated period. As soon as an Ordinance is promulgated, the Ministry requests the administrative Ministry **(Annexes IV-K & IV-L)** to get the Bill in replacement of the Ordinance drafted well in time and also take necessary action to fulfil the requisite procedural formalities for their introduction as also for consideration and passing in time so that the Bill in replacement of the Ordinance could be passed by both Houses as soon as possible during the ensuing session. The Ministry is also requested to take appropriate action as envisaged in Rule 71 of the Rules of Procedure and Conduct of Business in Lok Sabha or Rule 66 of the Rules of Procedure and Conduct of Business in the Rajya Sabha, depending upon where the Bill is proposed to be introduced, which provides that whenever a Bill seeking to replace an Ordinance with or without modification is introduced in a House, there shall be placed before the House along with the Bill, a statement explaining the circumstances which had necessitated immediate legislation by Ordinance. However, whenever an Ordinance which embodies wholly or partly or with modification the provisions of a Bill pending before either House is promulgated, such statement shall be laid on the Table of the House at the commencement of the session following the promulgation of the Ordinance.

For the purpose of laying of copies of Ordinances in two Houses, the Ministry, as soon as an Ordinance is promulgated, obtains 75 copies of the Ordinance, each in English and Hindi versions, from the Ministry of Law and Justice (Legislative Department). On receipt of copies of all the Ordinances promulgated before the commencement of each Parliament session, one copy each of the Ordinances in English and Hindi versions is submitted to the Minister of State for Parliamentary Affairs concerned for authentication. (Minister of State for Parliamentary Affairs, concerned with the Lok Sabha, authenticates copies of the Ordinances to be laid in the Lok Sabha whereas the Minister of State for Parliamentary Affairs concerned with the Rajya Sabha, authenticates copies of the Ordinances to be laid in the Rajya Sabha.) Thereafter, copies of the Ordinances as authenticated by the Ministers are sent to the Lok Sabha and Rajya Sabha Secretariats with the request to include an entry regarding laying of copies of the Ordinances on the Table of the Houses by the Ministers of State for Parliamentary Affairs, in the List of Business of the respective Houses for the first day of the session. Normally, the Minister of State for Parliamentary Affairs (Lok Sabha) lays the copies of the Ordinances in the Lok Sabha and the Minister of State for Parliamentary Affairs (Rajya Sabha) lays the copies in the Rajya Sabha. (Other procedural formalities for introduction as well as for consideration and passing of a Bill in replacement of an Ordinance are the same as explained in the preceding paras.)

Non-Legislative and Other Items

Discussion on any item of Non-Legislative Business, viz., Motion regarding statement made by the Minister, policy documents or reports of Statutory bodies and Motions, Resolutions on any other subjects/topics, sought to be moved by the Ministers can be listed in the Houses after the following procedural formalities have been fulfilled by the administrative Ministry:

(i) Notice of Motion (English and Hindi versions), duly signed by the Minister concerned for consideration/discussion of the policy document, etc. by the House, has been received in the Parliament Secretariat.

(ii) The Motion has been admitted by the Presiding Officer and has also been bulletined for information of the Members.

(iii) Copies of such documents/relevant literature, material etc., in English and Hindi versions, have been laid on the Table of the House in which the discussion is proposed to be listed. (Where it is not possible for the Ministry to lay copies of such documents in the House, before the proposed discussion, they may, with the permission of the Presiding Officer of the House concerned, circulate copies of such documents etc. to the Members and also lay a few copies thereof in the Parliament Library, for information of the Members.)

Order of Priority of Government Business

In case, all the items proposed to be included in the List of Government Business fulfil the requisite procedural formalities, they are prioritised in order of their importance and urgency. Normally, Bills seeking to replace Ordinances, Financial business etc. are given priority over other business. A sample list of business is at **Annex IV-M.**

Reference of Bills to Standing Committees

There are 24 departmentally related Standing Committees **(Annex IV-N)** consisting of Members of the Lok Sabha and the Rajya Sabha, under whose jurisdiction, various Ministries/ Departments have been placed. The functions of these Committees are examination and submission of reports to the Houses on (i) Demands for Grants of Ministries/Departments; (ii) National Long Term Policy Documents; (iii) Bills referred to them by the Presiding Officers of the respective Houses; and (iv) Annual Reports of Ministries/Departments. The Bills, other than the Finance Bills, Appropriation Bills and Bills of a trivial nature, after their introduction, are normally referred by the Presiding Officer to the Departmentally related Standing Committees for examination and report to the Houses. Where, however, the Bills are of an urgent nature and are required to be enacted early, the Minister concerned, citing the reasons underlying the urgency, may request the Presiding Officer of the House where the Bill is being introduced or has been introduced, not to refer the Bill to the Standing Committee for examination. In case of Bills introduced in the Lok Sabha, the consent of the Leaders of major Opposition Parties in that House to the effect that they have no objection to the proposal to not refer the Bill to the Standing Committee has also to be obtained and communicated to the Speaker/Parliament Secretariat while making such requests.

Financial Business

In terms of article 112 of the Constitution, the President, in respect of every financial year, causes to be laid before both Houses of Parliament, an Annual Financial Statement of the estimated receipt and expenditure of the Government of India. The Annual Financial Statement known as the 'Budget' is presented in two parts, the Railway Budget relating to Railway finance and the General Budget relating to Government of India finances except Railways. According to Rule 204 of the Rules of Procedure and Conduct of Business in Lok Sabha, the Budget is presented to the Lok Sabha on such day as the President may direct. By convention, the General Budget is presented on the last working day of February each year at 11.00 a.m. (Before 1999, the General Budget was presented at 5.00 p.m. on the last working day of February.) If on the last working day of February, the Houses are not scheduled to meet, the Houses are specifically summoned to meet on that day for presentation of the General Budget. However, in a year when the session of the Parliament commences later than February, viz., in an election year or otherwise, the General Budget may be presented on any day convenient to the Government during that session. The Railway Budget is normally presented three to six days in advance of the date of presentation of the General Budget.

The Railway Budget is presented to the Lok Sabha by the Minister of Railways and the General Budget is presented to the Lok Sabha by the Minister of Finance. While presenting the Budgets in the Lok Sabha, the respective Ministers deliver their speeches and thereafter lay the Annual Financial Statement, duly authenticated by them, on the Table of the House. After the presentation of the Budgets in the Lok Sabha, the Ministers lays the respective Annual Financial Statements on the Table of the Rajya Sabha on the same day. On the date of presentation of the General Budget, no other formal business is included in the Order Papers of the two Houses. Therefore, after presentation/laying of the General Budget, the two Houses are adjourned for the day. If any State is under President's Rule and it becomes necessary to have the Budget, Demands for Grants etc. of that State presented/approved by Parliament during that period, the Budgets etc. in respect of such States are also presented to Parliament by the Minister of Finance and approval of Parliament thereto obtained within the stipulated time.

Immediately after presentation of the General Budget in the Lok Sabha, the Minister of Finance introduces the Finance Bill to give effect to the financial proposals of the Government for the following financial year. As per second proviso to Rule 72 of the Lok Sabha Rules, the Motion for leave to introduce a Finance Bill cannot be opposed and it is forthwith put to vote. (The motion for leave to introduce an Appropriation Bill also cannot be opposed.) As per provision of the Provisional Collection of Taxes

Act, 1931, the Finance Bill has to be passed by Parliament and assented to by the President before the expiry of 75 days after the date on which it was introduced.

In an election year, the Railway and General Budgets may be presented twice - first to secure a Vote on Account for a few months i.e. an Interim Budget followed by the Annual financial statement for that year or the full-fledged Budget. Whenever the General Budget is presented twice in a financial year, the Finance Bill is also presented twice in that year - once in the outgoing Lok Sabha and the other in the new Lok Sabha or once in the First Session of the new Lok Sabha and another in its Second Session. A sample check list of activities to be undertaken in respect of obtaining the Vote on Account is at **Annex IV-O.**

Provisional Programme for Consideration of Financial Business

On the basis of advance information furnished by the Ministries of Railways and Finance regarding the Financial business to be brought by them before Parliament during the Budget Session, the Ministry of Parliamentary Affairs prepares a provisional programme of dates for presentation and general discussions on the Railway and General Budgets and related Financial business. Depending upon the availability of time, normally three to four sittings in each House are provided for general discussion on the Railway and General Budgets in the provisional programme, six sittings in the Lok Sabha for discussion and voting on the Demands for Grants of various Ministries/Departments and consideration and passing of the related Appropriation Bill and one sitting in the Rajya Sabha for consideration and return of the Appropriation Bill after it has been passed by the Lok Sabha, one sitting each in the two Houses for discussion and voting on the Demands for Grants (Railway) and consideration and passing of the related Appropriation Bill, three sittings in the Lok Sabha and two sittings in the Rajya Sabha for consideration and passing/return of the Finance Bill. The general discussion on the respective Budgets and the corresponding discussion and voting on the Demands for Grants on Account, the Supplementary Demands for Grants, if any, and the Excess Demands for Grants, if any, and the introduction, consideration and passing of the related Appropriation Bills, are normally clubbed together for discussion. In the Rajya Sabha, discussion and voting on any Demands of Grants etc. are not taken up. That

House considers and returns the related Appropriations Bills only, after they have been passed by the Lok Sabha. A statement indicating the detailed information regarding the time allotted to various items of Financial business is at **Annex IV-P.**

The provisional programme, after it has been approved by the Minister, is forwarded to the Ministries of Railway and Finance, about a fortnight before the commencement of the session, for their concurrence/suggestions regarding change in dates, etc., if any. After receipt of their comments/suggestions, the programme is finalised and copies thereof are sent to the two Parliament Secretariats and the Ministries of Railway and Finance for necessary action. On receipt of the programme, the Lok Sabha Secretariat, in terms of Rule 204 (1) of the Lok Sabha Rules, obtains the approval of the President to the dates of the presentation of the Railway and the General Budgets to the Lok Sabha. The two Secretariats, through their Bulletin Part II, then circulate the programme of their respective Houses to the Members for their information. On receipt of the programme from the Ministry of Parliamentary Affairs, the Ministries of Railway and Finance also take appropriate advance action for presentation/discussion of their Financial business in the two Houses, as per the programme.

After forwarding the programme to the two Parliament Secretariats etc., the Ministry of Parliamentary Affairs takes necessary action for obtaining allotment of time from the Business Advisory Committees of the two Houses to various items of Financial business included in the programme. After obtaining allotment of time, the Ministry, from time to time, issues the Lists of Government business *inter alia* providing those items for consideration in the two Houses, as far as possible, on the dates indicated in the programme. In case, however, it is not possible to stick to the dates indicated in the programme in respect of items other than the presentation of Budgets, those items are provided for consideration/discussion on the revised dates, preferably after taking the BAC of the House concerned into confidence.

So far as presentation/laying of the Railway and General Budgets in the two Houses is concerned, the two Parliament Secretariats include an entry in this regard in their printed Lists of Business only when the Ministry of Parliamentary Affairs intimates them through the Lists of Government business, the date and time of their presentation/laying in the Houses. In regard to presentation/laying of Demands for Grants/ Supplementary Demands of Grants etc., the Ministry does not make a request to the Secretariats and they themselves include an entry in this regard in the printed Lists of Business of their respective Houses on the basis of requests received by them from the Ministries concerned.

General discussions on the Railway and General Budgets are normally held in the two Houses before they adjourn for recess during the Budget Session. (However, there have been instances when the general discussions on the Budgets have been held after recess during the second part of the Budget Session.) After the general discussion on the Budgets is over, the two Houses are adjourned for recess for a period of about three weeks. During this period, the various Departmentally related Standing Committees, in terms of provisions of Rule 331(G) of the Rules of Procedure and Conduct of Business in Lok Sabha and Rule 272 of the Rules of Procedure and Conduct of Business in the Rajya Sabha, consider the Demands for Grants of various Ministries/Departments and present their separate reports on the Demands for Grants of each Ministry on reassembly of the two Houses after the recess. The Demands for Grants are considered by the Lok Sabha in the post-recess period in the light of the reports of the committees.

However, before the two Houses are adjourned for recess, Ministries/Departments are required to prepare the Detailed Demands for Grants, Performance Budget and Annual Reports of that financial year and make requisite copies thereof available to the two Parliament Secretariats, at least three days before the date on which the Houses are scheduled to adjourn for recess, for laying on the Table of the Houses/circulation to the Members of their respective Houses to enable them to make use of these documents during the deliberations of the Standing Committees. This requirement is generally brought to the notice of all Ministries/Departments sufficiently in advance of the commencement of the Budget Session of Parliament **(Annex V-Q)**.

The tentative dates for discussion of the Demands for Grants of various Ministries/Departments in the Lok Sabha, as recommended by the Business Advisory Committee, Lok Sabha, are circulated by the Ministry to the Ministries concerned

(Annex IV-R) immediately after the adoption of the report of the committee in this regard by the House, to enable them to prepare themselves for discussion in advance. Discussion and voting on Demands of various Ministries is proposed by the Ministry in the Lok Sabha on the dates, unless changed either by the BAC subsequently or agreed to in the House, as recommended by the BAC.

Procedure followed for Discussion and Voting on Demands for Grants of Ministries/Departments

Discussion and voting on the Demands for Grants of the selected Ministries/Departments is provided by this Ministry in the List(s) of Business of the Lok Sabha for such days as are recommended by the BAC, Lok Sabha. Discussion on the Demands for Grants of a Ministry is not initiated or moved by the Minister concerned in the House. As per practice, when the item regarding the Demands of the Ministry comes up for discussion as per entry in the List of Business for a particular day, it is assumed to have been moved and the Demands are proposed from the Chair for discussion by the House to save the time of the House. After the Demands have been proposed by the Chair, the discussion thereon is initiated by one of the Members of the House. On conclusion of the debate, it is replied to by the Minister concerned. Thereafter the cut motions moved by Members, if any, are put to the vote of the House. After the cut motions have been negatived or withdrawn by the Members concerned. Demands for Grants of the Ministry are put to the vote of the House and are adopted, normally by voice vote. This concludes the item regarding discussion and voting on the Demands for Grants of a Ministry. Discussion and voting on Demands for Grants of other selected Ministries/Departments continues in this manner until the day and time fixed by the BAC for guillotining of outstanding Demands. On the day and time recommended by the Business Advisory Committee for Guillotine, the Speaker puts every question necessary to dispose of all the outstanding matters in connection with Demands for Grants. Besides the Minister of Finance, all the Cabinet Ministers and Ministers of State holding independent charge, except those whose Ministries' Demands for Grants have been discussed and voted by the House, are requested by the Minister of Parliamentary Affairs **(Annex IV-S)** to remain present in the Lok

Sabha at the time of guillotining of outstanding demands. After the adoption of the Demands, the related Appropriation Bill is introduced, considered and passed by the House, normally without discussion.

The procedural formalities required to be fulfilled for listing of the Appropriation Bills and the Finance Bills in the two Houses are the same as for other Bills except that copies of Appropriation Bills, after they have been passed by the Lok Sabha, are not required to be scrutinised by the Legislative Department before messages regarding their passing are sent to the Rajya Sabha.

Important Rules/Precedents

(i) The relative precedence of various classes of business to be listed in the Order Paper of the Lok Sabha shall be in the same order as provided in the Direction 2 of the 'Directions by the Speaker'.

(ii) Immediately after presentation of the General Budget in the Lok Sabha, the Finance Bill is introduced by the Minister of Finance.

(iii) The two Houses of Parliament were convened on gazetted holidays for presentation of the General Budget in the years 1954, 1955, 1981, 1982, 1983, 1984, 1987, 1992 and 1999.

(iv) On the day on which the General Budget is presented to the Parliament, the two Houses are adjourned for the day immediately after presentation/laying of the Budgets in the Houses.

(v) General Budget, Railway Budget and Finance Bills were presented twice in the years 1957, 1962, 1966, 1971, 1977, 1980, 1991, 1996, 1998 and 2004

(vi) On a point of order as to whether a caretaker Government was competent to pilot Financial business in the Lok Sabha, raised by several Members in the Lok Sabha on 11 March, 1991, the Speaker ruled that "the Council of Ministers headed by the Prime Minister continues to function. There is no vacuum. Government is fully competent to pilot the Government Business".

(vii) Railway Budget/Demands for Grants (Railways) and General Budget/Demands for Grants (General) presented to the Lok Sabha on 26 and 28 February, 1997 by the Minister of Railways and Minister of Finance respectively in the outgoing Government headed by Shri H.D. Deve Gowda, were moved by the same Minister of Railways and Minister of Finance in the Lok Sabha under the subsequent Government headed by Shri I.K. Gujaral and were passed by the House on 2 and 6 May, 1997.

(viii) In terms of the Provisional Collection of Taxes Act, 1931, the Finance Bill has to be passed by the Parliament and assented to by the President before the expiry of 75 days after the day on which it was introduced.

(ix) The motion for leave to introduce a Finance and Appropriation Bill cannot be opposed. It is forthwith put to vote (Lok Sabha Rule 72).

(x) General discussion on the Railway Budget in the Rajya Sabha was taken up before the general discussion on the Railway Budget in the Lok Sabha in the years 1953-63, 1965, 1974, 1975, 1993 and 1998.

(xi) General discussion on the General Budget was taken up in the Lok Sabha before general discussion on the Railway Budget in the years 1957, 1962, 1995 and 2002; general discussion on the General Budget in the Rajya Sabha was taken up before the general discussion on the Railway Budget in the years 1952, 1957, 1966, 1987 and 1994.

(xii) Seventeen Departmentally Related Standing Committees for various Ministries/Departments were formally constituted w.e.f. 8 April, 1993 and twenty-four Departmentally Related Standing Committees were formally constituted on 20 July, 2004.

(xiii) All Cabinet Ministers and Ministers of State (Independent Charge) are requested to remain present in the Lok Sabha at the time of guillotining of the outstanding Demands relating to various Ministries/ Departments of Government of India.

CHECK LIST

A check list indicating steps to be taken at various stages in connection with the function relating to the planning and co-ordination of official business in the two Houses of Parliament is at **Annex IV-T.**

5

OTHER GOVERNMENT BUSINESS IN PARLIAMENT

The following items *inter alia* constitute other Government Business (excluding Financial business):

MOTION MOVED BY MINISTER FOR DISCUSSION ON A MATTER OF GENERAL PUBLIC IMPORTANCE

No discussion on a matter of general interest, except provided otherwise in the Constitution or the Rules of the respective Houses, can take place in the Houses except on a motion made with the consent of the Presiding Officer (Lok Sabha Rule 184, Rajya Sabha Rule 167)`. A motion may be in the form of a declaration of opinion or a recommendation; or it may be in the form so as to record approval or disapproval by the House of an act or policy of Government or to express concern or commend, to urge or request an action or to take note of a document or to consider a policy, statement or situation. Usually, notices are tabled in two forms: (i) the House takes note of a document, viz. report, statement, etc., laid on the Table of the House; and (ii) the House considers a policy or situation or statement or any other matter. The motions of the first type are submitted to the vote of the House at the end of the discussion and amendments seeking to approve or disapprove the report etc. can be moved thereto. The second type of motion is generally used when a policy or situation or statement or any other matter is to be taken into consideration. This category of motion is not put to the vote of the House at the close of the debate. However, if a Member, with the consent of the Presiding Officer, moves a substantive motion in substitution of the original motion, the vote of the House thereon is taken (Lok Sabha Rule 342).

The motion for discussion on a matter of general public

interest given by a Minister is treated as having been given under Rule 185 in the Lok Sabha and under Rule 168 in the Rajya Sabha. Normally, a motion moved by a Minister that the policy or situation or statement or any other matter be taken into consideration is not put to the vote of the House and is disposed of in a manner as laid down in the Lok Sabha Rule 342. The motion moved by a Minister that 'the House takes note of the report etc. laid on the Table of the House' is put to the vote of the House as provided in Lok Sabha Rule 191. In the Rajya Sabha, there is no Rule corresponding to Rule 342 in the Lok Sabha Rules and all the motions admitted in that House under Rule 168 are put to the vote of the House as provided for in Rajya Sabha Rule 173.

When a notice of a motion given by a Minister under the above Rules in the two Houses is admitted by the Presiding Officers, the Ministry of Parliamentary Affairs moves the Business Advisory Committee (BAC) of the concerned House for allocation of time for discussion on the motion. After the BAC has allotted the time, the motion is provided for discussion in that House on a day either convenient to the Government or as recommended by the BAC.

CONFIDENCE MOTION

Background

The Government seeking a vote of confidence of the House of the People is of recent origin. There is no rule in the Rules of Procedure relating to a Motion of Confidence in the Council of Ministers. The requirement of moving such motion was perhaps not visualised at the time of the framing of the Lok Sabha Rules. The necessity for debate through such a motion, which is in the nature of an exercise of demonstrating majority support in the Lok Sabha by the ruling party, arose in the late seventies with the advent of Governments obtaining a majority through splits in the political parties, and later on account of formation of coalition Governments as a result of hung Parliaments. In the absence of any rule in this regard, such Motions of Confidence have been entertained under the category of motions stipulated under Rule 184 which are meant for raising discussions on matters of public interest. Decisions on such motions are taken under Rule 191 by putting before the House all necessary questions.

Process

There is no requirement of seeking leave of the House as in the case of a No-Confidence Motion. The one line notice of motion **(Annex II-K)** has to be given by the Prime Minister. When admitted by the Speaker, it is bulletined. The date and time for its discussion and the time for putting the motion to vote in the House is normally decided in consultation with the Business Advisory Committee (BAC) of the House. After the BAC has made recommendations in this regard, the Ministry requests the Lok Sabha Secretariat to provide an entry in the List of Business of the House for discussion on the motion on the day(s) as recommended by the Committee. At the scheduled time on the given day, the Prime Minister moves the motion with a short speech. Thereafter, Members belonging to various parties/groups participate in the discussion. After the discussion on the motion has concluded, the Prime Minister replies to the debate. The motion is then put to the vote of the House and a decision is taken through the process of Division. If the motion is not adopted by the House, the Prime Minister has to tender the resignation of the Government which he heads.

Discussion on Statement made by Minister in the House

A statement on a matter of public importance on any subject, for which the Minister is responsible, can be made by the Minister with the consent of the Presiding Officer. In the Lok Sabha, the statement is made under Rule 372 read with direction 119 of the 'Directions by Speaker', and in the Rajya Sabha, the corresponding rule under which the statement can be made by a Minister is Rule 251. As per provisions of Rules of both the Houses, no question can be asked at the time the statement is made. However, by way of convention, Members of the Rajya Sabha are allowed to seek clarifications on a statement made by a Minister in that House, either at the time of making of the statement by the Minister or subsequently on any day during the session. If clarifications on a statement are not sought on the day the statement is made, an entry in the List of Business under the heading, "Clarifications on the statement made by the Minister for .... on..............regarding........" is also given by the Rajya Sabha Secretariat themselves and they normally keep on making this entry until the clarifications have been sought by the Members. In the Lok Sabha, there is no such convention. However, the Speaker, in exceptional circumstances, may either allow Leaders of various parties/groups or only a limited number of Members of the House, to seek clarifications on the statement made by a Minister on an important issue.

Whenever any Member or Minister concerned is keen to have a discussion on a statement made by the Minister, he/she can give a notice of his/her intention to move the motion that the statement made by the Minister may be discussed by the House. If the motion so given is admitted by the Presiding Officer, the discussion on the statement is provided after the Business Advisory Committee has recommended time and day for its discussion. Such motions are normally admitted under Rule 193 in the Lok Sabha and Rule 176 in the Rajya Sabha. The motion given notice of by a Minister is considered as Government Business and, therefore, the Ministry is required to request the Parliament Secretariat concerned to include the discussion in the List of Business of the concerned House on a day convenient to the Government or as recommended by the BAC of the House.

RESOLUTIONS

A Member or a Minister may move a resolution relating to a matter of general public interest (Lok Sabha Rule 172, Rajya Sabha Rule 156). A resolution may be in the form of a declaration of opinion, or a recommendation or may be in the form so as to record either approval or disapproval by the House of an act or policy of the Government, or convey a message; or commend, urge or request an action; or call attention to a matter or situation for consideration by Government; or in such other form as the Presiding Officer may consider appropriate.

The three broad categories under which Government resolutions may be classified are: (i) resolutions approving international treaties, conventions, or agreements of which the Government is a party, (ii) resolutions declaring or approving certain policies of the Government; and (iii) resolutions approving recommendations of certain committees, viz., recommendations of the Railway Convention Committee.

A Minister may address the notice of the resolution sought to be moved by him/her in either House to the Secretary-General of the concerned House. After the resolution has been admitted by the Presiding Officer, it is published in the Bulletin Part II of that House. Any Member can thereafter table notice(s) for moving amendment(s) to the resolution. Besides, after the resolution has been published in the Bulletin, the Ministry moves the BAC of the concerned House for allocation of time for discussion on the resolution. After the committee has allotted time for its discussion, the concerned Parliament Secretariat is requested to include the resolution for 'discussion and adoption' in the List of Business of that House for a day suitable to the Government. However, before the resolution is listed for consideration in the Order Paper of the House, the Minister concerned may ensure that all relevant documents and literature, wherever necessary, are circulated to the Members sufficiently in advance. The resolution can be taken up first in any House. It can also be taken up simultaneously in the two Houses provided it is not inconvenient to the Government. It is, therefore, not necessary that a message by one House regarding its adoption by that House should be sent to the other House. A copy of every resolution adopted by the House is sent by the Secretary-General of that House to the Minister concerned.

STATUTORY RESOLUTION SEEKING DISAPPROVAL OF ORDINANCES

Any Member of the House can give notice for moving a statutory resolution seeking disapproval of an Ordinance. Though it is not an item of Government Business, if, however, notice of a statutory resolution given notice of by a Member of the House seeking disapproval of an Ordinance is admitted by the Speaker, time has to be provided by the Government for discussion thereon. Not only time is to be provided by the Government for the purpose, an entry for its consideration, along with an entry for the consideration and passing of the Bill seeking to replace the Ordinance, after such Bill (if it is not already pending in either House even before promulgation of the Ordinance) has been introduced in either House, has also to be provided by the Ministry in the List of Business of the House where the resolution has been admitted.

PROCLAMATION ON FAILURE OF CONSTITUTIONAL MACHINERY IN A STATE (PRESIDENT'S RULE IN A STATE)

A Proclamation, issued by the President in respect of any State, under the provisions of article 356 of the Constitution, is required to be laid on the Table of the two Houses of Parliament. Along with the Proclamation, Government also generally lays on the Table of the Houses a summary of the Governor's report or the Governor's report *in extenso*, where the President has acted on such a report.

Article 356 (3) *inter alia* provides that such a Proclamation shall cease to operate at the expiration of two months from the date of its issue unless before the expiration of this period, it has been approved by resolutions of both Houses of Parliament. Therefore, if the Proclamation so issued is to be continued beyond two months, both the Houses of Parliament may have to approve it by a resolution. For this purpose, Government, after the Proclamation along with other requisite documents has been laid on the Table of the Houses, has to give a separate notice **(Annex V-A)** to the Secretary-Generals of the respective Houses indicating its intention to move a resolution seeking approval of the Proclamation by that House during the session following the promulgation of the Proclamation. After the allocation of time by the BAC of the respective Houses, the Ministry requests the two Secretariats to include the item regarding consideration of the resolution in the Lists of Business of the two Houses on a day either convenient to the Government or as recommended by the BACs. However, care should be taken to list the resolution in the two Houses sufficiently in advance of the expiry of the prescribed period of two months. There is no restriction in moving the resolution in any House first. There is also no restriction on the discussion on the resolution being taken up in the two Houses simultaneously unless it is inconvenient to the Government. The resolution has to be adopted by the Houses by a simple majority.

It has been held that an amendment to the resolution seeking to approve the President's Proclamation is out of order if the amendment is negative in character or is beyond the scope of the resolution, or is contradictory to the text of the resolution. An amendment seeking to give conditional approval to the

Proclamation is also inadmissible. A resolution seeking disapproval of the Proclamation is also inadmissible as there is no provision to this effect in article 356 of the Constitution. The House may adopt or not adopt a resolution as the resolution before the House cannot take any other form.

PROCLAMATION OF EMERGENCY

Proclamation of Emergency issued under article of 352 of the Constitution has to be laid on the Table of both Houses of Parliament. Such Proclamation ceases to operate at the expiration of one month unless before the expiration period it has been approved by resolutions of both Houses of Parliament. If any such Proclamation is issued at a time when the Lok Sabha has been dissolved or the dissolution of the Lok Sabha takes place during the period of one month and if a resolution approving the Proclamation has been passed by the Rajya Sabha, but no resolution with respect to such Proclamation has been passed by the Lok Sabha before the expiration of that period, the Proclamation ceases to operate at the expiration of thirty days from the date on which the Lok Sabha first sits after its reconstitution, unless before the expiration of the period of thirty days a resolution approving the Proclamation has been passed by the Lok Sabha.

When a notice in writing of a resolution seeking disapproval of a Proclamation or its continuance, signed by not less than one-tenth of the total number of Members of the Lok Sabha, has been given to the Speaker, if the Lok Sabha is in session, or, to the President, if it is not in session, a special sitting of the Lok Sabha shall be held within fourteen days from the date of receipt of the notice for considering the resolution. All resolutions for approval of or for further continuance of the Proclamation of Emergency may be passed by Parliament by a majority of the total membership and by a majority of not less than two-thirds of the Members present and voting in each House.

The life of the Lok Sabha may, while a Proclamation of Emergency is in operation, be extended beyond its normal period by Parliament by law for a period not exceeding one year at a time and not exceeding in any case beyond a period of six months after the Proclamation has ceased to operate.

After the Proclamation of Emergency has been laid on the

Table of the House and time for its consideration has been allotted by the BAC, the Ministry may request the Lok Sabha Secretariat to include the resolution given notice of by the Government and admitted by the Speaker, in the List of Business of the House for consideration and passing. After it has been passed by the Lok Sabha, the Ministry takes action on the lines of procedure followed for listing in the Lok Sabha, to list the resolution for consideration and passing in the Rajya Sabha.

PRESIDENT'S ADDRESS

Background

Under article 87 of the Constitution, at the commencement of the First Session after each general election to the House of People and at the commencement of the First Session of each year, the President shall address both Houses of Parliament assembled together and inform Parliament of the causes of its summons.

Process

About two months in advance of the President's address, the Prime Minister's Office requests the Secretaries of all Ministries/Departments to furnish, by a specified date, information on the following items for inclusion in the President's address to be delivered in the ensuing Parliament session:

(a) matters relating to Finance to be prepared in consultation with the Ministry of Finance;
(b) matters relating to Ordinances promulgated during the inter-session period; and
(c) matters relating to Legislative business together with the list of Bills proposed to be considered/introduced during the next session.

So far as the Ministry of Parliamentary Affairs is concerned, it is required to furnish necessary updated material, preferably in the form of a short statement in respect of the Ministry in general and on the above points in particular, to the PMO with a copy thereof to the Cabinet Secretariat, by a specified date. In order to obtain the information relating to various

Ministries/Departments in regard to item at (c) above, Secretaries of all the Ministries are addressed by the Ministry **(Annex V-B)** to furnish the requisite information for onward transmission to the PMO. On receipt of the information from the Ministries/ Departments, it is consolidated and passed on to the PMO along with (i) the requisite information relating to the Ministry of Parliamentary Affairs, if any; (ii) list of Ordinances promulgated, if any; and (iii) list of Bills pending on the conclusion of the last session of Parliament or the list of Bills pending on the dissolution of the last Lok Sabha.

On the occasion of the President's address, seats in the front rows in the Central Hall are reserved for the members of the Union Council of Ministers. In order to ensure that the seats reserved for Ministers do not remain vacant, the Ministry informally ascertains from the offices of the Ministers, as to whether they will attend the address. Names of Ministers, who are not in a position to attend the address, are intimated to the Lok Sabha Secretariat (Table Office) so that seats may not be reserved for them in the Central Hall.

Requisite number of copies of the President's address are made available to the Ministry of Parliamentary Affairs by the President's Secretariat on the morning of the day on which the President has to deliver his address to the Houses. After the President has addressed both Houses of Parliament, copies of the address are forwarded by the Ministry of Parliamentary Affairs to all Central Ministries/Departments for information.

DISCUSSION ON MOTION OF THANKS

About ten to fifteen days in advance of the date of the address, a provisional programme of dates of discussion on the Motion of Thanks on the President's address in the two Houses is chalked out. Normally, three to four days in the Lok Sabha and three days in the Rajya Sabha are provided for this purpose. After the programme has been approved by the Minister, it is communicated to the two Parliament Secretariats which bulletin it for the information of the Members.

Discussion on the Motion of Thanks in the two Houses is initiated by one of the Members, called mover, and seconded by another Member, who seconds the motion is called the seconder. Normally, the mover moves the motion in one language while the seconder seconds the motion in the other language i.e. if the mover moves the motion in English, the seconder will second it in Hindi and *vice versa.* It has been the practice that the Minister of Parliamentary Affairs, in consultation with the Prime Minister, decides the names of the movers and seconders to the motion in the two Houses. The Members so decided have to sign the notice of the motion addressed to the Secretary-General of each House **(Annexes II-N & O)** which has to be given to the respective Houses after the copy of the President's Address has been laid in the two Houses. For this purpose, a note requesting the Minister to select the mover and seconder in each House is submitted about a week in advance of the President's address, along with (i) the names of the Members who moved and seconded the motion in the two Houses during the last five years; and (ii) the draft of the notice of motion to be moved in each House (in English and Hindi). After the Minister has selected the Members, the notices of motions are got signed by the respective Members by the Minister's office. On receipt of the file in the Legislative I Section, the notices of motions, in original, are forwarded at the level of the Under Secretary to the Table Offices in the two Secretariats for further necessary action. The discussion on the motion in the two Houses is provided by the Ministry on the dates already communicated to the two Secretariats. Where, however, it is not possible to provide discussion on those dates, efforts are made to chalk out the revised dates and, after the Minister's approval, communicate them to the Parliament Secretariat concerned for bulletining them for the information of the Members.

Decisions

President's Address

(i) The Fourteenth Session of the XIII Lok Sabha was adjourned *sine die* on 23 December, 2003. The House was not prorogued thereafter and was reconvened to meet on 29 January, 2004. It was treated as the second part of the 14th Session as per past practice. However, a number of Members, through points of order, submitted in the House on 30 January, 2004 and 3 February, 2004 that the session which commenced on 29 January, 2004 was the First Session of the year 2004 and it should, therefore, have been addressed by the President in terms of article 87 of the Constitution. In his ruling given in the House on 3 February, 2004, the Speaker, Lok Sabha *inter alia* observed that as per the provisions of the Constitution, a session of the House comes to an end when the House is prorogued and since the House was not prorogued after its adjournment *sine die* on 23 December, 2003, this session could, at best, be treated as the second part of the 14th Session of the XIII Lok Sabha notwithstanding the fact that the calendar year had since changed. The Speaker, therefore, ruled out the points of order on the issue **(Annex V-C)**. On a writ petition (No.86/2004) filed on this issue by Shri Ramdas Athawale (Member of XIII Lok Sabha), the Supreme Court decided that........

> "......... Issue notice to learned Attorney General also. Learned Attorney General is present in Court. He seeks and is allowed four weeks time to obtain instructions. List after four weeks. However, it is clarified that the question shall have prospective bearing and not retrospective bearing in regard to dissolution of Parliament."

(ii) On 6 March, 1991, while concluding his reply to the Motion of Thanks on the President's address to both Houses of Parliament assembled together on 21 February, 1991, the then Prime Minister stated that the Council of Ministers had decided to tender their resignation and that he would be meeting the President immediately to convey to him their decision. The Speaker, thereupon, observed that in view of the decision of the Council of Ministers to resign, the Motion of Thanks on the President's address had become infructuous.

(iii) After the swearing in of the United Front Government under Shri H.D. Devegowda as Prime Minister on 1 June, 1996, the Leader of the House and the then Minister of Parliamentary Affairs, Shri Ram Vilas Paswan held a meeting of Leaders of Political Parties and Groups in Parliament on 9 June, 1996 to discuss the point as to whether the Motion of Thanks admitted on 27 May, 1996 be taken up during the reconvened sitting of the Lok Sabha on 10 June, 1996. The consensus in the meeting was that there was no need at that stage to discuss the Motion of

Thanks on the President's address as the Motion of Thanks apparently had become infructuous. Therefore, the Motion on the President's address was not taken up for discussion during the reconvened session of the Lok Sabha on 10 June, 1996.

(F.No.20(1)/96-Leg.I)

(iv) During the Budget Session, 2000, it was decided that in future while furnishing information received from various Ministries/Departments on the subject, the Ministry of Parliamentary Affairs shall furnish a para containing a brief summary of the Government legislative proposals/programmes for that year to the Cabinet Secretariat for incorporation in the President's address.

Government's Prerogative to Provide Discussion on Proclamation Regarding President's Rule

On 4 March, 1999 in the Rajya Sabha, the Leader of Opposition Dr. Manmohan Singh, and others made submissions *inter alia* desiring to know when the discussion on the Proclamation under article 356 in relation to the State of Bihar will be provided in the Rajya Sabha. The Members submitted that the resolution on this subject had already been passed by the Lok Sabha and, therefore, Government should make its position clear as to when the discussion on the Proclamation will be provided in the Rajya Sabha. They also expressed a fear that the Government might bypass the Rajya Sabha in this respect.

The Minister of Parliamentary Affairs (Shri P.R. Kumaramangalam), who intervened during these submissions, assured the House that in no circumstances would Government ever go against the constitutional provisions or political decorum. He further stated that on 8 March, 1999 the Government would inform the House as to what steps it proposed to take in the matter. However, the Members continued to make submissions on the subject and requested the Chair to give its ruling in the matter. In this connection, the Hon'ble Chairman gave the following ruling:

> "Hon'ble member, the basic issue is this. It has come up earlier also in the House and my distinguished predecessor, Chairman of the Rajya Sabha, on 4th November, 1986 had given his ruling and it is nearly the same as my ruling. He had said:

> 'You are aware that if the Government does not want to have the proclamation approved, they need not move the Resolution. And if they do not move the Resolution, the proclamation lapses. Therefore, there is nothing for discussion. It is only when the proclamation is continued that there is something for discussion in the House. When the Government is not coming forward with the proclamation, and if it lapses, there will be nothing for discussion. It is for the Government to decide. We cannot force the Government to decide just now. It is their right to decide'."

Statutory Resolution Seeking Disapproval of an Ordinance Adopted

(i) On 5 August, 1991, the Statutory Resolution seeking disapproval of the Code of Criminal Procedure (Amendment) Ordinance, 1991 and the motion for consideration of the Code of Criminal Procedure (Amendment) Bill, 1991 were moved by Shri S.S. Ahluwalia, MP, a Member of the ruling party, and Shri S.B. Chavan, Minister of Home Affairs, respectively. After a brief discussion, Shri S.S. Ahluwalia replied to the debate on the resolution and Shri S.B. Chavan, Minister of Home Affairs while intervening in the debate requested Shri S.S. Ahluwalia to withdraw the resolution. However, Shri Ahluwalia did not withdraw the resolution. Accordingly, the resolution was put to vote. Thirty nine votes each were cast in favour and against the resolution. In such a situation, the Chair, in terms of article 100 of the Constitution, exercised his casting vote in favour of the Statutory Resolution. Accordingly, the Statutory Resolution was adopted by 40 to 39 votes and further consideration and passing of the Bill was not proceeded with.

However, the above Bill was again introduced in the Rajya Sabha during the next session, viz., 160th Session, on 3 September, 1991. At the time of its introduction, some Members from the Opposition benches opposed the introduction of the Code of Criminal Procedure (Second Amendment) Bill, 1991, stating that the Bill was disapproved by the House in the 159th Session. The Chair overruled the objection and thereafter the Bill was introduced. The Bill was passed by the Rajya Sabha on 4 September, 1991 and by the Lok Sabha on 17 September, 1991 and was assented to by the President on 19 September, 1991.

(ii) On 7 August, 1997, the Statutory Resolution seeking disapproval of the Presidential and Vice Presidential Election (Amendment) Ordinance, 1997, moved by Shri Satish Aggarwal and motion for consideration of the Presidential and Vice Presidential Election (Amendment) Bill, 1997 moved by the Minister of State for Law and Justice were together taken up for discussion in the Rajya Sabha. After a brief discussion, the Statutory Resolution was put to vote and was adopted by the House. As a result of this further consideration and passing of the Bill was not proceeded with.

With a view to replace the Ordinance by an Act of Parliament, the above Bill was introduced in the Lok Sabha on 12 August, 1997 i.e. during the same Parliament session, as the Presidential and Vice Presidential Elections (Second Amendment) Bill, 1997. The Bill was considered and passed by the Lok Sabha on 13 August, 1997. This Bill could not have been taken up in the Rajya Sabha in the same session in the normal circumstances in view of the provisions of the Rule 228 of the Rajya Sabha Rules which *inter alia* provides that a motion must not raise a question substantially identical with one on which the Council has given a decision in the same session. Thereafter, on a motion moved by the Minister of Law and Justice, the Rule 228 in its application to the above Bill was suspended and the Bill was thereafter considered and passed by the Rajya Sabha on 14 August, 1998.

(iii) On 21 March, 2002, the Statutory Resolution seeking disapproval of the Prevention of Terrorism (Second) Ordinance, 2001 moved by Shri Kapil Sibal and the motion moved by the Minister of Home Affairs for consideration of the Prevention of Terrorism Bill, 2002 as passed by the Lok Sabha, were taken up together for discussion in the Rajya Sabha. After reply to the debate by the Minister of Home Affairs, the Statutory Resolution was put to the vote of the House and was adopted after division (Ayes 113, Noes 98). After the Statutory Resolution was adopted, the motion for consideration of the Bill was put to the vote of the House and was negatived after division (Ayes 98, Noes 113).

As the Prevention of Terrorism (Second) Ordinance, 2001 would have lapsed on 8 April, 2002 if not replaced by an Act of Parliament on or before the above date in terms of article 123 of the Constitution, it was decided to convene a Joint Sitting of the two Houses in terms of article 108 of the Constitution on 26 March, 2002 for deliberation and voting on the Prevention of Terrorism Bill, 2002 as passed by the Lok Sabha and rejected by the Rajya Sabha. The Bill was deliberated, during the Joint Sitting held on 26 March, 2002. On the motion for consideration for the purpose of deliberating on the Bill, the Division took place (Ayes: 425; Noes: 294). The motion for consideration was accordingly adopted. Thereafter, the motion moved by Minister of Home Affairs that the Bill be passed was adopted and the Bill was passed.

Discussion on the Working of Ministries in Rajya Sabha

During the second part of the Budget Sessions, a few sittings in the Rajya Sabha are devoted to discussion on working of some of the Ministries as recommended by the Business Advisory Committee of the House. Normally, discussion on the working of Ministries is taken up in the Rajya Sabha during more or less the same period when the Lok Sabha is busy with discussion and voting on the Demands for Grants (General) of Ministries/ Departments. With a view to selecting the Ministries/ Departments for this purpose, the Chairman, Rajya Sabha, convenes a meeting of the Business Advisory Committee, Rajya Sabha, during the last week of the first part of the Budget Session. Keeping in view the time (days) likely to be available for this purpose, the committee decides the number and names of Ministries/Departments whose working can be discussed by the House during the second part of the Budget Session to be held after recess and also allots time for discussion on the working of such Ministries/Departments. In the meeting, the names of various parties/groups, whose Members may initiate the discussion on the working of various Ministries selected for this purpose, are also decided. Sometimes, date(s) of discussion. Such Ministries/Departments and the order in which they should be taken up for discussion is also decided in the meeting.

As soon as the recommendations of the Business Advisory Committee about the names of Ministries/Departments to be discussed are announced in the House or the minutes of the meeting are received in the Ministry, the Ministries/Departments concerned are informed in order to enable them to make necessary preparation for the purpose in advance and also to ensure that the Minister concerned may make it convenient to remain present in the House on the probable date of discussion of his/her Ministry.

Discussion on the working of Ministries is included in the List of Business of the Rajya Sabha for the days and in the order in which it is intimated by the Ministry of Parliamentary Affairs to the Rajya Sabha Secretariat through daily Lists of Government Business. When this item comes for discussion in the House, the Member, in whose name the item is listed in the List of Business, is called by the Chair to initiate the discussion. After such a Member has made his speech, few other Members, who have given their names for participation in the debate, are called to speak. Minister concerned replies to the debate at the end. With this, the discussion on the working of a Ministry is over. There is no voting by the House on this item.

CHECK LIST

A check list indicating steps to be taken at various stages for transaction of other Government Business in two Houses is at **Annex V-D.**

6

CABINET COMMITTEE ON PARLIAMENTARY AFFAIRS

BACKGROUND

With the creation of a bicameral Parliament consisting of several representatives of the people, it was deemed desirable that the Cabinet should delegate the overall responsibility regarding detailed parliamentary matters to a small standing committee of the Cabinet, specialising in this task. A Parliamentary and Legal Affairs Committee was accordingly constituted in 1949. This committee was subsequently named as the Cabinet Committee on Parliamentary Affairs. The then Department of Parliamentary Affairs and now Ministry of Parliamentary Affairs has been providing secretarial assistance to the committee since 1954. Prior to 1954, the Ministry of Law had been providing secretarial assistance to the committee though secretarial assistance in regard to planning of Government Business in both Houses of Parliament was even then provided by the then Department of Parliamentary Affairs.

As per the First Schedule to the Government of India (Transaction of Business) Rules, 1961, the following functions have been assigned to the Cabinet Committee on Parliamentary Affairs:

(i) To watch the progress of Government Business in Parliament and to give such directions as may be necessary from time to time, in order to secure smooth and efficient conduct of such business;

(ii) to scrutinise, and to consider the attitude of the Government on non-official bills and resolutions to be presented to Parliament;

(iii) to maintain a review from an all-India point of view of legislations undertaken by State legislatures; and

(iv) to consider proposals to summon or prorogue the Houses of Parliament.

Under Rule 6 of the above Rules, the Prime Minister may, from time to time, modify the functions assigned to the committee.

The composition of the Cabinet Committee on Parliamentary Affairs, as last notified, is as under:-

1. Minister of Defence - **Chairman**
2. Minister of Agriculture and Minister of Consumer Affairs, Food & Public Distribution
3. Minister of Railways
4. Minister of Home Affairs
5. Minister of Chemicals & Fertilizers and Minister of Steel
6. Minister of Parliamentary Affairs and Minister of Urban Development
7. Minister of Road Transport & Highways and Minister of Shipping
8. Minister of Law & Justice

Special Invitees

1. Minister of State in the Ministry of Personnel, Public Grievances & Pension and Minister of State in the Ministry of Parliamentary Affairs
2. Minister of State in the Ministry of Defence and Minister of State in the Ministry of Parliamentary Affairs
3. Minister of State in the Prime Minister's Office
4. Minister of State in the Ministry of Rural Development and Minister of State in the Ministry of Parliamentary Affairs

(Ministers other than members of the committee, who are concerned with the subject matter under discussion in the meetings of the committee, are also invited, if necessary, to attend such meetings of the committee)

PROCESS

The Cabinet Committee on Parliamentary Affairs normally takes decisions on matters placed before it for consideration, through circulation of papers. However, whenever the Chairman of the committee, who is normally the Minister of Parliamentary Affairs, desires to convene a formal meeting of the Cabinet Committee on Parliamentary Affairs for consideration of any issues related to functions assigned to it, action is taken by the Ministry to convene the meeting of the committee. The meetings of the committee are normally held during the session period, though there have been occasions when meetings have been held during inter-session period also. The venue of the meeting is either the Minister of Parliamentary Affairs' Room in Parliament House or any place/room inside or outside Parliament House, convenient to him/her.

As per records available in the Ministry, only thirty formal meetings of the Cabinet Committee on Parliamentary Affairs, including four meetings during the tenure of the XIII Lok Sabha, have so far been held since 1978 **(Annex VI-A).** Except for these meetings, the decisions by the committee on various issues placed before it for consideration, were taken through circulation of papers.

The process followed for taking action on four functions assigned to the Cabinet Committee on Parliamentary Affairs has been dealt with *in seriatim,* as follows:

To watch the progress of Government Business in Parliament and to give such directions as may be necessary from time to time, in order to secure smooth and efficient conduct of such business

There have been very few occasions when the Cabinet Committee on Parliamentary Affairs reviewed either in formal meetings or through circulation of papers, the progress of the Government Business in the two Houses. Earlier, the Cabinet Committee on Parliamentary Affairs had been meeting sometimes for this purpose, but for the last few years, it has hardly been meeting to review the progress of Government Business in the Houses. It will be interesting to note that during the term of the XIII Lok Sabha, the committee did not meet even once, either formally or through circulation of papers, for this purpose. As per records available with the Ministry **(Annex VI-A),** the committee held its first meeting to discuss the Government Business for the Winter Session, 1983, on 7 November, 1983. Since 1983, the committee has so far held only thirteen meetings to *inter alia* review the Government Business.

This function now-a-days is normally taken care of by the Minister of Parliamentary Affairs himself/ herself. About a week before the commencement of every session of Parliament, the Minister of Parliamentary Affairs or one of the Ministers of State for Parliamentary Affairs, if the Minister is not available on the proposed date of the meeting, takes a meeting with Secretaries/ senior officers of various Ministries/Departments to finalise the Tentative List of Legislative and other Business to be taken up in the two Houses during the ensuing session. Besides, the Minister also takes review meetings with Secretary/senior officers of the Ministry, as and when necessary, before commencement of the session and on an almost daily basis during the session period and gives such directions, as may be necessary, for expeditious and smooth disposal of pending and new Government Legislative and other Business in the two Houses.

To scrutinise and to consider the attitude of the Government on Non-Official Bills and Resolutions to be presented to Parliament

This is the most important function of the committee. The committee has held a maximum number of meetings, formally as well as through circulation of papers, for consideration of matters relating to Private Members' Bills and Resolutions.

Private Members' Bills and Resolutions are taken up alternatively in the two Houses for two and a half hours on every Friday or any other day of the week during the session period as the Presiding Officer of the respective House may direct. If Private Members' Bills are taken up in one week, then the Private Members' Resolutions will be taken up during the next week and so on. Whenever the Private Members' Bills/ Resolutions are listed for consideration in the two Houses, the Government has to take a stand on their subject matter with the approval of the Cabinet Committee on Parliamentary Affairs. For this purpose, Ministries/Departments concerned are requested to furnish, with the approval of their Ministers, two copies of the 'Note for Consideration of the Cabinet Committee on Parliamentary Affairs', commonly called 'Brief', both in English and Hindi versions, indicating the Government's stand on the Private Members' Bills/Resolutions which have been listed for consideration in the two Houses for the day scheduled for such business (Ministries are requested to furnish two copies of the brief in each version, if the approval of the committee on the Ministry's proposal is to be taken through circulation of papers and thirty copies in each version, if there is a proposal to convene a formal meeting of the committee). The various stages at which the copies of the Brief are called from the Ministries/ Departments concerned can be seen in the following paras.

As soon as the result of the ballot in respect of Private Members' Bills to be taken up for consideration in the Lok Sabha on the days scheduled for Private Members' Bills is notified in the Parliamentary Bulletin by the Lok Sabha Secretariat, a letter **(Annex-VI-B)** is addressed by the Secretary, Ministry of Parliamentary Affairs, to the Secretaries of the Ministries/ Departments concerned with the Bills which secure the first ten positions in the ballot, requesting them to send the requisite copies of the Brief (English and Hindi versions), if not already sent, to this Ministry for consideration/approval of the Government's stand on such Bills by the committee. So far as the Private Members' Resolutions in the Lok Sabha and the Private Members' Bills and Resolutions in the Rajya Sabha are concerned, the names of Members, who have given notices for moving these items, are only balloted and the Members who secure the first few positions/places in the ballot are requested to intimate the title of the pending Bills/text of the Resolutions which they intend to move to the respective Parliament Secretariat so that such Bills/ Resolutions in their names could be listed for consideration in the Order Papers of the two Houses for the days specified for this purpose. As the Members furnish their replies in this regard when the List of Business is about to be sent to the Press for printing, no letter is addressed by the Secretary, Ministry of Parliamentary Affairs, after the results of the ballots in respect of Private Members' Resolutions in the Lok Sabha and the Private Members' Bills and Resolutions are notified by the Parliament Secretariat concerned.

Wherever, however, the requisite information from the Members in this regard becomes available to the Parliament Secretariat a couple of days or more in advance of the date of printing of the Lists of Business, an advance list of such business is obtained from the concerned Secretariat and Ministries/ Departments concerned therewith are requested **(Annex-VI-C)** to immediately furnish the requisite number of copies of the Brief in both the versions clearly and precisely indicating the

Government's stand on such Bills and Resolutions. Alternatively, as and when the printed Lists of Business of Private Members' Bills and Resolutions become available, which is normally two or three days in advance of the day on which they are to be taken up, Ministries/Departments, which have not already furnished Briefs on the Bills/Resolutions included in the list for consideration, are requested to immediately furnish Briefs on such Bills and Resolutions (Such communication is first faxed and then physically sent to the Parliament Unit of the Ministry to provide them maximum possible time to examine the Bills/ Resolutions and furnish the requisite information). Ministries/ Departments, from whom the Briefs are not received in time as specified in our communication, are also informally contacted at various levels, to expedite the same.

The 'Note for CCPA' **(Annex VI-D** for Bills and **Annex VI-E** for Resolutions) for consideration and approval of the Government's stand on the Private Members' Bills/Resolutions, listed for consideration in the two Houses and on which Briefs have been received from the Ministries/Departments concerned, is submitted normally a day before the day for which they are listed and approval of the committee is ordinarily obtained through circulation of papers (Bills/Resolutions on which Government's stand has already been approved by the committee are not included in such Notes). Whenever it is, however, decided to convene formal meetings of the committee for the purpose, the convenience of the Minister in regard to the date, time and venue of the proposed meetings is solicited. After getting the room reserved, if necessary, all the members of the committee are informed about it, along with the agenda of the meeting, preferably a day in advance of the day of the meeting. Arrangement for providing tea/coffee and pens/pads etc. is also made by the Ministry. In addition to the members of the committee, the concerned Ministries are also endorsed copies of the agenda with the request that they may depute their officers, preferably of the level of Joint Secretary or above to the meeting to brief the committee, if necessary, on the item(s) included in the agenda concerning those Ministries. The Secretary and other officers of the Ministry of Parliamentary Affairs also attend the meetings to render necessary secretarial assistance to the committee. Decisions taken by the committee, in the formal meetings or through circulation of papers, are communicated to the Ministries/Departments concerned first on the telephone followed by formal communications as normally decisions by the committee in such matters are taken on the day on which the Bills/Resolutions are scheduled to be taken up in the Houses.

A majority of the Private Members' Bills introduced in the two Houses involve expenditure from the Consolidated Fund of India when enacted and brought into operation and, therefore, require the recommendation of the President under article 117(3) of the Constitution before they are taken up in either House of Parliament. Similarly, some Bills sponsored by private Members require the recommendation of the President under article 117(1) of the Constitution before they are introduced in the Lok Sabha. In response to queries made by the Ministries on the scope of granting or withholding of such recommendation, the question was considered in consultation with the Ministry of Law and Justice who opined as under:

> "The recommendation of the President is for the introduction or moving of the Bill. The grant of this recommendation is an executive act to be performed on the advice of the Ministry. The fact that the Ministry advise recommendation only means that it has no objection to the introduction or moving of the Bill. It does not preclude the Government from opposing the passing of the Bill into law. It may, therefore, oppose the Bill on merits at any stage after introduction."

In view of the above, whenever references seeking advice from the Ministry in this regard are received, the Ministries are advised that the President's recommendation required under clause (1) and/or (3) of article 117 of the Constitution for the introduction/consideration of Private Members' Bill may ordinarily be granted unless very exceptional circumstances specially warrant withholding of the President's recommendation **(Annex VI-F).** As per recommendation of the Committee on Private Members' Bills and Resolutions, even the Private Members' Bills awaiting recommendation of the President under article 117(3) for their consideration in the Houses can be included in the List of Business to be transacted by the Houses. To avoid any embarrassment being caused to the administrative Ministry owing to listing of a Bill for consideration for which they have not obtained the requisite recommendation of the President, Ministries/Departments are required to take action for obtaining/ withholding of recomm-endation of the President as soon as they receive notices of such Bills from the Parliament Secretariat concerned **(Annex VI-G).**

Notwithstanding the opinion of the Ministry of Law and Justice in the matter **(Annex VI- F)**, Ministries/Departments, citing various reasons, have from time to time been making references to the Ministry of Parliamentary Affairs for soliciting the approval of the Cabinet Committee on Parliamentary Affairs to the Government stand to advise the President to withhold his recommendation for introduction/consideration of the Private Members' Bills by the two Houses under article 117(1)/(3) of the Constitution. In such cases and also on various related issues, decisions taken by the committee from time to time have been indicated under the heading 'Decisions'.

To Maintain a Review from an all-India point of view of Legislations undertaken by State Legislatures

As per records available in the Ministry, the committee has never undertaken a review of this nature since its constitution.

To Consider Proposals to Summon or Prorogue the Houses of Parliament

Summoning of the Houses

Since 1999, proposals regarding summoning the Houses of Parliament are being submitted to the Cabinet for consideration and decision. However, prior to 1999, such proposals were submitted to the CCPA and after approval by the committee, the approvals of the Prime Minister and the President were sought. After the President had approved the proposed dates of summoning of the Houses, the respective Parliament Secretariats were informed of the Government's decisions in the matter for further necessary action. The submission of such proposals was discontinued in 1999 following a observation made by the then Minister of Home Affairs that suchs proposals should be submitted to the Cabinet. As this function of the committee has almost been rendered dysfunctional since 1999, a proposal that the Cabinet Secretariat may be requested for deletion of this function from the list of functions assigned to the Committee, was submitted for consideration of the Minister of Parliamentary Affairs in 2003. However, after discussion with the Minister, it was decided not to pursue the proposal.

Prorogation of the Houses

As soon as the Houses are adjourned *sine die* on the conclusion of a Session, a Note for consideration of the CCPA **(Annex VI-H)** seeking its approval to the proposal to prorogue the Houses is submitted and approval of the committee is obtained through circulation of papers. After the committee has approved the proposal, the Secretary- Generals of the two Houses are informed of the Government's decision in the matter by the Secretary, Ministry of Parliamentary Affairs **(Annexes III-K & L).** Whenever the committee is not functional because of its non-constitution, e.g. on the conclusion of a short first Session of the Houses held after the constitution of a new Lok Sabha, proposals regarding prorogation of the Houses, after their approval by the Minister of Parliamentary Affairs, are submitted to the Prime Minister for his approval in terms of Rule 12 of the Government of India (Transaction of Business) Rules, 1961 (Rule 12 states that "The Prime Minister may, in any case or classes of cases permit or condone a departure from these rules, to the extent he deems necessary"). After the Prime Minister has accorded his approval to the proposal, the two Parliament Secretariats are informed in the usual manner.

DECISIONS

(i) With the approval of the Cabinet Committee on Parliamentary Affairs, the Ministries of Personnel, Public Grievances and Pensions and Urban Affairs and Employment approached the President to withhold his recommendations for consideration of (i) the Declaration of Assets by Civil Servants Bill, 1994 by Shri K. Ramamurthy, and (ii) the Slums and Jhuggi Jhopri Areas (Basic Amenities and Clearance) Bill, 1994 by Smt. Bhavna Chikhalia and Shri Suresh Pachouri, under article 117(3) of the Constitution. However, the President recommended all these Bills for consideration under article 117(3) of the Constitution. (F.No.44(3)/95-Leg.I)

(ii) The Cabinet Committee in its meeting held on 25 February,

1999 did not agree with the views of the Ministry of Urban Development and Poverty Alleviation for advising the President to withhold his recommendation under article 117 (3) of the Constitution for consideration of the Slum and Jhuggi Jhopri Areas (Basic Amenities and Clearance) Bill, 1977 in the Rajya Sabha by Shri Suresh Pachouri. (F.No.44(5)/98-Leg.I)

(iii) The State of Vidarbha Bill, 1999 by Shri Vilas Muttemwar relating to reorganisation of States, attracted the provision of article 3 of the Constitution, which *inter alia* provides that no such Bill can be introduced in either House of Parliament without the recommendation of the President after he has referred the Bill to the concerned State Legislature for expressing its views thereon within a specified period. On this Bill, the Ministry of Home Affairs had sought the approval of the C.C.P.A. to the following Government's stand:

> "The State of Vidarbha Bill, 1999 may not be referred to the State Legislature of Maharashtra for expressing its views thereon as required under article 3 of the Constitution."

The Minister of Home Affairs, who was invited to the meeting, was requested by the Minister of Parliamentary Affairs to reconsider their stand on the Bill. The Ministry of Home Affairs, however, subsequently stated that after reconsideration of the matter, it has been decided, with the approval of the Minister of Home Affairs, to reiterate their earlier stand on the Bill. The Committee accorded its approval to the Government's stand through circulation of papers vide CCPA Note No.15/2000 dated 22 November, 2000.

(F.No.70(2)/2000-Leg.I - Part-II and f.44(6)/2000-Leg.I)

(iv) On the State of Paschim Pradesh Bill, 2000, relating to the creation of a separate State of Paschim Pradesh by reorganising the present state of Uttar Pradesh, introduced in the Lok Sabha by Shri Chandra Vijay Singh, the Ministry of Home Affairs had sought the approval of the CCPA to the following Government's stand:

> "Bill be not referred to the State Legislature of UP for expressing its views thereon as required under article 3 of the Constitution of India."

The proposal was placed before the CCPA and the CCPA, through circulation of papers, approved the above stand of the Ministry of Home Affairs *vide* Note No. 3/2001 dated 8 March, 2001. (F.No.70(1)/2001-Leg.I)

(v) The Ministry of Home Affairs proposed that the President may be advised to withhold his recommendation under article 117(3) of the Constitution, for consideration of the States Reorganisation Commission Bill, 2000 by Shri Subodh Mohite in the Lok Sabha. The CCPA, through circulation of papers, approved the proposal of the Ministry of Home Affairs *vide* Note No.11/2001 dated 22 November, 2001.

(F.No.70(1)/2001-Leg.I Part-II)

(vi) The Ministry of Home Affairs proposed that the following Bills introduced in the Lok Sabha may not be referred to the respective State Legislatures for expressing their views thereon, as required under article 3 of the Constitution of India:

1. The State of Telangana Bill, 2001 by Dr. Y. Lakshmi Prasad.
2. The State of Gorakhaland Bill, 2001 by Shri Dawa Lama.
3. The State of Vidarbha Bill, 2000 by Shri Vijay J. Darda.

The proposals were placed before the CCPA and the CCPA approved the above stands of the Ministry *vide* Note No.11/2001 dated 22 November, 2001. (F.No.70(1)/2001-Leg.I Part-III)

CHECK LIST

A check list indicating steps to be taken at various stages in connection with the functions allocated to the committee is enclosed as **Annex VI-I.**

7

CONSULTATIVE COMMITTEES

BACKGROUND

Functioning of the Consultative Committees of Members of Parliament for various Ministries is one of the functions allocated to the Ministry of Parliamentary Affairs under the Government of India (Allocation of Business) Rules, 1961. In discharge of this function, the Ministry constitutes these committees and arranges their meetings.

The current Consultative Committees of Members of Parliament in their broad features owe their origin to a suggestion made by the late Prime Minister, Shri Jawaharlal Nehru, in a Note circulated to the members of the Cabinet in 1954. The late Prime Minister felt that there should be some kind of Standing Advisory Consultative Committees of Parliament to provide opportunities to Members to have some glimpse into the working of the Government. It was felt that this might also help in reducing the number of questions asked by Members. With this in view, informal Consultative Committees were constituted for the various Ministries/Departments of the Government of India in the year 1954.

In 1969, discussions were held with Leaders of Opposition Parties/Groups in Parliament and as per decisions taken during these discussions, detailed guidelines were drawn up for constitution and functioning of these committees. It was also then decided that these committees would be known as "Consultative Committees" retaining, however, the informal nature of deliberations in these committees. These guidelines were also subsequently approved by the Cabinet. These committees have since been functioning under these guidelines **(Annex VII-A).**

The main objective of these committees is to provide a forum for informal discussion between Members of Parliament, on the one hand, and Ministers and senior officers of the Government, on the other, hand on the policies, principles and programmes of the Government and the manner of their implementation. Discussions at the meetings of these committees are held in a free and frank manner, cutting across party lines.

THE PROCESS

Consultative Committees for various Ministries/ Departments are normally constituted after general election to the Lok Sabha and as and when necessary, thereafter. The constitution of these committees is generally timed with the summoning of the Budget Session of Parliament. The membership of these committees is voluntary and is left to the choice of the Members/Leaders of their parties/groups in the respective Houses. A Member of Parliament can be nominated on only one Consultative Committee. Members of Parliament belonging to both Houses are nominated on these committees by the Minister of Parliamentary Affairs.

Constitution of the Committees

After constitution of the Lok Sabha and allocation of portfolios to Ministers, the Minister of Parliamentary Affairs addresses a letter **(Annexes VII-B (i)-(iii))** to the Members of both Houses/ Leaders of their parties/groups in the respective Houses to furnish, in the prescribed proforma **(Annex VII-C),** the names of the three Consultative Committees in the order of their preferences, on which they or the members of their parties/groups may be nominated. So far as the Members of the main ruling party, Members of smaller parties with membership of less than 5 in the both Houses, nominated Members and Independent Members are concerned, they are addressed by the Minister individually in this connection **(Annex VII-B(i))**. As regards the allied, supporting and opposition parties having strength in two Houses of 5 Members and more, but not more than the number of Consultative Committees proposed to be constituted are concerned, the Minister addresses the Leaders of those parties to suggest the names of Members of their parties for nomination on the proposed Consultative Committees [**Annex VII-B(ii)**]. Further, so far as the allied, supporting and opposition parties/ groups having membership in the two House of 5 Members and more, but not more than the number of Consultative Committees proposed to be constituted are concerned, the Minister addresses Leaders of those parties/groups as in the letter **Annex VII-B(iii).**

Subject to availability of vacancies, Members are nominated on the Consultative Committees of their first, second or third preference, as the case may be, with the approval of the Minister of Parliamentary Affairs. The Secretary, Ministry of Parliamentary Affairs, notifies the constitution of these committees and their sub-committees as and when they are constituted.

The maximum limit of membership on a Consultative Committee is 40 from both the Houses. The Consultative Committee for a Ministry/Department is not constituted if a minimum of ten Members have not given their option for being nominated on that committee. Members having special interest in subjects concerning a particular Ministry/Department can be nominated as Permanent Special Invitees (PSIs) on Consultative Committees attached with such Ministries/Departments. The maximum limit for nomination of PSIs on a Consultative Committee is four from both the Houses. The Consultative Committees, so constituted, are notified and Members nominated thereon and all concerned are informed about it **(Annex VII-D).** At the time of dissolution of the XIII Lok Sabha, there were 30 Consultative Committees for various Ministries/Departments **(Annex VII-E).**

Special Invitees

Under the guidelines, a Member of Parliament who is not a member of the committee, may also suggest subject(s) for discussion at a meeting of the Consultative Committee. If his/her item(s) is/are included in the agenda, he/she is invited as a special invitee to the meeting, subject to the condition that he/she will not be entitled to payment of TA/DA for attending the meeting. It is necessary that in case any suggestions or subjects are received from a non-member, the Ministry concerned takes an expeditious decision regarding their inclusion in the agenda or otherwise so that he/she may be invited by the Ministry of Parliamentary Affairs to the meeting or informed about the non-inclusion of his/her items in the agenda, sufficiently in advance of the date of the meeting.

When the Ministry has fixed a subject for discussion for a meeting of the committee, a Member of Parliament, who is not a member of the committee, may be allowed, with the approval of the Minister of Parliamentary Affairs, to attend the meeting, if he expresses a desire to participate in the discussion on the subject of the agenda. When any such request is received by a Ministry from a non-member, it should be forwarded to the Ministry of Parliamentary Affairs for being placed before the Minister of Parliamentary Affairs for permission to allow such a Member to attend the meeting of the committee of which he is not a member. The Ministry should not take a decision on its own in the matter and should not extend an invitation to such a Member directly, but refer the request to the Ministry of Parliamentary Affairs.

Periodicity of the Meetings

Each Consultative Committee is expected to hold one meeting each during the session and inter-session period, the only exception being the Consultative Committee for the Ministry of Railways which meets only during the inter-session period. However, there are sixteen Zonal Informal Consultative Committees of the Ministry of Railways, each consisting of Members of both Houses belonging to the areas falling under the respective Railway Zones. These zonal committees, which are also constituted by the Ministry of Parliamentary Affairs, after the constitution of the Consultative Committees for various Ministries/Departments, are expected to meet once in a year during the session period.

The Ministries/Departments may also hold one meeting of their Consultative Committees in a calendar year during an inter-session period anywhere in India, if the Chairman of the committee, so desires **(Annexes VII-F & G).** At the beginning of each session/inter-session, the Ministry of Parliamentary Affairs requests the Ministries to indicate the dates convenient to their Ministers for holding the meetings of the committees attached to their Ministry **(Annexes VII-H & I).** The Ministries are expected to fix the dates of the meetings of their committees without waiting for a formal communication from this Ministry. The Minister in change of each Ministry/Department presides over the Consultative Committee attached to his/her Ministry. The meetings of the Consultative Committees are also attended by senior officers of the Ministry who assist the Minister during the meetings.

Venue of the Meetings

Normally, meetings of the Consultative Committees are held in Parliament/Parliament House Annexe, New Delhi. The committee rooms in these buildings are booked by the Ministry of Parliamentary Affairs. However, if no committee room is available in either of these buildings for the day on which the Ministry proposes to hold the meeting of their committee, the Ministry/Department concerned has itself to arrange for a venue/committee room for the meeting. However, during the session period, meetings of the committees have to be normally held in Parliament/Parliament House Annexe to enable Members to attend the session or move to Parliament in case their presence in the Lok/Rajya Sabha is required urgently. In case the meeting is arranged at a venue other than the Parliament/Parliament House Annexe, the concerned Ministry may have to make transport arrangements for the Members from the Parliament House to the venue of the meeting and back.

Agenda

The agenda for the meeting is decided by the Chairman of the committee either on the basis of suggestions received from the Members or in consultation with Members during the preceding meeting of the committee. Notes on agenda items, brief records/minutes of the preceding meetings, and Action Taken Report (ATR) on the minutes of the last meeting are prepared by the Ministry concerned. However, notices regarding the meetings of the committees, all the documents mentioned above and other relevant papers are circulated to the Members and all others by the Ministry of Parliamentary Affairs.

No decisions are taken in these meetings. However, where there is unanimity of views in the meeting, the Government may accept the views of the committee, subject to the following exceptions, viz.:

(i) any recommendation with financial implications;
(ii) any recommendation concerning Security, Defence, External Affairs and Atomic Energy; and
(iii) any matter falling within the purview of an autonomous institution.

In these meetings, Members are free to discuss any matter which can be discussed on the floor of the Houses. However, no reference to the discussions held in these meetings may be made on the floor of the Houses.

Time Schedule for Circulation of Papers

The agenda notes, minutes and the action taken reports are required to be supplied to this Ministry by the Ministry concerned well in advance of the meeting for circulation to the members of the committee. This Ministry has laid down a time schedule **(Annex VII-J)** for circulation of papers, which may be strictly adhered to by the Ministries/Departments in order to obviate any criticism from the members of the Consultative Committees.

Quorum

There is no requirement of presence of a minimum number of Members to constitute the quorum for holding meetings of Consultative Committees.

Press Briefings

The question of briefing of the Press about the deliberations of a Consultative Committee meeting was discussed between the Minister of Parliamentary Affairs and the Leaders/Chief Whips/Whips of various parties in Parliament on 30 April, 1974 and the following decision was taken:

> "While it was agreed that in the Consultative Committees the discussions should be free and frank, it was also decided that any information, which, in the opinion of the committee was of a classified and confidential nature, should not be reported to the press."

This decision was conveyed to all the Ministries/Departments in 1974 **(Annex VII-K).**

Entitlement for TA/DA

Regular members of the Consultative Committees (and not PSIs) are entitled to payment of TA/DA, as admissible to them under the Rules, for attending the meetings of the committees held during inter-session periods. However, sometimes, Members reach the place of the meetings of the Committees but cannot attend the meetings due to certain unavoidable circumstances. On the other hand, there may be occasions when the Members reach the place of meeting but the meeting has already been cancelled/postponed though the intimation regarding it was not received by the Members before they left their constituency etc. for the place of the meeting. To deal with such and other similar contingencies, certain guidelines **(Annex VII-L)** have been designed in consultation with the Ministry of Finance to examine the cases regarding entitlement of TA/DA Members as and when requests of this nature are received from them.

Other Services at the Meetings

Whenever meetings of the Consultative Committees are held in rooms where simultaneous translation facilities are available, the Ministry concerned has to make arrangements to provide simultaneous translation in Hindi and English. As regards translation from other languages, action may be taken by the Ministry concerned if a request is received from a member of the committee.

It is for the Ministry concerned to ensure that the microphones in the meeting room are in working condition. For this purpose, the Ministry has to contact the Lok Sabha/Rajya Sabha Secretariat, Junior Engineer (Sound/Electrical/A.C.), Parliament House/ Parliament House Annexe, well in advance of the meeting.

The Ministry has to supply necessary stationery items such as note pads/papers, pens/pencils, etc. to the members of the committee.

It is for the Ministry to make arrangements for refreshments and lunch/dinner if so decided to the members of the committee. For this purpose, they may contact the Chief Caterer, Parliament House/Parliament House Annexe in case the meetings are to the held in these buildings.

Sub-committees/Study Group

A Consultative Committee may decide to constitute a Sub-committee or Study Group for the purpose of going into any particular aspect of the working or a problem concerning the Ministry and to make a report thereon **(Annex VII-M).** The notification for setting up the Sub-committee or Study Group is issued by the Ministry with the approval of the Minister of Parliamentary Affairs. If the term of the Sub-committee/Study Group is to be extended, it also requires the approval of the Minister of Parliamentary Affairs.

DECISIONS

Strength of Committees

(a) The maximum membership of a Consultative Committee should be limited to forty. In addition, a maximum of four Members from both Houses can also be nominated as Permanent Special Invitees.

(b) The minimum membership of the Consultative Committee shall be ten.

Permanent Special Invitees

With the approval of the Minister of Parliamentary Affairs, the number of Permanent Special Invitees on a Consultative Committee has been raised from two to four Members, with effect from 19 September, 1998.

Request for Change of Consultative Committee not to be Entertained if it Brings down the Membership of the Committee below ten Members

The committee is normally constituted if there are ten or more Members who have been chosen to be nominated on the committee. It was decided that normally no request from a Member for change of a Consultative Committee be entertained if such request brings down the strength of the committee of which he/she is a member, below the minimum limit of ten members.

Nomination of Members of Parliament, who have not made/ subscribed oath/affirmation, on the Consultative Committee

It was decided with the approval of the Minister of Parliamentary Affairs that a Member who has not made and subscribed the oath or affirmation in the House can also be nominated to a Consultative Committee.

Keeping Consultative Committees under suspended animation under Caretaker Government

During the period of a caretaker Government, the Consultative Committees should be kept under suspended animation and a final decision in the matter may be left to be taken by the new Government whenever formed.

Exchange Vouchers for Members for Undertaking Air Journeys

Members desirous of traveling by air during the inter-session period for attending the meetings of Consultative Committees should obtain exchange vouchers from the respective Secretariat of Parliament.

Agenda Papers

Agenda papers are also be issued to Members who are in jail.

Meeting Presided over by a Member

As per guidelines, the Minister concerned with each Ministry/Department shall preside over the meeting of the Consultative Committee attached to his/her Ministry. It is, therefore, not desirable for a Minister to leave the meeting midway and request one of the members of the Consultative Committee to preside over the meeting. In a case of this nature, the violation of guidelines was brought to the notice of the Minister concerned.

Meetings of Consultative Committees outside Delhi during Inter-session Period

(a) With the approval of the Ministry of Finance, it has been decided that Ministries/Departments may hold one meeting of their Consultative Committee in a year during the inter-session period anywhere in India, if the Chairman of the committee so desires. This decision was conveyed to all Ministries/Departments *vide* this Ministry's circular No. F. 12(26)/94-CB dated 16 October, 1995.

(b) During the calendar year 2002, the Ministry of Civil Aviation convened two meetings of their Consultative Committee outside Delhi viz. one meeting was held at Mumbai on 28 January, 2002 as usual and the second meeting was held at Cochin on 10 July, 2002 with the approval of the Secretary, Ministry of Parliamentary Affairs.

Meeting of Consultative Committees held outside Delhi during the Session Period

No meeting of a Consultative Committee may be held outside Delhi during the session period. However, with the approval of the Minister of Parliamentary Affairs (P), the Ministry of Home Affairs was allowed to hold the meeting of its Consultative Committee at BSF Academy, Takenpur, Madhya Pradesh, on 8 March, 2003 during the recess of Budget Session, 2003 of Parliament.

Visits of the Consultative Committees outside Delhi to Project Sites of Major PSUs under the Concerned Ministries

With the concurrence of the Ministry of Finance, it has been decided that, if necessary, visits of the members of the Consultative Committees to project sites of major Public Sector Undertakings under the control of the concerned Ministry could be undertaken during Inter-session periods. A liaison officer may accompany the committee during such visits and the local officer may explain the progress of projects. Members of the Consultative Committee are entitled to TA and DA as admissible under the Salary, Allowances and Pensions of Members of Parliament Act, 1954 for participating in such visits.

'Year' for the Purpose of Outside Meetings Means 'Calendar Year'

In terms of this Ministry's Office Memorandum dated 11 February, 1997, the question whether 'year' for the purpose of 'holding meeting once in a year outside Delhi' be taken as Calendar or Financial year, it has been clarified that 'year' in this regard shall be taken as 'calendar year'.

Visits of the Committee in addition to Meeting Outside Delhi

(a) In August, 2001, the Ministry of Rural Development had proposed to arrange the visits of MPs of their Consultative Committee to the states of Andhra Pradesh, Maharashtra, Madhya Pradesh and Rajasthan to review the Land Reforms Schemes. Accordingly, a reference was made to the Ministry of Finance whether the visit of the Consultative committees to a place outside Delhi can be arranged in addition to one outside meeting of the committee in a calendar year. The Ministry of Finance, however, did not agree to the proposal.

(b) In August, 2002, the Ministry of Rural Development had

again proposed to arrange the visit of the members of their Consultative Committee to Palampur in Himachal Pradesh. A reference was made to Ministry of Finance seeking their advice on the point. The Ministry of Finance clarified the position as under:

> "The Consultative Committees attached to the Ministries having no major PSUs were allowed to hold one meeting outside Delhi once in a calendar year, keeping in view the visits of Members of Consultative Committees attached to the Ministries having major PSUs. The presumption of the Ministry of Parliamentary Affairs that visit of the Consultative Committee can be arranged outside Delhi in addition to one outside meeting in a calendar year, does not seem to be correct."

In view of the above, it was decided with the approval of the Secretary, Ministry of Parliamentary Affairs, that visits of CCs of Ministries having no major PSUs under their control may not be arranged outside Delhi in addition to one outside meeting in a calendar year.

Guidelines Regarding Constitution and Functioning of Sub-committees

The matter relating to constitution of Sub-committees of Consultative Committees was reviewed in the Ministry and with the approval of the Minister of Parliamentary Affairs, the following decisions with regard to the constitution and functioning of Sub-committees of Consultative Committees were taken:

"(a) Consultative Committees, being informal bodies, should not ordinarily set up Sub-committees.

(b) Instead of setting up Sub-committees for a detailed enquiry, they should get exhaustive information regarding any particular aspect of working of the Ministry. The Minister in-charge, who presides over the meetings of Consultative Committees, can direct the officials to furnish the relevant information.

(c) In rare cases, where the Members insist on constituting a Sub-committee, it can be constituted with the approval of the Minister in-charge and in consultation with the Ministry of Parliamentary Affairs. The term of a Sub-committee shall in no case exceed three months. No request for any extension of tenure of a Sub-committee beyond three months shall be entertained.

(d) The Sub-committees may meet only at Delhi; and in case they are required to visit places outside Delhi, the Members may kindly make the visit on the strength of their free railway/air passes."

These instructions were conveyed to all the Ministries/ Departments vide this Ministry's Office Memorandum No. 6-8/ 93-CB dated 21 November, 1994 **(Annex VII-M).**

Meetings of Sub-committee Held Outside Delhi

As per guidelines, the Sub-committees may meet only at Delhi; and in case they are required to visit places outside Delhi, the Members may make the visit on the strength of their free railway/air passes. The Sub-committee for Air India Ltd. of the Consultative Committee for the Ministry of Civil Aviation had convened two meetings outside Delhi i.e. at Mumbai on 28 March and 24-25 June, 2003, respectively, with the approval of Secretary, Ministry of Parliamentary Affairs. No representative from the Ministry of Parliamentary Affairs was deputed to attend those meetings.

Visit of Sub-committee Abroad Not Agreed to

The Sub-committee for Airports Authority of India (AAI) of the Consultative Committee for the Ministry of Civil Aviation desired to undertake a visit to one of the International Airports abroad in order to enable members of the Sub-committee to study the facilities available there and to give positive recommendations to the Consultative Committee. The request of the Sub-committee was rejected.

CHECK LIST

A check list of steps to be taken at various stages during constitution and functioning of the Consultative Committees is at **Annex VII-N.**

8

MONITORING REPLIES TO SPECIAL MENTIONS AND RULE 377 ISSUES

BACKGROUND

Under Rule 377 of the Rules of Procedure and Conduct of Business in Lok Sabha, Members are allowed to raise matters which are not Points of Order or which have not been raised during the same session under any other Rule. In the Rajya Sabha, Members are allowed to make a mention of matters of public importance under Rule 180A-E of the Rules of Procedure and Conduct of Business in the Council of States. Such matters raised in the Lok Sabha are commonly known as 'matters raised under Rule 377' and mentions made in the Rajya Sabha under Rule 180A-E as 'Special Mentions'.

Under the Government of India (Allocation of Business) Rules, 1961, the function regarding determination of policy and follow up action on the matters raised/special mentions made in the two Houses under the above Rules has been allocated to the Ministry of Parliamentary Affairs. In the Ministry, a new section, namely, Legislative II Section was created on 23 June, 1984 to *inter alia* attend to this new item of work in the Ministry. Until the creation of Legislative II Section, the work was being handled by Legislative I Section in the Ministry.

Normally, Ministers do not make statements on such matters in the House. However, if a Minister so desires, he may make a statement on these matters in the House with the permission of the Presiding Officer. Further, the Rules under which these matters are permitted to be raised by Members in the Houses do not provide for a reply by the Minister concerned to the Member who raises or makes a mention of such matters. Accordingly, no replies were normally sent by the concerned Ministers or

Secretaries to the Members who raised such matters. However, in a meeting of the Business Advisory Committee, Lok Sabha, held on 20 March, 1978, when a point was raised by Shri Vasant Sathe, MP, that Ministers seldom respond by way of clarifications to the important matters raised by Members under Rule 377 in the House, the Speaker observed that the Minister of Parliamentary Affairs might bring it to the notice of the Ministers that they might appropriately send a communication to the Members who raised matters under Rule 377 within one week of the matter being raised in the House. Accordingly, the Minister of Parliamentary Affairs had then brought the direction of the Speaker, Lok Sabha, to the notice of his colleagues in the Council of Ministers for information and necessary action. Subsequently, it was decided that replies by the Ministers concerned to Special Mentions raised in the Rajya Sabha may also be sent within a week of their being raised in the Rajya Sabha.

However, as the period of one week for sending replies to such matters was too short and as the Ministries were finding it difficult to send replies within this period, the Rules Committees of the Rajya Sabha and the Lok Sabha, which considered this matter in their meetings held on 27 January, 1987 and 2 March, 1989 respectively, *inter alia* recommended that one month's time be given to the Ministries to send replies to the Members concerned in respect of such matters raised by them in the two Houses. The time period then recommended by the committees in this regard is still being followed.

Normally, a Member can raise only one matter/special mention during a week. In the Lok Sabha, a maximum of 15 matters can be raised at a sitting of the House, while in the Rajya Sabha not more than six Special Mentions are admitted for a day. On the day when the Minister for Parliamentary Affairs makes a statement in the Lok Sabha regarding the Government Business to be taken in that House during the following week, matters under Rule 377 are not raised. In the Rajya Sabha, no such practice is followed. In the Lok Sabha, an entry titled 'Matters under Rule 377 is given in the List of Business if the matters given notices of by Members have been admitted for that day. However, in the Rajya Sabha, no entry in this regard is given in the List of Business. Members are permitted to raise these matters after completion of Question Hour and disposal of other formal items listed in the agenda.

In its meeting held on 29 May, 1984, the Rules Committee, Rajya Sabha, had *inter alia* recommended that the Minister of Parliamentary Affairs may, as in the case of Government Assurances, lay during each session a statement on the Table of the House indicating the action taken by the Government on the Special Mentions made by Members in the House. The matter was placed before the Cabinet Committee on Parliamentary Affairs through circulation of papers as well as by way of a formal meeting. However, the Committee could not arrive at a decision. Subsequently, the Minister of State for Parliamentary Affairs (Rajya Sabha) discussed the matter with the Chairman, Rajya Sabha, and the matter rested there. The Rules Committee, Rajya Sabha, in its meeting held on 27 January, 1987, however, again reiterated its earlier recommendation. The matter was re-examined and it was decided that as the replies to Special Mentions were already being sent to the Members concerned, the existing practice may continue. The Rajya Sabha Secretariat was informed of the Government's view in the matter.

PROCESS

Normally, on the day following the day on which these matters are raised in the Houses, relevant extracts from the proceedings of the Houses are sent by the Parliament Secretariats to the Ministries concerned with the advice to send replies to these matters to the Members concerned directly, under intimation to the Parliament Secretariat. A copy of such communications along with the relevant extracts, is also sent to the Ministry of Parliamentary Affairs. It is the respective Parliament Secretariat which decides as to which Ministry is administratively concerned with the subject matter of a Special Mention/Matters raised under Rule 377 and to whom the relevant extracts may be sent for necessary action. On the basis of the communications endorsed to this Ministry by the Parliament Secretariats, the Ministry of Parliamentary Affairs sends weekly statements, separately in respect of each House, containing the gist of matters raised by Members, as published in the Parliamentary Bulletins Part I of the respective Houses, to the Ministries/Departments concerned to enable them to cross check the matters raised in respect of their Ministry with reference to the extracts received by them from the two Parliament Secretariats with a view to ensuring that no item is lost sight of. In these weekly communications to the Ministries **(Annex VIII-A & B)**, they are *inter alia* requested to ensure that replies are sent to the Members concerned under intimation to the Parliament Secretariat and the Ministry within the stipulated period of one month from the day on which a matter is raised in the House.

The Ministry of Parliamentary Affairs, in consultation with the two Secretariats of Parliament, has consolidated certain instructions, issued by it from time to time, regarding the procedure to be followed for taking follow up action on these matters. These consolidated instructions/guidelines **(Annex VIII-C)** are circulated/brought to the notice of Ministries/Departments periodically to guide them in proper and expeditious disposal of these matters. The salient features of these guidelines are as follows:

(i) Prescribed time limit of one month for sending the reply should be strictly adhered to. Where it is not possible to do so, an interim reply may be sent to the Member concerned under intimation to the Parliament Secretariat and the Ministry of Parliamentary Affairs.

(ii) If the Ministry is not administratively concerned with the subject matter of a Special Mention etc. sent to it by the Parliament Secretariat, it shall take expeditious action to have the matter accepted by the Ministry to which it appears to concern. Until such acceptance has been received and communicated to the Ministry of Parliamentary Affairs, it shall continue to be pending against the Ministry to which it was originally sent.

(iii) On dissolution of the Lok Sabha, all pending matters raised in that House shall lapse. However, if a Member of the Lok Sabha resigns or passes away, the Ministry concerned shall be required to send replies in respect of matters raised by him/her to the Lok Sabha Secretariat and the Ministry of Parliamentary Affairs. Where, however, a Member, who had resigned, is re-elected to the same Lok Sabha, reply to the matter earlier raised by him will be sent to the Member under intimation to the Ministry.

(iv) There is no effect of dissolution of the Lok Sabha on

the Special Mentions raised in the Rajya Sabha. However, in the case of Special Mentions made by a Member who has subsequently retired, resigned or has passed away, no reply need be sent by the Ministry to anyone. However, if such a Member has been re-elected, he is required to be sent a reply in respect of the matter earlier raised by him in the House.

FOLLOW-UP ACTION

During each inter-session period, a review of the matters remaining pending in the two Houses is undertaken. A statement showing the pendency of these matters in various Ministries/ Departments is prepared year-wise, session-wise, in a tabular form, separately for each House. Simultaneously, statements showing the dates on which matters were raised, names of the Members who raised them and the gists of all pending matters in respect of two Houses are prepared in respect of each Ministry/ Department. After each review, a note reflecting the position of pendency etc. is submitted to the Minister along with a draft D.O. letter **(Annex VIII-D)** from the Minister to his/her colleagues in the Council of Ministers (Cabinet Ministers and Ministers of State with independent charge only) requesting them to ensure expeditious disposal of pending matters relating to Ministries/Departments under their charge. In case of Ministries/ Departments whose additional charge has been given to the Minister of Parliamentary Affairs, D.O. reminders to such Ministries/Departments are sent at Secretary's level. The statements containing *inter alia* the gists of the pending matters in respect of respective Ministries/Departments are invariably enclosed with such D.O. letters help Ministries/Departments identify their pending matters and take further follow-up action promptly.

Besides, the Secretary, Ministry of Parliamentary Affairs, also from time to time takes meetings, normally during inter-session periods unless the exigencies demand otherwise, with Secretaries/senior officers of concerned Ministries/Departments, to review and expedite disposal of such matters pending action in various Ministries/Departments. Whenever it is decided to have a series of such meetings with Ministries/Departments concerned, a D.O. letter as at **Annex VIII-E,** along with the statements containing the gist of pending matters, is sent from the Secretary, Ministry of Parliamentary Affairs, to the Secretaries of the concerned Ministries/Departments requesting them to attend or depute some senior officer to attend such meetings as per the schedule drawn up with the approval of the Secretary. Depending upon the magnitude of the pendency and the convenience of the Secretary, meetings are, normally, held over a period of three to four days. There are, normally, three time slots each day and a group of Ministries/Departments are clubbed together in each time slot in such a manner that the number of matters to be reviewed in each time slot are, as far as possible, the same. The outcome of the series of meetings so held, which normally results in significant reduction in the pendency of these matters, is then communicated to the Presiding Officers and the Secretary-Generals of the two Houses by the Minister of Parliamentary Affairs and the Secretary, Ministry of Parliamentary Affairs respectively.

During the course of the series of meetings taken by the Secretary, Ministry of Parliamentary Affairs, with Secretaries/ senior officers of various Ministries/Departments during 2003, the following clarifications in regard to the causes which normally result in inordinate delay in disposal of these matters were provided:

(i) Whenever a policy decision is required to be taken on issues raised in these matters, the Ministries may, instead of waiting till a final decision is taken in such matters, send replies to the Members furnishing factual information in the matter.

(ii) Whenever information asked for in these matters concerns State Governments, officers of the Ministry being deputed to such States in connection with some other work, can be given copies of the list of such pending matters so that they can meet the officers concerned in those States for obtaining/expediting the requisite information.

(iii) Whenever a matter is pending for more than one year for want of information from the State Governments, concerned officers from the States may be summoned by the Ministry for obtaining requisite information in the matter.

(iv) Whenever a matter pertains to some other Ministries/ Departments, it may be transferred to them with their consent, as in the case of Parliament Questions. Where, however, a matter concerns another Department/Unit of the Ministry, its transfer to the concerned Department/Unit may be done through internal discussions expeditiously.

(v) Copies of replies sent to the Members concerned may invariably be endorsed to the Parliament Secretariat concerned and the Ministry of Parliamentary Affairs.

It has been decided that for the purpose of holding review meetings in future, the Ministries concerned shall be divided into the following three categories:

Category 1: Secretaries of the Ministries, where there is a comparatively large pendency, especially matters pending for more than a year, may be requested to convene review meetings at their own level in the respective Ministries/Departments, which will be attended by the Secretary, Ministry of Parliamentary Affairs.

Category 2: The Secretary, Ministry of Parliamentary Affairs, will convene meetings with Secretaries/senior officers of the Ministries which have more than five matters (old as well as new) pending at the conclusion of the last Parliament session, in Parliament House, as in the past.

Category 3: D.O. letters from the Secretary, Ministry of Parliamentary Affairs, will be sent to the Secretaries of the Ministries/Departments where less than five matters are pending.

DECISIONS

(i) The Rules Committee of the Rajya Sabha, at its sitting held on 27 January,1987, observed that one month's time be given to the Ministries to send replies to the Members concerned in respect of Special Mentions raised by them. These observations were circulated to all the Ministries. [F.No.54(3)/84-Leg.II]

(ii) The Rules Committee of the Lok Sabha, at its sitting held on 2 March,1989, observed that one month's time be given to the Ministries to send replies to the Members concerned in respect of matters raised by them under Rule 377. [F.No.3(1)/88-Leg.II]

(iii) The recommendation of the Rules Committee of the Rajya Sabha was examined and it was decided that the Government did not feel it necessary to lay the statements containing the replies sent to MPs in respect of matters raised by them under Rule 377/Special Mentions on the Table of the Houses, as recommended by the Committee. [F.No.54(3)/84- Leg.II]

(iv) The suggestion for deletion of Special Mention involving information of a sensitive nature raised by Shri S.S. Surjewala, MP, on 21 December, 1993 was examined and it was decided to delete the Special Mention from the record. [F.No. 2(38)/93-Leg.II]

CHECK LIST

A check list indicating steps to be taken to deal with Special Mentions etc. is enclosed as **Annex VIII-F** .

9

MONITORING ASSURANCES

BACKGROUND

In the parliamentary system of governance, the Council of Ministers is responsible and accountable to the Legislature. The Executive acts with the approval and concurrence of the Legislature and the representatives of the people have the right to know about the various activities of the Government. The Government is duty bound to disclose such information except that the disclosure of which may not be in public interest. This flow of information from the Executive to the Legislature is an essential feature of the responsibility of the former to the latter.

The central objective of various practices and procedures adopted by the Legislature such as Questions, Calling Attention Motions, Short Duration Discussions, Debates, etc. is to obtain maximum information from the Government, on their acts of commission or omission, which enable the Legislature to judge its performance.

During the course of answers to Questions or during debates, various assurances - in the form of promises, undertakings or other such forms of expressions - are given by Ministers on the floor of the House. Such assurances are given due to non-availability of information, at that point of time, to meet the queries or points raised by the Members. There is a formalised list **(Annex IX-A)** of expressions or forms which are treated as constituting assurances given by Ministers. This list has been approved by the Committees on Government Assurances of the Lok Sabha and the Rajya Sabha. Apart from these listed standard expressions, other remarks or expressions may be treated as assurances on the basis of the context in which such remarks or expressions were made. It is to be noted that:

(a) the assurance though given (in response to a Question or demand from an individual Member or Members) is in essence an assurance given to the House as a whole; and conversely

(b) the assurance though given by an individual Minister ultimately devolves as a responsibility upon the Government as a whole.

Naturally, the Government would be anxious that the assurances given on the floor of the House by Ministers are duly fulfilled. Also, given the implied characteristics of assurances in so far as they ultimately constitute a pending matter between the Government and the House concerned, full efforts are made by the Government to fulfill the assurances expeditiously.

PROCEDURE

The Ministry of Parliamentary Affairs is the coordinating agency within the Government for its interaction with the Legislature. One of the specific functions assigned to the Ministry under the Government of India (Allocation of Business) Rules, 1961 **(Annex IX B)** is the implementation of assurances given by Ministers in Parliament. In fact, this has been one of the functions assigned to the Ministry (then Department) since its very inception in 1949.

The functions performed by the Ministry of Parliamentary Affairs in this regard essentially comprise the following three broad lines of action:

(i) culling out of assurances from the debates;
(ii) monitoring the state of fulfilment thereof; and
(iii) laying of implementation reports before the Houses.

The Implementation Branch of the Ministry looks after the work relating to assurances. It comprises two sections, one dealing with Lok Sabha assurances and the other with Rajya Sabha assurances.

The procedure followed by the Implementation Branch is briefly as under:

(a) On receipt of the debates of each day's proceedings,

the concerned section goes through them to identify the assurances. The extracts are submitted for approval and these are normally approved at the level of the Under Secretary. In cases where the assurances relate to MPs, Ministers *per se* or to the Ministry of Parliamentary Affairs itself, are approved at the level of the Secretary. Details of various levels at which matters relating to assurances are decided upon are provided in **Annex IX-B.**

(b) After approval, the extracts are sent to the concerned Ministries. The forwarding communication contains detailed instructions **(Annex IX-C)** to the Ministries on the various procedures and points to be noted while fulfilling the assurance. A list of such culled out assurances in respect of each day's debate is also forwarded to the respective Secretariats of Parliament with the request that these may be checked and the Ministry of Parliamentary Affairs may be informed whether all the assurances have been culled out. On receipt of their response, if any, additions/deletions, as may be required, are made.

(c) The entire process of culling out of the assurances and forwarding them to the concerned Ministries is to be completed within ten days of the date on which the assurance was given in the House.

(d) Each assurance is dealt with in a separate file.

(e) Periodic review of the stage of implementation is done and Ministries are reminded for expediting the fulfilment.

(f) On receipt of the Implementation Reports from the Ministries, sets are prepared for laying these on the Table of the respective Houses by the Minister(s) of Parliamentary Affairs. The laying is done periodically, usually twice in a session.

(g) After the Implementation Reports have been laid, the Members concerned are informed accordingly with a copy of the respective Implementation Report. The concerned Ministries are also informed about the laying of the Implementation Report.

(h) The Ministries/Departments often seek extension of

time beyond the stipulated period of three months for fulfilling the assurances. The Ministries approach the Committee on Government Assurances by directly writing to the Lok Sabha/Rajya Sabha Secretariats for the purpose and endorse a copy to the Ministry of Parliamentary Affairs.

(i) Sometimes Ministries/Departments also request dropping of the assurances giving cogent reasons for doing so. They write directly to the respective Secretariats and endorse a copy to the Ministry of Parliamentary Affairs.

(j) In cases where after the committee decides that a particular matter constitutes an assurance even after a Ministry represents that it is otherwise, the Chairman of the committee may refer the matter to the Speaker/ Chairman for guidance. The Reports of the two House Committees on Government Assurances are also received in the Implementation Branch and they are scrutinised with special reference to any recommendations or observations made therein which are of a general nature or which are specifically addressed to the Ministry of Parliamentary Affairs and due action is initiated thereon.

Committees on Government Assurances

The Committee on Government Assurances is an innovation of the Indian Parliament. Parliament made this innovation with a view to institutionalising the procedure to ensure the fulfillment of assurances given by Ministers in the Houses. Each House of Parliament has a Committee on Government Assurances. The Lok Sabha committee was first nominated by the Speaker on 1 December, 1953 and is reconstituted every year. The Rajya Sabha committee was first constituted on 1 July, 1972. The functions assigned to these committees under the Rules of Procedure and Conduct of Business of the respective Houses are to:

> "....scrutinize the assurances, promises, undertakings, etc., given by Ministers, from time to time, on the floor of the House and to report on

a. the extent to which such assurances, promises, undertakings, etc. have been implemented; and
b. where implemented whether such implementation has taken place within the minimum time necessary for the purpose."

In the matter of assurances, the decisions taken by the Committee on Government Assurances of the respective Houses are treated as final. Wherever necessary, the Chairman of the committee may refer the matter to the Speaker/Chairman, as the case may be, for guidance.

DECISIONS

(i) In cases where an assurance was not culled out either by the Ministry of Parliamentary Affairs or by the concerned Secretariat and the Ministry concerned subsequently sends an Implementation Report, the same is laid on the Table of the concerned House.

(F.No.II/P&AR(4)USQ 6632 LS/85)

(ii) In reply to a Question the Minister replied that he would send an answer to the Member. The Minister accordingly sent a reply to the Member. Subsequently, the Ministry supplied an Implementation Report enclosing therewith a copy of the letter sent by the Minister to the Member. The Implementation Report enclosing the said letter was laid on the Table of the House. (F.No.II/YAS(3) SQ 856-LS/85)

(iii) A question arose as to whether the dissolution of a Lok Sabha would have any effect on the assurances pending. The Ministry of Law was consulted and the Minister of Parliamentary Affairs wrote to the Committee on Government Assurances. The committee considered the matter and decided to keep alive the assurances pending at the time of dissolution of the Lok Sabha. The committee took the view that where the new Government does not agree with the policies of the previous Government, it can approach the committee for dropping such assurances.

(F.No.6(5)/91-Imp-I)

(iv) Statements made by Ministers during Zero Hour and matters raised under Rule 377 in Lok Sabha and Special Mentions in Rajya Sabha are not marked as assurances by Implementation Branch. Such matters are already being dealt with by the Legislative Branch of the Ministry of Parliamentary Affairs which separately takes up the matters with the Ministries concerned (in those cases the Ministries do not submit any Implementation Report to be laid before the concerned House). (approved by Secretary, M.P.A on 24.5.2000)

(v) Ministry sent an Implementation Report after the assurance was dropped by the Committee on Government Assurances. The Implementation Report was not laid on the Table of the House and was returned to the Ministry. (RS USQ 1850 dt.11.5.88 H&FW)

(vi) A question was raised by the Ministry of Railways whether it would be appropriate to furnish copies of Implementation Reports or even information collected in connection therewith to the Member of Parliament before the Implementation Report was laid on the Table of the House. The Ministry of Parliamentary Affairs advised that till such time as the Implementation Report is laid before the House they are to be treated as confidential and the Members are to be supplied the information by this Ministry only after it is laid on the Table of the House. (F.No.2(7)/77-Imp-I)

(vii) In reply to a Rajya Sabha Question addressed to the Ministry of Defence, it was stated that a Committee Report (The La Fontaine Committee Report on Air Accidents) was a classified document and necessary action to implement its recommendations has been taken. Many recommendations have already been implemented and action to finalise decisions on the remaining recommendations was in hand. This reply was marked as an assurance. However, subsequently the Ministry of Defence represented that this might not be treated as an assurance. They mentioned that the Minister of Defence had minuted that "There is no question of making the Report Public. Furthermore, I cannot see how the reply is being read as an assurance.

Ministry of Parliamentary Affairs may be advised accordingly". The matter for dropping the assurance was taken up with the Committee on Government Assurances and the committee agreed to drop the assurance. (USQ No. 221 Dated 24.07.1985)

CHECK LIST

A check list of steps to be taken at various stages is at **Annex IX -D.**

10

SALARIES, ALLOWANCES AND FACILITIES FOR MPs

The first Legislative Assembly of India came into being in 1920 after the passing of the Government of India Act, 1919 in implementation of the reforms known as the Montague Chelmsford Reforms.

ALLOWANCES ADMISSIBLE TO MEMBERS OF LEGISLATIVE ASSEMBLY

The Members of the Legislative Assembly were at that time entitled to Daily Allowances as indicated below:

Year	Daily Allowance
Upto March, 1921	Rs. 15 per day (for each day of residence at the place where the Assembly met).
From March, 1921	Rs. 20 per day.
1928	Provision of daily allowance was extended to cover any period of residence on duty.
(Budget Session) 1945	Rs. 30 per day as daily allowance
	Rs. 15 per day as conveyance allowance
April, 1948	Rs. 45 per day (by merger of two allowances) Free of Income Tax.
1949	Rs. 40 per day (A voluntary cut of Rs. 5 imposed).

EXTENSION OF FACILITIES TO MEMBERS GENERALLY ON THE RECOMMENDATIONS OF JOINT COMMITTEE ON SALARY AND ALLOWANCES OF MEMBERS OF PARLIAMENT

6 June, 1952: The Speaker announced the appointment of a Joint Committee of two Houses on payment of Salary and Allowances of Members of Parliament.

4 August, 1952: The Joint Committee submitted its recommendations.

27 March, 1954: The Minister of Parliamentary Affairs moved the resolution for approval and acceptance of the recommendations of the Joint Committee but after some discussion, the House adopted that in view of abolition of First Class on Railways, the question of TA admissible to Members or grant of free passes should be examined by the Joint Committee and the report submitted again to Parliament.

20 April, 1954: The Joint Committee presented its second report to the House.

May, 1954: The Bill on the basis of the recommendations of Joint Committee was passed by the Lok Sabha on 14 May, 1954 and Rajya Sabha on 19 May, 1954. The Parliament enacted a law called "The Salary and Allowances of Members of Parliament Act, 1954".

Commencement of Act 1 June, 1954: The Salary and Allowances of Members of Parliament Act came into being.

Entitlement to Members of Parliament from the commencement of Act, 1954 onwards as amended from time to time: A Statement showing the admissibility of Salary, Allowances, Pension and other facilities to Members of Parliament from the enactment of the Act i.e.,

1954 onwards as amended from time to time is at the **Annex X-A** and another statement showing the facilities extended to ex-MPs is at **Annex X-B.**

IMPORTANT RULINGS/DECISIONS RELATING TO ADMINISTRATION OF ACTS

Facilities for Railway accommodation to the Chairman of Parliamentary Committee etc on par with the Ministers/high officials

"The suggestion that the Chairman of the Estimates Committee and the Public Accounts Committee should be provided with a four berthed compartment for journeys undertaken by them in Rail on official purposes, as in the case of Ministers and high officials, was not agreed to by this Department". (This suggestion was made in the meeting of the General Purposes Committee held on 9 December, 1995).

(File No.55(L) 56)

Attachment of Salary of Members of Parliament

A suggestion was mooted by the Lok Sabha Secretariat that the Code of Civil Procedure should be amended in order to vest powers in the two Secretariats of Parliament for compulsorily attaching from the salaries of Members of Parliament such sum as ordered by the court. This matter was examined in the Department and it was decided that:

> "the Attachment of a Member's salary should take its normal course provided under the Law and Civil Procedure Code need not be amended."

(File No.F. 115(L) 56-PA)

Entitlements of Members of Lok Sabha to Daily Allowance on adjournment *sine die* and Dissolution of the House

The second Lok Sabha was dissolved on 31 March 1962 but according to the Programme, the session was to continue up to 30 March 1962. In the circumstances, the question arose whether the MPs would be entitled to DA for three days succeeding the date of adjournment *sine die* of the session i.e. up to 2 April 1962, notwithstanding the dissolution of the Lok Sabha on 31 March 1962. After examination of the matter in consultation with the Ministry of Law and justice, the Department held the following view:

> "Members are entitled to the daily allowance for three days succeeding the date of adjournment sine die notwithstanding the fact that he ceases to be a Member on the dissolution of the House. The right granted to him by the statute is not lost by supervening dissolution."

(File No.F. 108(L)/62-PA)

Admissibility of Daily Allowance to an MP during the period of suspension from the services of the House

"When a Member is suspended from the remainder of the session, he cannot be said to be residing for that period for the purpose of attending the session for the simple reason that he is precluded from attending the session for the period. The Member cannot, in the circumstances claim daily allowance for this period. However when the Member is not suspended for the remainder of the session for when the suspension is for longer period, the provisions for dealing with such situations may be made in the Rules."

(File No .F. 108(L)/62-PA.)

Association of Minister of Parliamentary Affairs as Member and Chairman of the Joint Committee on Salaries and Allowances of Members of Parliament

"There is no illegality involved in the nomination of Minister of Parliamentary Affairs as member and Chairman of the Joint Committee on Salaries and Allowances of MPs."

(File No. F. 108 (L)/62- PA.)

Facility of Free Transport in State Nationalised Bus Service offered to Members of Parliament by State Governments

A reference from the Governments of Kerala and Maharashtra was received in the Department seeking clarifications as to whether any impropriety was involved in allowing MPs from that State to travel free of cost in State Transport Department Buses.

The opinion held by this Department in this regard was that it was entirely a question covering a State's own policy and that State should feel free to decide the question on its own merits and any Member having a free ride in a State bus during the period of ride was not holding any office of profit. However, the Ministry of Law which was approached for its views opined that MPs are not entitled to any concessions having pecuniary benefits beyond what is provided in the Members Salaries and Allowances Act, 1954. Therefore, after exchanges of views with the Ministry of Law, the following advice was tendered to the Government of Maharashtra:

> "MPs cannot be singled out by the State Government for grant of such facilities as free travels to visit Government Undertaking etc. But they can be included in the distinguished visitors to whom such facilities may be extended by the State Government."

(File No.F. 4(6)/65- R&C & 4 (15)/75- R&C)

Payment of Salary to MPs detained under Defence of India Rules

"The Members of Parliament are entitled to salary in terms of the Salaries and Allowances of Members of Parliament Act, 1954, which did not debar a Member detained under the Defence of India Rules from getting his salary."

(File No. 4(1)/68-R&C)

Free Rail travel facilities for MPs and Ministers—utilisation of spouse pass by Ministers as an MP

The Law Ministry explained provision of Section 6B (iii) of the Salary, Allowances and Pension of MPs Act, 1954 and the Rule 8 (1) (i) of the Ministers (Allowances, Medical Treatment and other Privileges) Rules, 1957.

(File No.4(1)/77-R&C)

Supply of typewriters at DGS&D rate contract and used typewriters of the Ministry of Defence on fixed price to MPs

"The typewriters by the DGS&D are supplied at the rate contract only to the Govt. Deptts. and not to the individuals.

However, if Lok Sabha/ Rajya Sabha Sectts. indent the typewriters with the DGS&D, the same can be supplied at the rate contract. The used typewriters as per practice followed in the Ministries/ Departments, are disposed off through auction."

(File No. 4(5)/79- WS)

T.A. admissible to wife of a deceased MP for winding up establishment in Delhi

"Though there is no specific provision in the Act, yet the Ministry of Finance in a number of cases have agreed to allow to and fro first class Railways pass to the wife of the deceased MP for winding up their establishment in Delhi."

(File No. 4(7)/79-R&C also F. No.4(4)/83-WS)

Annuity paid under the Oriental Pension Fund to be taken into account while determining Parliamentary Pension to ex-MPs

The Oriental Pension Fund is a purely pension scheme. Annuity paid under Oriental Pension Fund Scheme is to be treated as pension for determining parliamentary pension payable to ex-MP in terms of Section 8A (i) of the Salary, Allowances and Pension of Members of Parliament Act,1954.

(File No. 4(14)/79-WS)

Payment of Pension to Shri Narsingh Narayan Panday, ex-MP

Shri Panday was allowed to draw pension of Rs. 200 from State Government of U.P. and Rs. 300 from Central Government for his services rendered as MP.

(File No. 4 (14)/79-WS Vol. I)

Rail-*cum*-Road or Air-*cum*-Road T.A. for journey undertaken under Section 5 of the Act

"Members would be entitled to get rail-*cum* road-or air-*cum*-road T.A. beyond the nearest airport even if he visits any place outside his constituency for reaching his place of destination."

(File No. 4 (9)/81- R&C)

Payment of Pension to ex-MPs - entitlement regarding

On his appointment as Government Advocate/Chairman of Board etc.

"Since the honorarium as also fee is a payment made for services rendered, the honorarium and the retainer's fee can therefore be treated as remuneration within the meaning of the Section 8A (2) (iii) of the Salary, Allowances and Pension of MPs Act and as such the pension under Section 8A (I) of the Act *ibid* will not be admissible."

On appointment on honorarium basis as Professor in the Gujarat Vidyapith, Ahmedabad

"Since the Gujarat Vidyapith is neither a Municipal Committee nor a District Governmental body nor a corporation owned or controlled by the Central Government or any State Government or a local body, the Section 8A (2) (iii) of the Salary, Allowances and Pension of MPs Act, would not apply and as such the pension payable under Section 8A (i) of the Act *ibid.* would be admissible to the person appointed as Professor in addition to the honorarium."

(File No. 4 (13)/81-WS)

If the election of a Member is declared void will the period of such membership be counted for the purpose of determining pension

"*Prima facie,* it would appear that members whose election has been declared void may not be entitled to pension. However, each individual case may be dealt with on its merits depending upon the facts of each case."

(File No. 4 (14)/81-R&C)

Telephone facility to Ministers in their constituency residences

Ministers of Government of India would be entitled to a free telephone connection in their constituency residences, in their capacity as a Member of Parliament, with a maximum ceiling of * 7,500 free local calls in a year. The expenditure in respect of

---

*Limit raised from time to time, along with increase in free local calls admissible to MPs.

installation, rental and call charges is to be borne by the Ministry/ Department concerned.

(File No. 4(20)/82-WS also F. No. 4 (6)/86- WS S.No. 28)

Meaning of Session *vis-a-vis* commencement, adjournment, adjournment *sine die,* prorogation or dissolution for the purposes of determining intermediate journeys

"A Session once it has commenced on the basis of summons comes to an end only when the House is prorogued or dissolved by the President and the intermediate journeys admissible to MPs under the provisions of the Act shall be regulated in accordance with this interpretation."

(File No. 4(25)/82-WS)

Pension to Members of Legislative Assembly, Pondicherry, whose tenure falls short by up to maximum of 90 days - concurrence for the introduction of a Bill

"In view of the peculiar circumstances and history of the Legislative Assembly of the Union territory of Pondicherry, the Department agreed that the approval of the Central Government may be accorded to introduction of the Bill in the Legislative Assembly, Pondicherry, which seeks to provide the coverage to short fall of a period of 90 days for grant of pensionary benefits to MLAs."

(File No. 4(35)/82 -WS)

Payment of D.A. to Ministers without amending the Minister's Act

According to Ministry of Law, it would be necessary to amend the Minister's Act to enable them to get D.A.

(File No. 4 (31)/82- WS)

House Rent Allowances to MPs when on tour as Chairman of the Committee/Board etc.

"In accordance with the provisions of the Salary, Allowances and Pension of Members of Parliament Act, 1954, when an MP appointed as Chairman of the Committee etc. proceeds on tour in connection with the work of the Committee he shall not be entitled to House Rent Allowances for meeting the actual expenditure incurred by him on house rent."

(File No. 33(6)/82-R&C)

Payment of Special Allowances of Rs. 100 and Medical Allowances of Rs. 10 to the ex-MPs from Bihar who were Freedom Fighters

Special Allowances of Rs. 100 and Medical Allowances of Rs. 10 paid by the State Government of Bihar to ex-MPs from Bihar who are also freedom fighters will not attract the provision of Section 8A (iii) of the Salary, Allowances and Pension of Members of Parliament Act, 1954.

(File No. 4(3)/83-WS)

Commuted value of Pension to be taken into account while determining Parliamentary Pension

Pension means full amount of pension sanctioned and not the balance left after commutation. Commuted value of pension which an ex-MP received for his services as a Government servant is also to be taken into account while determining the parliamentary pension in terms of Section 8A of the Salary, Allowances and Pension of MPs Act, 1954.

(File No. 4(3)/83-WS)

Payment of to and fro T.A. to the spouse of the deceased Member to wind up establishment in Delhi

The Ministry of Finance agreed to the payment of to and fro T.A. to the spouse of the deceased Member for winding up establishment in Delhi on the presumption that the spouse was not in Delhi when the Member expired (equal to and fro rail fare).

(File No. 4(4)/83- WS also. No F.. 4(7)/79-R&C -S.No.10 ante)

Payment of air fare for spouse of a Minister

Payment of air fare in respect of journey performed under Section 6B (iii) of the Salary, Allowances and Pension of MPs Act, 1954, by the spouse of a Member who happens to be a Minister will be borne by the respective Secretariat of Parliament.

(File No. 4(8)/83-WS)

Payment of T.A./D.A. to MPs as representatives of workers' organisations

The case of MPs for payment of T.A./D.A for attending meetings/conferences as representatives of the workers' organisations but not appointed by the Government as such on these committees etc. was examined in consultation with the Ministry of Law and Ministry of Finance. It was decided that they are not entitled to T.A. under Section 4 of the Salary, Allowances and Pension of Members of Parliament Act, 1954 as they are not appointed by the Government.

(File No. 4(8)/83-WS) Vol. II)

Extension of certain facilities to Ex-MPs

The question of extending certain facilities to ex-MPs such as rail travel facilities, accommodation at concessional rates, etc. was examined in consultation with the Ministry of Law. The Ministry of Law opined that it is for the consideration of the Government whether some public purpose is served by extending these facilities under article 282 of the Constitution and that *prima facie* it seems that no public purpose is served by extending any such facilities to ex-MPs.

(File No. 4(8)/85-WS)

Grants of pension to Shri V.K. Saklecha, ex-MP being ex-MP and ex-MLA

Shri V.K. Saklecha was a Member of the Rajya Sabha for about 5 years. Shri Saklecha was in receipt of pension by virtue of his being ex-MLA @ Rs. 450 p.m. The opinion of the Law Minister was sought as to whether he will get pension under the Central Act after adjusting the amount of Rs. 450. Our view was that Shri Saklecha was entitled only to a pension of Rs. 450 p.m. as an ex-MLA as it was higher than the parliamentary pension of Rs. 300 p.m. to which he is entitled under Section 8A of the Central Act. However, after the amendment of the aforesaid Section in December, 1985 the minimum pension of an ex-MP has been raised to Rs. 500 p.m. The Ministry of Law clarified that from the date of amendment of the said Section, Shri Saklecha is entitled to receive pension of Rs. 500 p.m.—Rs.50 p.m. as parliamentary pension in addition to pension of Rs. 450 p.m.as an ex-MLA. The Ministry of Law agreed with our views *in toto*.

(File No. 4(1)/86-WS)

Telephone facilities to Ministers in their Constituencies/usual places of residence

The Minister of Government of India would be entitled to a telephone connection either in his usual place of residence or at a place selected by him, being a place situated within the State which he represents or within the State in which he resides, in his capacity as a Member of Parliament with a maximum ceiling of *15,000 free local calls. The Minister would also be allowed to adjust the trunk call bills within the monetary equivalent of 15,000 local calls in a year.

In case where the telephone at the constituency/usual place of residence is in a flat rate exchange, the Minister would be allowed to adjust the charges for trunk calls made from this telephone to the extent of Rs. 3,000 per year (equivalent of 7500 local calls).

(File No. 4(6)/86-WS also F.No. 4(20)/WS S.No. 16 ante)

Grant of pension *(ex-gratia)* by the State Government to Smt. Usha Khan in addition to Parliamentary Pension

The short point for consideration was whether pension *(ex-gratia)* granted by the Government of Rajasthan to Smt. Usha Khan on account of meritorious service rendered by her late husband is liable to be adjusted for calculating pension payable to her by virtue of her being an MP. The opinion given by the Law Ministry in the case is as under:

> "the intention underlying the provision appears to be that a person who receiving pension as of right and who can enforce it in a Court of Law alone, is covered by it, and not persons who receive *ex-gratia* payments from the Government."

(File No. 4(9)/86-WS)

Grant of Honorarium to ex-MPs who are in receipt of Parliamentary Pension (case of Shri R.S. Panjhazari)

"The expression 'honorarium' is used in cases, where some special work is done and in consideration thereof certain payments are made. Normally, such special work may be of an occasional or intermittent character. The facts in the reference would appear to bring it under the category of honorarium.

As regards the house rent allowance and the conveyance allowance and the presumption raised by Department now that

---

*Limit raised along with increase of free local calls admissible to MPs.

as it is clarified by the Department that ex-MP has his permanent residence at Patiala and has to maintain a house himself at Delhi for the assignment, it would appear that as stated by the Department these allowances are compensatory in nature and are not remuneration."

(File No. 4(11)/86-WS)

TA for intermediate journeys to Members of Parliament under Section 5 of the Act

The opinion of the Ministry of Law was sought as to whether the restriction of not more than 15 days' absence during session of Parliament for claiming TA by MPs as contemplated under section 5 (1) will still be applicable in view of amended Section 5 (2) of the Act. It was clarified by the Ministry of Law that limitation of performing the intermediate journey within the prescribed limit of 15 days as specified in sub-section 1 of the Section 5 of the Act operates only when the concerned House of Parliament is in Session or a sitting of a committee is taking place. The conditions referred to in Section 5 (1) do not govern the TA admissible under Section 5 (2), newly inserted by the 1985 (Amendment Act). Section 5 (2), therefore, will be applicable irrespective of the fact whether a House of Parliament is in session and/or there is a sitting of committee or not. In view thereof, the condition of "absence of less than 15 days" contemplated in sub-section (I) of Section 5 will not be applicable.

(File No. 4(12)/86-WS)

Payment of Honorarium to Minister for use of his copyright

A question arose as to whether Shri P. V. Narasimha Rao, Minister of Human Resource Development , who had contributed an article on "Copyright and Peace" to the World Intellectual Property Organisation may accept a honorarium of 5,000 Swiss Francs from that Organisation for this assignment. The matter was examined in consultation with the Ministry of Home Affairs and the Ministry of Law who opined that there can be no objection to the payment for the use of his copyright. There is nothing in the Code of Conduct disentitling a Minister from receiving honorarium for intellectual work.

(File No. 4(27)/86-WS)

Drawal of Salary by a Chief Minister from the State and Constituency Allowance from the Centre by virtue of his being a Member of Parliament

A reference was examined in consultation with the Ministry of Law and Justice whether a Member of Parliament, while holding office of a Chief Minister in a State Government, can draw his salary from the State Government and Constituency Allowance from the Centre by virtue of his being an MP. The case related to Shri Bansi Lal, Chief Minister of Haryana. The opinion of the Ministry of Law was:

> "that there will be no legal objection to the Member of Parliament drawing constituency allowance as a Member of Parliament during this period unless there is any bar to his drawing such allowance under a parliamentary Law or State Law. In the instant case, there appears to be no such bar."

(File No. 4 (29)/86 -WS)

Entitlement of Shri Sitaram Kesari, Minister of State to draw Pension in addition to salary and allowance under the provisions of the Act

"In the light of the observations of the Supreme Court in M. Karunanidhi *Vs.* UOI AIR 1979 S.C. 898 at 915 that a Minister gets a salary for the public work done, or the public duty performed by him and that the said salary is paid to the Minister from the Government funds, the Minister would appear to be entitled to remuneration from the Government. If that be so, the case squarely falls under Section 8A(2) (iii)."

(File No. 4 (1) /87-WS)

IMPORTANT RULINGS/DECISIONS RELATING TO ADMINISTRATION OF ACTS

Free furnished residence to Chairman of Financial Committees

The recommendations of the Joint Committee on Salaries and Allowances of MPs made on 28 June, 1967 for provision of free furnished residence for the Chairman of 3 Financial Committees was not agreed to by Ministry of Law and Ministry of Finance.

Ministry of Law opined that it would be discrimination to other MPs. Ministry of Finance opined that the matter may not rest there and it will become difficult to deny the same concession to the Chairman of the other Parliamentary Committees.

(File No. 4(3)/67-WS)

Average days for attending Sessions, sittings of Committee

The Joint Committee on Salaries and Allowance of MPs recommended on 11 November, 1992 that the average days for attending sessions and sittings of committee in a year be taken as 250 and not 300 while calculating the financial implications for DA to MPs.

(File No. 4(3)/92-WS)

Extention of free travel facility to spouse of ex-MPs

Extract from reply from Minister of Railways (Shri C.K. Jaffer Sharief) (No.E (W) 92 PS5-7/3 dated June /July 3,1992):

> "The long standing demand of ex-MPs for grant of free rail facility has already been agreed to. As an additional benefit and further also directed Railways for inclusion of an attendant in second class on subsequent requests. You will, therefore, appreciate that in view of financial crunch and heavy demand for accommodation and consequent over-crowding in trains, it would not be possible to enlarge the scope of concessions further for inclusion of spouse also, which would mean a further increase in number of persons from initial one to three."

(F.No. 4(11)/92-WS)

Rail travel facilities to ex-MPs /companions

Instructions were also subsequently issued by the Ministry of Railways on 27 February, 1996 that the First Class Complimentary Card Passes issued to former Members of Parliament may be made available for travel in II AC Class in Rajdhani and Chair Car in Shatabdi Express trains for self along with a companion in the same class without payment of difference of fare. They can also secure reservation in these trains from the General Quota available at the counters. (Ministry of Railways O.M. No. E (W) 95PS5-7/7 dated 29.2.1996).

(File No. 4 (2) /95-WS)

PART-II

Constitution of Joint Parliamentary Committee

Joint Parliamentary Committee (FRM) was constituted by the Speaker, Lok Sabha, w.e.f. 1 June , 1993 to suggest facilities and remuneration for Members of Parliament.

(File No. 4(5)/93 -WS)

Condoning the shortfall in the period of membership upto 15 days for grant of pension (Case of Shri Bansi Lal, ex-MP)

Amendment of the Act was sought for granting discretionary powers to Speaker/Chairman for condoning the shortfall in the period of membership (up to 15 days) for grant of pension.

Ministry of Law *inter alia* opined :

"There would not be any legal objection to the proposed amendment *ibid*. However also suggested that a decision in respect of period sought to be condoned may, in the first instance, be taken on the basis of some reasonable criteria. It is observed that in the present case the ex-MP's 18th year is falling short by 15 days. There could be other cases where such period could be 16 or 20 days.Therefore, before initiating a formal amendment proposal, a decision regarding period in question would appear to be necessary."

(File No. 4(8)/93-WS)

Enhancement of CGHS Contribution

To a reference received from the Ministry of Health and Family Welfare regarding enhancement of CGHS Contribution of MPs to Rs. 50 per month, the Ministry responded as under:

> "..... it is for the Ministry of Health and Family Welfare to take a policy decision regarding the scale of contribution under the CGHS. However, if the scale of contribution in case of Members of Parliament is to be related to the level of services rendered, it would be necessary to amend Rule 3 of the Medical Facilities (MPs) Rules, 1959 framed under the Salary, Allowances and Pension of Members of Parliament Act, 1954. The

> Ministry also opined that the contribution from Members of Parliament should in no case be more than the contribution to be made by the Ministers as a Minister is entitled to receive a salary per mensem and an allowance for each day during his tenure as such Minister at the same rates as are specified in Section 3 of the Salary, Allowances and Pension of Members of Parliament Act, 1954 with respect to Members of Parliament.

In regard to ex-MPs, referring to the Ministry of Health and Family Welfare O.M. No. F. 4-96/74-CGHS (P) dated 6 June, 1976, it was *inter alia* stated :

> ".... as the contribution under CGHS to be made by ex-MPs was fixed through executive instructions issued by the Deptt of Health, it is for that Deptt. to take a decision in the matter and issue the necessary instructions."

(F.No. F.4 (24)/94-WS)

Increase in ceiling on supply of furniture to Members of Parliament

The ceiling on supply of durable furniture was raised from Rs. 12,000 to Rs. 24,000 per Member of Parliament and the corresponding ceiling for non-durable furniture was raised from Rs. 3,000 to Rs. 6,000 per Member of Parliament for recovery of concessional rate of hire charges. Recovery of rent for the furniture supplied to Members of Parliament will be made at the following rates subject to 25 per cent rebate:

Durable furniture

Nine per cent per annum of the cost of furniture up to the value of Rs. 24,000 and 13.75 per cent per annum of the cost of furniture beyond the value of Rs. 24,000.

Non-durable furniture

At the rate of 16.5 per cent per annum of the cost of furniture up to the value of Rs. 6,000 and 24.5 per cent per annum of the cost of furniture beyond the value of Rs. 6,000.

(*vide* Directorate of Estates O.M. No. 18012 (2)/84- Pol. III dated 12th November,1996 effective from 1 December, 1996).

(F.No. 4 (12)/96-WS)

Amendment of the Salaries and Allowances of Officers of Parliament Act, 1953 to provide for pension, housing and medical facilities to the spouse of the Speaker of the House of the People, dying while holding such office

Consequent to the death of Shri G.M.C. Balayogi, former Speaker of Lok Sabha, on 3 March, 2002 the Salary and Allowances of Officers of Parliament Act,1953 has been amended as under to provide for pension, medical and housing facilities to the spouse of the Speaker dying while holding such office retrospectively from 3 March, 2002.

> 7A (i) "There shall be paid a family pension to the spouse of the Speaker of the House of the People who dies while holding such office at the rate of fifty per cent of the salary last drawn by him for the remainder of life of such spouse from the date of death of the Speaker:
>
> Provided that the spouse of such Speaker shall not be entitled to receive pension available to the spouse of any Member of Parliament who dies during his term of office as such Member for a period of five years from the date of death of the Member under sub-section (1A) of Section 8A of the Salary, Allowances and Pension of Members of Parliament Act,1954.
>
> Without prejudice to the provisions of clause (a) of sub-section (2) of Section 4 and subject to any rules made in this behalf under section 11, such spouse shall be entitled to the use of unfurnished residence without payment of licence fee for the remainder of her life.
>
> Subject to any rules made in this behalf under Section 11—such spouse, for the remainder of her life, and the minor children of such Speaker, shall be entitled to medical attendance and treatment, free of charge."

To execute the above provision of the Act of the Officers of Parliament (Pension, Housing and Medical Facilities to the Spouse of the Speaker of the House of the People, dying while holding such Office) Rules, 2002 have been framed and printed in the Gazette of India *vide* Notification No.535 (E) dated 31 July, 2002 to be effective from 3 March, 2002.

(F. No. 13(2)/2002-WS)

Increase in Sumptuary Allowance of Officers of Parliament and Leaders of Opposition in Parliament

The Sumptuary Allowance shall be paid to :

The Speaker of the House of the People and Leaders of the Opposition in Parliament at the same rate at which the sumptuary allowance is payable, under Section 5 of the Salaries and Allowances of Ministers Act,1952, to every other Minister who is a member of the Cabinet ; the Deputy Chairman and the Deputy Speaker at the same rate at which the sumptuary allowance is payable, under Section 5 of Salaries and Allowances of Ministers Act, 1952 to a Minister of State.

(F.No. 13 (2)/2002-WS)

Recovery of Salary and Allowances of Shri V. C. Shukla for his membership of X Lok Sabha

The election of Shri V.C. Shukla to the X Lok Sabha was declared null and void by the Jabalpur High Court of Madhya Pradesh on the Election Petition filed against him *vide* its order dated 20 February, 1996 in Election petition No.1 of 1991. Though he had appealed against this judgement in the Supreme Court, but by the time the Court decided on his appeal, the X Lok Sabha was dissolved and realising that the appeal was infructuous, he withdrew the appeal from the Supreme Court. While calculating his pension, the Lok Sabha Secretariat ignored his membership for the X Lok Sabha keeping in view the fact that the judgement of the Jabalpur High Court was valid as no judgement had come against it on the basis of appeal filed by Shri Shukla in Supreme Court.

The matter was referred to Ministry of Law and Justice, (Department of Legal Affairs) and on a later stage to the Solicitor General of India. Both of them had opined that in the absence of any judgement by the Higher Court against it, the judgement of

Jabalpur High Court of Madhya Pradesh was valid and Shri V.C. Shukla was not entitled to the pension for his membership of the X Lok Sabha.

On a reference from the Lok Sabha Secretariat and in view of the opinion rendered by Ministry of Law and Justice, (Department of Legal Affairs) and the Solicitor General of India against the grant of pension of Shri V.C. Shukla for his membership for X Lok Sabha, the matter was again referred to Ministry of Law and Justice, (Department of Legal Affairs) asking whether Shri Shukla was entitled to the salary and allowances which he received from Lok Sabha Secretariat as an MP and also as a Member of the Union Council. The Solicitor General of India was also approached in the matter for his esteemed opinion. The opinion rendered by the Solicitor General of India (Shri Harish N. Salve) on 23 February, 2002 is as under :

> "for the period prior to the judgement of the High Court any recovery of the salary, even if legally possible, would be highly unjust and unfair for the period after the judgement of the High Court, the government should not, in fairness, considering the factors indicated above, seek a recovery of the salary paid to him."

(File No. 4(9)/2000-WS)

11

WELFARE OF MEMBERS OF PARLIAMENT

The Ministry of Parliamentary Affairs looks after the welfare of ailing Members of Parliament admitted for treatment in hospitals in Delhi. Arrangements are made with the leading hospitals in Delhi to obtain day-to-day information by fax and/ or telephone regarding health condition of the ailing Members. The information is communicated to Ministers/Ministers of State/senior officers in the Ministry of Parliamentary Affairs as well as to the concerned parliamentary party offices. This information is also made available on this Ministry's official website (http://www.mpa.nic.in/). The officers of this Ministry pay visits to the hospitals to enquire about the health condition of the Members and to render any assistance required by them. The Minister/Ministers of State for Parliamentary Affairs and senior officers also make courtesy calls on the ailing Members admitted in hospitals as and when required. Format of daily report is at **Annex XI-A.**

In the unfortunate event of the passing away of a Member of Parliament in Delhi, the Ministry of Parliamentary Affairs renders all necessary assistance to the bereaved family members for transporting the mortal remains of the deceased Member to the place of last rites chosen by the family. The entire expenditure on embalming, coffin box, its sealing, and hearse van etc. is borne by the Ministry of Parliamentary Affairs. Cost of transportation between the place of death and the place of last rites of the deceased MP, TA for one member of the family accompanying the body of the deceased MP is also borne by this Ministry (MHA O.M.No.25/1/84-Public dated 13 August, 1985).

A check list of procedure followed for transportation of dead body of the Member of Parliament is at **Annex XI-B.**

Under the Foreign Contribution (Regulation) Act, 1976, it is *inter alia,* incumbent on Members of Parliament going abroad to obtain political clearance from the Ministry of External Affairs and prior permission of the Ministry of Home Affairs, where such visits involve acceptance of "foreign hospitality" from a foreign government or organisation. This Ministry informs Members from time to time, about the procedure to be followed in this respect. Necessary assistance sought for by Members in this regard is also provided/extended.

12

APPOINTMENT OF MEMBERS OF PARLIAMENT ON COMMITTEES, ETC.

BACKGROUND

Committees, Councils, Boards, Commissions, etc. are appointed/constituted by the Government from time to time to deal with specified items of business requiring expert or detailed consideration and to aid and advise the Government. Such Committees etc. are composed of expert officials and non-officials and may include Members of Parliament who have specialisation/expertise/experience in the field.

The subject of 'Nomination of Members of Parliament on Committees and other bodies set up by the Government' has been allocated to the Ministry of Parliamentary Affairs under the Government of India (Allocation of Business) Rules, 1961 made by the President under article 77(3) of the Constitution. By virtue of this, Members of Parliament are to be selected and nominated on all Government bodies by the Minister of Parliamentary Affairs only. However, in the case of statutory bodies, where the statute provides that the Members of Parliament will be nominated by the Speaker, Lok Sabha, or the Chairman, Rajya Sabha, the nominations are made by the Speaker or the Chairman, as the case may be. In the case of Speaker, Lok Sabha, such nominations are processed by the Lok Sabha Secretariat directly. In case the nomination is to be made by the Chairman, Rajya Sabha, the Rajya Sabha Secretariat makes a reference to the Ministry of Parliamentary Affairs for obtaining the recommendations of the Minister of Parliamentary Affairs.

This function has been entrusted specifically to the Minister of Parliamentary Affairs for the reasons that (a) there should be a single authority through which all nominations of Members of

Parliament on various bodies set up by the Government are made, (b) the Minister of Parliamentary Affairs being the Government Chief Whip is eminently suited to discharge this function as he is in the know of the interest, aptitude, experience, suitability and availability of Members of Parliament in relation to the proposed assignments, and (c) certain uniform, fair and objective norms would be observed for equitable distribution of membership of various Government bodies among the Members belonging to different sections of both the Houses of Parliament to avoid a situation where some Members come to be over-burdened with assignments while others have none.

Hindi Salahkar Samities are constituted by various Ministries/Departments of the Government of India to advise them on matters relating to the progressive use of Hindi in official work and other allied issues. The bye-laws of these Samities *inter alia* provide for nomination of four Members of Parliament-two each from the Lok Sabha and Rajya Sabha.

Considering all aspects of the matter, the Ministry with the approval of the Minister of Parliamentary Affairs, has laid down guidelines for nomination of Members of Parliament on committees etc.; consolidating all existing instructions on the subject **(Annex-XII-A).** A proforma has also been prescribed for the Ministries for sending their proposals for nomination of Members of Parliament **(Annex- XII-B).**

PROCESS

Wherever bye-laws/rules regarding constitution of such committees etc. *inter alia* provide for nomination of Members of Parliament thereon, Ministries concerned request this Ministry to move the Minister of Parliamentary Affairs for nomination of requisite number of Members on the committees. On receipt of the proposal from the Ministry concerned, if the required information has not been received in the prescribed proforma, the Ministry concerned is requested to furnish it accordingly.

On receipt of complete information, the case is submitted to Minister of Parliamentary Affairs for nomination of requisite number of Members of Parliament through Minister of State (Lok Sabha) and Minister of State (Rajya Sabha), who suggest the names of Members of the Lok Sabha and Rajya Sabha respectively, for approval of the Minister. Main points contained in the proposal and certain factual information - details of Members who were earlier nominated on that body and their availability (facts regarding expiry of term of Rajya Sabha Members/ resignation, demise of any of the earlier Members) - are provided in the note.

Names of the Members nominated by Minister of Parliamentary Affairs are then communicated to the Ministry with the request to notify their nomination on the body and supply to them all the necessary literature including the constitution, function and programme of work etc. of that body under intimation to this Ministry **(Annex-XII-C).**

Letters are also sent to the Members concerned informing them of their nomination on the body by the Minister of Parliamentary Affairs and to let this Ministry know if they, for any reason, would find it difficult to serve on that body **(Annex-XII-D).**

Under the Parliament (Prevention of Disqualification) Act, 1959, Members nominated on such committees etc. can draw only 'compensatory allowance' and no other remuneration for attending meetings of such committees, bodies etc. Compensatory allowance according to that Act means:

> "Any sum of money payable to the holder of an office by way of daily allowance, such allowance not exceeding the amount of daily allowance to which a Member of Parliament is entitled under the Salary, Allowances and Pensions of Members of Parliament Act, 1954 (30 of 1954), any conveyance allowance, house rent allowance or traveling allowance for the purpose of enabling him to recoup any expenditure incurred by him in performing the functions of that office."

This is *inter alia* informed to the Members concerned through the aforesaid letter. The Ministry concerned is also advised to make suitable provisions for the purpose.

To fill up the vacancy of a Member of Parliament, if any, on such bodies, on account of the death, resignation or retirement of any Member nominated on the body, the case for nomination of another Member on it is processed on the same lines.

It has been observed that Ministries/Departments normally

delay the constitution of various Government bodies on which Members of Parliament are nominated by the Ministry. They also take time in sending necessary literature relating to these bodies, viz., notification regarding their constitution, functions, programme of work, etc. to the Members of Parliament concerned. Members have, on several occasions, complained to the Minister of Parliamentary Affairs in this regard. Ministry of Parliamentary Affairs takes up the matter with the Ministries/Departments concerned from time to time to expedite the requisite information/literature to Members concerned under intimation to the Ministry. Periodically, a D.O. letter at the Secretary/Joint Secretary level is also sent to all Ministries/Departments to impress upon them the necessity of quickly sending the reguisite information/literature in the matter to MPs etc.

DECISIONS

Nomination of Members of Parliament on Committees, Councils, Boards, Commissions, etc. set up by the Government

Minister of Parliamentary Affairs nominates Members of Parliament on Committees, Councils, Boards, Commissions, etc. constituted/set up by the Government of India in any Ministry.

(No.F.1-1/95-CB)

Vigilance and Monitoring Committees for different District Rural Development Agencies (DRDAs)

With a view to constituting the Vigilance and Monitoring Committees in 581 districts in the country, the Minister of Parliamentary Affairs was requested to nominate Member(s) of the Lok Sabha in each district where he/she has been elected, for being nominated as Chairman/Member of the respective District committee. Instead of nominating individual Members for each committee, 'guidelines' for nominating Members as Chairman/Co-Chairman were formulated with the approval of Minister of Parliamentary Affairs which were communicated to the Ministry of Rural Development for making nomination thereon as per the guidelines **(Annex XII-E).**

(No.F.2-29(2)/2002-CB)

Nomination of a Minister on a Committee

Members of Parliament are nominated on various committees, councils, etc. constituted by the Government as per provisions contained in this Ministry's O.M.No.1-1/96-CB dated 24 May, 1999. Members of Parliament nominated on statutory bodies cease to be members of such bodies on their becoming Ministers, Speaker, Deputy Speaker, Lok Sabha, and Deputy Chairman, Rajya Sabha. However, the Ministry of Youth Affairs and Sports had suggested the name of a Minister, namely Shri Arun Jaitley, Minister of Law Justice and Commerce and Industry, for being nominated on the Preparation Committee for '2004 Olympic Games (Athens)' and Minister of Parliamentary Affairs approved the proposal.

(No.F.2-40(1)/2003-CB)

CHECK LIST

A check list indicating the points to be checked while processing a case of nomination of Members on committees, etc. is at **Annex XII-F.**

13

HANDLING OF PARLIAMENTARY WORK IN MINISTRIES

The Ministry of Parliamentary Affairs serves as an important link between the two Houses of Parliament and the Ministries/ Departments, and helps the Ministries in handling parliamentary work in various ways.

Manual of Parliamentary Procedures in the Government of India

The Ministry reviews and updates instructions issued from time to time regarding parliamentary procedures for the Ministries of the Government of India. The Ministry has recently reviewed and updated the manual and the updated manual is also available to the Ministries on the Ministry of Parliamentary Affairs' website (http://www.mpa.nic.in) and in the form of a CD, apart from the revised printed edition.

Planning and Co-ordination of Government Business

The Ministry plans and coordinates the Government legislative and other business in Parliament, and reviews it from time to time as per requirement/preparedness of the Ministries. There is a separate chapter on 'Legislative and Financial Business of the Government' in this Handbook **(Chapter-4).**

Ordinances

The Ministry arranges for laying by the Minister/Minister of State for Parliamentary Affairs, copies of the ordinances issued by the Ministries during the Inter-session period, on the Table of both the Houses of Parliament. (Details are provided in **Chapter-4** on **'Ligislative and Financial Business of the Government'.)**

Private Members' Business

The Ministry co-ordinates action in respect of approval of the Government stand by the Cabinet Committee on Parliamentary Affairs on Private Members' Bills and Resolutions in the two Houses of Parliament (This is discussed in **Chapter-6** on **'Cabinet Committee on Parliamentary Affairs').**

Allotment of Rooms

The Ministry has forty eight rooms in Parliament House for allotment to Ministers during the Parliament sessions for the facility in handling Parliamentary business **(Annex-XIII-A).** The Ministry allots rooms in the Parliament House to Ministers/ Ministers of State (MOS) for various Ministries before each session of Parliament with the approval of the Minister of Parliamentary Affairs. Private Secretaries to the Ministers, Lok Sabha/Rajya Sabha Secretariats, President's Secretariat, Prime Minister's Office, Cabinet Secretariat and all others concerned are intimated **(Annex XIII-B).**

As the number of rooms available are much less than the number of Ministers, it is not possible to allot rooms to all the Ministers. The order of precedence for allotment of rooms to Ministers is as under :

(1) Cabinet Ministers
(2) Ministers of State (Independent Charge)
(3) Ministers of State

(Note: Four rooms (9-12) are set apart for the Prime Minister's Office and one room (27) for the Leader of the House in the Rajya Sabha. The Minister for Parliamentary Affairs occupies two rooms, viz., 14 and 15. Certain rooms are also set apart for Ministers of State, Parliamentary Affairs. Two rooms are reserved for the Leaders of Opposition in the Lok Sabha and the Rajya Sabha i.e. room Nos. 43 and 44).

The Ministry has, however, been taking up the matter with the Speaker, Lok Sabha, for providing more rooms for allotment to all the Ministers.

Roster of Attendance

In order to ensure the presence of some Minister(s) to represent the Government in the two Houses all the time when the House sits, the Ministry of Parliamentary Affairs prepares a roster of attendance of Ministers/Ministers of States (Independent Charge)/ Ministers of State, in the two Houses, before every Parliament session and the Ministers/Ministers of State are informed in advance by the Minister of Parliamentary Affairs **(Annex XIII-C).** A circular is also sent to all others concerned **(Annex XIII-D).**

Coordination of work in respect of States under the President's Rule

When any of the State(s) is(are) under President's Rule, important Legislative business in respect of the State(s) may be taken up in the two Houses of Parliament. The Ministry of Parliamentary Affairs coordinates action in that regard in consultation with the Ministries concerned/Ministry of Home Affairs/Ministry of Law and Justice.

Training Courses

The Ministry organises short duration training courses in Parliamentary Practices and Procedures for the officers of Ministries for providing procedural guidance and practical tips [Details are provided in **Chapter 16** on **'Training of Officials (Ministries/Departments, State Governments)'].**

Matters raised during Zero Hour

Members of Parliament, with the permission of the Presiding Officers, raise various urgent matters of public importance during Zero Hour. The Ministry forwards relevant extracts from the proceedings of the House to the Ministries for their information and such action as they deem necessary **(Annex XIII-E).** In cases where there is a direction from the Presiding Officer or an assurance from the Minister/Minister of State, Parliamentary Affairs, the related extracts are forwarded to the Minister concerned by the Minister/Minister of State, Parliamentary Affairs, the same day **(Annex XIII-F).** For this purpose, an official from Legislative-II Section is deputed to the Official Galleries of each House during Zero Hour. Besides, one Under Secretary of the Ministry is also deputed to the Official Gallery of each House during Zero Hour to take note of important developments in the Houses and bring the same to the notice of the Minister of Parliamentary Affairs **(Annexes XIII-G & H).**

Matters raised under Rule 377/Special Mentions

The Ministry forwards to the Ministries concerned, weekly lists of the matters raised in the two Houses to enable them to counter-check the position with the extracts received from the Lok Sabha/Rajya Sabha Secretariat. The Ministry has also formulated procedural guidelines to facilitate processing and replies to these matters. The Ministry reviews pending matters from time to time, sends reminders to Ministries, organizes meetings with Secretaries/senior officers concerned to expedite replies to pending matters (Details are provided in **Chapter-8** on **'Monitoring Replies to Special Mentions and Rule 377 Issues').**

Nomination of Members of Parliament on Government Bodies

The Minister of Parliamentary Affairs nominates Members of Parliament on the Committees, Commissions, Boards, etc. set up by the Government and the Hindi Salahkar Samities of various Ministries. (Details are provided in **Chapter-12** on **'Appointment of Members of Parliament on Committees etc.')**

Election of Members of Parliament on Parliamentary Financial Committees and Committee on Welfare of Scheduled Castes and Scheduled Tribes

The three Financial Committees, viz., the Public Accounts Committee, the Estimate Committee and the Committee on Public Undertakings, and the Committee on the Welfare of Scheduled Castes and Scheduled Tribes are constituted for a term of one year. While the Estimate Committee consists of Members of the Lok Sabha only, the remaining three committees consist of Members of both the Houses. The Members are elected on these committees from amongst the Members of the House(s) according to the principle of proportional representation by means of a single transferable vote, after Motions to this effect **(Annexes XIII-I to O),** which are moved by the Minister of Parliamentary Affairs in the Lok Sabha and by the Minister of

State for Parliamentary Affairs from the Rajya Sabha, in the Rajya Sabha, have been adopted by the respective Houses. Further, when any vacancy(ies) occurs on these committees due to resignation or demise of the Members serving on the committees, such vacancies are filled through the process of election after Motion(s) to that effect moved by the Minister of Parliamentary Affairs or the Minister of State for Parliamentary Affairs, as the case may be, has/have been adopted by the Lok Sabha in case of a vacancy relating to a Member of the Lok Sabha and by both Houses in case of a vacancy relating to the Rajya Sabha.

Implementation of Assurances

The Ministry coordinates action in culling out and forwarding the extracts of assurances given by the Ministers in the Lok Sabha/ Rajya Sabha, scrutinises the Implementation Reports received from the Ministries, arranges for laying of the sets of Implementation Reports duly authenticated by the Minister/ Minister of State for Parliamentary Affairs on the Tables of both the Houses. The Ministry also reviews pending assurances and reminds the Ministries concerned from time to time to expedite fulfilment of the parliamentary assurances. Further, the Ministry processes the reports of Committees on Government Assurances, Lok Sabha and Rajya Sabha and takes up the matter with the Ministries for further necessary action. (Details are provided in **Chapter-9** on **'Monitoring Assurances'.)**

Compliance of Recommendations of Parliamentary Committees

The Ministry processes the recommendations of general nature contained in the reports of the following Parliamentary Committees (Lok Sabha and Rajya Sabha) impressing upon the Ministries the need for their strict compliance:

(i) Committees on Papers Laid;
(ii) Committees on Subordinate Legislation; and
(iii) Committees on Petitions.

Advice to Ministries

References are often received from the Ministries for advice on various parliamentary/constitutional matters such as parliamentary privileges, anti-defection law, code of conduct for

Members of Parliament, declaration of assets and liabilities by the Members, expenditure on a sitting of Parliament, official dealings between Members of Parliament and administration, attendance before Parliamentary Committees, provision of papers to them, etc. Though these subjects do not exactly relate to the functions allotted to the Ministry of Parliamentary Affairs under the Government of India (Allocation of Business) Rules, 1961, the Ministry examines the requests with reference to rules, conventions, precedents, legal opinions in consultation with the Ministry of Law and other Ministries concerned and sends suitable replies.

General Instructions

In order to ensure compliance with various instructions, directions of the Speaker, Lok Sabha/Chairman, Rajya Sabha in respect of supplying factual information about Paliament Questions/Calling Attention Notices, copies of annual reports, etc., circulars are issued to the Ministries from time to time. Whenever D.O. letters/instructions on such and other important matters are issued to Ministries/Departments, copies thereof should be endorsed to concerned officers/sections in the Ministries for necessary action. For example, copy of D.O. letters issued under the signature of the Secretary to Secretaries of various Ministries/Departments on the above matters may be endorsed to the Joint Secretary. Similarly, copy of D.O. letters/ instructions issued to Ministries/Departments under the signature of Joint Secretary may be endorsed to the concerned Deputy Secretary in the Ministry and copies of such communications issued under the signature of Deputy Secretary may be endorsed to concerned Under Secretary and Section Officer in the Ministry.

Addresses and Telephone Numbers of Officers dealing with Parliamentary Work

The Ministry compiles a directory of office addresses and telephone numbers (office and residence) of officers dealing with parliamentary work in various Ministries and in the Lok Sabha/ Rajya Sabha Secretariats, and provides it to the Ministries for facilitating contact and reference. Telephone numbers of Joint Secretary (Parliament) and Parliamentary Units of various

Ministries/Departments are also available on the website of the Ministry.

Notes on Emerging Trends

About a week before the commencement of every Parliament session, a list of issues likely to be raised by Members in the two Houses is submitted by Legislative-II Section for the information of the Minister. Ministries/Departments concerned with these and other issues, which in the opinion of the Ministries/ Departments are important and can be raised in the Houses, are requested to furnish Brief Notes thereon to the Prime Minister's Office and the Ministry of Parliamentary Affairs to enable the Minister of Parliamentary Affairs, in his capacity as the Government Chief Whip, to reply to any point which may be raised in the Houses on the above issues **(Annex XIII-P).** A copy each of the Brief Notes, as and when received from the Ministries/ Departments, is submitted to the Minister of Parliamentary Affairs and the Minister of State for Parliamentary Affairs from the Rajya Sabha.

14

ALL INDIA WHIPS' CONFERENCE

BACKGROUND

In a parliamentary form of Government, the Whips, who are drawn from various political parties, are vital links in the internal organisation of parties inside the Legislature. The expression "Whips" is derived from the term 'Whipper-in' employed by a hunt to look after the hounds and keep them together in the field. The term 'Whipper-in' was originally used in Parliament as in the hunting field for a Member who discharged this duty for his party, but, in due course of time, it became reduced to 'Whip'. In this sense the Oxford Dictionary defines a 'Whip' as a member of a particular party in Parliament whose duty is to secure the attendance of members of that party on the occasion of an important division. Later, the term was applied to the call or appeal made by such a person, and is defined by the dictionary as "the written appeal issued by a Parliament 'Whip' to summon the members of his party".

The efficient and smooth working of the parliamentary machine depends, to a very large extent, upon the office of the Whip. The Whips are responsible for carrying on, efficiently and smoothly, the organisation of the parties inside the Legislatures. The Whips have to keep a vigilant eye on the proceedings of the House and have to be ready to meet any emergency in the House.

Origin and History

In view of the important role played by the Whips in the smooth running of the parliamentary machine, an idea of providing a suitable forum for periodical meetings and mutual exchange of views amongst the Whips in Parliament as well as the State Legislatures was conceived as early as in 1952. Accordingly, the first Conference of Whips was held at Indore on 13 September, 1952. The object of convening the conference was to establish a suitable link amongst the Whips who were concerned with the practical working of Legislatures, to discuss matters of common concern, and to evolve standards to strengthen the institutions of parliamentary democracy.

The Whips, Conference provides a useful forum to the Whips of various political parties - ruling as well as opposition, at the Centre as well as in the States - to sit together, exchange their views, thoughts and experiences, discuss difficulties confronted by them in the discharge of their parliamentary duties and evolve certain well-considered norms for efficient working of the parliamentary machine in the country. A statement showing the details of All India Whips, Conferences held so far is at **Annex XIV-A**.

THE PROCESS

The Ministry of Parliamentary Affairs organises the conference of Whips of All India Political Parties, at the Centre as well as in the States, for which a suitable venue and date are decided well in time. The Whips' Conference usually makes a number of recommendations for smooth and efficient working of Parliament and the State Legislatures in the light of the experience gained by the Whips. The Central Ministry of Parliamentary Affairs forwards the recommendations to the (i) the State Chief Ministers; (ii) Ministers in-charge of Department of Parliamentary Affairs in the State Governments; and (iii) Presiding Officers of the State Legislatures and all the invitees to the conference, for information and necessary action.

The recommendations generally fall into three categories, namely, (i) those requiring action by the Central Government; (ii) those which require action by the State Governments, and (iii) those which are to be implemented by the State Legislatures.

Accordingly, the Ministry of Parliamentary Affairs requests the concerned authorities to intimate action taken by them on the recommendations concerning them. It has been observed that the State Government Legislatures have generally taken a keen interest in the implementation of recommendations. Some recommendations are implemented, some accepted in principle or implemented in spirit, if not in letter, and others are commented upon by them. The replies/comments received are consolidated in a statement and are submitted to the next conference for the information of the delegates, as Implementation

Reports from State Governments and State Legislatures. Similarly, an Implementation Report showing the action taken on the recommendations of the preceding conference by the Central Government is also provided to the succeeding conference for information.

The proceedings of a Whips' Conference together with the Implementation Reports of the Central and State Governments are printed in the form of a brochure and made available to the delegates of the next conference.

After the date for holding of the conference is decided in consultation with the hosting State Government, the Central Ministry of Parliamentary Affairs has to take, broadly speaking, the following steps:

(a) To chalk out the programme of the conference;
(b) To prepare items of agenda and notes thereon;
(c) To request the State Governments/Legislatures to expedite their Implementation Reports;
(d) To request the Chief Ministers for nominating delegates;
(e) To write to Leaders of the Opposition in Parliament for nominating delegates;
(f) On receipt of information on (d) and (e) above, to send invitation letters to the delegates;
(g) To request the President, the Vice-President, the Prime Minister, the Speaker, the Deputy Speaker, the Deputy Chairman and the Chief Ministers to send messages for the conference;
(h) To prepare Implementation Reports in respect of the recommendations of the previous conference, of (i) the Centre, (ii) State Governments and State Legislatures;
(i) To take appropriate steps for publicity and press coverage of the conference; and
(j) To request the Indian Airlines Corporation and the Railway Board for necessary reservations for delegates and the staff.

The 12th All India Whips' Conference, held at Srinagar on 21 & 22 August, 1997, had, *inter alia,* recommended **(Annex XIV-B)** setting up of a Monitoring Group under the Chairmanship of the Union Minister of Parliamentary Affairs to oversee the progress of implementation of the recommendations of the 12th All India Whips' Conference.

In pursuance of the above recommendation, a Monitoring Group, to watch the progress of implementation of the recommendations made by the said conference, was constituted on 7 April, 2000 initially for a period of one year. In its first meeting held on 17 May, 2000, the Monitoring Group constituted two Sub-committees i.e. Sub-committee "A" and Sub-committee "B," on 23 May, 2000 for going to the various States to study and assess the state of implementation of the recommendations of the All India Whips' Conference. The Sub-committees were required to submit their reports within three months from the dates of their first meetings. The terms of the Monitoring Group and Sub-committees have been extended from time to time. The extended term of the Sub-committees was up to 31 January, 2004 and that of the Monitoring Group up to 16 February, 2004. Updated composition of the Monitoring Group and its two Sub-committees is at **Annexes XIV-C and D.**

Sub-committee "A" of the Monitoring Group held its meetings as under:

1. On 28.6.2000 — Himachal Pradesh at Shimla
2. On 29.6.2000 — Haryana and Punjab at Chandigarh
3. On 11.6.2001 — Uttar Pradesh at Lucknow
4. On 12.6.2001 — Delhi
5. On 13.6.2001 — Rajasthan at Jaipur
6. On 6.1.2004 — Delhi
7. On 29.1.2004 — Delhi

The meeting of Sub-committee "B" was held at Calcutta on 5 July, 2000 covering the state of West Bengal and at Delhi on 30 January, 2004.

DECISIONS

All India Whips, Conference held at Bangalore in January, 1994 made the following recommendation:

"Chief Whips of recognised Opposition parties in Parliament and the State Legislatures should be provided secretarial assistance and facilities of telephone and office accommodation in the premises of Legislatures by giving them statutory recognition (secretarial assistance means one stenographer Grade 'B' and one peon)".

After due consideration of the matter as a whole and to implement the recommendation of the All India Whips' Conference, it was decided to provide secretarial and telephone facilities to the Leader and Chief Whip of each party which has a strength of not less than fifty Members in respect of the Lok Sabha and twenty five Members in respect of the Rajya Sabha and of each group which has a strength of not less than twenty members in respect of the Lok Sabha and fifteen Members in respect of the Rajya Sabha.

The Leaders and Chief Whips of Recognised Parties and Groups in Parliament (Facilities) Bill, 1998 was passed by the Lok Sabha on 18 December, 1998 and by the Rajya Sabha on 21 December, 1998. It was assented to by the President on 7 January, 1999.

The Leaders and Chief Whips of Recognised Parties and Groups in Parliament (Telephone and Secretarial Facilities) Rules, 1999 were framed under the Act and notified in the gazette on 5 February, 1999. These rules were laid on the Table of the Lok Sabha on 26 February, 1999 and on the Table of the Rajya Sabha on 8 March, 1999.

The Cabinet in its meeting held on 8 February, 2000 approved the proposals for amendment to the Leaders and Chief Whips of Recognised Parties and Groups in Parliament (Facilities) Act, 1998 and the rules made thereunder.

The Leaders and Chief Whips of Recognised Parties and Groups in Parliament (Facilities) Amendment Bill, 2000 was passed by both the Houses of Parliament and was assented to on 7 June, 2000 as Act No. 18 of 2000.

The Leaders and Chief Whips of Recognised Parties and Groups in Parliament (Telephone and Secretarial Facilities) Amendment Rules, 2000 were framed and were notified on 3 July, 2000.

CHECK LIST

A check list for arranging All India Whips' Conferences is at **Annex XIV-E.** Samples of Letters to be sent to the participants etc. are at **Annexes XIV-F** to **XIV-I.**

15

CREATING AWARENESS ABOUT PARLIAMENTARY SYSTEM AND PROCEDURES

BACKGROUND

The 4th All India Whips' Conference, held at Bombay in 1962, made the following recommendation:

> "The Committee recommends that Government should encourage holding of mock Parliaments (now Youth Parliament) in educational institutions and through Panchayats in rural areas."

In pursuance of the above recommendation and with a view to develop a democratic ethos among the younger generations, the scheme of Youth Parliament competition was introduced in the Higher Secondary Schools of the National Capital Territory (NCT) of Delhi by the Ministry of Parliamentary Affairs in collaboration with the Directorate of Education, Government of NCT of Delhi in the year 1966-67. To broaden the base and reach of this activity, the schools run by the NDMC were also brought under the ambit of this scheme in the year 1995.

In the year 1978, Kendriya Vidyalayas located in and around Delhi were inducted into the ongoing Youth Parliament Competitions in the Higher Secondary Schools under the Directorate of Education, Government of NCT of Delhi. Gradually, owing to increase in the number of participating schools, a separate scheme was launched in 1983 for the Kendriya Vidyalayas in and around Delhi on the lines similar to those of the scheme for Senior Secondary Schools under the Directorate of Education, Government of NCT of Delhi. In the year 1988, the scheme of Youth Parliament was launched at the national level in the Kendriya Vidyalayas as part of the celebrations of Pandit Jawaharlal Nehru's birth centenary and forty years of India's Independence.

In the year 1997, the schemes of Youth Parliament were launched at the national level in Jawahar Navodaya Vidyalayas and Universities/Colleges, as part of the celebration of the Golden Jubilee year of India's Independence, on the pattern of the national scheme for Kendriya Vidyalayas.

PROCESS

Youth Parliament competitions under the various schemes are organised as under:

Youth Parliament Competition Scheme for recognised educational institutions in the NCT of Delhi

(a) In the first instance, the officers of the Ministry of the Parliamentary Affairs hold a meeting with officers of the Directorate of Education, Government of NCT of Delhi and NDMC to finalise the modalities of holding the competition during the year. Thereafter, an Orientation Course for the benefit of the teachers in-charge of the activity in the schools sponsored by the Directorate of Education and the NDMC is conducted. The schedule of the competition is finalised by the Ministry of Parliamentary Affairs in consultation with the officers of the Directorate of Education and the NDMC.

(b) Youth Parliament competitions in the participating schools are evaluated by a Committee of Judges consisting of a Member of Parliament or an ex-Member of Parliament, an officer of the Ministry of Parliamentary Affairs and an officer of the Directorate of Education, Government of the NCT of Delhi. The committee awards prizes and certificates to select students on the basis of their performance in the competition. Members/ex-Members of Parliament associated with the evaluation of these competitions are paid DA for the day they are associated as one of the judges.

(c) The school winning first place in the competition is required to give a repeat performance at the Prize Distribution Function organised by the Ministry of Parliamentary Affairs on a suitable date, time and venue. The prizes are distributed by a high dignitary. All prize winning students and teachers in charge of the activity and the Principals of the schools are invited to the Prize Distribution Function. The expenditure in this regard is borne by the Ministry of Parliamentary Affairs.

(d) A copy of the scheme is at **Annex XV-A** and check list for organising Youth Parliament competition is at **Annex XV-B.**

National Youth Parliament Competition Scheme for Kendriya Vidyalayas

(a) In the first instance, the officers of the Ministry of Parliamentary Affairs hold a meeting with officers of the Kendriya Vidyalaya Sangathan (KVS) to finalise the modalities of holding the competition during the year. Thereafter, to acquaint the teachers in-charge of organising a Youth Parliament in the participating Vidyalayas with the concept and background of the scheme, the Ministry of Parliamentary Affairs, in cooperation with KVS, organises Orientation Courses as per schedule decided at the meeting. All the teachers in-charge of the activity in the schools sponsored by the KVS for participation in the competition take part in the Orientation Course, along with officers of the KVS.

(b) There are 18 regions of the KVS. The competition is held in two phases - first at the Regional Level and then at the National Level. The competitions at the Regional Level are held among such vidyalayas of the respective regions as are sponsored for the competition by the Kendriya Vidyalaya Sangathan from that region. This is conducted under the supervision of the Kendriya Vidyalaya Sangathan authorities. The competition at the National Level is held among the Kendriya Vidyalayas which win first position in their respective regions.

(c) The competitions at the Regional Level are evaluated by a Committee of Judges consisting of :

1. An MP/ex-MP/MLA/MLC/ex-MLA/ex-MLC;
2. An officer of the Kendriya Vidyalaya Sangathan of the respective regions; and
3. The Principal of a non-participating vidyalaya of the region or some local prominent educationist.

(d) Competition at the National Level i.e. among all the 18 regional first Kendriya Vidyalayas, is evaluated by a Committee of Judges consisting of :

1. An MP/ex-MP;
2. An officer of the Ministry of Parliamentary Affairs; and
3. An officer of the Kendriya Vidyalaya Sangathan (HQ).

Members/ex-Members of Parliament associated with the evaluation of these competitions are paid DA for the day they are associated as one of the judges.

(e) The institution standing first at the National Level is required to give a repeat performance at the Prize Distribution Function organised by the Ministry of Parliamentary Affairs at a suitable date, time and venue. The prizes are distributed by a high dignitary. All prize winning students of the schools winning first position in their respective regions are invited to the function in which escort teachers and principals of the schools also participate. Officers of KVS are also invited to the function. The expenditure in this regard is borne by the Ministry of Parliamentary Affairs.

(f) A copy of the scheme is at **Annex XV-C** and check list for organizing the Youth Parliament Competition under this scheme is at **Annex XV-D.**

National Youth Parliament Competition Scheme for Jawahar Navodaya Vidyalayas (JNVs)

(a) In the first instance, the officers of the Ministry of Parliamentary Affairs hold a meeting with officers of the Navodaya Vidyalaya Samiti (NVS) to finalise the modalities of holding the competition during the year. Thereafter, to acquaint the teachers in-charge of organising the Youth Parliament in the participating vidyalayas with the concept and background of the scheme, the Ministry of Parliamentary Affairs, in cooperation with NVS, organises Orientation Courses as per the schedule decided in the meeting.

(b) There are eight regions of the NVS. The competition is held in two stages - first at the Regional Level and then at the National Level. The competitions at the Regional Level are held among such vidyalayas of the respective regions as are sponsored for the competition by the Navodaya Vidyalaya Samiti from that region. This is conducted under the supervision of the Navodaya Vidyalaya Samiti authorities. The competition at the National Level is held among the Navodaya Vidyalayas which stand first in their respective regions.

(c) The competitions at the Regional Level are conducted by the NVS and are evaluated by a Committee of Judges consisting of:

1. An MP/ex-MP/MLA/MLC/ex-MLA/ex-MLC;
2. An officer of the Navodaya Vidyalaya Samiti of the respective regions; and
3. Principal of a non-participating vidyalaya of the region or some prominent local educationist.

(d) The competitions at the National Level are evaluated by a Committee of Judges which consists of:

1. An MP/ex-MP;
2. An officer of the Ministry of Parliamentary Affairs; and

3. An officer of the Navodaya Vidyalaya Samiti (HQ).

Members/ex-Members of Parliament associated with the evaluation of these competitions are paid DA for the day they are associated as one of the judges.

(e) The institution winning first place at the National Level is required to give a repeat performance at the Prize Distribution Function to be held at a venue to be decided by the Ministry of Parliamentary Affairs. The Ministry fixes a date, time and venue for the function. The prizes are distributed by a high dignitary. Invitations to the prize winners, participating institutions and such of the other institutions, etc. as are considered necessary are sent by the Ministry of Parliamentary Affairs. The expenditure in this regard is borne by the Ministry of Parliamentary Affairs in accordance with the rules and regulations applicable to them.

(f) A copy of the scheme is at **Annex XV-E** and check list for organising the Youth Parliament Competition is at **Annex XV-F.**

National Youth Parliament Competition Scheme for Universities/Colleges

(a) All the universities recognised by the Ministry of Human Resource Development, who sponsor their nominees for attending the Orientation Course to be conducted by the Ministry of Parliamentary Affairs prior to the start of the competition, are eligible for participation. The participating institutions are divided into different groups. The competition is held in two stages - firstly, at the Group Level and secondly, at the National Level among the winners (Group Level first) of various groups. The schedules of the Group and National Level Competitions are finalised by the Ministry of Parliamentary Affairs. For the purpose of organizing the Group Level competition, the Ministry of Parliamentary Affairs nominates a coordinator from amongst the participating institutions to coordinate and conduct the competition in respect of the group allotted to him/her and submit a report thereon to the Ministry.

(b) The Group Level competitions are evaluated by a panel of Judges consisting of:

1. An MP/ex-MP/MLA/ex-MLA/MLC/ex-MLC;
2. A coordinator appointed from amongst the institutions participating in that group; and

[*Note:* For evaluating the performance of the coordinator's own institution, another nominee from amongst the other participating institutions of that group will sit on the panel of Judges instead of the coordinator.]

3. An academician of repute from a non-participating institution.

(c) At the National Level competition, the performances of the teams are evaluated by a panel of Judges consisting of :

1. An MP/ex-MP/MLA/ex-MLA/MLC/ex-MLC;
2. An officer of the Ministry of Parliamentary Affairs; and
3. An academician of repute from a non-participating institution.

Members/ex-Members of Parliament associated with the evaluation of these competitions are paid DA for the day they are associated as one of the judges.

(d) The institution winning first at the National Level is required to give a repeat performance at the Prize Distribution Function to be held at a venue to be decided by the Ministry of Parliamentary Affairs. The Ministry fixes a date, time and venue for the function. The prizes are distributed by a high dignitary. Invitations to the prize winners, participating institutions and such of the other institutions, etc. as are considered necessary are sent by the Ministry of

Parliamentary Affairs. The expenditure in this regard is borne by the Ministry of Parliamentary Affairs in accordance with the rules and regulations applicable to them.

(e) A copy of the scheme is at **Annex XV-G** and check list for organizing the Youth Parliament competition under this scheme is at **Annex XV-H.**

Financial Assistance to State/UT Governments for conducting Youth Parliament

In view of the laudable objectives of the scheme, the 7th All India Whips' Conference, held at Madras in 1969, recommended that the scheme should be extended to all the States/Uts of the country and the Ministry should give all possible help to encourage its implementation by offering financial assistance to the States and Union territories which organise the Youth Parliament competitions. Consequently, a scheme of financial assistance was evolved by the Ministry in 1972-73, according to which financial assistance up to a ceiling of Rs.1,000 was given to the States/Uts implementing the scheme. This amount was raised to Rs. 3,000 in 1982, Rs. 5,000 in 1987 and Rs. 10,000 in 1993. As per the recommendations of the 11th All India Whips, Conference held at Bangalore in 1994, the ceiling of the financial assistance to the States/Uts was raised to Rs. 25,000 with effect from 16 August, 1994. Thereafter, the 12th All India Whips, Conference held at Srinagar in 1997, recommended for enhancing the financial assistance to rupees two lakh which was taken up with the Ministry of Finance, which agreed to raise the ceiling of financial assistance to rupees one lakh per annum only and the amount was accordingly raised to rupees one lakh per annum with effect from 21 January, 1999.

This Ministry also provides financial assistance to different institutions as per the details given below:

S.No.	**Institutions**	**Amount**
1.	Jawahar Navodaya Vidyalayas	up to Rs.5,000 per participating school

2.	Universities/Colleges	up to Rs.5,000 per participating institution at both Group as well as National Levels.

The Ministry of Parliamentary Affairs reimburses the transportation expenditure up to a maximum of Rs.30,000 to the first prize winning vidyalaya in the competition, attending the prize distribution function to stage their repeat performance, through the Navodaya Vidyalaya Samiti.

In regard to the National Youth Parliament competition in Universities/Colleges, the Ministry of Parliamentary Affairs also reimburses, within permissible limits, actual TA/DA expenses incurred in connection with journeys undertaken by the group coordinators nominated for coordinating the Group Level competitions in respect of each group during the first stage of the competition. Escort teacher and students of prize winning institutions securing first position at the Group Level competitions, attending the Prize Distribution Function are also reimbursed train fare restricted to II-AC class for escort teacher and IInd Sleeper class for students from their actual place of residence to Delhi and back. Similarly, an amount up to Rs. 30,000 is reimbursed to the team winning first place at the National Level in the competition, towards TA expenses for travelling to give their repeat performance at the Prize Distribution Function. A copy of the scheme of financial assistance is at **Annex XV-I.**

DECISIONS

Payment of D.A. to MP/ex-MP for acting as a Judge in the Youth Parliament Competition

MP/ex-MP who acts as a judge in the Youth Parliament competition will be paid Daily Allowance @ Rs. 500 and Rs. 300 respectively for the day he is associated as a judge. In case, however, an ex-MP stays in a hotel on the day he is associated as a judge, he will be paid D.A. @ Rs. 350 per day. These orders take effect from 14 September, 2001 in case of MPs and from 13 October, 1998 in the case of ex-MPs.

Award of Certificates to the Teachers/Professors who Participate in the Orientation Courses on 'Youth Parliament'

It was decided to award certificates of participation to the teachers/professors of the Government of NCT of Delhi and NDMC schools, Kendriya Vidyalayas, Jawahar Navodaya Vidyalayas and the universities/colleges who participate in the Orientation Courses organised by the Ministry of Parliamentary Affairs for the Youth Parliament competitions.

Whether Honorarium be Paid to the Officers of the Ministry of Parliamentary Affairs and the Directorate of Education, Government of NCT of Delhi and the Kendriya Vidyalaya Sangathan who are Associated as Judges in the Youth Parliament Competition

On a proposal received from the Directorate of Education in this connection, the matter was referred to the Ministry of Finance for their concurrence. However, that Ministry did not agree to the proposal.

16

TRAINING OF OFFICIALS

BACKGROUND

In order to improve the functioning of Parliament Units in various Ministries/Departments and for better handling of parliamentary work, a need was felt to organise Orientation Programmes in Parliamentary Practice and Procedure for the officers and staff working in the Parliament Units of various Ministries at the Centre. The Ministry of Parliamentary Affairs, with the approval of the Ministry of Personnel, Public Grievances and Pensions, have been organising Short Duration Training Courses in Parliamentary Practice and Procedure for the officers of the Ministries since 1985. Initially, these courses were conducted for officers/staff of Parliament Units. Subsequently, officers other than those working in Parliament Units were also covered and officers of the level of Under Secretary were also invited for such training programmes. So far, thirty four such training courses have been held.

The faculty for these courses consists of the officers of this Ministry. Officers who deliver lectures on various subjects in these courses are paid a token honorarium. The rates of honorarium are based on the rate of honorarium paid by the Bureau of Parliamentary Studies and Training (BPST), Lok Sabha, for their courses and are revised from time to time whenever any revision is made by them.

On a request from the Ministry of Road Transport and Highways, the 34th Orientation Course was organised exclusively for the Chief Engineers/Superintending/Executive Engineers/ officers of that Ministry.

Besides these Orientation Courses, a half-day Workshop of Joint Secretaries on Managing Legislative Business was conducted on 28 October, 2003 in collaboration with the Ministry of

Personnel, Public Grievances and Pensions to acquaint the Joint Secretaries/senior officers concerned in the Ministries/ Departments with the detailed procedures involved in the legislative process, from the conceptual stage of legislation till it becomes an Act of Parliament, is notified in the gazette and comes into force. Guest Speakers from the Ministry of Law and Justice, the Lok Sabha and Rajya Sabha Secretariats were also invited for this Workshop.

In pursuance of the recommendations made by the All India Whips' Conferences, from time to time, the Ministry has also been holding training programmes in Parliamentary Practice and Procedure for the officers of State/Union territory Governments for exchange of knowledge and information about procedures and practices prevalent at the Centre and in various States which may eventually lead to better performance and standardisation of procedures. Eleven such courses have been held till now.

PROCESS

The process of holding training courses for officers of Ministries at the Centre comprises various steps:

(1) A decision is taken for conducting the training course and on the probable dates/period.

(2) A circular is issued to Ministries calling for nominations for the training course **(Annex XVI-A).**

(3) Draft programme for the course is submitted and finalised **(Annex XVI-B).**

(4) Expenditure involved on tea/refreshment/lunch, training folders, training material, honorarium, etc. is estimated and a proposal is sent for approval of Internal Finance Division after its approval by Secretary/Joint Secretary.

(5) Availability of a committee room is informally ascertained from Lok Sabha/Rajya Sabha Secretariat and a note is sent for booking of the committee room.

(6) A circular to officers of this Ministry is submitted/ issued intimating programme/assignment of lectures.

(7) A note is sent to Under Secretary (Administration) for printing of following background material or

certificates **(Annex XVI-C)** if adequate copies are not available:

(i) Orientation Course in Parliamentary Practice and Procedure - Background Material.

(ii) Brochure on Transaction of Business in Parliament.

(8) Acceptance of nominations received is communicated to Ministries requesting them to direct the officers to report at the Reception Office, Parliament House on ....(date) at..............(time). If necessary, passes are collected by the Ministry in advance.

(9) Position of receipt of nominations is reviewed/ submitted with reminder, if necessary.

(10) Communication of exact dates of the course, if not mentioned in earlier letter or if there has been a change subsequently.

(11) Contacting Ministries concerned on phone at whatever stage it is necessary.

(12) A note is sent to Accounts and Purchase Section for supply of required number of copies of Rules of Procedure, Lok Sabha/Rajya Sabha and the Constitution of India (small size), stationery/plastic folders etc.

(13) A letter is sent to the Caretaker, Parliament House, and other agencies concerned for arrangements for the course.

(14) A proposal/menu for serving tea, refreshment, lunch, etc. is submitted for approval and letter sent to Railway Catering, Parliament House for serving it as per approval.

(15) A letter is sent to Reception Officer/Deputy Director, Parliament House Security, for arranging casual entry passes for participants/arranging for a tour of Parliament House, Parliament House Annexe and Parliament Library Building.

(16) Arrangements are made for a group photograph of participants with the Secretary, Joint Secretary and other officers concerned.

(17) An official is deputed at the Reception gate/outside to receive the trainees, if necessary.
(18) A list of participants is prepared from time to time.
(19) Attendance Sheets are prepared for attendance of the participants.
(20) Copies of the Feedback Form (Appreciation Sheet) are prepared **(Annex XVI-D).**
(21) Copies of objective type test are prepared **(Annex XVI-E).**
(22) Folders with training material, writing pads, pen, etc. are kept ready for distributing to participants and are sent a day in advance to Secretary, Joint Secretary, Deputy Secretary, Under Secretary, other officers concerned who have to deliver lectures.
(23) Certificates are prepared and submitted for signature of Secretary.
(24) Copies of the group photograph are obtained and are kept along with certificates in a proper cover.
(25) Feedback Forms are given to participants and collected, duly filled in by them, on the last day.
(26) A report is submitted regarding training course conducted - indicating main points, duration, dates of the programme, number of officers who attended along with a statement showing the suggestions contained in the Feedback Forms and comments thereon.
(27) A letter to Department of Personnel and Training is submitted/sent regarding the training - for training programme for Central Ministries only **(Annex XVI-F).**
(28) A note is sent to the Administration Section for sanctioning honorarium, indicating the names of officers, number of lectures delivered by them and the rate at which honorarium is admissible and copy of approval by the Secretary.
(29) Bills for catering and photographs are obtained from the Railway Catering Unit, Parliament House, and the photographer, necessary entries are made in the expenditure register and the bills are sent to Accounts and Purchase Section for payment.

(30) Necessary entries are made in the records being maintained by the section concerned and the records are updated.

(31) Two copies of the group photograph are kept for the Annual Report of the Ministry.

Additional steps/check points in respect of training for officers of State and Union territory Governments/Assembly Secretariats:

(1) With a view to have close interaction, nominations of two officers of Deputy Secretary/Under Secretary level, each from some of the States whose officers have not attended any training course in this Ministry or had not attended it for a long time, are called for with necessary information in the prescribed proforma **(Annex XVI-G).** While taking decision about conducting the course, decision is also taken as to the States to be included.

(2) A copy each of the letters to Chief Secretaries concerned for sending nominations/ subsequent communications, is also endorsed to the respective Resident Commissioners in Delhi with a request to make arrangements for boarding and lodging of the officers nominated by the States.

(3) The officers forwarding the nominations are requested to direct the nominated officers to bring with them:

   (i) Photocopy of the journey tickets.

   (ii) Letter from competent authority certifying that the officer is entitled to travel by the mode/class he/she has actually used for the journey performed to attend the training course, also specifying the mode/class of entitlement (Where, however, an officer undertakes to and/or fro journey for the above purpose, by a higher class to which he is not entitled, he/she is paid TA/DA by the class to which he/she is entitled under the rules unless he/she brings a certificate from the Head of his Department permitting him/her to undertake the journey by the higher class).

(4) A note is sent to Under Secretary(Administration) for drawing advance for payment of TA/DA to the officers attending the training course before conclusion of the course. TA/DA forms are provided to the participants. The Accounts and Purchase Section is contacted for deputing the Accountant/Cashier for making the payment. It is also ascertained whether payment of TA/DA has been made to all the participants.

(5) The following arrangements are made for the participants for local sightseeing for a day:

(i) Conveyance is arranged through the General Section.
(ii) A programme of local sightseeing is drawn up.
(iii) A note for contingency advance is sent to Under Secretary (Administration) and the advance is drawn to meet incidental expenses/entry tickets, etc.
(iv) An official is deputed to accompany the trainees.

(6) Account of the expenditure from contingent advance is submitted and the balance is deposited with the cashier.

DECISIONS

(i) Approval of the Department of Personnel and Training was obtained for organising training programmes for officers of Ministries/Departments dealing with parliamentary work.

(F.No.89(3)/82-Leg.II)

(ii) The Lok Sabha Secretariat, *vide* their U.O. Note dated 29 January, 1988, pointed out that the training courses conducted by this Ministry are duplication as they were also conducting such courses in BPST. They were informed that the nature of their training courses was academic and general, whereas the training imparted by this Ministry was pragmatic.

(F.No.4(2)/88-Leg.II)

(iii) As per instructions of the Department of Official Language, it was decided to supply training literature bilingually.

(F.No.4(30)/88-Leg.II)

(iv) In the 5th Short Duration Course (SDC), conducted by this Ministry from 24 to 26 June, 1987, officers up to the level of Under Secretary were invited for the first time. Also invited for the first time were officers other than those working in Parliament Units. (F.No.F.4(2)/87-Leg.II)

(v) It was decided that three new subjects viz., (i) Questions, (ii) Parliamentary Committees, and (iii) Drafting of Statements made by Ministers may also be covered during the short duration training courses. (F. No.F.4(3)/87-Leg.II)

(vi) Keeping in view the suggestions made by the participants of the 19th Short Duration Training Course held from 21 to 24 September, 1992, it was decided that the duration of the courses may be increased from four half-days to five half-days and additional lectures on the new subjects viz. (i) Evolution of Parliamentary form of Government in the country, and (ii) Laying of Papers, Statements by Ministers and Private Members' Bills and Resolutions also be covered. It was also decided to cover the role of this Ministry in the Welcome Address on the opening day. The Constitution of India is covered suitably in the lecture on evolution of Parliamentary form of Government.

(F. No.F.4(5)/92-Leg.II)

(vii) In the 26th Short Duration Training Course, a suggestion was made by the participants that these courses should be organised for three full days instead of five half-days. Accordingly, with effect from the 27th SDC held from 8 to 10 November, 1995, the courses are being conducted for three full days.

(F. No.F.4(6)/92-Leg.II)

(viii) With a view to implement the recommendation of the Tenth All India Whips' Conference, 1988 for conducting a training course for officers of States/Union territories in Parliamentary Practice and Procedure, the proposal of conducting Training Courses for officers of States/Union Territories was made and approval of the Department of Personnel and Training was obtained. The first Training Course was held from 21 to 28 December, 1994. (F.No.4(2)/92-Leg.II)

(ix) On the basis of the rates of honorarium of the Bureau of Parliamentary Studies and Training (BPST), Lok Sabha, for their training courses as revised with effect from 19 May, 1998, the rates of honorarium for the training courses, organised by this Ministry were revised with the approval of the Secretary, Ministry of Parliamentary Affairs dated 6 October, 1998, effective from the 31st Orientation Course, conducted from 9 to 11 September, 1998 as follows :

(i)	Minister/Members of Parliament and officers of the rank of Joint Secretary and above	Rs. 500 per lecture
(ii)	Officers of the rank of Under Secretary and above but below Joint Secretary	Rs. 300 per lecture
(iii)	Officers below the rank of Under Secretary	Rs. 200 per lecture

(F.No.4-A(1)/98-Leg.II)

CHECK LIST

A check list indicating the steps to be taken at various stages in connection with the Organisation of Training Courses in Parliamentary Practices and Procedure is enclosed as **Annex XVI-H.**

17

GOODWILL DELEGATIONS

In the continuously and rapidly changing international scenario, the need to project and propagate our national policies, programmes and achievements, problems in the proper perspective among various countries as well as understanding their points of view has been felt for a long time. The parliamentarians of a country play a significant role in determining the policy of the country and strengthening of relations with other countries. More particularly, it is indeed useful and necessary for a democratic and developing country like India to select some Members of Parliament and distinguished personalities and utilise their services in projecting our policies, programmes and achievements in different fields with their counterparts and other opinion makers in other countries and secure their support in favour of India.

With these objectives in view, the Ministry of Parliamentary Affairs sponsors Government Goodwill Delegations of Members of Parliament to other countries and receives similar Government sponsored delegations of parliamentarians under the exchange programme from other countries through the Ministry of External Affairs.

The check lists of procedure followed for Goodwill Delegations sent Abroad is at **Annex XVII-A** and for receiving a Foreign Delegation in India is at **Annex XVII-B.**

The Ministry of Parliamentary Affairs assists the other Ministries/Departments on various occasions viz., Government functions/occasions where MPs are invited.

The Ministry of Parliamentary Affairs assists the Members of Parliament, on request, in coordination with Ministry of External Affairs/our Missions abroad in respect of extending courtesies, during their private visits abroad.

Protocol services are rendered and usual courtesies are extended to various foreign Parliamentary Delegations visiting India under the Inter-Parliamentary Union (IPU), Commonwealth Parliamentary Association (CPA), etc., for calling on Minister/Ministers of State for Parliamentary Affairs and exchanging views on the functioning of Parliament and other matters of mutual interest. Mementos/gifts are presented to the foreign delegates by the Hon'ble Minister/Ministers of State for Parliamentary Affairs.

Foreign Parliamentary Delegations visiting India under Inter-Parliamentary Union, Commonwealth Parliamentary Association, etc. call on Minister/Ministers of State for Parliamentary Affairs for exchange of views on functioning of Parliament and other matters of mutual interest. In this connection, following arrangements are made by this Ministry :

(i) To collect details regarding the composition of the delegation along with the bio-data of the delegates and facts sheets about the country of the delegation;

(ii) To collect material from the Ministry of External Affairs regarding the Talking Points for the Minister during his meeting with the delegation;

(iii) To prepare a note on the functioning of the Ministry of Parliamentary Affairs;

(iv) To prepare the folders containing the material collected/prepared for Minister/Ministers of State, Secretary, Joint Secretary and other concerned senior officers;

(v) To arrange for briefing of the Minister and to invite an officer of Ministry of External Affairs for briefing the meeting;

(vi) Procurement and packing of gifts to be presented to the delegates;

(vii) Arrangement of bouquets, if desired by the Minister; and

(viii) Arrangement of passes for the delegates, officers of the Ministry of External Affairs and their vehicles for entry in Parliament House premises.

18

MISCELLANEOUS PROCESSES

In this chapter, the processes in regard to the following activities of the Ministry have been covered:

(i) Press Conferences held by the Minister of Parliamentary Affairs.
(ii) Convening of meetings of the Cabinet Committee on Parliamentary Affairs.
(iii) Night Duty arrangements.
(iv) Appointment and functions of the Parliamentary Secretary.
(v) Arrangements to be made for new Ministers.

PRESS CONFERENCES HELD BY THE MINISTER OF PARLIAMENTARY AFFAIRS

The Minister of Parliamentary Affairs normally holds a Press Conference on the eve as also on the last day of every Parliament session. As soon as the date of convening the conference is indicated by the Minister, the following action is taken by the Ministry:

(i) Information Officer, PIB attached to the Ministry, is informed of the date, time and, if possible, the venue of the conference.
(ii) The Lok Sabha/Rajya Sabha Secretariat, as the case may be, is requested to reserve suitable Committee Room and Banquet Hall for the day of the conference.
(iii) A note seeking direction from the Minister's office in regard to the items of refreshment to be served in the conference and the approximate number of persons for whom the arrangement has to be made, is submitted.

(iv) Invitation cards, if necessary, are printed in consultation with the Minister's office and made available to the Information Officer for extending invitations, on behalf of the Minister, to media persons.

(v) On obtaining the approval of the Minister's office for the items proposed to be served as refreshment in the conference, approval of the IFD for the expenditure involved in holding the conference is sought and, simultaneously, orders are placed with the Manager, Railway Catering, Parliament House, for serving the refreshment at the specified time and venue on the day of the conference. When it is not possible to obtain the prior approval of the IFD, the proposal for obtaining the *ex post facto* approval of the IFD is sent to them after the bill has been received from the Caterer.

(vi) After reservation of the Committee Room requested for has been confirmed, a note from JS to the Ministers of State for Parliamentary Affairs requesting them to make it convenient to attend the conference at the specified time, date and venue is sent. They are also requested to attend the 'briefing' meeting scheduled before the conference, if the Minister for Parliamentary Affairs so desires.The Information Officer is also informed/confirmed regarding the venue of the conference. In addition, Security Officer, Lok Sabha and Rajya Sabha Secretariat, Junior Engineers (Electrical/Sound/ Airconditioning) and Caretaker are informed about the conference.

(vii) Press release is drafted and is submitted for approval. After its approval, requisite number of copies of the release are prepared for circulation to the media persons after or during the conference.

(viii) Talking Points for the Minister, in addition to the Press Release, are also required to be prepared.

(ix) Labels/Sign Boards indicating the direction/location of venue of the conference are prepared and affixed/ displayed at prominent posts/positions to help the invitees to reach the venue of the conference conveniently.

(x) Manager, Railway Catering, J.Es. (Electrical, Sound and AC), Caretaker, Parliament House/Parliament House Annexe are telephonically contacted/reminded to ensure that they have made/are making necessary arrangements/position of services at the venue of the conference, as per the programme.

(xi) Secretary and Joint Secretary brief the Minister about half an hour before the conference or at such other time, as may be fixed by the Minister for the purpose.

(xii) Name plates of the Minister, Ministers of State for Parliamentary Affairs, Secretary and Joint Secretary are carried to the venue of the conference and are placed on the table facing their chairs in the conference room. Besides, the concerned officers and staff of the Legislative I Section and the Section Officer, Legislative II Section attend the conference.

(xiii) In case the Conference is being held during the inter-session period or on holidays, the Reception Officer, Lok Sabha/Rajya Sabha Secretariat, as the case may be, are requested to issue entry passes to media persons carrying proper PIB ID Cards, for entry into the Parliament House/Parliament House Annexe, as the case may be, for attending the conference.

(xiv) As soon as the conference is over, the press release is distributed to the members of the media and is also placed on the website of the Ministry.

(xv) On receipt of the bills from the Lok Sabha Secretariat towards reservation of the Committee Room, Banquet Hall, and from the Railway Catering Service for refreshment served in the conference, they are verified and are sent to the A&P Section in the Ministry for payment of the bill.

(xvi) On the day following the day of the conference, the press clippings from various newspapers containing reports of the conference are submitted by the Legislative II Section of the Ministry for information of the senior officers/Minister.

CONVENING THE MEETINGS OF THE CABINET COMMITTEE ON PARLIAMENTARY AFFAIRS

The following action is taken by the Ministry for convening the meeting of the Cabinet Committee on Parliamentary Affairs (CCPA):

(i) A proposal is submitted for obtaining the convenience of the Minister of Parliamentary Affairs and Chairman, CCPA regarding the date and time for holding the meeting of the committee.

(ii) After the Chairman has confirmed the date and time for the meeting, the availability of a suitable Committee Room is first ascertained informally and, in case the desired venue for the purpose is available, the Parliament Secretariat or the Department concerned is sent a note requesting reservation of the committee room for the purpose.

(iii) In case the meeting is proposed to be held in Room No.9, Parliament House, the request for reservation of the room is sent to the Cabinet Secretariat and copies thereof are endorsed to the Joint Secretary (Security) and Caretaker, Parliament House. No formal confirmation regarding reservation of the room is issued by the Cabinet Secretariat. It is only confirmed informally on telephone.

(iv) Notices regarding the meeting are issued to all the members/special invitees in the committee indicating the date, time, venue and items of the agenda for the meeting as in the format at **Annex XVIII-A.**

(v) PSs. to all the Ministers, who are members/special invitees of the committee, are telephonically contacted to ascertain whether the notice and other papers regarding the meeting have been received by them and whether the Ministers will attend or not attend the meeting.

(vi) Notices regarding the meeting are also sent to the Secretary/senior officers of the Ministry/Department administratively concerned with the topics, if any, included in the agenda of the meeting.

(vii) Before each meeting, it is ensured that name plates of all the members of the committee and other officers of the rank of the Secretary, who have been invited to its meeting are ready. Wherever necessary, new name plates are obtained before the meeting.

(viii) Requisite items of stationery, viz. scribbling pads, sharpened pencils, etc. in requisite number are obtained from the A&P Section before the meeting and are placed before the members/officer in the committee room.

(ix) Orders in regard to tea/coffee/juice and other items to be served in the meeting are placed with the Manager, Catering Service, Parliament House/ Parliament House Annexe, sufficiently before the meeting, after obtaining the approval of the senior officers.

(x) Some spare copies of the brief on the agenda and other relevant papers circulated to the members, along with the relevant file, are taken to the meeting for use of the members/for reference, if necessary.

(xi) After the meeting, minutes as in the format at **Annex XVIII-B** are drafted and after their approval by the Minister of Parliamentary Affairs, they are submitted to the Chairman of the committee for his/her approval (in case where the Minister of Parliamentary Affairs is not himself/herself the Chairman of the committee).

(xii) After approval of the minutes by the Chairman of the committee, they are circulated to all the members/ special invitees of the committee and other officers (of the rank of Secretary only) from various Ministries who attend the meeting.

(xiii) Thereafter, necessary action on the agenda item is initiated/taken by the Ministry as per decision(s) taken in the meeting.

NIGHT DUTY ARRANGEMENTS

In order to attend to important parliamentary papers on holidays and after normal office hours during the Parliament sessions, the Ministry makes appropriate arrangements. For this purpose, one clerk and one peon are put on roster duty on holidays and during the night in the General Section of the Ministry. The roster duty starts three days before the commencement of a Parliament session and ends two days after both the Houses of Parliament are adjourned *sine die*.

Before the commencement of every Parliament session, a roster is drawn to put the staff on holidays and night duty on a weekly rotation basis. The staff on such duty is required to attend to important parliamentary papers received in the Ministry urgently and send these papers to concerned senior officers for necessary action without delay. The staff on roster duty is also required to perform any other emergent duty for the smooth functioning of the Ministry.

APPOINTMENT AND FUNCTIONS OF PARLIAMENTARY SECRETARY

In the United Kingdom, a Minister who is a member of one House, cannot go to the other House of Parliament. Therefore, a member of the House other than the one to which a Minister belongs, is appointed as Parliamentary Secretary to help his Minister and deputise for the Minister in that House. The Parliamentary Secretary has a status below that of a Cabinet Minister and a Minister of State. He is a paid servant and as he is not a Minister, who must be careful not to speak or to conduct himself as if he was a member of the Government.

In India, the institution of the office of Parliamentary Secretary has no statutory origin nor does it derive authority from the Constitution of India. The office of the Parliamentary Secretary in India was first created in 1951, purely for the purpose of assisting the Minister in parliamentary work. Unlike the Ministers, the oath to the Parliamentary Secretaries is administered by the Prime Minister and not by the President. The appointment of a Parliamentary Secretary is entirely at the discretion of the Prime Minister, who decides when and who should be appointed as a Parliamentary Secretary. The functions of a Parliamentary Secretary are as under:

(i) He will assist the Minister in his official work.
(ii) He will represent the Department/Ministry in the House to which he belongs.
(iii) He will perform such functions as may be assigned to him by the Minister.

Note: Since an oath of secrecy is administered to a Parliamentary Secretary, he has access to official papers.

According to the Government of India (Allocation of Business Rules), 1961, the Ministry of Home Affairs is concerned with:

(i) Issue of Notification of appointment and resignation of the Parliamentary Secretaries; and

(ii) Salaries and Allowances of Parliamentary Secretaries, whereas the Ministry of Parliamentary Affairs is concerned with the functions of Parliamentary Secretaries.

Shri Satish Chandra and Shri S.N. Mishra, the then Members of Parliament, were the first Parliamentary Secretaries appointed w.e.f. 11 June, 1951 by late Shri Jawaharlal Nehru, the then Prime Minister. Shri Nakul Nayak was appointed as the last Parliamentary Secretary to the Prime Minister on 24 November, 1990. Thereafter, no Parliamentary Secretaries have been appointed.

A Brochure with the title "Study Report on the Parliamentary Secretary" is available in the Ministry.

List of Parliamentary Secretaries appointed from time to time is at **Annex XVIII-C.**

ARRANGEMENTS FOR NEW MINISTERS

When a new Goverment is formed, new Ministers/Ministers of State/Deputy Ministers for Parliamentary Affairs are to be briefed about the functioning of the Ministry. For this purpose, an Induction Note or a Brief is prepared by the Legislative Division of the Ministry for handing over to the new incumbents by the Secretary. The material for the Induction Note/Brief is provided by all the divisions of the Ministry.

As soon as the portfolios of the new Ministers are known, Secretary, Ministry of Parliamentary Affairs, and other senior officers of the Ministry call on the Minister/Ministers of State for Parliamentary Affairs to ascertain from them the date and time when they would like to formally assume the charge of the Ministry. At the appointed time, Ministers are welcomed by the senior officers of the Ministry by presenting them bouquets and a brief meeting is held with them. The Ministers are also shown their office rooms in the Parliament House. Ministers are also given a copy of the Salaries and Allowances of Ministers Act, 1952 and the rules made thereunder and other instructions governing their entitlement of staff, official car and other facilities.

As per the convenience of the Minister, a Powerpoint presentation about the Ministry, its functions, its annual action plan, etc. is arranged in the office of the Minister. The Ministers of State are formally invited to be present during this presentation.

As soon as the Ministers take charge, a note is submitted by the Administration Division to the Minister of Parliamentary Affairs regarding allocation of work among the Ministers and Ministers of State/Deputy Ministers, a for Parliamentary Affairs as the case may be. After appproval of the Minister, necessary orders in this regard are circulated to all concerned.

Posts are created on the personal staff of Ministers and Ministers of State as per their entitlement. A Cabinet Minister is entitled to a set of 15 posts on his personal staff. In situations where the Cabinet Minister is holding charge of two independent Ministries, he/she is entitled to a set of fifteen posts on his personal staff separately from each of the two Ministries. An MOS is entitled to a set of thirteen posts on his personal staff. But the MOSs, even though not entitled to additional personal staff for a dual charge, as a general rule, are given an additional set of three posts for discharging the onerous responsibilities relating to the Parliament by the Ministry of Parliamentary Affairs, after obtaining the approval of the Department of Personnel and Training. After the posts have been created, appointments as desired by the Minister/MOSs are made. In cases where appointments are made in relaxation of the upper age limit, the approval of the Hon'ble Prime Minister is obtained through the Ministry of Personnel, Public Grievances and Pensions, Department of Pensions, CS Division. Verification of character antecedents in respect of appointees on the personal staff are also obtained from the concerned authorities wherever required, specially in the case of persons who do not belong to an organised cadre of the Central/State Government.

COST OF SITTING OF PARLIAMENT PER DAY/PER HOUR

The sum of the revised Budget Estimates of the Lok Sabha Secretariat, Rajya Sabha Secretariat and the Ministry of Parliamentary Affairs for the last financial year are divided by the total number of sittings of the two Houses held during the financial year. The figure so arrived is expenditure per sitting of the Parliament. If we divide this figure by 6 (assuming that each sitting of the Parliament, on an average, is for 6 hours), it will give cost of sitting of Parliament per hour.

The cost worked out above, however, does not include the

expenditure incurred by the various Ministries/Departments and by their respective subordinate units, in collecting and supplying information of Parliament and also the expenditure incurred by the Ministries/Departments, such as, Railways, Posts, Banking, etc. for providing special facilities to MPs. On the other hand, it also does not include the time spent by the various Parliamentary Committees, Standing Committees etc.

ARRANGING DINNERS DURING LATE SITTING OF PARLIAMENT

As and when the sitting of House(s) of Parliament is anticipated to go beyond 8 p.m. for transaction of urgent government business, the Minister of Parliamentary Affairs, if he/she considers necessary, directs the Ministry to make arrangement for dinner for Members, press personnel, officers and staff on duty etc. Occasionally, arrangements for light snacks/refreshments are also made.

The number of persons for whom food is arranged is normally 350 in case of MPs, press personnel and officers of the rank of Under Secretary and above and 700 in case of staff on duty including security personnel, when the Lok Sabha alone sits late. The corresponding number is 250 and 700 respectively, when the Rajya Sabha alone sits late. In case of late sitting of both Houses of Parliament, the number of persons for whom food is arranged is 600 (MPs, Press and Officers) and 1000 (other persons) respectively. However, these numbers may vary depending upon the number of Members likely to remain present in the House(s) during late hours and the nature of business under discussion. The procedure to be followed for making arrangement/supply of food to the officers and staff on duty during late hours was decided in a meeting taken by the Joint Secretary, Ministry of Parliamentary Affairs, with the officers of the Lok Sabha and Rajya Sabha Secretariats on 18 September, 1995. (Minutes of the meeting are at **Annex XVIII-D.)**

Besides, transport arrangements are also made by the Ministry by hiring 4 buses from Delhi Transport Corporation whenever the proceedings of the House(s) are likely to continue beyond 10.00 p.m.

The entire expenditure on serving food and hiring transport on such occasions is borne by the Ministry of Parliamentary Affairs.

In the meeting of the Business Advisory Committee (BAC) of the Lok Sabha held on 2 May, 2002, it was agreed that food might be provided to Members, staff and officers on duty whenever the House sits late. It was also agreed that food would be arranged by the Lok Sabha Secretariat instead of the Ministry of Parliamentary Affairs.

A check list of procedure followed for making arrangement for dinner and transport is at **Annex XVIII-E.**

19

मंत्रालय की राजभाषा संबंधी गतिविधियां

राजभाषा नीति एवं राजभाषा अधिनियम, 1963 को कार्यान्वित करने के लिए मंत्रालय में वर्ष 1973 में एक हिन्दी प्रकोष्ठ की स्थापना की गई थी। जैसे-जैसे मंत्रालय में हिन्दी का प्रयोग बढ़ा, उसके साथ-साथ हिन्दी के प्रयोग को प्रोत्साहन देने एवं राजभाषा विभाग द्वारा जारी अनुदेशों के कार्यान्वयन को सुनिश्चित करने के लिए एक पूर्ण हिन्दी अनुभाग गठित करने की आवश्यकता महसूस की गई। अतः वर्ष 1973 में स्थापित हिन्दी प्रकोष्ठ को वर्ष 1976 में हिन्दी अधिकारी के अधीन एक पृथक हिन्दी अनुभाग का रूप प्रदान किया गया।

मंत्रालय में हिन्दी के प्रगामी प्रयोग के बारे में राजभाषा विभाग (गृह मंत्रालय) द्वारा जारी अधिनियमों, नियमों, आदेशों, अनुदेशों आदि का अनुपालन सुनिश्चित करने के लिए मंत्रालय के हिन्दी अनुभाग द्वारा अपेक्षित कार्रवाई की जाती है। वर्तमान में मंत्रालय द्वारा राजभाषा संबंधी निम्नलिखित गतिविधियों का संचालन किया जा रहा है:

कर्मचारियों के लिए टिप्पण–आलेखन नकद पुरस्कार योजना

राजभाषा विभाग द्वारा चालू की गई हिन्दी टिप्पण-आलेखन की नकद पुरस्कार योजना को वर्ष 1984 में मंत्रालय में लागू किया गया। कर्मचारियों द्वारा हिन्दी में मूल टिप्पण और आलेखन के प्रयोग को बढ़ावा देने के लिए मंत्रालय में हिन्दी अनुभाग द्वारा यह पुरस्कार योजना चलाई जाती है। योजना का क्षेत्र, पात्रता, अवधि, पुरस्कार, पुरस्कार देने के लिए मापदंड, मूल्यांकन समिति से संबंधित जानकारी तथा हिन्दी में किए गए काम का ब्यौरा रखने वाला प्रपत्र **परिशिष्ट-19डी** में दिया गया है।

हिन्दी पखवाड़ा और उसके दौरान आयोजित की जाने वाली प्रोत्साहन प्रतियोगिताएं

मंत्रालय में प्रतिवर्ष सितम्बर मास के दौरान हिन्दी सप्ताह अथवा हिन्दी पखवाड़ा मनाया जाता है और इसके दौरान अधिकारियों/कर्मचारियों के लिए स्थल पर हिन्दी टिप्पण-आलेखन की लघु प्रतियोगिता आयोजित की जाती है। इसके अतिरिक्त लिपिकों के लिए हिन्दी टंकण की एक प्रतियोगिता का भी आयोजन किया जाता है। हिन्दी दिवस अर्थात 14 सितम्बर को हिन्दी सप्ताह/पखवाड़े का समापन समारोह आयोजित किया जाता है तथा इस दौरान आयोजित की गई प्रतियोगिताओं में पुरस्कार जीतने वाले अधिकारियों/कर्मचारियों को पुरस्कृत किया जाता है।

हिन्दी कार्यशालाएं

मंत्रालय में कर्मचारियों को हिन्दी टिप्पण और प्रारूपण का प्रशिक्षण देने के लिए वर्ष में तीन बार हिन्दी कार्यशालाओं का आयोजन किया जाता है। इन कार्यशालाओं में मंत्रालय के कार्य से संबंधित प्रायः सभी विषयों को हिन्दी में करने का प्रशिक्षण दिया जाता है। इन कार्यशालाओं का इस प्रकार आयोजन किया जाता है कि वर्ष के दौरान प्रत्येक सहायक/अनुसंधान सहायक/उच्च श्रेणी लिपिक को कम से कम एक बार अवश्य ही प्रशिक्षण दिया जा सके। इस प्रकार मंत्रालय के सभी डीलिंग हैंडों को इन कार्यशालाओं में हिन्दी में काम करने का कई बार प्रशिक्षण दिया जा चुका है। इसके परिणामस्वरूप उनकी हिन्दी में कार्य करने की क्षमता में दिन-प्रति-दिन विकास होता गया है।

हिन्दी के प्रगामी प्रयोग के संबंध में तिमाही प्रगति रिपोर्ट

प्रत्येक तिमाही में मंत्रालय के सभी अनुभागों द्वारा हिन्दी के प्रगामी प्रयोग के संबंध में तिमाही प्रगति रिपोर्ट हिन्दी अनुभाग को **परिशिष्ट-19इ** में दिए गए प्रोफार्मा में भरकर भेजी जाती है। हिन्दी अनुभाग मंत्रालय के सभी अनुभागों द्वारा भेजी गई तिमाही प्रगति रिपोर्ट को समेकित कर राजभाषा विभाग को आवश्यक कार्रवाई हेतु भेजता है।

राजभाषा नीति के कार्यान्वयन के लिए वार्षिक कार्यक्रम

सरकारी काम-काज में हिन्दी के प्रगामी प्रयोग के क्षेत्र में महत्वपूर्ण प्रगति हुई है। किन्तु अभी भी शत-प्रतिशत लक्ष्य प्राप्त नहीं किए जा सके हैं। संसद

द्वारा पारित राजभाषा संकल्प, 1968 के अनुपालन में राजभाषा हिन्दी के प्रसार और विकास की गति बढ़ाने के लिए तथा संघ के विभिन्न राजकीय प्रयोजनों के लिए उत्तरोत्तर प्रयोग हेतु राजभाषा विभाग प्रतिवर्ष एक वार्षिक कार्यक्रम जारी करता है और उसी के अनुसार हिन्दी अनुभाग द्वारा मंत्रालय के लिए भी एक वार्षिक कार्यक्रम तैयार किया जाता है और उसे सभी अनुभागों को इस अपेक्षा के साथ भेजा जाता है कि सभी अनुभाग उनसे संबंधित मदों पर आवश्यक कार्रवाई करें ताकि कार्यक्रम में की गई सभी सिफारिशों का कार्यान्वयन सुनिश्चित हो सके। संसदीय कार्य मंत्रालय का वर्ष 2003-2004 के लिए वार्षिक कार्यक्रम **परिशिष्ट-19एफ** में दिया गया है।

राजभाषा कार्यान्वयन समिति

मंत्रालय में हिन्दी के प्रगामी प्रयोग को सुनिश्चित करने के लिए संयुक्त सचिव की अध्यक्षता में एक राजभाषा कार्यान्वयन समिति गठित की गई है। मंत्रालय में अधिकारियों की संख्या सीमित होने के कारण सभी अनुभाग अधिकारियों तथा इससे ऊपर के अधिकारियों को इसका सदस्य बनाया गया है। इस समिति को सामान्यतः निम्नलिखित कार्य सौंपे गए हैः

1 हिन्दी के प्रयोग संबंधी आदेशों के कार्यान्वयन की समीक्षा करना और इस बारे में कार्रवाई करना।

2 तिमाही प्रगति रिपोर्टों की समीक्षा तथा इसे समय पर भेजना सुनिश्चित करना।

3 कार्यान्वयन में आने वाली कठिनाइयों की समीक्षा करके यथावश्यक सुझाव देना।

4 हिन्दी, हिन्दी टंकण और आशुलिपि प्रशिक्षण के लिए उपयुक्त संख्या में कर्मचारी भेजना सुनिश्चित करना।

इस समिति की प्रत्येक तिमाही में नियमित रूप से एक बैठक आयोजित की जाती है जिसमें तिमाही प्रगति रिपोर्ट की समीक्षा के साथ-साथ हिन्दी के प्रयोग संबंधी आदेशों के कार्यान्वयन को सुनिश्चित किया जाता है।

हिन्दी सलाहकार समिति

सरकार की राजभाषा नीति के सुचारू कार्यान्वयन के बारे में सलाह देने तथा मंत्रालय में हिन्दी के प्रयोग को बढ़ावा देने के उद्देश्य से संसदीय कार्य

मंत्री की अध्यक्षता में हिन्दी सलाहकार समिति का गठन किया जाता है जिसका कार्यकाल 3 वर्ष होता है। संसदीय कार्य मंत्रालय में हिन्दी सलाहकार समिति के गठन संबंधी आदेश को राजभाषा विभाग द्वारा अनुमोदित किए जाने पर हिन्दी सलाहकार समिति का गठन सर्वप्रथम वर्ष 1984 में किया गया।

उपरोक्त के अतिरिक्त सरकारी कार्यों के लिए हिन्दी का प्रयोग राजभाषा अधिनियम, 1963 तथा उसके अधीन बनाए गए नियमों एवं राजभाषा विभाग द्वारा समय-समय पर जारी आदेशों/अनुदेशों द्वारा शासित किया जाता है।

BIBLIOGRAPHY

1. Barnhart, Gordon (1999): *Parliamentary Committees - Enhancing Democratic* Governance, Cavendish Publishing, London.
2. Commonwealth Parliamentary Association (1997): *Guidelines for the Training of Parliamentary Staff,* CPA, London.
3. Constitution of India.
4. Gupta, Ram Kishore (ed.) (1993): *Parliamentary Companion - A Work for Reference and Record,* Shikha Publication, New Delhi.
5. Jha, Radha Nandan: *Some Aspects of Parliamentary Procedure,* Sharda Prakashan, Patna.
6. Kashyap, Subhash C. (1986): *Parliaments of the Commonwealth,* Lok Sabha Secretariat.
7. Kashyap, Subhash C. (2003): *Parliamentary Procedure - The Law, Privileges, Practice and Precedents* (Two Volumes), Universal Law Publishing Company, New Delhi.
8. Kaul, M.N. & Shakdher, S.L.: *Practice and Procedure of Parliament,* Metropolitan Book Company Pvt. Ltd.
9. Lochrie, James (2003): *Meeting Procedures - Parliamentary Law and Rules of Order for the 21st Century,* The Scarecrow Press, Lanham.
10. Lok Sabha Secretariat: *Rules of Procedure and Conduct of Business in Lok Sabha.*
11. Lok Sabha Secretariat: Directions by the Speaker, Lok Sabha.
12. Lok Sabha Secretariat: *Government and Parliament : Procedure to be Followed by Ministries in Connection with Parliamentary Work.*
13. Lok Sabha Secretariat (1991): *Dictionary of Constitutional and Parliamentary Terms.*
14. Lok Sabha Secretariat (1992): *Unparliamentary Expressions.*

15. Lok Sabha Secretariat (1999): *Demarcation of Responsibilities in Government of India.*
16. Lok Sabha Secretariat : Information Folder-Bureau of Parliamentary Studies and Training.
17. Lok Sabha Secretariat : Abstract Series: Table Office.
18. Malhotra, G.C. (1998): *Motions of Confidence and No-Confidence,* Published for Lok Sabha Secretariat (by Metropolitan).
19. May, Erskine (1976): *Treatise on the Law, Privileges, Proceedings and Usage of Parliament,* Butterworths , London.
20. May, Erskine (1997): *Parliamentary Practice.*
21. Rajya Sabha Secretariat: *Rules of Procedure and Conduct of Business in the Council of States.*
22. Rajya Sabha Secretariat (2001): *Rulings and Observations from the Chair (1952-2000).*
23. Rajya Sabha Secretariat (1995): *Parliament in India - An Introduction.*
24. Rajya Sabha Secretariat (2000): *Rajya Sabha and Its Secretariat - A Performance Profile, 1999.*
25. Rajya Sabha (1999): *Practice & Procedure Series .*
26. Rama Devi, V.S. & Gujar, B.G. : *Rajya Sabha at Work,* Rajya Sabha Secretariat.
27. Sturgis, Alice (1993): *The Standard Code of Parliamentary Procedure,* (third ed.), Mcgraw-Hill, New York.
28. Staskiewicz, Wieslaw (1995) : Rules of Procedure and Parliamentary Practice-The Proceedings of the International Conference on Parliamentary Rules of Procedure and Parliamentary Practice, Chancellory of the Sejm of the Republic of Poland, Warsaw.
29. Surya Prakash, A. (1995): *What Ails Indian Parliament ? An Exhaustive Diagnosis,* Indus, New Delhi.

ANNEX I-A

No.F. 34/6/49-Public
GOVERNMENT OF INDIA
MINISTRY OF HOME AFFAIRS

New Delhi, the 16th May, 1949

NOTIFICATION

The Governor General is pleased to announce the creation with immediate effect of a Department of Parliamentary Affairs under the Minister of State for Parliamentary Affairs. This Department will take over from the Ministry of Law the work in connection with the functions of the Government Chief Whip and other Parliamentary Affairs.

Sd: H.V.R. IENGER
SECRETARY TO THE GOVERNMENT OF INDIA

ANNEX I-B

ALLOCATION OF FUNCTIONS TO THE MINISTRY OF PARLIAMENTARY AFFAIRS

1. Dates of summoning and prorogation of the two Houses of Parliament: Dissolution of Lok Sabha, President's Address to Parliament.
2. Planning and coordination of Legislative and other Official Business in both Houses.
3. Allocation of Government time in Parliament for discussion of Motions given notice of by Members.
4. Liaison with Leaders and Whips of various Parties and Groups represented in Parliament.
5. Lists of Members of Select and Joint Committees on Bills.
6. Appointment of Members of Parliament on Committees and other bodies set up by Government.
7. Functioning of Consultative Committees of Members of Parliament for various Ministries.
8. Implementation of assurances given by Ministers in Parliament.
9. Government's stand on Private Members' Bills and Resolutions.
10. Secretarial assistance to the Cabinet Committee on Parliamentary Affairs.
11. Advice to Ministries on procedural and other parliamentary matters.
12. Coordination of action by Ministries on the recommendations of general application made by parliamentary committees.
13. Officially sponsored visits of Members of Parliament to places of interest.
14. Matters connected with powers, privileges and immunities of Members of Parliament.
15. Parliamentary Secretaries - functions.
16. Organisation of Youth Parliament Competitions in schools/colleges throughout the country.
17. Organisation of All India Whips' Conference.

18. Exchange of Government Sponsored Delegations of Members of Parliament with other countries.
19. Determination of policy and follow-up action in regard to matters raised under Rule 377 of the Rules of Procedure and Conduct of Business in Lok Sabha and by way of Special Mentions in Rajya Sabha.
20. Manual of Parliamentary Procedures in the Government of India.
21. The Salaries and Allowances of Officers of Parliament Act, 1953 (20 of 1953).
22. The Salary, Allowances and Pension of Members of Parliament Act, 1954 (30 of 1954).
23. The Salary and Allowances of Leaders of Opposition in Parliament Act, 1977 (33 of 1977).
24. The Leaders and Chief Whips of Recognised Parties and Groups in Parliament (Facilities) Act, 1998 (5 of 1999).

ANNEX I-C
(As on 2.06.2004)

COMPOSITION OF CABINET COMMITTEE ON PARLIAMENTARY AFFAIRS

Composition

1. Shri Pranab Mukherjee, Minister of Defence—Chairman
2. Shri Sharad Pawar, Minister of Agriculture and Minister of Consumer Affairs, Food and Public Distribution
3. Shri Lalu Prasad, Minister of Railways
4. Shri Shivraj V. Patil, Minister of Home Affairs
5. Shri Ram Vilas Paswan, Minister of Chemicals and Fertilizers and Minister of Steel
6. Shri Ghulam Nabi Azad, Minister of Parliamentary Affairs and Minister of Urban Development
7. Shri T.R. Baalu, Minister of Road Transport and Highways and Minister of Shipping
8. Shri H.R. Bhardwaj, Minister of Law and Justice

Special Invitees

1. Shri Suresh Pachouri, Minister of State in the Ministry of Personnel, Public Grievances and Pension and Minister of State in the Ministry of Parliamentary Affairs.
2. Shri B.K. Handique, Minister of State in the Ministry of Defence and Minister of State in the Ministry of Parliamentary Affairs.
3. Shri Prithviraj Chavan, Minister of State in the Prime Minister's Office.
4. Smt. Suryakanta Patil, Minister of State in the Ministry of Rural Development and Minister of State in the Ministry of Parliamentary Affairs.

Functions

1. To watch the progress of Government business in Parliament and to give such directions as may be necessary from time to time, in order to secure smooth and efficient conduct of such business;
2. To scrutinise and to consider the attitude of the Government on non-official bills and resolutions to be presented to Parliament;
3. To review legislations undertaken by State Legislatures from an all-India point of view; and
4. To consider proposals to summon or prorogue the Houses of Parliament.

ANNEX I-D
(As on 31.12.03)

ORGANISATIONAL STRUCTURE OF MINISTRY OF PARLIAMENTARY AFFAIRS (AS ON 31.12.2002)

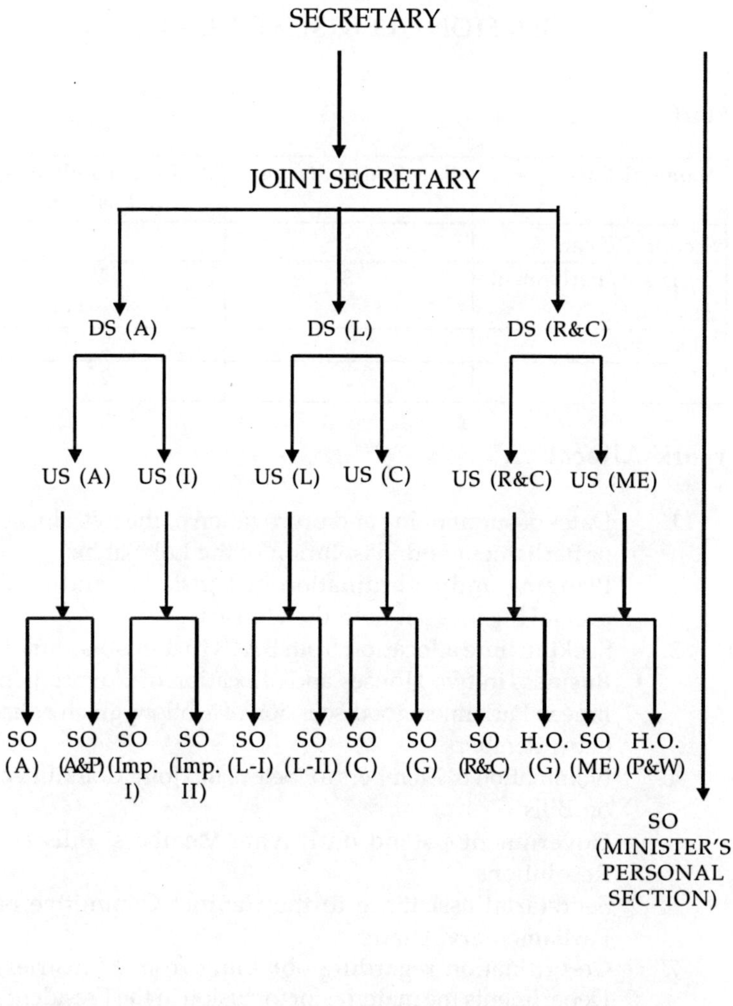

ANNEX I-E

LIST OF SECTIONS, STAFF STRENGTH AND WORK ALLOCATION

SECTION : LEGISLATIVE - I

Staff

Name of Post	Sanctioned Strength	Actual Incumbent(s) in Position
Section Officer	1	1
Assistant/Parliament Assistant	3	2
UDC	1	2
LDC	2	2

Work Allocation

1. Dates of summoning and prorogation of the two Houses of Parliament and dissolution of the Lok Sabha.
2. Planning and co-ordination of legislative and other official business in both the Houses.
3. Seeking time allocation from BACs to the Government Business in two Houses and allocation of Government time in Parliament for discussion of Motions given notice of by Members.
4. Nomination of Members for Select and Joint Committees on Bills.
5. Government's stand on Private Members' Bills and Resolutions.
6. Secretarial assistance to the Cabinet Committee on Parliamentary Affairs.
7. Co-ordination regarding obtaining from Ministries/ Departments the material for inclusion in the President's address.

8. Ordinances—their laying and other related correspondence.
9. Simultaneous laying of papers and documents in both Houses of Parliament.
10. General directions for the guidance of Ministries in the preparation of their Annual Reports.
11. Preparation of a Directory showing telephone numbers and addresses of Officers dealing with parliamentary work in various Ministries/Departments.
12. Maintenance of statistics relating to Parliament Questions addressed to the Ministry.
13. Recommendations of a general nature of the Committees on Papers Laid on the Table of the Lok Sabha and the Rajya Sabha.
14. Recommendations of the Rules Committees of the Lok Sabha and the Rajya Sabha.
15. Calling Attention Notices - forwarding notices in respect of the Rajya Sabha only to Ministries.
16. Allotment of rooms to Ministers in Parliament House.
17. Keeping a watch on the day-to-day progress of business transacted by the two Houses of Parliament by deputing Gallery Assistants in Official Galleries of the Houses.
18. Maintenance of a complete and up-to-date statistical record about the discussions and debates on legislative, financial and other miscellaneous matters in each session of both the Houses of Parliament to be utilised at the time of the preparation of the Annual Report of the Ministry.
19. Coordination of work relating to States under President's Rule.
20. Preparation of roster for attendance of Ministers in the Lok Sabha and the Rajya Sabha.
21. Vote of Confidence in the Council of Ministers.
22. The Government of India (Allocation of Business) Rules, 1961.
23. Statement on Government Business by Ministers of Parliamentary Affairs in the Lok Sabha and the Rajya Sabha.
24. Appointment of Speaker *pro tem* and other persons before whom Members can subscribe oath or affirmation.

SECTION : LEGISLATIVE - II

Staff

Name of Post	Sanctioned Strength	Actual Incumbent(s) in Position
Section Officer	1	1
Assistant	3	2
UDC	1	1
LDC	2	1

Work Allocation

1. Determination of policy and follow-up action in regard to matters raised under Rule 377 in the Lok Sabha and by way of Special Mentions in the Rajya Sabha.
2. Review/revision/updating of the Manual of Parliamentary Procedures in the Government of India and advice/correspondence relating to the Manual and instructions therein etc.
3. Organising Orientation Courses in Parliamentary Practice and Procedure for officers of various Ministries/ Departments.
4. Organising Orientation Courses in Parliamentary Procedure and Practice for Officers of State Governments.
5. Advance study of the likely emerging trends in Parliament.
6. Action on the recommendations of general nature in reports of Committees on Petitions of the Lok Sabha and the Rajya Sabha.
7. Sending extracts to Ministries/Departments concerned in regard to matters raised during Zero Hour in the Lok Sabha and the Rajya Sabha.
8. Culling out of press clippings on important topics from the daily newspapers.

SECTION : COMMITTEE

Staff

Name of Post	Sanctioned Strength	Actual Incumbent(s) in Position
Section Officer	1	1
Assistant	3	1
UDC	2	3
LDC	2	1

Work Allocation

1. Appointment of Members of Parliament on committees and bodies set up by Government.
2. Functioning of Consultative Committees of Members of Parliament for various Ministries.
3. Constitution and functioning of Informal Consultative Committees for various Railway Zones.
4. Payment of TA/DA to Members of Parliament in connection with the meetings of Consultative Committees.
5. Organising meetings of Consultative Committees and Zonal Railway Informal Consultative Committees. Each Consultative Committee is required to hold six meetings in a year. Informal Consultative Committees meet once in a year.
6. Booking of suitable committee room in Parliament House/Parliament House Annexe for arranging the meetings of the above committees.
7. Issuing of agenda notes in English and Hindi, minutes of the meetings, action taken reports on the minutes and notices regarding meetings to the Members.
8. Arranging for various facilities in the committee rooms such as chairs, air-conditioning, sound system, etc.
9. Maintenance of various nomination registers, various profession-wise lists and bio-data of Members of Parliament.
10. Maintenance of name plates of Members which are placed in front of Members during the committee meetings.

SECTION : IMPLEMENTATION - 1

Staff

Name of Post	Sanctioned Strength	Actual Incumbent(s) in Position
Section Officer	1	1
Assistant	3	2
UDC	1	2
LDC	2	2

Work Allocation

1. Reading of proceedings of the Lok Sabha, and culling out of assurances/undertakings/promises given by the Ministers on the floor of the House.
2. Forwarding relevant extracts of the assurances to the Lok Sabha Secretariat for information and to the Ministries concerned with the subject matters of assurances for implementation within the stipulated time of three months.
3. Processing of requests of the Ministries/Departments regarding grant of extension of time for fulfilment of assurances and moving the Lok Sabha Secretariat for obtaining necessary extension.
4. Processing the casenes regarding deletion of the assurances given on the floor of the Lok Sabha.
5. Processing the Implementation Reports received from the Ministries/Departments in fulfilment of assurances and making necessary arrangements for laying of sets of Implementation Reports on the Table of the House.
6. Intimating fulfilment of assurances to the Members of Parliament concerned.
7. Intimation of laying of assurances to Ministries/ Departments concerned.
8. Advising Ministries/Departments on various procedural matters connected with implementation of assurances.
9. Maintenance of copies of sets of Implementation Reports laid on the Table of the House.

10. Processing the reports of the Committee on Government Assurances of the Lok Sabha and communicating the decisions/observations of the committee to Ministries/Departments for compliance.

SECTION : IMPLEMENTATION - II

Staff

Name of Post	Sanctioned Strength	Actual Incumbent(s) in Position
Section Officer	1	1
Assistant	3	2
UDC	1	Nil
LDC	2	2

Work Allocation

1. Reading of proceedings of the Rajya Sabha, and culling out of assurances/undertakings/promises given by the Ministers on the floor of the House.
2. Forwarding relevant extracts of the assurances to the Ministries/Departments concerned for implementation within the prescribed time limit of three months and to the Secretariat of the House, for information.
3. References regarding extension of time limit for fulfilment of assurances and requests for deletion of assurances.
4. Processing the Implementation Reports received from the Ministries/Departments in fulfilment of assurances and making necessary arrangement for laying of sets of Implementation Reports on the Table of the House.
5. Intimating fulfilment of assurances to the Members of Parliament concerned.
6. Intimation of laying of assurances to Ministries/Departments concerned.
7. Advising Ministries/Departments on various procedural matters connected with implementation of assurances.
8. Maintenance of copies of sets of Implementation Reports laid on the Table of the House.
9. Processing the reports of the Committee on Government Assurances of the Rajya Sabha and communicating the decisions/observations of the committee to Ministries/Departments for compliance.

SECTION : RESEARCH AND CONFERENCE

Staff

Name of Post	Sanctioned Strength	Actual Incumbent(s) in Position
Section Officer	1	1
Assistant	3	2
UDC	1	Nil
LDC	2	2

Work Allocation

1. Writing of Brochures.
2. Advice to Ministries/State Governments on constitutional matters and matters relating to rules/ conventions of Parliament.
3. Preparation of notes on various parliamentary and constitutional matters.
4. Maintenance of library and also selection and purchase of books for library.
5. Conducting of Youth Parliament Competitions in schools under the Government of NCT of Delhi and the NDMC.
6. Conducting of National Youth Parliament Competitions in Kendriya Vidyalayas.
7. Conducting of Orientation Courses for organisers of Youth Parliament Competitions in States.
8. Conducting training on Youth Parliament Competitions to officers of State Governments deputed to the Ministry.
9. Training in parliamentary matters to parliamentary fellows of ICPS and representatives of State Governments.
10. Training of foreign nationals under Colombo Plan.
11. Conducting of National Parliamentary Quiz Contest for Delhi Schools and Kendriya Vidyalayas.

SECTION : MEMBERS' EMOLUMENT

Staff

Name of Post	Sanctioned Strength	Actual Incumbent(s) in Position
Section Officer	1	1
Assistant	1	2
LDC	2	2

Work Allocation

I. Functions relating to "Work Study"

1. To deal with work pertaining to OandM.
2. All correspondence with the Department of Administrative Reforms and Public Grievances relating to O&M matters.
3. Issue of instructions and providing guidance to all sections in the Ministry relating to O&M procedures, as outline in the Manual of Office Procedure and also relating to instructions issued by the Department of Administrative Reforms from time to time.
4. Coordinating work relating to recording, indexing and weeding out of old files done by sections, collection of progress reports from sections and submission of consolidated report to the Secretary, Ministry of Parliamentary Affairs/National Archives of India.
5. Induction Material of the Ministry.
6. Annual inspections of sections.
7. Record Retention Schedule.
8. Periodical returns relating to O&M activities.
9. Organisational History of the Ministry.

II. Functions relating to administration of the Salary, Allowances and Pension of Members of Parliament Act, 1954

1. Administration and interpretation of the Salary, Allowances and Pension of Members of Parliament Act, 1954 and the rules made thereunder.

2. To examine cases of facilities/amenities to MPs in connection with the above and to seek Law Ministry's advice etc. from time to time.
3. Preparation of note in regard to Government's stand on the agenda of the meetings of the Joint Committee on Salaries and Allowances of Members of Parliament.
4. To examine and process the recommendations of the Joint Committee on Salaries and Allowances of Members of Parliament.
5. Advice to Ministries/State Governments regarding TA/DA entitlement of MPs for attending meetings of Government committees.

III. Administration of the Salary and Allowances of Leaders of Opposition in Parliament Act, 1977 and the rules framed thereunder.

IV. Administration of the Salaries and Allowances of Officers of Parliament Act, 1953 and the rules framed thereunder.

V. Work relating to functions of Parliamentary Secretaries.

VI. Conducting of National Youth Parliament Competitions in Jawahar Navodaya Vidyalayas.

VII. Conducting of National Youth Parliament Competitions in universities and colleges.

VIII. Conducting of National Parliamentary Quiz Contests in Jawahar Navodaya Vidyalayas and Universities/Colleges.

IX. Miscellaneous correspondence.

SECTION : PROTOCOL AND WELFARE

Staff

Name of Post	Sanctioned Strength	Actual Incumbent(s) in Position
Section Officer	1	1
UDC	1	1
LDC	1	1

Work Allocation

1. To render assistance to ailing Members of Parliament and their families whenever required. Inform the Members of the family of ailing Members if they are not in Delhi.
2. To keep the Minister/Ministers of State/Deputy Minister/Secretary and other concerned officers including Party Offices in Parliament House informed vide Daily Report about the illness of Members. Visits to ailing MPs admitted in Delhi Hospitals. Submission of the report of visit for information of HMPA.
3. In the unfortunate event of the passing away of a Member, to take up the work of transporting the dead body according to the wishes of the family of the deceased and to render all assistance that may be required by them. Embalming of body, arrangement of coffin, arranging of death certificate and police clearance, arrangement of wreath for paying homage to the deceased Member and transportation of body to Airport/Railway Station for onward journey to the place of last rites to be taken care of.
4. Officially sponsored visits of Members of Parliament to places of interest.
5. To assist the nodal Ministries for receiving MPs on important national occasions such as investiture ceremonies, oath-taking ceremonies of high dignitaries including the President-elect and co-ordination for issuance of passes to MPs. Ushering in duties during

various national occasions such as Independence day, Republic Day, and Beating Retreat ceremony etc.

6. Film shows and other entertainment programmes for Members of Parliament
7. Extending usual courtesies/protocol services to foreign parliamentary delegations calling on Minister/MOSs of Parliamentary Affairs.
8. Liaison with leaders of various parties/groups represented in Parliament.
9. Arrangement of dinner/refreshment to Members of Parliament during late sittings of Houses and on other occasions.
10. Work relating to sending Government sponsored delegations of Members of Parliament abroad and also receiving similar foreign delegations in India under exchange programmes.
11. Transport arrangements (DTC services) for MPs in case of late sittings of Parliament beyond 10.00 p.m.
12. Nomination of Members of Parliament on various Government Sponsored Delegations.
13. Clearance of visits of State Governments sponsored Foreign Delegations.
14. Meeting of the Minister of Parliamentary Affairs with Chief Whips of various political parties in Parliament.
15. Committee on Subordinate Legislation, Lok Sabha and Committee on Subordinate Legislation, Rajya Sabha for processing of recommendations of a general nature.
16. Holding of All India Whips' Conference and to ensure the implementation of recommendations of the conference by the State Governments and various agencies.
17. The Leaders and Chief Whips of Recognised Parties and Groups in Parliament (Facilities) Act, 1998 and rules made thereunder.

SECTION : ADMINISTRATION

Staff

Name of Post	Sanctioned Strength	Actual Incumbent(s) in Position
Section Officer	1	1
Assistant	3	3
LDC	2	2

Work Allocation

1. Establishment matters viz. recruitment, promotion, appointments, etc.
2. Recruitment Rules : framing and amendments.
3. Creation/continuation and conversion of posts, confirmation and quasi permanent, seniority list.
4. All matters connected with the allocation of work amongst the Ministers and appointment etc. of the personal staff of Ministers including rules and instructions on the subject.
5. Implementation of orders regarding reservation for Scheduled Castes/Tribes, Ex-servicemen, released Emergency Commissioned Officers, Physically Handicapped Persons, OBCs, etc.
6. Maintenance of Service books and Personal Files, Grant of Leave, Increments, Pay Fixation, Character Verification, Medical Examination, etc.
7. Assured Career Progression Scheme.
8. Training of staff except Hindi training.
9. Implementation of the recommendations of Pay Commission.
10. Security arrangements, punctuality and vigilance cases.
11. Matters connected with Office Council.
12. Conduct, Classification, Control and Appeal Rules.
13. Various types of returns on different subjects.
14. Postings/transfer of staff.
15. Nomination for Family Pension, DCRG, GPF, CGEIS, etc.
16. Retirement.

17. Review of cases of officers/staff who have attained the age of 50/55 years and have completed 30 years of service.
18. Vigilance cases and matters connected with Conduct Rules.
19. Calling and processing of property returns.
20. Grant of special rewards, increments, personal pay, honorariums, etc.
21. Work related to CGHS facility, Library membership, etc.
22. Deputation to ex-cadre posts.
23. Annual Confidential Reports.
24. Hiring and maintenance of air-conditioners, room-coolers, etc.
25. Supply of electric fans, heaters, etc.
26. Air-conditioning of rooms allotted to the secretary.
27. Cleanliness, caretaking jobs.
28. Modernisation of office—providing partitions, cupboards, etc.
29. Procurement and supply of liveries to Group C and D employees.
30. Allotment of Government accommodation.
31. Computerisation in the Ministry, computer training of staff.
32. E-governance, e-readiness.
33. Secretarial assistance to Steering Committee to examine annual action plan - e-readiness.
34. Co-ordination of matters regarding new initiatives undertaken by the Ministry.
35. Parliament Questions regarding the subjects allotted to the section.
36. Posting of staff for night duty/roster duty.
37. Compilation of Annual Report of the Ministry.

SECTION : ACCOUNTS AND PURCHASE

Staff

Name of Post	Sanctioned Strength	Actual Incumbent(s) in Position
Section Officer	1	1
Assistant	Nil	2
UDC	3	1
Accountant	1	1
LDC	1	1

Work Allocation

1. All budget matters, control over expenditure, reconciliation of accounts.
2. Attending to audit parties, settlement of audit objections.
3. Pay bills.
4. Processing and preparation of TA bills, LTC bills, OTA bills, Tuition Fee bills, CEA bills, Medical Reimbursement bills, Hospitality and Entertainment bills, Advances bills, Conveyance charges bills etc.
5. GPF - allotment of GPF account numbers, sanction of advances, maintenance of accounts and other related matters.
6. Financial matters, economy instructions, watch and review the progress of expenditure against sanctioned grants.
7. Screen the proposals for supplementary demands for grants.
8. Advise the Ministry on all financial matters.
9. To identify, in particular, specific savings for creation of posts and to maintain a register for this purpose.
10. To keep closely associated with the formulation of important expenditure proposals from their initial stages.
11. To screen all expenditure proposals requiring to be referred to Finance Ministry for concurrence or comments.
12. Submission of expenditure returns and other returns on related subjects.

13. Installation of telephones and settlement of telephone bills, providing mobile telephones and settlement of bills.
14. Salary, TA bills of Ministers/Members of Parliament/ Non-official members, etc.
15. Income Tax calculation and deduction.
16. Sanction of advances of TA/LTC/Festival/House Building/Car/Scooter and Cycle etc.
17. All types of purchases including computers, fax machines, photocopying machine, staff-cars, scooters, room-coolers, air-conditioners, etc.
18. Maintenance/AMC of all equipment except vehicles.
19. Settlement of air-passage bills.
20. Assisting officers in connection with annual income tax returns.
21. Last Pay Certificate.
22. Calculation and deduction of interest on advances.
23. Preparation of pension papers.
24. Screening Committee proposals regarding delegations/ foreign tours undertaken.
25. Parliament Questions regarding tours, expenditure, etc.
26. Periodical returns.
27. Purchase, maintenance and disposal of furniture, stationery and other items.
28. Disposal of unserviceable stores by auction.
29. Purchase of books, periodicals, etc.
30. Obtaining forms, engagement diaries, calendars, photographs of leaders etc. from Government agencies and local purchase of such items.
31. Washing and issue of linen such as towels, curtains, sofa covers, etc.
32. Recaning of chairs.
33. Preparation of rubber stamps, name plates, etc.
34. Screening the proposals of incoming delegations from the financial angle.
35. Making provision for filling the equivalent value of stamps in the franking machine.
36. Any other items of work assigned.

SECTION : GENERAL

Staff

Name of Post	Sanctioned Strength	Actual Incumbent(s) in Position
Section Officer	1	1
Assistant	Nil	1
UDC	2	1
LDC	2	2

Work Allocation

1. Maintenance of staff cars and three wheeler scooters.
2. Binding of parliamentary debates.
3. Receipt and Dispatch work of the Ministry.
4. Repair of duplicating machines/addressograph machines/cycles and typewriters.
5. Issue of passes/identity cards/validation slips.
6. Printing work.

HINDI ANUBHAG

Staff

Name of Post	Sanctioned Strength	Actual Incumbent(s) in Position
Hindi Officer	1	1
Hindi Translator Gd. I	1	1
H.T. Grade II	2	1
UDC	1	1
LDC	2	1

Work Allocation

1. Translation of official correspondence from English into Hindi and *vice versa*.
2. Translation of Reports/Brochures brought out by the Ministry from time to time.
3. Implementation of Official Language Policy of the Government of India.
4. Follow-up action on the instructions issued by the Department of Official Language (M/o Home Affairs) from time to time.
5. Implementation of decisions taken by the Central Hindi Committee.
6. Implementation of decisions taken by the Central Official Language Implementation Committee.
7. Official Language Implementation Committee of the Ministry: Arrangements for holding quarterly meetings, preparation of minutes and undertaking follow-up action on the decisions taken at its meeting.
8. Progressive use of Hindi - compilation of Quarterly Reports for onward transmission to Department of Official Language.
9. Implementation of Yearly Programme for use of Hindi as issued by the Department of Official Language.
10. Hindi Salahkar Samiti of the Ministry : Constitution, arrangements for quarterly meetings, preparation of minutes and follow-up action on the decisions taken at its meetings.

11. Hindi Workshop - arrangement of a workshop during every inter-session period.
12. Parliament Questions regarding progressive use of Hindi in the Ministry.
13. Correspondence with MPs regarding progressive use of Hindi in the Ministry.
14. Hindi Fortnight/Week/Day in the Ministry.
15. Sansadiya Hindi Pustak Puruskar Yojana.
16. Compilation and providing data regarding progressive use of Hindi in the Ministry to:

    (a) Parliamentary Committee on Official Language.
    (b) Department of Official Language.

17. Implementation of various incentive schemes for progressive use of Hindi i.e. cash prizes for original noting-drafting in Hindi etc.

OTHER PERSONNEL

I. Section : Minister's Personal Section

Name of Post	Sanctioned Strength	Actual Incumbent(s) in Position
Assistant	1	1 (The post of Assistant in the Minister's Personal Section has been upgraded to the grade of SO w.e.f. 18.1.2001)
UDC	Nil	1
LDC	2	Nil

II. Other Officials

Name of Post	Sanctioned Strength	Posts filled	
		On Regular Basis	On ad-hoc/ Deputation
Principal PS	1	Nil	1
Private Secretary	1	1	Nil
Research Assistant	2	Nil	2
Personal Assistant	4	3	1
Stenographer	6	3	2
Staff Car Driver Gr.I	2	2	Nil
Staff Car Driver Gr.II	2	2	Nil
Staff Car Driver (Ordinary Grade)	3	2	Nil
Despatch Rider	1	1	Nil
Gestetner Operator	1	1	Nil
Addressographer	1	1	Nil
Jamadar	2	1	Nil
Daftari	5	5	Nil
Peon	17	10	7
Farash	1	1	Nil
Sweeper	1	1	Nil
Chowkidar	1	1	Nil

III. Summary of Staff Position

Total Posts	Posts Filled		Posts Vacant
	On Regular Basis	On ad-hoc/ Deputation	
130	96	29	5

ANNEX I-F

MINISTRY OF PARLIAMENTARY AFFAIRS
(WORK STUDY SECTION)

No.F. 1(3)/97-WS Dated : 5t January, 1998

Sub : Decentralisation of powers in respect of cases in each section of the Ministry of Parliamentary Affairs - Instructions regarding review of

Departmental instructions regarding decentralisation of power in respect of cases in each section of the Ministry of Parliamentary Affairs were issued to all sections and officers for information and necessary action *vide* this section circular No. F. 1(3)/93-WS dated 28th April, 1994. These instructions have since been reviewed and a copy of the revised instructions on the above subject is forwarded herewith for information, compliance and necessary action.

Hindi version will follow.

Sd/-
(G.K. Ahuja)
Under Secretary (WS)

To

1. PPS to Secretary
2. PS to JS
3. PSs/PA to DS(A)/DS(L)/DS(RandC)
4. All Under Secretaries
5. All Section Officers

REVISED INSTRUCTIONS REGARDING THE DECENTRALISATION OF POWER IN RESPECT OF DISPOSAL OF CASES IN EACH SECTION OF MINISTRY OF PARLIAMENTARY AFFAIRS

Implementation (I & II) Sections

1. Assurances may be culled out after approval of Under Secretary. However, assurances relating to MPs, Ministers and the assurances relating to the Ministry of Parliamentary Affairs may be culled out after approval of Secretary.
2. Cases of extension of time for implementation of assurances should normally be processed after approval of the Under Secretary. However, cases in which assurances were extracted with the approval of senior officers may be processed with the approval of Joint Secretary.
3. Cases relating to dropping of assurances may be processed after obtaining the approval of Joint Secretary.
4. Cases relating to scrutinising and laying of the Implementation Reports in respect of assurances should normally be decided at the level of Under Secretary. However, Implementation Reports in respect of assurances relating to MPs, Ministers and any other important Implementation Report may be laid on the Table after approval of Secretary.
5. All cases of assurances pending five years or more should be put up to Joint Secretary.
6. Recommendations of a general nature made by the Committee on Government Assurances may be processed after the approval of Secretary.
7. Intimation about the implementation of assurances may be sent at the level of Section Officer in respect of Ministries/Departments and at the level of Under Secretary in respect of Members of Parliament.

I. Committee Section

1. ***Consultative Committees***

   Constitution of the Consultative Committees is to be decided at the level of the Minister. Constitution of the committees is to be notified by the Secretary.

2. ***Additions/Deletions of Members to/from Committees***

   Subsequent additions/deletions of the names of MPs to/from Consultative Committees is to be approved by the Minister. Notification in regard thereto is to be issued by the Under Secretary.

3. ***Issue of notices to Members regarding Consultative Committee meetings***

   All circulars regarding the meetings of the Consultative Committees will be issued by the Under Secretary. However, in case of meetings chaired by the Prime Minister, the first circulars will be issued by the Under Secretary with the approval of Deputy Secretary.

4. All other routine circulars such as circulation of agenda/minutes/action taken reports etc. will be issued by the Under Secretary.
5. Routine letters regarding (i) fixing the venue of the meetings, (ii) other arrangements connected with the meetings and (iii) forwarding to the Secretariats attendance of MPs at the meetings etc. will be issued by the Section Officer. Likewise, suggestions received from Members for inclusion of item(s) in the agenda of the meetings will be forwarded to the Ministries concerned without delay, by the Section Officer who will also find out and report whether the items suggested by the Members have been included in the agenda or not.

II. Appointment/Nominations of Members of Parliament on the Committees and other Bodies set up by the Government

1. All cases of nomination of Members of Parliament on Governmental Committees/Councils/Bodies, Boards etc. must be submitted to the Minister for his approval.
2. Consent of Members of Parliament, wherever necessary, nominated by the Minister may be obtained at the Under Secretary's level.
3. Intimation about nomination of Members of Parliament as approved by the Minister may be intimated to the concerned Ministries at the Under Secretary's level.
4. Intimation about vacancies caused on the Government Committees/Councils/Boards etc. owing to retirement, resignation, unfortunate death of a Member may be conveyed to the concerned Ministries/Departments at the level of Under Secretary.

General Section

Submission of log-books for scrutiny

1. It has been decided that hereafter the log-books of staff cars/three wheeler scooters should be submitted to Under Secretary well in time for scrutiny every month.
2. The log-books should be submitted to Deputy Secretary/IFA at the end of each quarter.

Expenditure on the maintenance of staff cars

1. It has been decided that the Under Secretary in charge of General Section may have the authority in respect of items of work entrusted to General Section to accord administrative approval up to Rs. 2,000. After execution of the required jobs, bills/cases which involve expenditure not exceeding Rs. 2,000 may be marked by US to US(A) for financial approval and signing of payment orders recorded on the Bill(s).
2. Deputy Secretary may have the authority to accord

administrative approval in respect of various items of work entrusted to General Section to the tune of Rs. 10,000. After execution of jobs, the bills/cases which involve expenditure exceeding Rs. 2,000 may be submitted to DS(A) for financial approval and to US(A) for signing the payment orders recorded on the bill(s).

3. Bill(s)/case(s) which involve expenditure exceeding Rs. 10,000 and up to 100,000 will be submitted to Joint Secretary for administrative and financial approval.
4. Bill(s)/case(s) involving expenditure exceeding Rs. 100,000 will be submitted to Secretary for approval. Bill(s)/case(s) at S.Nos. 3 and 4 above after execution of jobs, will be marked to US(A) for signing of payment orders recorded on the bill(s).

Welfare Section

1. Cases regarding sanctions for expenditures to be incurred (i) in purchasing gifts to be given to foreign delegates, (ii) on serving dinner to MPs and staff in cases of late sitting of the House(s) of Parliament, and (iii) in the event of death of an MP in Delhi will be submitted up to Joint Secretary.
2. Cases regarding sanctions for expenditure to be incurred on serving refreshments to MPs during meetings of Leaders; call on meetings with foreign delegations, etc. may be submitted up to Deputy Secretary.
3. Cases relating to medical treatment of MPs in foreign countries will be submitted to Joint Secretary.
4. Cases relating to visits of MPs to foreign countries will be submitted to Joint Secretary.
5. Cases relating to installation of statues/portraits in Parliament House may be submitted to Deputy Secretary.
6. Cases relating to invitation to MPs in connection with ceremonies such as Independence Day, Republic Day, Prime Minister's Rally, Oath taking by President and Vice-President and Iftar parties will be submitted to Joint Secretary.

Research and Conference Section

I. *Youth Parliament Work*

1. All the work connected with Youth Parliament will be co-coordinated by the Section Officer and Under Secretary.

II. *Youth Parliament Competitions - Annual Prize Distribution Functions, etc.*

1. The date for holding the Prize Distribution Function of the Youth Parliament will be decided at Joint Secretary's/ Secretary's level.
2. The sanction of expenditure etc. within the approved limits will be decided at the level of Deputy Secretary. Only cases for which special sanction is required will be submitted to Joint Secretary/Secretary for approval.

III. *National Parliamentary Quiz Contest*

1. All time schedules and dates of various examinations held under the contests viz., dates of holding the zonal and national contests will be decided at the level of Joint Secretary/Secretary.
2. After the programme and scheme of the contest have been forwarded by the H.M. to C.Ms, etc. in the States/ UTs, follow-up action will be taken at the level of the Secretary/Joint Secretary/Deputy Secretary. However, all correspondence and decisions in matters of a routine nature will be taken at the Under Secretary's level.
3. Questionnaire for the zonal level contests will be finalised at the level of Minister. Questions for national level contests will have to be cleared/finalised by the Secretary/Minister.
4. Answer sheets of zonal level examinations will be evaluated under direct supervision of the Deputy Secretary.

IV. *All India Whips' Conferences*

1. Decisions and venue of holding the All India Whips' Conference will be decided by the Secretary with the approval of H.M.
2. Action taken reports/implementation reports of the recommendations of the preceding conferences will be finalised at the level of the Secretary. The agenda of the conferences and notes on various items included therein will be finalised at the level of Joint Secretary/Secretary with the approval of the Minister.
3. All correspondence with the State Governments etc. in connection with the conference, except of routine nature, will be done with the approval of the Joint Secretary/ Secretary. Under Secretary will, however, attend to all correspondence and take decisions on matters of routine nature.
4. Recommendations of the conference concerning the Centre will be processed and action taken at the level of the Joint Secretary/Secretary, with the approval of the Minister.

V. *Research Work*

1. Finalisation of subjects will be submitted to Joint Secretary/Secretary for approval.
2. Final draft brochures will be submitted for Joint Secretary's/Secretary's approval. Monitoring of the work relating to preparation of brochures will be submitted to Deputy Secretary and finalised at Deputy Secretary's level quarterly.

VI. *Queries from the States*

1. All correspondence of a routine nature will be decided at the Under Secretary level. However, cases where a legal opinion has to be expressed will be submitted to Deputy Secretary/Joint Secretary/Secretary for consideration and approval.
2. Reports of the Committee on Subordinate Legislation are to be submitted to Joint Secretary/Secretary for his information. Cases involving recommendations of a

general nature which have to be brought to the notice of all Ministries/Departments of the Government of India for compliance are to be submitted to Joint Secretary/ Secretary for approval.

Members' Emoluments Section

I. *Administration of the three Acts*

1. All routine queries regarding administration of the Salary, Allowances and Pension of Members of Parliament Act; the Salaries and Allowances of Officers of Parliament Act; and the Salary and Allowances of Leaders of the Opposition in Parliament Act will be dealt with at the Under Secretary's level.
2. Replies to Members of Parliament will be put up to Secretary/Minister for approval.
3. Cases relating to the meetings/recommendations of the Joint Committee on Salaries and Allowances of Members of Parliament will be submitted to Secretary.
4. Follow up action in regard to the recommendations of the Joint Committee will be submitted and decided at Secretary's level.

II. *Organisation and Method*

1. Normally all communications received from the Department of Administrative Reforms and Public Grievances and also from the National Archives of India are to be submitted and disposed of at the O&M officer i.e. Deputy Secretary's level.
2. Half-yearly position with regard to weeding out, recording and indexing of files and their pendency is to be submitted to Joint Secretary.
3. Work Study Programme for the whole year is decided at Secretary's level.
4. Work Study reports of work load assessed of a particular section is submitted to Secretary for his approval.
5. Periodical Reports meant for Department of Administrative Reforms and Public Grievances and National Archives of India may be approved at Deputy Secretary's level.

Hindi Section

1. All translation and typing work in Hindi will primarily be disposed of at the level of the Hindi Officer.
2. Work relating to the constitution of the Hindi Salahkar Samiti will be put up to Secretary/Minister for approval. The nomination/deletion of *ex-officio* members on/from the Hindi Salahkar Samiti is taken at Secretary's level. In respect of nomination/deletion of members other than *ex-officio* members the decision is taken at the level of Minister.
3. Prize schemes for original books on the subjects of the Ministry and on parliamentary subjects to be approved at Secretary's level.
4. All India Essay Competition on subjects relating to parliamentary democracy to be approved at Secretary level.
5. Organising Hindi week to be approved at Secretary's level.
6. Hindi Training to employees of the Ministry relating to:

   (i) Hindi Language Training;
   (ii) Hindi Typing/Stenography;
   (iii) Intensive Hindi training to officers; and
   (iv) Training of bilingual electronic typewriter.

Decision on these items is taken at Joint Secretary level.

Administration Section

	Cases	Levels of decision taking
1.	***Appointments***	
	Group 'A'	Minister
	Group 'B'	Secretary
	Group 'C'	Joint Secretary
	Group 'D'	Joint Secretary
2.	***Promotion, Confirmation, Deputation etc.***	Recommendation of concerned DPC obtained and submitted to appropriate appointing authority for orders.

3.	***Creation of Posts*** (After approval of Finance Minister and Cabinet's approval)	Secretary/Minister
4.	***Reservation Orders***	
	Reservation in Services of SC/ST (de-reservation and carry forward of reserved vacancy) through Liaison Officer i.e. Joint Secretary of our Ministry.	Secretary

5. ***T.A.***

The controlling officers for the purpose of TA are as under:

1. *One's own controlling officers*

   All Officers of the rank of Under Secretary and above will be their own controlling officers.

2. *In other cases*

   In respect of non-gazetted and gazetted staff below the rank of Under Secretary the concerned Under Secretary is the Controlling Officer.

6. ***LTC***

As mentioned under 'TA'.

7. ***Grant of Leave, etc.***

As regards grant of leave, the Head of Office being in-charge of Administration Section may continue to exercise the powers of granting leave on the recommendation of the officer(s) concerned. The practice of allowing persons to proceed on leave/re-join duty after leave may, however, continue to be exercised by the officer(s) concerned.

8. ***All Policy Matters (All subjects)*** Secretary

9. ***Sanction of Casual Leave***

Category of staff	*Sanctioning Authority*
Staff working in a Section	i) For 3 days by S.O. ii) From 4 to 7 days by Branch Officer iii) More than 7 days by Deputy Secretary
Section Officer	i) For 3 days by Under Secretary ii) More than 3 days by Deputy Secretary.
Under Secretary	i) Up to 3 days by Deputy Secretary ii) More than 3 days by Jt. Secretary
Deputy Secretary	i) Up to 3 days by Joint Secretary ii) More than 3 days by Secretary
Joint Secretary	Secretary

10. ***Punctuality in Attendance***

Instructions have been reiterated emphasising the need for punctuality in attendance. Instructions in this regard will continue to be issued by Administration Section with the approval of Deputy Secretary/Joint Secretary.

Accounts and Purchase Section

1. Powers of the Head of the Department may continue to be vested in the Secretary as hithertofore.
2. Under Secretary (Admn.) declared as Head of Office may accord financial sanction upto Rs. 5,000 under the Delegation of Financial Powers Rules.

3. Financial powers for sanctioning a contingent expenditure up to Rs. 1,00,000 in respect of various items of work has been delegated to Joint Secretary. DS(A) exercises delegated financial power for sanctioning expenditure up to Rs. 25,000.
4. Cases involving Contingent expenditure above Rs. 1,00,000 will require approval of Secretary.

5.	House Building Advance	Secretary
6.	All conveyance advances except cycle advance	Secretary
7.	Cycle Advance	US(A) being Head of Office
8.	G.P.F. Advance	- do -
9.	G.P.F. Advance/withdrawals (for special reasons)	DS(A)
10.	GPF withdrawal exceeding three-fourth of balance	Secretary
11.	Grant of advances of all other types except those mentioned at S.Nos. 5, 6 and 9 above	US(A)
12.	For budgetary provision etc. (cases to be submitted through IFA)	Secretary

Legislative-I Section

1. *Government Business for a session of Parliament*

(i) The initial circular calling for items of Government Business which a Ministry/Department desires to take up for consideration in a session of Parliament will be issued over the signature of Secretary of the Ministry. It will be addressed to all Secretaries (by name) heading the Ministries/Departments.

(ii) Reminders to defaulting Ministries will be issued by the Under Secretary.

2. *No-Day-Yet Named Motions*

Ministries concerned with subject matter of admitted No-Day-Yet Motions are requested to indicate whether they have any objection to the discussion being arranged thereon. Such communications will be issued over the signature of Under Secretary.

3. *Calling Attention Notices*

Section Officer (Leg.I) will forward copies of Calling Attention Notices received from Rajya Sabha Secretariat to P.S. to Minister concerned with the subject matter.

4. *Committee on Papers Laid*

Reports to be submitted to the Joint Secretary/Secretary for information. Cases involving recommendations of a general nature which have to be brought to the notice of all Ministries/Departments for compliance are to be submitted to Joint Secretary/Secretary for approval.

Legislative-II Section

1. *Matters raised in Lok Sabha under Rule 377 and by way of Special Mentions in Rajya Sabha*

(i) Dispatch of lists and follow-up action in regard to matters raised under Rule 377 in Lok Sabha and by way of Special Mentions in Rajya Sabha are to be disposed of at Under Secretary's level.

(ii) Cases of delayed action on references from Members of Parliament are to be submitted to Secretary. Cases involving policy matters have to be submitted to Secretary.

2. *Manual of Parliamentary Procedures in the Government of India*

Policy matters/review of chapters relating to the Manual are to be submitted to Secretary.
Examination of references/rendering advice, etc. to be submitted/decided at Joint Secretary's level.

3. ***Training of Officers dealing with Parliamentary work in Ministries/Departments***

Policy matters relating to organisation of training of officers of various Ministries/Departments are to be submitted to Secretary. Subsequent follow-up action is to be taken at Under Secretary's level. Dates of conducting the courses, programme of training courses are to be submitted to the Joint Secretary.

4. ***Training of officers of Department of Parliamentary Affairs in the States/Union territories***

Policy matters relating to organisation of training of officers of Department of Parliamentary Affairs in the States/Union territories and the dates of conducting courses are to be submitted to Secretary. Subsequent follow-up action is to be taken at Deputy Secretary's level.

5. ***Advance study of emergent trends in Parliament***

Details about the advance study of emerging trends in Parliament are to be submitted to Secretary/Minister.

6. ***Committee on Petitions***

Reports of the Committee on Petitions involving any action are to be submitted to Joint Secretary/Secretary for his approval.

7. ***Press clippings on important Parliamentary and other matters***

All Press Clippings on important parliamentary and other matters including last week in Parliament are to be submitted to the Secretary.

8. ***References from Members of Parliament***

All miscellaneous references from Members of Parliament are to be submitted to the Secretary.

Legislative-III Cell

1. ***Matters raised in Lok Sabha and Rajya Sabha during Zero Hour***

   (i) Distribution of lists of matters raised during Zero Hour in the Lok Sabha and the Rajya Sabha to offices of the Ministers/Sr. Officers to be monitored/ensured at Under Secretary's level.

   (ii) Matters raised during Zero Hour in the Lok Sabha and the Rajya Sabha, where there are either any directions from the Chair or any assurance from Minister(s) of Parliamentary Affairs are to be forwarded to the concerned Minister(s) at Minister's level.

   (iii) Cases involving policy matters are to be submitted to Secretary.

2. Copies of proceedings of the Lok Sabha/Rajya Sabha (during Zero Hour), where references to PM/PMO are made, are to be forwarded to PMO at Section Officer's level.

No.F. 1(2)/92-IFC
Government of India
Ministry of Parliamentary Affairs

92, Parliament House,
New Delhi.

Dated : 9th January, 2002

ORDER

In terms of sub-rule (3) of Rule (13) of Delegation of Financial Powers Rules, 1978, Head of Department i.e. Secretary, Ministry of Parliamentary Affairs delegates his powers to Joint Secretary, Ministry of Parliamentary Affairs for incurring contingent expenditure up to Rs. 1,00,000 (Rs. One Lakh only) in each case in respect of the following four items of expenditure:

1. Fixture and furniture - purchase and repair;
2. Motor vehicle - Maintenance, upkeep and repair;
3. Expenditure on purchase, hire, upkeep and repair of all office equipments including typewriters, electronic typewriters, intercom equipments, calculators, photo copiers and addressographs; and
4. Expenditure on maintenance of computers of all kinds.

Such delegation shall carry with it all the conditions and restrictions prescribed in the Delegation of Financial Powers Rules, 1978.

Sd/- (G.K. Ahuja)
Deputy Secretary to the Govt. of India
Tele : 3034763

Copy to:

1. All Officers/Sections of the Ministry
2. Pay and Accounts Officer, PAO, Cabinet Affairs, New Delhi

No.F.15(1)/2003-AandP
Government of India
Ministry of Parliamentary Affairs

8, Parliament House,
New Delhi.

January 9, 2004

ORDER

The undersigned re-delegates his powers to the Subordinate Officers of the Ministry of Parliamentary Affairs as per details below:

1. For incurring contingent expenditure to the following Subordinate Officers up to the extent specified against them:

S.No.	Subordinate Officers	Financial limit
1.	Joint Secretary	Rs. 1,00,000 (Rupees One Lakh only)
2.	Deputy Secretaries	Rs. 25,000 (Rupees Twenty Five Thousand only)
3.	Under Secretaries	Rs. 5,000 (Rupees Five Thousand only)

Such re-delegation shall carry with it all the conditions and restrictions prescribed in the Delegation of Financial Powers Rules, 1978 and should be exercised in consultation with IFD.

2. For sanctioning GPF advance/withdrawal for special reasons to Deputy Secretary (Admn.).

Such re-delegation shall also carry with it all the conditions and restrictions prescribed in the General Provident Fund (Central Services) Rules, 1960.

Sd/- (V.K. AGNIHOTRI)
SECRETARY

Copy to:

1. All Officers/Sections of the Ministry
2. Pay and Accounts Officer, PAO, Cabinet Affairs, New Delhi

ANNEX I-G

LIST OF SECRETARIES OF THE MINISTRY OF PARLIAMENTARY AFFAIRS

S. No.	Name of the Secretary	Period		Remarks
		From	To	
1.	Shri S.L. Shakdher	16.5.49	26.11.52	The post was equivalent to an Under Secretary to the Government of India
2.	Shri Prem Chand	27.11.52	9.2.54	The post was equivalent to a Deputy Secretary to the Government of India
3.	Shri N.K. Bhojwani	9.2.54 (AN) 10.11.55	4.9.55 31.12.58	-do-
4.	Shri S.P. Advani	5.9.55	9.11.55	-do-
5.	Shri Kailash Chandra	1.1.59	16.3.67	The post was equivalent to a Deputy Secretary upto 28.11.63 and upgraded to the status of Joint Secretary to the Government of India w.e.f. 29.11.63
6.	Shri H.N. Trivedi	28.3.67	31.12.75	The post was equivalent to a Joint Secretary to the Government of India.
7.	Shri K.N. Krishnan	25.3.76	5.2.82	The post was equivalent to a Joint Secretary up to 2.6.80 and upgraded to the status of Additional Secretary to the Government of India w.e.f. 3.6.80.
8.	Shri Ishwari Prasad	5.2.82 (AN)	29.2.88	The post was equivalent to an Additional Secretary up to 18.2.84 and upgraded to the status of Secretary to the Government of India w.e.f. 18.2.84. It was personal to the incumbent.

Contd. ...

Contd....

9.	Shri B.N. Dhoundiyal	11.4.88	28.2.91	The post of Secretary, MPA, is of the status of Secretary to the Government of India
10.	Shri R. Srinivasan	28.2.91 (AN)	31.8.92	-do-
11.	Shri M.M. Rajendran	16.9.92	20.5.93	-do-
12.	Shri P.C. Hota	20.5.93	31.8.95	-do-
13.	Shri R.C. Tripathi	1.9.95	31.8.97	-do-
14.	Shri S.A.T. Rizvi	1.9.97	24.2.99	-do-
15.	Shri L.D.Mishra (Addl. charge)	25.2.99	15.3.99	-do-
16.	Shri S.A.T. Rizvi	16.3.99	1.8.2000	-do-
17.	Shri R.D. Kapoor	17.8.2000	2.11.2000	-do-
18.	Dr. M. Rehman	2.11.2000	31.7.2002	-do-
19.	Shri L.M. Goyal	26.8.2002	31.5.2003	-do-
20.	Sh. V. Lakshmi Ratan	1.6.2003	24.6.2003	-do-
21.	Dr. V.K. Agnihotri	24.6.2003	-	-do-

ANNEX I-H

STATEMENT SHOWING CABINET MINISTERS/MINISTERS OF STATE HOLDING CHARGES OF THE MINISTRY OF PARLIAMENTARY AFFAIRS

S. No.	Name of the Cabinet Minister/Minister of the State In charge	Period		Name of the Minister of State	Period	
		From	To		From	To
1.	Shri Satya Narain Sinha	*26.2.49	25.1.50			
		31.1.50	6.5.50			
		13.5.50	13.5.52			
		13.5.52	17.4.57			
		17.4.57	10.4.62			
		10.4.62	27.5.64			
		27.5.64	9.6.64	Shri Jagannath Rao	14.2.66	13.3.67
		9.6.64	11.1.66			
		11.1.66	24.1.66			
		24.1.66	13.3.67			
2.	Dr. Ram Subhag Singh	13.3.67	14.2.69	Shri I.K. Gujral	18.3.67	14.2.69
3.	Shri K. Raghuramaiah	*14.2.69	26.6.70	Shri Om Mehta	30.6.70	18.3.71
		26.6.70	18.3.71		18.3.71	24.3.77
4.	Shri Raj Bahadur	18.3.71	5.2.73			
5.	Shri K. Raghuramaiah	5.2.73	24.3.77			
6.	Shri Ravindra Verma	26.3.77	28.7.79	Shri Larang Sai	14.8.77	28.7.79
				Dr. Ram Kripal Sinha	14.8.77	28.7.79
7.	Shri K. Gopal	*4.8.79	14.1.80			

Contd.....

8.	Shri Bhishma Narain Singh	14.1.80	29.1.83	Shri P. Venkatasubhaiah	16.1.80	2.9.82
				Shri Sitaram Kesri	3.3.80	15.1.82
9.	Shri Buta Singh	29.1.83	31.12.84	Shri H.K.L. Bhagat	2.9.82	31.10.84
				Shri Kalpnath Rai	29.1.83	31.10.84
				Shri N.K.P. Salve	4.11.84	31.12.84
10.	Shri H.K.L. Bhagat	31.12.84	2.12.89	Shri Ghulam Nabi Azad	31.12.84	12.5.86
				Mrs. Margaret Alva	31.12.84	25.9.85
				Shri Sitaram Kesri	25.9.85	22.10.86
				Smt. Shiela Dikshit	12.5.86	2.12.89
				Shri M.M. Jacob	22.10.86	2.12.89
				Shri P. Namgyal	4.7.89	2.12.89
				Shri R.K. Malaviya	4.7.89	2.12.89
11.	Shri P. Upendra	5.12.89	10.11.90	Shri Satyapal Malik	23.4.90	10.11.90
12.	Shri. Satya Prakash Malaviya	21.11.90	21.6.91			
13.	Shri Ghulam Nabi Azad	21.6.91	18.1.93	Shri M.M. Jacob	21.6.91	17.1.93
				Sh. P.R. Kumaramanglam	21.6.91	2.12.93
14.	Shri V.C. Shukla	18.1.93	17.1.96	Shri Abrar Ahmed	18.1.93	2.4.94
				Smt. Margaret Alva	19.2.93	16.5.96
				Shri Mukul Wasnik	19.2.93	16.5.96
				Shri Eduardo Falerio	2.12.93	19.9.95
				Shri Rameshwar Thakur	17.4.94	22.12.94
				Shri Mallikarjun	17.4.94	16.5.96
15.	Shri Ghulam Nabi Azad	18.1.96	16.5.96	Shri Matang Singh	10.2.95	16.5.95
				Shri S.S. Ahluwalia	19.9.95	10.5.96
				Shri Vilas Muttemwar	19.9.95	10.5.96

Contd.....

16.	Shri Pramod Mahajan	16.5.96	1.6.96(FN)			
17.	Shri Ram Vilas Paswan	1.6.96(FN)	29.6.96	Shri Beni Prasad Verma	1.6.96	29.6.96
18.	Shri Srikanta Kumar Jena	29.6.96(AN)	21.4.97	Sh. P. Venkateshwarlu	29.6.96	21.4.97
		21.4.97	19.3.98		21.4.97	26.5.97
				Shri S.R. Balasubramoniyan	29.6.96	21.4.97
					1.5.97	19.3.98
				Smt. Jayanthi Natrajan	9.6.97	19.3.98
				Sh. M.P. Veerandra Kumar	26.5.97	9.6.97
19.	Shri Madan Lal Khurana	19.3.98	30.1.99	Shri R.K. Kumar	19.3.98	22.5.98
				Shri Ram Naik	19.3.98	5.5.99
				Shri Dilip Ray	19.3.98	13.10.99
20.	Shri P.R. Kumaramangalam	30.1.99	13.10.99	Shri M.A. Naqvi	16.2.99	13.10.99
				Shri Santosh Gangwar	16.2.99	13.10.99
21.	Shri Pramod Mahajan	13.10.99	29.1.03	Shri Phaggan Singh Kulaste	13.10.99	22.11.99
				Shri Sriram Chauhan	13.10.99	22.11.99
				Shri Dilip Ray	13.10.99	22.11.99
				Shri Santosh Gangwar	13.10.99	29.1.03
				Shri O. Rajagopal	22.11.99	29.1.03
22.	Smt. Sushma Swaraj	29.1.03	22.5.04	Smt. Bhavanaben D Chikhalia	29.1.03	22.5.04
				Shri Vijay Goel	29.1.03	24.5.03
				Shri O. Rajagopal	30.1.03	22.5.04
				Sh. S. Gangwar	24.5.03	22.5.04
23	Shri Ghulam Nabi Azad	23.5.04		Shri Suresh Pachouri	23.5.04	
				Shri B.K. Handique	23.5.04	
				Smt. Suryakanta Patil	23.5.04	

* During these periods, Shri Sinha and Shri K. Raghuramaiah were appointed Minister of State In charge of the Department and Shri K. Gopal, Minister of State In charge of the Ministry.

STATEMENT SHOWING DEPUTY MINISTERS HOLDING CHARGE OF THE MINISTRY OF PARLIAMENTARY AFFAIRS

Sl. No.	Name of the Deputy Minister	Period From	To
1.	Shri Satya Narain Sinha*	1.10.48	26.2.49
2.	Shri V.C. Shukla	24.1.66	14.2.66
3.	Shri Rohan Lal Chaturvedi	18.3.67	14.11.67
4.	Shri J.B. Muthyal Rao	8.3.67	14.11.67
5.	Sardar Iqbal Singh	14.2.69	8.7.70
6.	Sardar Raghubir Singh Panjhazari	30.6.70	18.3.71
7.	Sh. P. Parthasarthy	30.6.70	18.3.71
8.	Shri B. Shankaranand	2.5.71	24.3.77
9.	Shri Kedar Nath Singh	2.5.71	10.10.74
10.	Shri Mallikarjun	17.11.80	31.10.84
		4.11.84	31.12.84
11.	Shri Kalpnath Rai	15.1.82	29.1.83
12.	Shri P. Namgyal	25.6.88	3.7.89
13.	Shri R.K. Malaviya	25.6.88	3.7.89
14.	Shri Jagdip Dhankar	23.4.90	5.11.90

*(Shri Sinha was Chief Whip with status of Deputy Minister and attached to PM)

ANNEX I-I

F.No 9(3)/97-Admn
Government of India
Ministry of Parliamentary Affairs

92, Parliament House,
New Delhi

Dated: 27.05.2004

Subject: Allocation of work among the Minister of Parliamentary Affairs and the Ministers of State in the Ministry of Parliamentary Affairs

The Minister of Parliamentary Affairs has approved that MOS Shri Suresh Pachouri will be incharge of work in respect of Rajya Sabha and MOS Shri B.K. Handique and Smt. Suryakanta Patil will be incharge of items of work in respect of Lok Sabha, as indicated in Annexes. Files, including those of policy matters and Bills, in respect of the Lok Sabha/Rajya Sabha, shall be routed through the MOS concerned.

2. For the sake of internal working in the Ministry and for marking files, abbreviations for the three Ministers of State will be as follows:-

1. Shri Suresh Pachouri — MOS (SP)
2. Shri B.K. Handique — MOS (BH)
3. Smt Suryakanta Patil — MOS (SK)

(V.K. AGNIHOTRI)
SECRETARY TO THE GOVT. OF INDIA

To

1. PS to HMPA
2. PS to MOS (SP)
3. PS to MOS (BH)
4. PS to MOS (SK)

Copy to:- Cabinet Secretariat,
(Shri K.L. Sharma, Deputy Secretary)
Rashtrapati Bhawan

ANNEX I-I(I)

ALLOCATION OF WORK AMONG THE MINISTER AND MINISTERS OF STATE MINISTER

I. To be overall incharge of all functions allocated by the President to the Ministry of Parliamentary Affairs under article 77(3) of the Constitution, viz.

a. Dates of summoning and prorogation of the two Houses of Parliament, dissolution of the Lok Sabha, President's address to Parliament.
b. Planning and coordination of legislative and other Official Business in both Houses.
c. Allocation of Government time in Parliament for discussion of motions given notice of by Members.
d. Liaison with Leaders and Whips of various parties and groups represented in Parliament.
e. Lists of members of Select and Joint Committees on Bills.
f. Appointment of Members of Parliament on committees and other bodies set up by Government.
g. Functioning of Consultative Committees of Members of Parliament for various ministries.
h. Implementation of assurances given by Ministers in Parliament.
i. Government's stand on Private Members' Bills and Resolutions.
j. Secretarial assistance to the Cabinet Committee on Parliamentary Affairs.
k. Advice to Ministries on procedural and other parliamentary matters.
l. Coordination of action by ministries on recommendations of general application made by Parliamentary Committees.
m. Officially sponsored visits of Members of Parliament to places of interest.

n. Matters connected with powers, privileges and immunities of Members of Parliament.
o. Parliamentary Secretaries—functions.
p. Organisation of Youth Parliament Competitions in schools/colleges throughout the country.
q. Organisation of All India Whips' Conference.
r. Exchange of Government Sponsored Delegations of Members of Parliament with other countries.
s. Determination of policy and follow up action in regard to Matters raised under Rule 377 of the Rules of Procedure and Conduct of Business in Lok Sabha and by way of Special Mentions in the Rajya Sabha.
t. Manual of Parliamentary Procedures in the Government of India.
u. The Salaries and Allowances of the Officers of Parliament Act, 1953 (20 of 1953).
v. The Salary, Allowances and Pension of Members of Parliament Act, 1954 (30 of 1954).
w. The Salary and Allowances of Leaders of Opposition in Parliament Act, 1977 (33 of 1977).
x. The Leader and Chief Whips of Recognised Parties and Groups in Parliament (Facilities) Act, 1998 (5 of 1999).

2. To assist the Leaders of the Lok Sabha and the Rajya Sabha in carrying out the functions allotted to the Leaders of the two Houses in the Rules of Procedure and Conduct of Business in the Lok Sabha and the Rajya Sabha.
3. To liaise with Leaders of Opposition parties/groups in Parliament.
4. To advise the Prime Minister on parliamentary matters.
5. All matters relating to establishment and administration of the Ministry.
6. Approval of replies to Starred Questions relating to both the Houses.
7. Approval of daily List of Government Business for the Lok Sabha and the Rajya Sabha.

ANNEX I-I(II)

MINISTER OF STATE (RAJYA SABHA) (SHRI SURESH PACHOURI)

1. To assist the Leader of the Rajya Sabha in carrying out the functions allotted to the Leader of the Rajya Sabha in the Rules of Procedure and Conduct of Business in that House in consultation with the Minister of Parliamentary Affairs.
2. To keep the Minister posted with the various suggestions emanating from Members of the Rajya Sabha.
3. To be in attendance in the Rajya Sabha throughout the period of session.
4. To be constantly in touch with the Leaders and Chief Whips of the Opposition parties/groups for smooth functioning of the Rajya Sabha and to keep the Minister posted about their views and trends on various matters.
5. To assist the Minister in planning and coordination of Legislative and other business in the Rajya Sabha.
6. To maintain quorum in the Rajya Sabha.
7. To assist the Minister in deciding the lists of speakers on debates in the Rajya Sabha.
8. To attend to the work pertaining to Parliamentary Committees of the Rajya Sabha and assist the Minister in regard to nomination thereon.
9. To assist the Minister in the nomination of Members of the Rajya Sabha on Government Committees and Bodies.
10. To keep the Ministers informed of their business in the Rajya Sabha and ensure their attendance.
11. To scrutinise and lay statements of Implementation Reports on assurances on the Table of the Rajya Sabha.
12. To assist the Minister in the election of Members of the Rajya Sabha on committees and for this purpose to prepare Whips, as necessary.

13. To assist the Minister in matters relating to changes desired by Members of the Rajya Sabha on the Consultative Committees.
14. Claims of TA/DA of Members of the Rajya Sabha in connection with meetings of Consultative Committees.
15. To assist the Minister in allocation of Government time in the Rajya Sabha for discussion of motions given notice of by Members with the approval of Minister.
16. Approval of answers to the Rajya Sabha Unstarred Questions.
17. To assist the Minister in follow-up action *vis-à-vis* Special Mentions in the Rajya Sabha.
18. Any other work entrusted to him by the Minister of Parliamentary Affairs.

ANNEX I-I (III)

MINISTER OF STATE (LOK SABHA)
(SHRI B. K. HANDIQUE)

1. To keep the Minister posted with the various suggestions emanating from Members of the Lok Sabha.
2. To be in attendance in the Lok Sabha throughout the period of session.
3. To be constantly in touch with the Chief Whips of the Opposition parties/groups for facilitating smooth functioning of the Lok Sabha.
4. To assist the Minister in planning and coordination of Legislative and other Official Business in the Lok Sabha.
5. To maintain quorum in the Lok Sabha (especially for Congress MPs).
6. To assist the Minister in deciding the lists of speakers on debates in the Lok Sabha.
7. To assist the Minister in nomination of the Members of the Lok Sabha on Government committees and bodies.
8. To assist the Minister in the election of Members of the Lok Sabha to various committees and for this purpose prepare Whips, as necessary.
9. To keep the various Ministers informed of their business in the Lok Sabha and ensure their attendance.
10. To look after the work pertaining to Youth Parliament Competitions.
11. To look after the work of Consultative Committees (List of Ministries/ Departments will be allocated after the constitution of these committees).
12. To assist the Minister in matters relating to changes desired by Members of the Lok Sabha on the Consultative Committees mentioned above.
13. Claims of TA/DA of Members of the Lok Sabha in connection with meetings of the Consultative Committees referred to above.
14. Approval of answers to Unstarred Questions in the Lok Sabha.

15. To assist the Minister in the follow up action with regard to Matters raised under Rule 377 of the Rules of Procedure and Conduct of Business in the Lok Sabha in respect to Ministries mentioned in Appendix 'A'.
16. Any other work entrusted to him by the Minister of Parliamentary Affairs.

ANNEX I-I (IV)

MINISTER OF STATE (LOK SABHA)
(SMT. SURYAKANTA PATIL)

1. To keep the Minister posted with the various suggestions emanating from Members of the Lok Sabha.
2. To be in attendance in the Lok Sabha throughout the period of session.
3. To be constantly in touch with the Chief Whips of the Opposition parties/groups for facilitating smooth functioning of the Lok Sabha.
4. To assist the Minister in planning and coordination of Legislative and other Official Business in the Lok Sabha.
5. To maintain quorum in the Lok Sabha (especially for UPA allies except Congress).
6. To assist the Minister in deciding the lists of speakers on debates in the Lok Sabha.
7. To attend to the work pertaining to Parliamentary Committees of the Lok Sabha and assist the Minister in regard to nomination thereon.
8. To assist the Minister in the election of UPA Members of the Lok Sabha to various committees and for this purpose prepare Whips, as necessary.
9. To keep the various Ministers informed of their business in the Lok Sabha and ensure their attendance.
10. To scrutinise and lay statements of Implementation Reports on assurances on the Table of the Lok Sabha, with the approval of the Minister.
11. To look after the work of Consultative Committees (List of Ministries/ Departments will be allocated after the constitution of these committees).
12. To assist the Minister in matters relating to changes desired by Members of the Lok Sabha on the Consultative Committees mentioned above.
13. Claims of TA/DA of Members of the Lok Sabha in connection with meetings of the Consultative Committees mentioned above.

14. Matters concerned with All India Whips' Conference and Commonwealth Whips' Conference.
15. To assist the Minister in the follow-up action with regard to matters raised under Rule 377 of the Rules of Procedure and Conduct of Business in the Lok Sabha in respect to Ministries mentioned in Appendix 'B'.
16. Any other work entrusted to her by the Minister of Parliamentary Affairs.

ANNEX II-A

STATEMENT INDICATING THE DURATION AS MP IN RESPECT OF SOME SENIOR MEMBERS ELECTED TO XIV LOK SABHA

S.NO.	NAME	TENURE	DURATION IN YEARS and MONTHS		
			LS	RS	TOTAL
1.	Shri A.B. Vajpayee, BJP	2nd Lok Ṣabha (1957 - 62) Rajya Sabha (1962 - 67) 4th - 7th LS (1967-84) Rajya Sabha (1986-1991) 10th - 13th LS (1991-2004)	33-7	9-11	43-6
2.	Shri Chandra Shekhar, SJP	6th and 7th LS, (1977-84) 9th to 13th LS, (1989-2004) Rajya Sabha, (1962-77)	20-4	15	35-4
3.	L.K. Advani, BJP	Rajya Sabha (1970-1989) 9th - 10th LS(89-1996) 12th - 13th LS (1998-04)	11	19-8	30-8
4.	Shri Somnath Chatterjee, CPI(M)	5th to 13th Lok Sabha, 1971-2004	29-9	—	29-9
5.	Shri Pranab Mukerjee, INC	Rajya Sabha (1969-1984)(1993-2004)	—	28-9	28-9
6.	Shri Giridhar Gomang, INC	5th - 12th LS (1971-1999)	26-8	-	26-8
7.	Shri Manabendra Shah, BJP	2nd - 4th LS (1957-1970) 10th - 13th LS (1991-2004)	25-4	-	25-4
8.	Shri Balasaheb Vikhe Patil, INC	5th - 9th LS (1971 - 1991) 12th - 13th LS (1998 - 2004)	24-8	-	24-8

Contd. .....

9.	Shri George Fernandes, JD(U)	4th LS (1967-70) 6th - 7th LS (1977-1984) 9th - 13th LS (1989-2004)	24 -1	-	24 -1
10.	Shri M.H. Gavit, INC	7th -13th LS (1980-2004)	22-9	-	22-9
11.	Shri Basudeb Acharya, CPI(M)	7th to 12th LS (1980-2004)	22-6	-	22-6
12.	Shri Sanat Kumar Mandal, RSP	7th - 13th LS (1980-2004)	22-6	-	22-6
13.	Shri Hannan Mollah, CPI(M)	7th - 13th LS (1980-2004)	22-6	-	22-6
14.	Shri P.A. Sangma, AITC	6th - 8th LS (1977-89) 10th -13th LS (1991-2004)	22-3	-	22 -3
15.	Shri Santosh Mohan Dev, INC	7th - 11th LS (1980-1997) 13th LS (1999-2004)	21-8	-	21-8
16.	Dr. Laxminarayan Pandeya, BJP	5th and 6th LS (1971-79) 9th to 13th LS (1989-2004)	21-3	-	21-3
17.	Shri Kamal Nath, INC	7th - 10th LS (1980 - 1996) 12th - 13th LS (1998 - 2004)	21-3	-	21-3
18.	Shri Manoranjan Bhakta, INC	6th - 12th (1977 - 1999)	20 -10	-	20 -10
19.	Shri Ram Vilas Paswan, LJSP	6th and 7th LS (1977-84) 9th to 13th LS (1989-2004)	20-4	-	20-4
20.	Shri Anil Basu, CPI(M)	8th - 13th LS (1984 - 2004)	19	-	19
21.	Shri Rupchand Pal, CPI (M)	7th LS (1980-84) 9th - 13th (1989-2004)	19	-	19
22.	Shri Satyanarayan Jatiya, BJP	7th LS (1980-1984) 9th - 13th LS (1989 - 2004)	19	-	19

ANNEX II-B

MINISTRY OF PARLIAMENTARY AFFAIRS
(LEGISLATIVE-I SECTION)

Subject: Appointment of Speaker *pro tem* and three other newly elected Members of the Lok Sabha as persons before any of whom the Members of the new Lok Sabha may make or subscribe oath/affirmation.

With the dissolution of the Thirteenth Lok Sabha and the constitution of the Fourteenth Lok Sabha, it has become necessary to appoint a Member of the Lok Sabha to perform the duties of the office of the Speaker in terms of article 95(1) of the Constitution and also to appoint persons under article 99 of the Constitution before any of whom the new Members may make and subscribe oath or affirmation. For this purpose, a Speaker *pro tem* and three other MPs are nominated.

The names of the MPs appointed in the past to act as the Speaker *pro tem* can be seen in the detailed list at ______. The list also indicates the names of those who were nominated to administer oath to the MPs.

Normally, the seniormost amongst MPs is nominated as the Speaker *pro tem*. However, the list at ______, the seniormost MP in the XIV Lok Sabha is Shri ______, the former Prime Minister of India. It is, therefore, suggested that Shri ______, the next in terms of seniority among the Lok Sabha MPs, may be appointed as the Speaker *pro tem*.

As regards nomination of three other MPs to assist the Speaker *pro tem* in making or subscribing oath or affirmation to the newly elected MPs, it is suggested that the following three MPs, at Sr.No.3 to 5 of the seniority list at ______, may be nominated:

1. Shri
2. Shri
3. Shri

( )

SECRETARY

MINISTER OF PARLIAMENTARY AFFAIRS

PRIME MINISTER

ANNEX II-C

MINISTRY OF PARLIAMENTARY AFFAIRS
(LEGISLATIVE-I SECTION)

No.F.77(*)/2004-Leg.I
Dated: *.*.2004

Subject: Appointment of Speaker *pro tem* and persons for administration of oath or affirmation to Members of the Lok Sabha.

The Prime Minister has recommended that the following appointments may be made :

(a) Shri _______, a Member of the Lok Sabha, as Speaker *pro tem* to perform the duties of the office of the Speaker until a new Speaker is elected; and

(b) S/Shri _______, _______ and _______, Members of the Lok Sabha, as persons before any of whom the new Members may make and subscribe oath or affirmation.

The President may please approve the aforesaid appointments. Two draft orders relating to these proposals are also placed below.

If the above proposals are agreed to, arrangements will be made, after ascertaining the convenience of the President, for Shri _________ to be sworn in as Speaker *pro tem* by the President on ___, _____, 2004 at 9.30 a.m., sufficiently before the start of the
(day) (date)
sitting of the Lok Sabha at 11.00 hours on the same day.

( )
Minister of Parliamentary Affairs

THE PRESIDENT OF INDIA

DRAFT ORDER

Dated:

Whereas the office of the Speaker will become vacant immediately before the commencement of the first meeting of the House of the People on ____, 2004 and the office of the Deputy Speaker is also vacant.

In exercise of the powers conferred upon me by clause (1) of article 95 of the Constitution of India, I hereby appoint Shri …………, a member of the House of the People, to perform the duties of the office of the Speaker from the commencement of the said meeting and until the Speaker shall have been chosen by the House.

PRESIDENT OF INDIA

DRAFT ORDER

Dated:

I hereby appoint S/Shri ________, ___________,________ and ______ to be the persons before any of whom Members of the House of the People may make and subscribe the oath or affirmation in accordance with the provisions of article 99 of the Constitution of India.

PRESIDENT OF INDIA

ANNEX II-D

MINISTRY OF LAW AND JUSTICE
(DEPARTMENT OF LEGAL AFFAIRS)

Article 95(1) of the Constitution provides that while the office of Speaker is vacant, the duties of his office shall be performed by the Deputy Speaker or if the office of Deputy Speaker is also vacant, by such Member of the House of the People as the President may appoint for the purpose. Article 93 provides that the House of the People shall, as soon as may be, choose two Members of the House respectively Speaker and Deputy Speaker.

Unless all the Members are administered oath/affirmation and article 93 is acted upon, during any vacancy in the office of the Speaker as well as Deputy Speaker, the person appointed by the President is to perform the duties of the office of the Speaker. The person appointed by the President acts a Speaker *pro tem* till the regular Speaker is elected. For the conduct of proceedings for the different periods of the session, there may not be any legal or constitutional bar to appoint separate Members of the House as Speaker *pro tem* if the situation so requires.

In this view, the proposal to obtain President's approval for appointment of Shri Somnath Chatterjee to perform the duties of Speaker on 2nd and 3rd June, 2004 and of Shri Balasaheb Vikhe Patil on 4th June, 2004, when the motion for election of Sh. Somnath Chatterjee as Speaker is likely to be taken up, appears to be constitutionally and procedurally in order.

May kindly see

Sd/-
(A.P. AGRAWAL)
JS and LA
27.5.2004

Sd/-
(Law Secretary)

ANNEX II-E

Dated:

DRAFT ORDER

Whereas the office of the Speaker will become vacant immediately before the commencement of the first meeting of the House of the People on ____, 2004 and the office of the Deputy Speaker is also vacant;

And whereas appointment of Shri Somnath Chatterjee as Speaker *pro tem* is only upto the commencement of the sitting of the House of the People on the 4th of June, 2004;

Now, therefore, in exercise of the powers conferred upon me by clause (1) of article 95 of the Constitution of India, I hereby appoint Shri Balasaheb Vikhe Patil, a Member of the House of the People, to perform the duties of the office of the Speaker from the commencement of the sitting of the House of the People on the 4th of June, 2004 till the election of the Speaker by the said House.

PRESIDENT OF INDIA

ANNEX II-F(I)

D.O. No. F 77(1)/99-Leg.I

Dated:

Will you kindly recall my telephonic request which you had kindly accepted regarding your appointment as Speaker *pro tem* ? Accordingly, on the recommendation of the Government, you have been appointed as Speaker *pro tem* by the President and you will be administered the oath by the President at 9.30 a.m. on ___, the
(day)

____, 2004 at Rashtrapati Bhavan.
(date)

With kind regards,

Yours sincerely,

(Minister of Parliamentary Affairs)

Shri
Member of Parliament
(Lok Sabha)
New Delhi.

ANNEX II-F(II)

D.O. No. F 77(1)/99-Leg.I

Dated:

I am glad to inform you that the President has appointed you as one of the persons to assist Shri ___, Speaker *pro tem* until the new Speaker is elected.

With kind regards,

Yours sincerely,

(Minister of Parliamentary Affairs)

Shri
Member of Parliament
(Lok Sabha)
New Delhi.

ANNEX II-G

MINISTRY OF PARLIAMENTARY AFFAIRS
(LEGISLATIVE-I SECTION)

Subject: Appointment of Speaker *pro tem* and persons before any one of whom Oath or Affirmation can be made.

The President has appointed:-

(a) Shri ____________, a Member of the Lok Sabha, as Speaker *pro tem* to perform the duties of the office of the Speaker until a new Speaker is elected; and

(b) S/Shri ________, _______ and ______, Members of the Lok Sabha, as persons before any of whom the new Members may make and subscribe oath or affirmation.

Original orders signed by the President are enclosed for necessary action. It is presumed that the Members concerned will be informed accordingly by the Lok Sabha Secretariat.

The President will administer oath/affirmation to Shri ______ at _______ on _________. It is requested that Shri _______ may be informed accordingly and necessary arrangements may also kindly be made for the oath taking.

The appointment of Shri __________ as Speaker *pro tem* may be notified in the gazette.

( )
UNDER SECRETARY
Tel.No.

Lok Sabha Secretariat (Table Office)
MPA U.O.No.F.......... dated :

ANNEX II-H

MINUTE TO MINUTE PROGRAMME FOR SWEARING-IN OF SPEAKER *PRO TEM*

0840 hrs.	Secretary, Ministry of Parliamentary Affairs reports to HMPA
0845 hrs.	HMPA proceeds to the House of Shri Somnath Chatterjee (21, Ashoka Road, next to Kerala House, New Delhi - 110001) JS, Ministry of Parliamentary Affairs reaches the residence of Shri Somnath Chatterjee with two bouquets.
0900 hrs.	HMPA reaches the residence of Shri Somnath Chatterjee. HMPA and Secretary, MPA, present bouquets to Shri Somnath Chatterjee
0910 hrs 0920 hrs	HMPA escorts Shri Somnath Chatterjee to Rashtrapati Bhawan Arrival of HMPA and Shri Somnath Chatterjee at Rashtrapati Bhawan
0930 hrs.	Swearing-in Ceremony of the Speaker *pro tem* in Yellow Drawing Room, Rashtrapati Bhawan
1000 hrs	Speaker *pro tem* is escorted by Secretary General, Lok Sabha to Parliament House
1010 hrs	Speaker *pro tem* is presented a bouquet by HMPA at Gate No.3, Parliament House.

ANNEX II-I

MOST IMMIDIATE

MINISTRY OF PARLIAMENTARY AFFAIRS

No.F. 57(2)/2004-Leg.I

Dated:

Subject: Summoning of the First Session of the __________ Lok Sabha and the 201st Session of the Rajya Sabha - Approval of the President.

The Cabinet in its meeting held on ____ 2004 have decided that First Session of the Fourteenth Lok Sabha may be summoned to meet on ___, the ___, 2004 and ___ Session of the Rajya Sabha may be summoned to meet on ___, the ____, 2004 and subject to exigencies of Government Business, both the Houses may conclude their sessions on ___, the ____, 2004 .

It has further been decided to recommend to the President to address both Houses of Parliament assembled together in the Central Hall of Parliament at 11.00 a.m. on _____, the _____, 2004 and inform Parliament of the causes of its summons under article 87(1) of the Constitution. The communication received from the Cabinet Secretariat in this regard is enclosed along with relevant Note for Cabinet.

The President may kindly approve the date of commencement of the First Session of the Fourteenth Lok Sabha and the 201st session of the Rajya Sabha and the date and time of delivery of the President's Address. After the President's approval, the Lok Sabha and the Rajya Sabha Secretariats will be informed for taking further action in the matter.

( )

MINISTER OF PARLIAMENTARY AFFAIRS

THE PRESIDENT

ANNEX II-J

D.O.No. 6(*)/98-Leg.I

March ,1998

I am directed to say that it has been decided to take up the Motion of Confidence in the Council of Ministers in the Lok Sabha on_____, 1998. A draft motion is attached. I am to request that the Prime Minister be moved to approve it. Immediately thereafter it may kindly be sent to the Lok Sabha Secretariat for further necessary action.

Yours sincerely,

( )
Minister of Parliamentary Affairs

Shri
Principal Secretary to the Prime Minister,
Prime Minister's Office,
New Delhi.

ANNEX II-K

To

The Secretary-General,
Lok Sabha,
New Delhi.

Sir,

I hereby give notice of my intention to move the following Motion in the current Session of Lok Sabha:

"That this House expresses its Confidence in the Council of Ministers".

Yours faithfully,

( )
PRIME MINISTER

Copy to:

1. Minister of Parliamentary Affairs
2. Secretary, Ministry of Parliamentary Affairs

ANNEX II-L

D.O.No.F. 3(1)/2004-Leg.I

Dated :

Dear Mr. Speaker,

The Prime Minister has directed me to inform you that he has nominated Shri _________, Minister of _______________ as the Leader of the House.

With kind regards,

Yours sincerely,

(   )
MINISTER OF PARLIAMENTARY AFFAIRS

Shri
Speaker,
Lok Sabha,
New Delhi.

ANNEX II-M

D.O.No.F. 77(1)/2004-Leg.I

Dated :

Dear Mr. Chairman,

The Prime Minister has directed me to inform you that he has nominated Shri _________, Minister of _______________ as the Leader of the House.

With kind regards,

Yours sincerely,

( )

MINISTER OF PARLIAMENTARY AFFAIRS

Shri
Chairman,
Rajya Sabha,
New Delhi.

ANNEX II-N

Dated:

To

The Secretary-General,
Lok Sabha,
New Delhi.

Sir,

I give notice of my intention to move the following Motion during the current Session of Lok Sabha, namely:

"That the Members of the Lok Sabha assembled in this session are deeply grateful to the President for the Address which he has been pleased to deliver to both Houses of Parliament assembled together on __________."

Yours faithfully,

(__________)
M.P. (Lok Sabha)

I second the Motion

(__________)
M.P. (Lok Sabha)

ANNEX II-O

Dated:

To

The Secretary-General,
Rajya Sabha,
New Delhi.

Sir,

I give notice of my intention to move the following Motion during the current Session of Rajya Sabha, namely:

"That the Members of the Rajya Sabha assembled in this session are deeply grateful to the President for the Address which he has been pleased to deliver to both Houses of Parliament assembled together on __________."

Yours faithfully,

(___________)
M.P. (Rajya Sabha)

I second the Motion

(___________)
M.P. (Rajya Sabha)

ANNEX II-P

LOK SABHA
MOTION FOR ELECTION OF SPEAKER

Place:
Date:

To

The Secretary-General,
Lok Sabha,
New Delhi.

Sir,

Under Rule 7 of the Rules of Procedure and Conduct of Business in the Lok Sabha, I give notice of the following motion which I propose to move in the House on the ....

"That Shri____________________________ a member of this House, be chosen as the Speaker of this House."

Yours faithfully,

Signature......................
Name.........................
(in block letters) M.P.

I second the above Motion.

Signature......................
Name.........................
(in block letters) M.P.

I am willing to serve as Speaker, if elected.

Signature......................
Name.........................
(in block letters) M.P.

ANNEX II-Q

To be published in the Gazette of India, Extraordinary, Part I, Section I, Dated the __________.

GOVERNMENT OF INDIA
MINISTRY OF PARLIAMENTARY AFFAIRS

No.F.____________ New Delhi, the ________

NOTIFICATION

In pursuance of the powers conferred by Section 9 of the Salary and Allowances of Leaders of Opposition in Parliament Act, 1977 (No. 33 of 1977), the Central Government hereby notify that consequent on the dissolution of the House of the People on ___________, Shri/Smt. __________has ceased to be the Leader of Opposition in the House of the People with effect from that date.

( )
SECRETARY

To,

The Manager,
Government of India Press,
Mayapuri, Ring Road,
New Delhi.

ANNEX II-R

To be published in the Gazette of India, Extraordinary, Part I, Section I, Dated the ___________.

GOVERNMENT OF INDIA
MINISTRY OF PARLIAMENTARY AFFAIRS

New Delhi, the __________

NOTIFICATION

No.F. _______________ - WHEREAS, in pursuance of the provisions of Section 2 of the Salary and Allowances of Leaders of Opposition in Parliament Act, 1977 (No. 33 of 1977), the Speaker of the House of the People has recognized Shri/Smt. ___________as the Leader of the Opposition in the House of the People with effect from_____________.

NOW, THEREFORE, in exercise of the powers conferred by Section 9 of the said Act, the Central Government hereby notify Shri/Smt.__________ as the Leader of the Opposition in the House of the People with effect from __________for the purposes of the said Act.

( )
SECRETARY

To,

The Manager,
Government of India Press,
Mayapuri, Ring Road,
New Delhi.

ANNEX II-S

To be published in the Gazette of India, Extraordinary, Part I, Section I, Dated the __________.

GOVERNMENT OF INDIA
MINISTRY OF PARLIAMENTARY AFFAIRS

New Delhi, the ________

NOTIFICATION

No.F. ____________ - WHEREAS, in pursuance of the provisions of Section 2 of the Salary and Allowances of Leaders of Opposition in Parliament Act, 1977 (No. 33 of 1977), the Chairman of the Council of States has accorded recognition to Shri/Smt. ___________, as the Leader of Opposition in the Council of States with effect from ____________.

NOW, THEREFORE, in exercise of the powers conferred by Section 9 of the said Act, the Central Government hereby notify Shri/Smt.__________ as the Leader of the Opposition in the Council of States with effect from ___________ for the purpose of the said Act.

( )
SECRETARY

To,

The Manager,
Government of India Press,
Mayapuri, Ring Road,
New Delhi.

ANNEX II-T

To be published in the Gazette of India, Extraordinary, Part I, Section I, Dated the __________.

GOVERNMENT OF INDIA
MINISTRY OF PARLIAMENTARY AFFAIRS

New Delhi, the __________

NOTIFICATION

No.F. ______________ - In pursuance of the powers conferred by Section 9 of the Salary and Allowances of Leaders of Opposition in Parliament Act, 1977 (No. 33 of 1977), the Central Government hereby notify that consequent on his appointment as Prime Minister of India on____________, Shri/Smt.____________ has ceased to be the Leader of Opposition in the Council of States with effect from that date.

( )
SECRETARY

To,

The Manager,
Government of India Press,
Mayapuri, Ring Road,
New Delhi.

ANNEX II-U

F.No.55(2)/2004-Leg.I
Government of India
Ministry of Parliamentary Affairs

90, Parliament House,
New Delhi

Dated:

OFFICE MEMORANDUM

Subject: Allotment of Room in Parliament House to the Leader of the Opposition in Rajya Sabha.

The undersigned is directed to state that Room No. 43 in Parliament House has been allotted to Shri ____________, the Leader of the Opposition in the Rajya Sabha.

Private Secretary to the Leader of the Opposition is requested kindly to inspect the room and arrange furniture, telephone, draperies etc. with the assistance of the Caretaker, Parliament House and the Engineering Supervisor (Telephone), Parliament House. The Caretaker, Parliament House, is not responsible for the loss of articles. Personal staff of the Leader of the Opposition may therefore ensure that nothing is left unlocked in the room or the varandah adjacent thereto. Similarly telephone, when it is not in use, may be removed from varandah and kept inside the room properly secured with lock and key, so as to prevent unauthorised calls being made.

In case any additions/alterations are desired to be made in the room, P.S. to the Leader of the Opposition is requested kindly to take up the matter with the Deputy Secretary (Admn.), Ministry of Parliamentary Affairs for further necessary action.

The Caretaker, Parliament House, the Engineering Supervisor (Telephone) are being advised to arrange for furnishing of the room and installation of Telephone etc. in consultation with Private Secretary of the Leader of the Opposition.

( )
Under Secretary to the Govt. of India
Tel. No. 3034728

P.S. to the Leader of the Opposition in Rajya Sabha.

Copy forwarded for necessary action to:-

1. The Caretaker, Parliament House for furnishing the room in consultation with the Private Secretary to the Leader of the Opposition in Rajya Sabha.
2. Engineering Supervisor (Telephone), Parliament House, for installation of telephone in room of the Leader of the Opposition in Rajya Sabha in consultation with the Private Secretary to the Leader of the Opposition.
3. Lok Sabha Secretariat.
4. Rajya Sabha Secretariat.
5. Joint Secretary, Rajya Sabha Secretariat.
6. Assistant Director (WG), Lok Sabha Secretariat.
7. The President's Secretariat
8. The Prime Minister's Office.
9. The Cabinet Secretariat
10. Executive Engineer, P.W.D.II, C.P.W.D., New Delhi.
11. The Assistant Engineer I and III, Parliament Works Division No. II, Parliament House, New Delhi.
12. The Reception Officer, Parliament House, Lok Sabha and Rajya Sabha Secretariats.
13. The Chief Watch and Ward Officer, Lok Sabha Secretariat.
14. P.S. to Minister
15. P.S. to MOS (SP)
16. PS to MOS (SK)
17. PS to MOS (BK)
18. PPS to Secretary
19. PS/PA to JS/DS(L)/DS(A)/DS(RandC)/US(L)/US(A)/US(RandC)
20. SO(A)/SO(RandC)/SO(WS)

( )
Under Secretary to the Govt. of India
Tel. No. 3034728

ANNEX III-A

STATEMENT SHOWING THE INTERVAL OF LESS THAN 21 DAYS BETWEEN THE ISSUE OF SUMMONS TO MEMBERS OF LOK SABHA AND DATES OF COMMENCEMENT OF SESSIONS SINCE 1990

Session	Date on which Summons issued	Date of Commencement of Session	Interval (In days)
Ninth Lok Sabha			
Fourth	October 25,1990	November 7,1990	12 days
Fifth	November 10,1990	November 16,1990	05 days
Seventh	January 31,1991	February 21, 1991	20 days
Tenth Lok Sabha			
First	June 29, 1991	July 9, 1991	09 days
Second	November 4, 1991	November 20, 1991	15 days
Fourth	June 18,1992	July 8, 1992	19 days
Sixth	February 3, 1993	February 22, 1993	18 days
Seventh	July 9, 1993	July 26, 1993	16 days
Eighth	November 12, 1993	December 2, 1993	19 days
Ninth	February 3, 1994	February 21, 1994	17 days
Tenth	May 26, 1994	June 13, 1994	17 days
Eleventh	July 8,1994	July 25, 1994	16 days
Twelfth	November 18, 1994	December 7, 1994	18 days
Thirteenth	February 1, 1995	February 13, 1995	11 days
Fifteenth	November 14, 1995	November 27, 1995	12 days
Sixteenth	February 6, 1996	February 26, 1996	19 days
Eleventh Lok Sabha			
*First (Pt.I)	May 18,1996	May 22, 1996	03 days
(Pt.II)	June 4, 1996 (Reconvened)	June 10, 1996	05 days
Second	June 25, 1996	July 10, 1996	14 days
Third	November 2,1996	November 20, 1996	17 days

Fourth	February 3, 1997	February 20, 1997	16 days
Sixth (Pt.II)	November 28, 1997	December 2, 1997	03 days

Twelfth Lok Sabha

*First	March 21,1998	March 23, 1998	01 day

Thirteenth Lok Sabha

*First	October 16,1999	October 20,1999	03 days
Third	February 2, 2000	February 23, 2000	20 days
Fifth	November 4,2000	November 20,2000	15 days
Sixth	January 31, 2001	February 19,2001	18 days
Eighth	October 30,2001	November 19,2001	19 days
Tenth	June 28,2002	July 15,2002	16 days
Eleventh	October 31,2002	November 18,2002	17 days
Twelfth	January 30,2003	February 17,2003	17 days
Thirteenth	July 1, 2003	July 21, 2003	19 days
Fourteenth	November 12,2003	December 2, 2003	19 days
(Pt.I)	January 20, 2004	January 29, 2004	08 days
(Pt.II)			

Fourteenth Lok Sabha

*First	May 28,2004	June 2, 2003	04 days
Second	June 18, 2004	July 5, 2004	16 days

* First Session of New Lok Sabha

ANNEX III-B

INFORMATION REGARDING JOINT SITTINGS OF TWO HOUSES HELD SO FAR

1. May 6, 1961 to discuss Dowry Prohibition Bill, 1959 following disagreement between the two Houses over certain amendments to the Bill (Joint sittings were held on May 6 and 9, 1961).
2. May 16, 1978 to discuss the Banking Service Commission (Repeal) Bill, 1977 passed by Lok Sabha and rejected by the Rajya Sabha; (one day only).
3. March 26, 2002 to deliberate and vote on the Prevention of Terrorism Bill, 2002 as passed by the Lok Sabha and rejected by the Rajya Sabha;(one day only).

ANNEX III-C

MOST IMMEDIATE

MINISTRY OF PARLIAMENTARY AFFAIRS

No.F. 57(*)/2004-Leg.I

Dated:

Subject: Summoning of the ______ Session, 2004 of Parliament - Approval of the President.

The Cabinet in its meeting held on ______, 2004 have decided that both Houses of Parliament may be summoned to meet for the _________ Session, 2004 on ___________ and, subject to exigencies of Government Business, both the Houses may conclude their sessions on _________.

It has been proposed that during this period, both Houses may go into recess from _________ to _____________to enable the Departmentally related Parliamentary Standing Committees to consider the 'Demands for Grants' of Ministries/ Departments and prepare their reports. The communication received from the Cabinet Secretariat in this regard is enclosed along with relevant Note for Cabinet.

The President may kindly approve the date of the commencement of the ______ Session, 2004 of Parliament. After the President's approval, the Lok Sabha and the Rajya Sabha Secretariats will be informed for taking further action in the matter.

( )
MINISTER OF PARLIAMENTARY AFFAIRS

PRESIDENT OF INDIA

ANNEX III-D

MINISTRY OF PARLIAMENTARY AFFAIRS

No.F. 57(*)/2004-Leg.I Dated:

To

The Secretary-General,
Lok Sabha,
New Delhi.

Subject: Commencement and duration of ______Session of the ______ Lok Sabha.

Sir,

I am directed to inform you that the Government have decided that the ______Session of the ______ Lok Sabha be summoned to meet on ______and subject to exigencies of Government Business, the session may conclude on ______. During this period, the Hon'ble Speaker may be moved to kindly adjourn the Lok Sabha on ______to meet again on ______to enable Departmentally related Parliamentary Standing Committees to consider the 'Demands for Grants' of Ministries/Departments and prepare their reports.

The date of the commencement of the session was conveyed to the President by the Minister of Parliamentary Affairs and the President has approved it.

Yours faithfully,

( )
Secretary

Copy for information to:

1. Cabinet Secretary
2. Secretary to the President

( )
Secretary

ANNEX III-E

MINISTRY OF PARLIAMENTARY AFFAIRS

No.F. 57(*)/2004-Leg.I Dated:

To

The Secretary-General,
Rajya Sabha,
New Delhi.

Subject: Commencement and duration of the ____Session of the Rajya Sabha

Sir,

I am directed to inform you that the Government have decided that the___Session of the Rajya Sabha be summoned to meet on _______ and subject to exigencies of Government Business, the session may conclude on _________. During this period, the Hon'ble Chairman may be moved to kindly adjourn the Rajya Sabha on __________ to meet again on _________ to enable Department-related Parliamentary Standing Committees to consider the 'Demands for Grants' of Ministries/Departments and prepare their reports.

The date of the commencement of the session was conveyed to the President by the Minister of Parliamentary Affairs and the President has approved it.

Yours faithfully,

( )
Secretary

Copy for information to:

1. Cabinet Secretary
2. Secretary to the President

( )
(Secretary)

ANNEX III-F

MINISTRY OF PARLIAMENTARY AFFAIRS

No. F. 57(*)/200 -leg.I   Dated:

Subject: Summoning of Parliament for a Joint Sitting to consider the Prevention of Terrorism Bill, 2002.

The Prevention of Terrorism Ordinance, 2001 (No.12 fo 2001), was promulgated by the President on ______. The Prevention of Terrorism Bill, 2002, which was intended to replace the said Ordinance, was introduced in the Lok Sabha on ______. The Lok Sabha passed the Bill on the ______. The Rajya Sabha at its sitting held on the _______ adopted a Statutory Resolution disapproving the Ordinance and rejected a motion for consideration of the Bill as passed by the Lok Sabha. As a result, under Rule 134 (ii) of the Rules of Procedure and Conduct of Business in the Rajya Sabha, the Bill shall be deemed to have been rejected by the Rajya Sabha.

Clause (1) of article 108 of the Constitution, *inter alia* provides that if, after a Bill has been passed by one House and transmitted to the other House, the Bill is rejected by the other House, then, the President may notify to the Houses by message his intention to summon them to meet in a Joint Sitting for the purposes of deliberating and voting on the Bill.

It has become necessary that the two Houses may deliberate and vote on the Bill in a Joint Sitting in terms of article 108 of the Constitution. As the two Houses are in session, the President is requested kindly to notify to the two Houses by message his intention to summon them to meet in a Joint Sitting for the purposes of deliberating and voting on the Bill.

The Prime Minister has agreed that the two Houses may have a Joint Sitting on ______.

A draft message is submitted to the President for his approval and signature.

(__________)
MINISTER OF PARLIAMENTARY AFFAIRS

PRESIDENT OF INDIA

ANNEX III-G

MINISTRY OF PARLIAMENTARY AFFAIRS

D.O.NO.F. 57( )/200 -Leg.I Dated:

I am enclosing herewith a message from the President under article 108 of the Constitution notifying his intention to summon the Rajya Sabha and the Lok Sabha to meet in a Joint Sitting for the purposes of deliberating and voting on the Prevention of Terrorism Bill, 2002

The Prime Minister has agreed that the Joint Sitting may be held on ____ at 11.00 a.m.

I hope your Secretariat would take the necessary steps after you have read out the Message to the Lok Sabha for summoning the Members of both the Houses in accordance with the Rules of Procedure and Conduct of Business.

Yours sincerely,

( )

MINISTER OF PARLIAMENTARY AFFAIRS

Shri
Speaker, Lok Sabha,
New Delhi.

Dated:

MESSAGE

WHEREAS at its sitting on the ____, the Lok Sabha passed the Prevention of Terrorism Bill, 2002, and transmitted the same to the Rajya Sabha.

AND WHEREAS the Rajya Sabha at its sitting on the _____, rejected the said Bill.

NOW, THEREFORE, in exercise of the powers conferred by clause(1) of article 108 of the Constitution, I, _________, President of India, hereby notify my intention to summon the Rajya Sabha and Lok Sabha to meet in a joint sitting for the purposes of deliberating and voting on the said Bill.

PRESIDENT OF INDIA

The Speaker, Lok Sabha.

ANNEX III- H

MINISTRY OF PARLIAMENTARY AFFAIRS

D.O.NO.F.57( )/200 -Leg.I

Dated:

I am enclosing herewith a message from the President for the Rajya Sabha under article 108 of the Constitution notifying his intention to summon the Rajya Sabha and the Lok Sabha to meet in a Joint Sitting for the purposes of deliberating and voting on the Prevention of Terrorism Bill, 2002

The Prime Minister has agreed that the Joint Sitting may be held on ____ at 11.00 a.m.

Yours sincerely,

( )

MINISTER OF PARLIAMENTARY AFFAIRS

Shri

Chairman, Rajya Sabha,

New Delhi.

Dated:

MESSAGE

WHEREAS at its sitting on the ____ , the Lok Sabha passed the Prevention of Terrorism Bill, 2002, and transmitted the same to the Rajya Sabha.

AND WHEREAS the Rajya Sabha at its sitting on the _____, rejected the said Bill.

NOW, THEREFORE, in exercise of the powers conferred by clause(1) of article 108 of the Constitution, I, _________, President of India, hereby notify my intention to summon the Rajya Sabha and Lok Sabha to meet in a joint sitting for the purposes of deliberating and voting on the said Bill.

PRESIDENT OF INDIA

The Chairman, Rajya Sabha.

MINISTRY OF PARLIAMENTARY AFFAIRS
(LEGISLATIVE - I SECTION)

F.No. 57(*)/98-Leg.I   Dated :

Subject: Prorogation of both Houses of Parliament

Lok Sabha and Rajya Sabha are scheduled to adjourn *sine die* on ______.

It is proposed that both the Houses of Parliament may be prorogued after adjournment *sine die* on ______.

(   )
SECRETARY

MINISTER OF PARLIAMENTARY AFFAIRS

HONOURABLE PRIME MINISTER

ANNEX III-J

No.F. 57(*)/200 -Leg.I
Government of India
Ministry of Parliamentary Affairs

8, Parliament House,
New Delhi.

Dated:

To

The Secretary-General,
Lok Sabha,
New Delhi.

Subject: Prorogation of Lok Sabha

Sir,

I am directed to inform you that Government have decided that the Lok Sabha which adjourned *sine die* on ______, be prorogued.

Yours faithfully,

( )
SECRETARY

ANNEX III-K

No.F.57(*)/200 -Leg.I

GOVERNMENT OF INDIA
MINISTRY OF PARLIAMENTARY AFFAIRS

8, Parliament House,
New Delhi.

Dated:

To

The Secretary General,
Rajya Sabha,
New Delhi

Subject: Prorogation of Rajya Sabha.

Sir,

I am directed to inform you that Government have decided that the Rajya Sabha which adjourned *sine die* on ______, be prorogued.

Yours faithfully,

( )
SECRETARY

ANNEX III-L

MINISTRY OF PARLIAMENTARY AFFAIRS

To

Secretary to President of India
Rashtrapati Bhawan,
New Delhi.

F.17(1)/2003-Leg.I

5 February, 2004

Subject: Dissolution of the Thirteenth Lok Sabha

Sir,

This is to inform you that the Fourteenth Session of the Lok Sabha and 200th session of the Rajya Sabha have been adjourned today *sine die* after completing the essential Financial Business, including the Vote on Account (Railways and General) 2004-05 and the Finance Bill, 2004.

Yours faithfully,

Sd/-
(V.K. Agnihotri)

ANNEX III-M

CHECK LIST

1. It may be ensured that period between last sitting of the Houses in one session and the date appointed for its/ their first sitting in the next session shall not in any case exceed six months.
2. Note for the Cabinet regarding summoning of next session of Parliament should be submitted sufficiently in advance so that summons for the Parliament Session could as far as possible be issued at least 21 days in advance of the date of commencement of the session in order to provide 21 clear days for tabling the questions by the Members of the Lok Sabha.
3. In case of First Session after general election and First Session of the year, approval of the Cabinet is also obtained to the time, date of the President's address to the two Houses of Parliament assembled together.
4. In case of urgency, Cabinet Secretariat may be requested to furnish an authority regarding approval of the Ministry's proposal regarding summoning of the session by the Cabinet, so that further action, viz., obtaining the approval of the President to the proposal can be taken in time.
5. Approval of the Prime Minister to the proposal regarding prorogation of the Houses could be obtained whenever the Cabinet Committee on Parliamentary Affairs has not been constituted.
6. The approval of the Prime Minister has to be obtained to the proposal to convene the Joint Sitting of the two Houses of Parliament in terms of article 108 of the Constitution whenever any request in this regard is received from any Ministry.
7. First Session of the new Lok Sabha and the corresponding session of the Rajya Sabha may not be convened on the same day.

8. When Cabinet's recommendation regarding dissolution of the Lok Sabha is sent to the President for his orders, the Secretary, Ministry of Parliamentary Affairs, may inform the Secretary to the President that the essential financial and legislative business has been transacted by both the Houses.

ANNEX IV-A

D.O.No.F.66(1)/2004-Leg.I Dated:

The............ Session, 200- of Parliament is likely to commence during the middle of .... It is necessary to keep various items of Government Business ready for presentation in the said session.

I shall be grateful if information about the Bills as also other items of Government Business which your Ministry/Department proposes to bring in Parliament during the forthcoming session is forwarded to us in the enclosed proforma, latest by -----------, so as to enable us to prepare a tentative programme for the session in time. While forwarding the proposals, it may kindly be ensured that the titles of Bills are given in both English and Hindi without abbreviations of words and the purport of Bills is indicated in the proforma, in a self- explanatory manner. A list indicating the titles of the Bills pending in Parliament is enclosed.

I also request you to furnish information/comments on the following issues:

(i) whether you have any policy paper or discussion which could be scheduled in the Rajya Sabha in the beginning of the Budget Session;
(ii) introduction of new Bills in the Rajya Sabha;
(iii) scheduling of Bills pending in the Lok Sabha and the Rajya Sabha as reported by the Standing Committees; and
(iv) action being taken with regard to Bills pending with the Standing Committees and the likelihood of their being ready for discussion/passage.

Requisite details in this regard may be incorporated in the remarks column of the proforma.

Yours sincerely,

( )
Secretary

All Secretaries of the Ministries/Departments

ANNEX IV-B

BUSINESS FOR THE .... SESSION,.....(YEAR) OF PARLIAMENT
MINISTRY/DEPARTMENT OF ....
PART-I LEGISLATIVE BUSINESS

Sl. No.	Title of the Bill (English and Hindi versions)	Purport in brief (To be self-explanatory	Present State of preparedness			Probable date by which the Bill is likely to be introduced	Whether the Bill is required to be passed during the Session	Names and Telephone Numbers of the officers concerned with the Bill	Remarks
			Draft Cabinet Note ready	Concurrence/ views of concerned Ministries obtained	Cabinet approval obtained				
1	2	3	4	5	6	7	8	9	10

N.B. Bills, both pending (excluding those which are not proposed to be proceeded with during the Session) and proposed, may be arranged in the order in which they are proposed to be taken up in Parliament.

PART-II NON-LEGISLATIVE BUSINESS

MATTERS OF PUBLIC IMPORTANCE OR REPORTS REQUIRED TO BE DISCUSSED IN PARLIAMENT

Sl. No.	Subject	Whether the relevant document/ Report has been made available to Members; if so, when?	If the relevant document/ Report has not been presented, when it is likely to be ready	Remarks
1	2	3	4	5

N.B. If there is a time bound item, it may be so stated.

ANNEX IV-C

MINISTRY OF PARLIAMENTARY AFFAIRS

Legislative and other proposals for the ____ Session of _______ Lok Sabha and _____ Session of Rajya Sabha

Sl.No.	Title	Purport	Cabinet Note ready or not	Cabinet approval obtained	Bill ready	Priority
	Ministry or Department of					
	Legislative Business					
1.						
2.						
3.						
	Non-Legislative Business					
1.						
2.						

ANNEX IV-D

D.O. No.F. 66(1)/2003-Leg.I

Dated:

I am sending herewith a list of Bills proposed by various Ministries/Departments for the ensuing session of Parliament commencing from...................... .

As in the past, the list may be scrutinised and this Ministry informed of the position in regard to Bills which might be ready for introduction by (a) the first week of the session, (b) the middle of the session, and (c) by the close of the session. So far as the introduction of the Bills in replacement of Ordinances is concerned, I shall be grateful if you could ensure their introduction positively on the opening day of the session.

I shall be grateful for an immediate reply.

Yours sincerely,

(   )
Secretary

Shri
Secretary,
Ministry of Law and Justice,
Legislative Department,
Shastri Bhavan,
New Delhi.

ANNEX IV-E

D.O. No.F. 66(6)/2003-Leg.I Dated:

A meeting of the Secretaries to the Government of India in various Ministries/Departments will be held at .... a.m. on Monday, the .... in Room No. ...., Parliament House, New Delhi to consider the items of Government Business proposed by the Ministries/Departments for the ensuing ...... Session, 200 of Parliament. List of items(s) concerning your Ministry/Department, which will be considered in the meeting is enclosed.

Smt/Shri.........., Minister of Parliamentary Affairs, will chair the meeting

I shall be grateful if you could kindly make it convenient to come personally.

Yours sincerely,

( )
Secretary

To all concerned Secretaries (by name)

ANNEX IV-F

MINISTRY OF PARLIAMENTARY AFFAIRS

Tentative List of Government Legislative and Other Business expected to be taken up during the .... Session of ....Sabha

I - LEGISLATIVE BUSINESS

Bills Pending in Rajya Sabha

S.No.	Name of the Bill	Status/Purport	Motion proposed to be moved during the Session

Bills Originating in Lok Sabha and Pending Before Standing Committees

S.No.	Name of the Bill	Status/Purport	Motion proposed to be moved during the Session

Bills Originating in Rajya Sabha and Pending before Standing Committees

S.No.	Name of the Bill	Status/Purport	Motion proposed to be moved during the Session

New Bills

S.No.	Name of the Bill	Purport	Motion proposed to be moved during the Session

II - OTHER BUSINESS

Financial Business
Non-Financial Business

ANNEX IV-G

No.F._______
Government of India
Ministry of Parliamentary Affairs

8, Parliament House,
New Delhi

Dated:

To

The Secretary General,
Lok Sabha,
New Delhi.

Sir,

With the permission of the Hon'ble Speaker, the Minister of Parliamentary Affairs proposes to make a statement about Government Business in the Lok Sabha during the week commencing _______.

150 copies of the statement (English and Hindi versions) are enclosed.

Yours faithfully,

( )
SECRETARY

Copy to:

1. PS to Minister of Parliamentary Affairs
2. PS to MOS(SP)
3. PS to MOS(BK)
4. PS to MOS(SK)
5. PPS to Secretary
6. PA to DS(L)/US(L)

( )
UNDER SECRETARY

ANNEX IV-H

No.F.______________
Government of India
Ministry of Parliamentary Affairs

8, Parliament House,
New Delhi

Dated:

To

The Secretary General,
Rajya Sabha,
New Delhi.

Sir,

With the permission of the Hon'ble Chairman, the Minister of State in the Ministry of Parliamentary Affairs proposes to make a statement about Government Business in the Rajya Sabha during the week commencing __________.

15 copies of the statement (English and Hindi versions) are enclosed.

Yours faithfully,

( )
SECRETARY

Copy to:-

1. PS to Minister of Parliamentary Affairs
2. PS to MOS(SP)
3. PS to MOS(BK)
4. PS to MOS(SK)
5. PPS to Secretary
6. PA to DS(L)/US(L)

( )
UNDER SECRETARY

ANNEX IV-I

TIME TABLE OF GOVERNMENT BUSINESS IN LOK SABHA: BUDGET SESSION (PART-I)

Date: 16 July 2004

Date	Subject	Nature of Business	Duration Hrs-Mts	Cumulative Total Hrs-Mts
1	2	3	4	5
14.07.04 (Wednesday)	General Budget	General Discussion (Time Allotted: 12 hrs)	2-33	2-33
15.07.04 (Thursday)	(i)General Budget ; (ii) Vote on A/c	(i), (ii) General Discussion (Time Allotted :12 hrs.)	—	2.33
16.7.04 (Friday)	(i) Statements by Home Minister on : (a) Flood Situation in Bihar and Assam; and (b) Rape of three Dalit women in Madhya Pradesh. (ii) Statement by Minister of Parliamentary Affairs regarding Government Business. (iii) General Budget; (iv) Vote on A/c (v) Pvt. Members' Business	(i) Statement after laying of papers (ii) Statement (iii) General Discussion (iv) Discussion on Resolutions	10 mts 10 mts 15 mts 1½ 2½	4-03

Contd. ....

Date	**Subject**	**Nature of Business**	**Duration** **Hrs-Mts**	**Cumulative Total Hrs-Mts**
1	2	3	4	5
19.07.04 (Monday)	(i) Farmers' Suicides	(i) Short Notice Question	1	—
	(ii) Financial package for Drought in Maharashtra	(ii) PM's Statement (Immediately) after Short Notice Question (Subject to PM's convenience)	½	—
	(iii) General Budget, Vote on A/c and related Demands	(iii) General Discussion	3½	7-33
20.07.04 (Tuesday)	(i) General Budget, Vote on A/c and related Demands	(i) Further General Discussion and Reply by Minister (ii) Vote on Accounts Demands to be voted and passing of Appropriation Bills, etc.	4½ **House may sit upto 6.30.p.m.	12-03
21.07.04 (Wednesday)				
22.07.04 (Thursday)				
23.07.04 (Friday)	PRIVATE MEMBERS' BUSINESS	BILLS	2½	—

HMPA
MOS (SP)/MOS(SK)/MOS(BK)

(V.K.Agnihotri)
Secretary

ANNEX IV-J

TIME TABLE OF GOVERNMENT BUSINESS IN RAJYA SABHA: BUDGET SESSION (PART-I)

Date: 16 July 2004

Date	Subject	Nature of Business	Duration Hrs-Mts	Cumulative Total Hrs-Mts
1	2	3	4	5
16.07.04 (Friday)	(i) Resolution regarding nomination of Members in Railway Convention Committee	(i) Resolution	½	—
	(ii) Statement by MOS (SP) regarding Government Business (after laying of pagers	(i) Statement	10 mts	—
	(iii) Statement by Home Minister regarding criminal case against Shri Shibu Soren (at 2 p.m.)	(iii) Statement	1	—
	(iv) PRIVATE MEMBERS' BUSINESS	(RESOLUTIONS)		

Date	Subject	Nature of Business	Duration Hrs-Mts	Cumulative Total Hrs-Mts
1	2	3	4	5
19.07.04 (Monday)	(1) Financial package for Drought in Maharashtra	(i) PM's Statement (2.00 p.m. Subject to PM's convenience)	1	—
	(ii) General Budget	(ii) General Discussion	2	2
	(iii) Flood situation in Bihar and Assam	(iii) Statement **(To Be Decided)**	1**	—
20.07.04 (Tuesday)	General Budget	General Discussion	4**	6
21.07.04 (Wednesday)	General Budget	General Discussion	4**	10
22.07.04 (Thursday)	(i) General Budget	(i) General Discussion	1	11
		Reply by Minister	1	12
		Return of Appropriation Bills, etc. (without discussion)	1	13
	(ii) Railway Budget	(ii) Return of Railway Appropriation Bill; (without discussion)	1**	—
23.07.04	PRIVATE MEMBERS BUSINESS	BILLS		

** House may sit upto 6 p.m. subject to recommendation of BAC

HMPA (V.K.Agnihotri)
MOS (SP)/MOS(SK)/MOS(BK) Secretary

ANNEX IV-K

MINISTRY OF PARLIAMENTARY AFFAIRS

D.O. No.F. 78(*)/2003-Leg.I Dated:

As you are aware, the Delimitation (Amendment) Ordinance, 2003 (Ordinance No.6 of 2003) relating to your Ministry was promulgated by the President on ______________.

I shall be grateful if necessary procedural formalities for introduction of the Bill seeking to replace the above Ordinance are completed by your Ministry well in time so that the Bill could be introduced in the Lok Sabha/Rajya Sabha on the opening day of ensuing Winter Session.

I also request that after introduction of the Bill, notice of Motion for consideration and passing of the Bill may also be sent to the Secretary-General, Lok Sabha/Rajya Sabha under intimation to this Ministry to enable this Ministry to provide for its consideration at an early date.

It may not be out of place to point out here that according to article 123(2)(a) of the Constitution of India, the Ordinance shall cease to operate at the expiration of six weeks from the reassembly of Parliament, if the Bill seeking to replace the Ordinance is not passed by both Houses of Parliament and assented to by the President before expiry of the above period.

Yours sincerely,

( )
(SECRETARY)

Shri
Secretary,
Ministry of Law and Justice,
Legislative Department,
Shastri Bhawan,
New Delhi.

ANNEX IV-L

No.F.78(*)/2003-Leg.I
Government of India
Ministry of Parliamentary Affairs

90, Parliament House,
New Delhi.
Dated:

OFFICE MEMORANDUM

Subject: The National Tax Tribunal Ordinance, 2003 (Ordinance No. 3 of 2003)

The National Tax Tribunal Ordinance, 2003 (Ordinance No. 3 of 2003) was promulgated by the President on _____. As usual, this Ministry will make arrangements for its laying by the Minister of Parliamentary Affairs on the opening day of the ensuing session in pursuance of article 123(2)(a) of the Constitution.

The Ministry of Law and Justice, Department of Legal Affairs are requested to intimate to this Ministry whether it is proposed to get the above Ordinance replaced by an Act of Parliament. If so, the Bill in replacement of the Ordinance may kindly be got drafted well in time and notice for its introduction duly signed by the Minister may be sent to the Secretary-General of the House in which the Bill is sought to be introduced so that this may be introduced in the beginning of the ensuing session of Parliament. The Ministry may also take appropriate action as envisaged in Rule 71 (1)/ 66(1) of the Rules of Procedure and Conduct of Business in the Lok /Rajya Sabha which provides that whenever a Bill seeking to replace an Ordinance with or without modification is introduced in the House, there shall be placed before the House along with the Bill, a statement explaining the circumstances which had necessitated immediate legislation by Ordinance. The Ministry is also requested to supply the requisite number of copies of the statement to the Lok Sabha/Rajya Sabha Secretariat for circulation to Members of Parliament and five copies to this Ministry.

(_________)
UNDER SECRETARY TO THE GOVT. OF INDIA
Tel.No.

Ministry of Law and Justice,
(Department of Legal Affairs),
(Shri _______, Under Secretary)
A Wing, 4th Floor, Shastri Bhawan,
New Delhi.

Copy to Official Language Wing, Legislative Department (Shri _________, Superintendent), Bhagwan Das Road, New Delhi with the request that 75 copies of the Hindi version of the Ordinance may kindly be sent to this Ministry immediately.

(_______)
UNDER SECRETARY TO THE GOVT. OF INDIA
Tel.No.

ANNEX IV-M

MINISTRY OF PARLIAMENTARY AFFAIRS (LEGISLATIVE - I SECTION)

Subject: List of Government Business for Lok Sabha

Lok Sabha Secretariat are requested kindly to issue the Lists of Government Business for the following days:

I. List of Government Business for ___________(day and date)

"Oath or Affirmation"

II. List of Government Business for ______(day and date)

(i) Oath or Affirmation, if necessary;
(ii) Election of the Speaker, Lok Sabha.

( )
Deputy Secretary

Lok Sabha Secretariat (Table Office)

MPA U.O.No.F.63(*)/2004-Leg.I dated:

Copy to:

PS to Minister of Parliamentary Affairs
PS to MOS(SP)
PS to MOS(SK)
PS to MOS (BK)
PPS to Secretary
PS to Joint Secretary
PA to DS(L)/US(L)

( )
Under Secretary

ANNEX IV-N

MINISTRIES/DEPARTMENTS UNDER JURISDICTION OF THE STANDING COMMITTEES

Sl. No.	Name of the Committee	Ministries/Departments
1	2	3
	Part-I	
1.	Committee on Commerce	(1) Commerce and Industry
2.	Committee on Home Affairs	(1) Home Affairs (2) Development of North Eastern Region
3.	Committee on Human Resource Development	(1) Human Resource Development (2) Youth Affairs and Sports
4.	Committee on Industry	(1) Heavy Industries and Public Enterprises (2) Small Scale Industries (3) Agro and Rural Industries
5.	Committee on Science and Technology, Environment and Forests	(1) Science and Technology (2) Space (3) Ocean Development (4) Atomic Energy (5) Enviroment and Forests
6.	Committee on Transport, and Tourism and Culture	(1) Civil Aviation (2) Shipping, Road Transport and Highways (3) Tourism (4) Culture
7.	Committee on Health and Family Welfare	Health and Family Welfare
8.	Committee on Personnel, Public Grievances, Law and Justice	(1) Law and Justice (2) Personnel, Public Grievances and Pensions

1	2	3
	Part-II	
9.	Committee on Agriculture	(1) Agriculture (2) Food Processing Industries
10.	Committee on Information Technology	(1) Communications and Information Technology (2) Information and Broadcasting
11.	Committee on Defence	Defence
12.	Committee on Energy	(1) Non-Conventional Energy Sources (2) Power
13.	Committee on External Affairs	(1) External Affairs (2) Overseas Indian Affairs
14.	Committee on Finance	(1) Finance (2) Company Affairs (3) Planning (4) Statistics and Programme Implementation
15.	Committee on Food, Consumer Affairs and Public Distribution	Consumer Affairs, Food and Public Distribution
16.	Committee on Labour	(1) Labour and Employment (2) Textiles
17.	Committee on Petroleum and Natural Gas	(1) Petroleum and Natural Gas
18.	Committee on Railways	Railways
19.	Committee on Urban Development	(1) Urban Development (2) Urban Employment and Poverty Alleviation
20.	Committee on Water Resources	Water Resources
21.	Committee on Chemicals and Fertilizers	Chemicals and Fertilizers
22.	Committee on Rural Development	(1) Rural Development (2) Panchayati Raj
23.	Committee on Coal and Steel	(1) Coal and Mines Steel (2) Steel
24.	Committee on Social Justice and Empowerment	(1) Social Justice and Empowerment (2) Tribal Affairs

ANNEX IV-O

CHECK LIST OF STEPS FOR VOTE ON ACCOUNTS

Sl.No.	Steps	Target Date	Agency
1 (a)	Sending note for convening BAC of Lok Sabha on 29.1.2004 and of Rajya Sabha on 30.1.2004.	23.01.2004	Ministry of Parliamentary Affairs
1 (b)	(i) Holding of BAC of Lok Sabha (ii) Holding of BAC of Rajya Sabha	29.01.2004 (11.30 am) 30.01.2004 (12.30 pm)	Lok Sabha Secretariat/MPA Rajya Sabha Secretariat/MPA
2	Preparation of the Appropriation Bills and Finance Bill	26.01.2004(R) 30.01.2004(G)	Ministry of Finance/Ministry of Railways/Legislative Department
3	Obtaining President's Recommendation under article 113(3) read with articles 116 and 115 in respect of presentation/making following Demands: (a) Demands for Grants (Vote on Account) (b) Supplementary Demands for Grants (c) Demand for Excess Grants	27.01.2004(R) 30.01.2004(G)	Ministry of Finance/Ministry of Railways/President's Secretariat
4	Obtaining President's Recommendation under article 117(1) and 117(3) for introduction and consideration in Lok Sabha: (a) Appropriation Bills (Railways and General) (b) Finance Bill (Recommendation under article 274 will also be required)	27.01.2004(R) 30.01.2004(G) 27.01.2004(R) 30.01.2004(G)	Ministry of Finance/Ministry of Railways/President's Secretariat Ministry of Finance/President's Secretariat

Contd......

5	Sending the following Notices to Lok Sabha regarding Vote on Accounts (Railways) etc. and related Appropriation Bills I-Vote on Accounts and other Demands (a) Notice indicating date etc. of presentation of Demands (Vote on Accounts) etc. to the House. (b) President's Recommendation under article 113(3) II-Appropriation Bills (a) Notice for introduction (b) Notice for consideration and passing (c) President's recommendation under article 117(1) and 117(3) (d) Request to Speaker to allow consideration of Appropriation Bills immediately after their introduction	28.01.2004(R)	Ministry of Railways/Lok Sabha Secretariat
6	1. Supplying documents relating to Interim Railway Budget 2. Supply of printed copies of the Appropriation Bills (Railways) relating to Vote on Accounts, Supplementary Demands and Demands for Excess Grants, if any	30.01.2004 (Early morning) 30.01.2004 (In the afternoon)	Ministry of Railways/Lok Sabha/ Rajya Sabha Secretariat/ Directorate of Printing, Ministry of Railways/Legislative Department/Lok Sabha Secretariat/ Directorate of Printing (Lok Sabha Secretariat has agreed to supply requisite number of copies of the Appropriation Bills to the Rajya Sabha Secretariat after they have been passed by the Lok Sabha

Contd......

7	Sending the following Notices to Lok Sabha regarding Vote on Accounts (General) etc., relating to Appropriation Bills and Finance Bill. I-Vote on Account and other Demands (a) Notice indicating date etc. of presentation of Demands (Vote on Accounts) etc. to the House; and (b) President's Recommendation under article 113(3). II-Appropriation Bills (c) Notice for Introduction; (d) Notice for consideration and passing; (e) President's Recommendation under article 117(1) and 117(3); and (f) Request to Speaker to allow consideration of Appropriation Bills immediately after their introduction. III-Finance Bill (a) Notice for Introduction; (b) Notice for consideration and passing; and (c) President's Recommendation under articles 117(1), 117(3) and 274.	31.01.2004 (G)	Ministry of Finance/Lok Sabha Secretariat
8	1. Supply of documents relating to Interim Budget (General), including the Finance Bill.	03.2.2004 (Early morning)	Ministry of Finance/Lok Sabha Rajya Sabha Secretariat/Legislative Department/Directorate of Printing

Contd......

	2. Supply of Appropriation Bills (General) relating to Vote on Accounts, Supplementary Demands and Demands for Excess Grants. 3. Supply of printed copies of Finance Bill as passed by Lok Sabha.	03.2.2004 (In the afternoon) 04.02.2004 (After the Bill is passed by LS)	Ministry of Finance/Lok Sabha/ Rajya Sabha Secretariat/ Legislative Department /Directorate of Printing (Lok Sabha Secretariat has agreed to supply requisite number of copies of the Appropriation Bills to the Rajya Sabha Secretariat after they have been passed by Lok Sabha). Ministry of Finance/Directorate of Printing/Legislative Department/ Rajya Sabha Secretariat.
9	Presentation of following relating to Railways Budget in Lok Sabha (and their laying in the Rajya Sabha): (a) Vote on Accounts (Interim Budget); (b) Supplementary Demands for Grants; and (c) Demands for Excess Grants.	30.01.2004 11:00 hrs (LS) 14:15 hrs (RS)	Ministry of Railways/Lok Sabha get Secretariat/Rajya Sabha Secretariat/ MPA
10	1. Presentation of following relating to General Budget in Lok Sabha (and their laying in the Rajya Sabha): (a) Vote on Accounts (Interim Budget); (b) Supplementary Demands for Grants; (c) Demands for Excess Grants if any; and (d) Introduction of Finance Bill, 2004. 2. Discussion and Voting on Railways Vote on Accounts (Interim Budget) and other Demands etc. in Lok Sabha. 3. Introduction, consideration and passing of the Appropriation Bills (Railways) in Lok Sabha.	03.01.2004 11.00 hrs (LS) 12.30 hrs (RS) 03.02.2004 03.02.2004	Ministry of Finance/Lok Sabha Secretariat/Rajya Sabha Secretariat/MPA Ministry of Railways/Lok Sabha Secretariat/MPA. Ministry of Railways/Lok Sabha Secretariat/MPA.

Contd......

	4. Sending of the Messages regarding passing of the Appropriation Bills (Railways) in the Lok Sabha to the Rajya Sabha	03.02.2004	Lok Sabha/Rajya Sabha Secretariats.
	5. Reading out of messages in Rajya Sabha.		
	6. Obtaining President's Recommendation for consideration of Appropriation Bills under article 117(3) and communicating the same to the Rajya Sabha Secretariat on the same day along with notices for consideration and passing and request for relaxation of Rule 123.	03.02.2004 03.02.2004	Rajya Sabha Secrretariat Ministry of Railways/President's Secretariat/Rajya Sabha Secretariat/MPA.
11	General Discussion on Interim Railway Budget in the Rajya Sabha.	03.02.2004	Ministry of Railways/Rajya Sabha Secretariat/MPA.
12	1. Discussion and Voting on General Vote on Accounts (Interim Budget) and other Demands etc. in the Lok Sabha. 2. Introduction, consideration and passing of the Appropriation Bills (General) in the Lok Sabha. 3. Consideration and passing of the Finance Bill, 2003. 4. Sending of Messages regarding passing of Appropriation Bills (General) and Finance Bill in the Lok Sabha to the Rajya Sabha.	04.02.2004 04.02.2004 04.02.2004 04.02.2004	Ministry of Finance/Lok Sabha Secretariat/MPA -do- -do- Lok Sabha/Rajya Sabhs Secretariats.

Contd......

	5. Reading out of messages in the Rajya Sabha. 6. Obtaining President's Recommendation for consideration of Appropriation Bills and Finance Bill under article 117(3) and communicating the same to the Rajya Sabha Secretariat on the same day along with notices for consideration and passing and request for relaxation of Rule 123.	04.02.2004 04.02.2004	Rajya Sabha Secretariat Ministry of Finance/Rajya Sabha Secretariat/President's Secretariat/MPA.
13.	1. Consideration and return of Appropriation Bills (Railways) in Rajya Sabha. 2. General Discussion on Interm General Budget in Rajya Sabha.	04.02.2004	1. Ministry of Railways/Rajya Sabha Secretariat/MPA/ 2. Ministry of Finance/Rajya Sabha Secretariat/MPA.
14.	Consideration and return of the Appropriation Bills (General) and Finance Bill, 2003 as passed by Lok Sabha in Rajya Sabha.	05.02.2004	Ministry of Finance/Rajya Sabha Secretariat/MPA.

ANNEXE IV-P

TIME ALLOTTED TO VARIOUS ITEMS OF FINANCIAL BUSINESS

Item	LS	RS
General Discussion on Railway Budget; Discussion and Voting on Demands for Grants on Account (Railways); Supplementary Demands for Grants (Railways), if any; Demands for Excess Grants (Railways), if any; and Introduction, consideration and passing of the related Appropriation Bills*	3-4 days	3-4 days
General Discussion on General Budget; Discussion and Voting on Demands for Grants (General); Supplementary Demands for Grants (General), if any; Demands for Excess Grants (General), if any; and Introduction, consideration and passing of the related Appropriation Bills*	3-4 days	3-4 days
Discussion and Voting on Demands for Grants for various Ministries/ Departments in Lok Sabha only and Introduction, consideration and passing of the related Appropriation Bill*	6 days	1 day
Discussion and Voting on Demands for Grants (Railways) and Introduction, consideration and passing of the related Appropriation Bills*	1 day	1 day
Consideration and passing of the Finance Bill	3 days	2 days

* In the Rajya Sabha, Demands for Grants are not discussed, only related Appropriation Bills are discussed and returned.

ANNEX IV-Q

MINISTRY OF PARLIAMENTARY AFFAIRS

D.O.No.F.19(1)/2003-Leg.I

Dated:

As you are aware, the Budget Session, 200... of Parliament is scheduled to commence on .... During the session, both Houses of Parliament are scheduled to adjourn on Friday, the .... to meet again on Monday, the .... to enable the Department-related Standing Committees to consider the Demands for Grants of the Ministries/Departments and prepare their Reports.

In this context, your attention is specifically invited to the provision of Rule 331(G) of the Rules of Procedure and Conduct of Business in Lok Sabha and similar provision in the Rules of Procedure and Conduct of Business in the Council of States (Rule 272) which provide for mandatory consideration of the Demands for Grants of each Ministry/Department by the respective Standing Committee of Parliament. In order to ensure, therefore, that the Government do not face any adverse criticism on account of non-availability of Detailed Demands for Grants to Members of Parliament, it is essential that the Detailed Demands for Grants relating to your Ministry/Department are laid on the Table of Lok Sabha latest by .... without fail.

Further, in accordance with the extant instructions and practice, the Annual Report as well as the Performance Budget of your Ministry/Department also need to be circulated to the Members of Parliament through the Lok Sabha and the Rajya Sabha Secretariats respectively, latest by .... These would be made use of by the Members of Parliament during the deliberations of the Standing Committees.

I shall, therefore, be grateful if the required number of copies of the Detailed Demands for Grants, Performance Budget and the Annual Report in respect of your Ministry/Department are made available to the Lok Sabha and Rajya Sabha Secretariats latest by .... to enable them to ensure their timely circulation to the Members of Parliament.

Yours sincerely,

( )
Secretary
Ministry of Parliamentary Affairs

Secretaries of all Ministries/Departments

ANNEX IV-R

MINISTRY OF PARLIAMENTARY AFFAIRS

D.O. No.F. ________ Dated:

Dear

BAC, Lok Sabha, in its ________ report adopted by the House on ________has recommended *inter alia* that, the Demands for Grants of the Ministry of ________ for ________ may be discussed and voted on ________ in the Lok Sabha.

I am informing you in advance so that you may make it convenient to be present in the House on that day.

With regards,

Yours sincerely,

( )
Minister of Parliamentary Affairs

Shri________
Minister of ________
Government of India,
New Delhi.

ANNEX IV-S

MINISTRY OF PARLIAMENTARY AFFAIRS

D.O. No. F. 17(*)/200 - Leg.I

Dated:

As you are aware, guillotine to the outstanding Demands for Grants of various Ministries/Departments will be applied at __p.m. on ________.

I shall be grateful if you could make it convenient to be present in the Lok Sabha to answer any points which may be raised by the Members concerning your Ministry/Department at the time of guillotining of Demands.

With regards

Yours sincerely,

(   )
Minister of Parliamentary Affairs

Cabinet Ministers/ Minister of State (Independent Charge)

ANNEX IV-T

CHECK LIST

1. D.O. letters by Secretary have been addressed to the Secretaries of various Ministries/Departments regarding Government Business to be taken up during the next session of Parliament, within a week of the prorogation of the preceding Parliament session.
2. Monitoring of receipt of Government Business from various Ministries/Departments has been undertaken from time to time and reminders issued to Ministries/ Departments from whom the information has not been received within the prescribed time.
3. Note seeking convenience of the Minister for taking the meeting with Secretaries/Senior Officers of the Ministries/Departments regarding finalisation of Government Business in the next session, has been submitted about four to five weeks in advance of the session. And before the meeting of the Minister with the Secretaries.
4. Meeting of Secretary with Legislative Secretary regarding scrutiny of the Government Business received from various Ministries/ Departments, has been informally fixed about four to five weeks in advance of the session.
5. After issue of Summons for the next session of the two Houses, communications to various Ministries/ Departments requesting them to send notices of Motions for consideration and passing of the Bills pending in the two Houses on the conclusion of the last session, have been sent.
6. Lists of Business of the two Houses for first two to three days of the session, proposal regarding convening the meeting of Business Advisory Committee, Lok Sabha, and tentative lists of Government Business etc. for the two Houses, have been issued to the Parliament Secretariats about two to three days in advance of the session.

7. Draft statements regarding Government Business, to be taken up in the two Houses during the following week, have been submitted for approval of the Minister on every Thursday/penultimate sitting of the House in a week.
8. Proposals for allocation of time to items included in the weekly statement made by the Minister to which time has not been allotted earlier, are submitted for approval of the Minister, immediately after the statements have been made in the Houses.
9. Whether note regarding proposals for Lists of Business *inter alia* indicates against each item, the time allotted by the Business Advisory Committee and whether the Bills, if included in the proposal, has/have already been examined by the Standing Committees.
10. Whether the introduction of the Finance Bill has been included in the List of Business of the Lok Sabha for the day on which the General/Interim Budget is proposed to be presented to the Lok Sabha.
11. Whether the items regarding Bills seeking to replace Ordinances, Financial Business etc. have been given priority over other items in the proposals regarding the Lists of Business.
12. Whether the recommendation of the Business Advisory Committee regarding the date on which the Constitution (Amendment) Bills may be taken up in the two Houses and the time for Division/voting, have been obtained before their listing.

ANNEX V-A

MOST IMMEDIATE

MINISTRY OF PARLIAMENTARY AFFAIRS

DO No.

Dated:

To

The Secretary-General,
Lok Sabha/Rajya Sabha,
New Delhi.

Sir,

I beg to give notice of the following Resolution which I propose to move during the ensuing Session of the Lok Sabha/Rajya Sabha:

"That this House approves the Proclamation issued by the President on .... under article 356 of the Constitution in relation to the State of ...."

Yours faithfully,

( )
HOME MINISTER

Dated:

No.
Copy forwarded to:
Ministry of Parliamentary Affairs, New Delhi.
Parliament Section, M.H.A., New Delhi.

DEPUTY SECRETARY

ANNEX V-B

No.F. 20(2)/2003- Leg. I
Government of India
Ministry of Parliamentary Affairs

87, Parliament House,
New Delhi
Dated:

OFFICE MEMORANDUM

Subject: Legislative proposals for inclusion in the President's Address to the two Houses of Parliament during Budget Session, 2004

Attention of the Ministry of Home Affairs etc. is invited to Prime Minister's office D.O.No. H-11020/1/2003/PM(Parl.) dated 15 December, 2003, wherein the Ministries have been requested to supply material for the President's address to be delivered to the two Houses of Parliament during the Budget Session, 2004.

In order to enable this Ministry to prepare a note on the legislative programme for inclusion in the President's Address, the Ministry of Home Affairs etc. are requested to kindly furnish to this Ministry latest by Thursday, the 22 January, 2004, the details of legislative business proposed to be brought forward by them during the Budget Session, 2004 of Parliament. Where it is not possible to indicate the title of a Bill, a general description indicating the purport thereof may be given.

Ministries may kindly include only such important legislative measures which will be positively introduced during the Budget Session, 2004. They are also requested to mention specifically as to which of their legislative proposals merit mention in the President's address.

In case no material is received by the above date, it will be presumed that the Ministry/Department have no legislative proposals to merit mention in the President's address. However, it would be appreciated if 'NIL' reply is sent by the date mentioned above.

The receipt of this Office Memorandum may kindly be acknowledged.

(__________)
JOINT SECRETARY TO THE GOVT. OF INDIA

TELE:23034734

To

Secretaries of all Ministries/Departments,
Government of India

Copy to :-

R & C and M E Sections of this Ministry. They are requested to kindly supply requisite information, if any, immediately.

ANNEX V-C

RULING BY THE SPEAKER-REGARDING PROPRIETY OF (I) TERMING 'VOTE ON ACCOUNT' AS THE 'INTERIM BUDGET' IN THE ORDER PAPER OF THE DAY; AND (II) CONVENING OF THE FIRST SESSION OF THE YEAR ON 29 JANUARY, 2004 WITHOUT THE PRESIDENTIAL ADDRESS.

The Speaker, after hearing Shri Priya Ranjan Dasmunsi, Prof. Vijay Kumar Malhotra, Sarvashri Sudip Bandyopadhyay, Ramdas Athawale, Somnath Chatterjee, Shivraj V. Patil, Dr. Raghuvansh Prasad Singh, Sarvashri Chandrashekhar, S. Jaipal Reddy, Smt. Sushma Swaraj, Minister of Parliamentary Affairs and Shri Arun Jaitley, Minister of Law and Justice, gave the following ruling:

"Let me at the outset make it clear that the rulings of the Speaker are generally in accordance with the rules, the rule book and also the Constitution of India. At times, it so happens that the issue requires ruling of the Chair and in such circumstances the precedents are seen. If the precedents are not available, then the Presiding Officer has to make up his own mind and give a ruling on the issues which are raised. In this particular case, fortunately, there are rules of procedure as well as definitions to guide us. I have gone through Erskine May's Parliamentary Practice. I would like the House to listen carefully to the ruling which I am now going to give.

Firstly, let me refer to Erskine May who has given, fortunately, a definition of the term 'prorogation'. He has said:

'A prorogation terminates a session; an adjournment is an interruption in the course of one and the same session'.

Therefore, the point which was raised here about prorogation has been made clear by this definition.

Shri Priya Ranjan Dasmunsi, at the outset, when he started his argument on the issue, had said that this cannot be treated as an Interim Budget. Therefore, I had to go through the precedents to see whether this can be treated as an interim Budget or not. I find that this was treated as an interim Budget in the past also. For instance, I would like to bring it to the notice of the House that on 11 March, 1996 the general discussion on the Interim Budget was listed in the List of Business. Not only this; there are also several instances when Vote-on-Account was called an Interim Budget. Therefore, calling this a Vote-on-Account or calling this an Interim Budget does not really make much difference.

But that was not the main point which was raised today. The main point which was raised by Shri Somnath Chatterjee was about the very holding of this Session and this point was also raised in the House by Shri Varkala Radhakrishnan and some other Members on 30 January, 2004 and the Hon'ble Minister of Parliamentary Affairs had responded to the points raised by the Members on that day. Shri Somnath Chatterjee has contended that what was commenced on 29 January, 2004 was the first Session of the year. I would like to clarify that there is no mention of adjournment *sine die* of the House in the Constitution. As per the provisions of the Constitution, a Session of the House comes to an end when the House is prorogued. As the House was not prorogued after its adjournment *sine die* on 23 December, 2003 this Session can, at best, be treated as the second part of the Fourteenth Session of the Thirteenth Lok Sabha, notwithstanding the fact that the calendar year has since changed.

I am giving an illustration; I am giving a precedent regarding the Third Lok Sabha. On 11 December, 1962 the House adjourned to meet on 21 January, 1963.

This was treated as Part-II of the same Session. I may inform the House that in the past also there have been occasions when after adjournment *sine die* of the House, the Lok Sabha was re-convened before prorogation.

For example, the Eighth Session of the Eighth Lok Sabha was adjourned *sine die* on 12 May, 1987, but the House was not prorogued .... and was reconvened after a gap of 75 days on 27 July, 1987 as the second part of the Session. Similarly, the 14 Session of the Eighth Lok Sabha was adjourned *sine die* on 18 August, 1989, but the House was not prorogued and was reconvened on 11 October, 1989 after a gap of 53 days as the second part of the 14th Session.

There are several other similar instances also. I have already made a reference to the case when the House was adjourned and thereafter, though it was reconvened in the next year, it was not treated as the fresh Session. Therefore, I must make it clear that in this particular case also, this Session can be treated as the second part of the Winter Session.

After listening to the arguments, I have treated this as the second part of the Winter Session. Since under the provisions of the sub-clause (a) of clause (2) of article 85 of the Constitution, the power to prorogue the House vests in the Hon'ble President - please remember that this power is with the Hon'ble President - I am not inclined to allow any more discussion on the issue and I hold both the points of order out of order."

ANNEX V-D

CHECK LIST

Statements

1. For consideration by the House of a policy, report, statement etc., it may be ensured by the administrative Ministry that copies of such documents have either been laid on the Table of the Houses or copies thereof have already been made available to the Members of Parliament.

2. Whenever discussion on a statement made by the Minister in the Lok Sabha is admitted for discussion, the Ministry concerned should supply 450 copies in English and 250 copies in Hindi of such statement to the Lok Sabha Secretariat for circulation to Members. In case such discussion is admitted in the Rajya Sabha, 240 copies in English and 30 copies in Hindi may be supplied to the Rajya Sabha Secretariat for circulation to the Members of the Rajya Sabha.

Resolution

1. Whenever a resolution given notice of by a Minister is admitted, the Ministry concerned may ensure that all relevant documents and literature, wherever necessary, are circulated to the Members sufficiently in advance of the listing of the Resolution in the List of Business.

Proclamation of Emergency

1. A Proclamation issued by the President in respect of any State under article 356 of the Constitution may be laid in the two Houses of Parliament along with a summary of the Governor's report or the Governor's

report *in extenso* where the President has acted on such a report.

2. A Proclamation issued under article 356, unless they are not proposed to be continued beyond two months, must be approved by a Resolution of both Houses of Parliament within a period of two months from the date of its issue.

3. A Proclamation of Emergency issued under article 352, must be approved by a Resolution by both Houses of Parliament within a period of one month from the date of its issue unless it is not proposed to be continued after one month.

President's Address

1. Information called for by the Prime Minister's Office for incorporation in the President's address should be supplied to the Prime Minister's Office, with a copy thereof endorsed to the Cabinet Secretariat, by the prescribed date.

2. The requisite number of copies of the President's address may be obtained from the President's Secretariat and copies thereof forwarded to all the Ministries/ Departments for information as soon as copies of the address have been laid in the two Houses.

3. The Motion of Thanks to be moved and seconded by the Members in the respective Houses must be given to the Parliament Secretariat, in the prescribed format, duly signed by the concerned Members, as soon as copies of the address have been laid on the Table of the Houses.

ANNEX VI-A

DETAILS REGARDING THE MEETINGS HELD BY CCPA

Sl. No	Date of meeting	Subject	MPA at that time
1	27.7.1978	To consider and approve Government stand on Private Members' Bills/Resolution.	Sh. Ravindra Verma
2	3.8.1978	-do-	-do-
3	6.3.1979	-do-	-do-
4	18.4.1979	Rules Committee of the House	-do-
5	7.11.1983	To discuss the Government Business for Winter Session,1983	Sh. Buta Singh
6	9.12.1983	To discuss the Government Business for remaining part of Winter Session, 1983	-do-
7	17.7.1984	(i) Report of Justice Vaidialingam (ii) Government Business for 23 and 24 July, 1984	-do-
8	16.8.1984	Government Business for the remaining part of Monsoon Session of Parliament	-do-
9	8.5.1985	To consider and approve Government's stand on Private Members' Bills	Sh. H.K.L. Bhagat
10	24.4.1986	(i) To consider and approve Government's stand on Private Members' Bills/Resolutions (ii) Action taken by the Government on the Special Mentions. (iii) To consider withholding of the President's recommendation	-do-
11	17.5.1990	To discuss the tentative programme of the Budget Session	Sh. P. Upendra
12	21.5.1990	- do -	- do -
13	19.7.1990	To discuss the tentative programmeof Government Business.	- do -
14	19.12.1990	To discuss the Government Business for Winter Session	Sh. Satya Prakash Malaviya

Contd......

15	19.1.1991	Prorogation of Houses and commencement and duration of Budget Session - to discuss tentative programme also.	- do -
16	27.11.1991	To consider the Government Business for Winter Session	Sh. Ghulam Nabi Azad
17	5.12.1991	To consider the Constitution Amendment Bills, relating to Panchayati Raj and Urban Local Bodies.	- do -
18	6.6.1992	To consider commencement and duration of Monsoon Session	- do -
19	10.8.1992	To consider the setting up of Parliamentary Standing Committees	- do -
20	6.11.1994	(i) To consider the commencement and duration of Winter Session (ii) To hold meetings of Consultative Committees outside Delhi.	Sh. V.C. Shukla
21	20.3.1995	To consider withholding of the President's recommendation for consideration of three Bills under article 117(3) of the Constitution.	-do-
22	10.12.1998	(i) To consider and approve Government's stand on Private Members' Bills/Resolutions (ii)To review progress of the Government Business	Sh. M.L. Khurana
23	15.1.1999	(i) To consider and decide the date of commencement and duration of the Budget Session, 1999 (ii) Date and time of Presentation/ Laying of Railway and General Budgets in the two Houses.	-do-
24	25.2.1999	(i) To consider and approve the Government's stand on Private Members' Bills/Resolutions (ii) Did not agree with the view of Ministry for advising the President for withholding his recommendation under article 117(3) of the Constitution	Sh. P.R. Kumaramangalam

Contd......

25.	2.12.1999	To consider and approve the Government's stand on Private Members's Bills/Resolutions	Sh. Pramod Mahajan
26.	9.12.1999	-do-	-do-
27.	16.12.1999	-do-	-do-
28.	22.12.1999	-do- (ii)Prorogation of both Houses of Parliament.	-do-
29.	8.6.2004	Prorogation of 1st Session of 14th Lok Sabha and 201st Session of Rajya Sabha	Shri Ghulam Nabi Azad
30.	19.8.2004	Government's stand of Private Member's Bills	-do-

ANNEX VI-B

MINISTRY OF PARLIAMENTARY AFFAIRS

D.O.No.F.

Dated:

As you are aware, Private Members' Business viz., Private Members' Bills/Resolutions are transacted in either House of Parliament on the last working day of each week during Parliament sessions. Whenever the Private Members' Bills/Resolutions are listed for consideration, the Government has to take a stand on their subject matter with the approval of the Cabinet Committee on Parliamentary Affairs serviced by this Ministry.

A copy of the Lok Sabha Bulletin Part II No. ____ dated___ containing the list of 20 Bills which secured first twenty positions in the ballot and which subject to notices being received from the Members concerned, are likely to be listed for consideration in Lok Sabha during the ___ is enclosed. You are requested to forward two copies of the Brief (English and Hindi versions) indicating Government's stand on ___ (Sl.No. ____ in the enclosed list) which concern your Department, finalised at the level of your Minister, latest by ____ to enable this Ministry to place them before the Cabinet Committee on Parliamentary Affairs for its consideration.

It may also kindly be noted that as soon as the priorities of the Private Members' Bills and Resolutions are notified in the Parliamentary Bulletins after the ballots, the Ministry may, without waiting for any communication from this Ministry, prepare the briefs on the Bills/Resolutions concerning it and send requisite number of copies thereof (English and Hindi versions) to this Ministry to enable us to seek the approval of the Cabinet Committee on Parliamentary Affairs to the Government's stand on the Bills/ Resolutions. It is hoped that this arrangement will obviate the problem of the submission/supply of briefs as also the consequential embarrassment to the Government for its inability to obtain the approval of the Cabinet Committee before consideration of the Private Members' Bills and Resolutions in the two Houses.

Yours sincerely,

( )
Secretary

To

Secretaries of Ministries/Departments concerned

ANNEX VI-C

OUT TODAY
MOST IMMEDIATE
BY SPECIAL MESSENGER

No.F.
Government of India
Ministry of Parliamentary Affairs

90, Parliament House,
New Delhi.

Dated:

OFFICE MEMORANDUM

Subject: Private Members' Bills/Resolutions in Lok Sabha/Rajya Sabha

The attached/following Bill/Resolution tabled by Shri/Smt. .... which primarily concerns the Ministry/Department of .... will be set down for discussion in .... Sabha on Friday, the............. .

It is requested that two copies of the brief (Hindi and English versions) on Government's stand on the Bill/Resolution may kindly be sent to this Ministry latest by .... for consideration by the Cabinet Committee on Parliamentary Affairs. The brief may contain the following information:

GIST OF BILL/RESOLUTION

1. Schemes/Projects, and/or Acts, if any, catering to the requirement of the Bill/Resolution.
2. Geographical spread of the above Schemes/Projects/applicability of the Acts.
3. If the above Schemes/Projects/Acts are under implementation, the facts and figures showing three years' achievements.

4. Constraints, if any, identified in the implementation of the above Schemes/Projects/Acts.
5. Steps taken to remove the constraints.
6. Fresh/new proposals contained in the Bill/Resolution.
7. View of the Ministry regarding the fresh/new proposals clearly stating the reasons, if any, in support or against each of the said fresh/new proposals.
8. Clear statement on whether Ministry supports or opposes the Bill/Resolution. (This should be mentioned in the brief itself).
9. The fact that the Government's stand on the Bill/Resolution has been approved by the Minister should invariably be indicated in the brief as well as in the forwarding letter.

If the brief is not received in this Ministry by ...., it may not be possible to place it before the CCPA in their next meeting.

( )

UNDER SECRETARY TO THE GOVT. OF INDIA

Ministry/Department of .....
(Parliament Section)
New Delhi.

ANNEX VI-D

MINISTRY OF PARLIAMENTARY AFFAIRS (LEGISLATIVE I SECTION)

Note for Cabinet Committee on Parliamentary Affairs

(Note No._____ dt._______)

Subject: Approval of Government's Stand on Private Members' Bills in the Lok Sabha/ Rajya Sabha.

LOK SABHA

A copy of the List of Private Members' Business (Bills) for Lok Sabha for _______________, is at Annex 'A'. It contains ____ Bills, of which ____ Bills are for introduction and remaining ___ Bills are for consideration and passing. The Bills listed for consideration and passing are as under:-

BILLS

(i)
(ii)
(iii)
(iv)

The Bill mentioned at sl. no.___ above has been discussed in part and has so far taken ___ hrs ___mts. against allotment of _____ hrs ____ mts. The Government's stand on the Bill mentioned at sl. no. ___ has already been approved by the CCPA. Briefs in respect of the Bills mentioned at sl.nos. _____have been received from the Ministries concerned. Briefs in respect of the Bills mentioned at sl. no. _____have not yet been received from the Ministry of _______________.

RAJYA SABHA

A copy of the List of Private Members' Business (Bills) for the Rajya Sabha for ______________ is at Annex 'B'. It contains _____ Bills, of which ______ Bills are for introduction and remaining ____ Bills are for consideration and passing. The Bills listed for consideration and passing are as under:-

BILLS

(i)
(ii)
(iii)
(iv)

The Bill mentioned at sl. no.___ above has been discussed in part and has so far taken ___ hrs ___mts against the allotment of _____ hrs ____ mts. The Government's stand on the Bill mentioned at sl. no. ___ has already been approved by the CCPA. Briefs in respect of the Bills mentioned at sl.nos. _____have been received from the Ministries concerned. Briefs in respect of the Bills mentioned at sl. no. _____have not yet been received from the Ministry of _______________.

A statement indicating the titles of the Private Members' Bills, names of the Member-in-charge, Purport of the Bills, Ministry concerned, Government's stand and reasons, therefor, in respect of the Bills mentioned at sl. nos. __________ in para ___ in the Lok Sabha and at sl. no.______ in para ___ in the Rajya Sabha which have been received is at Appendix.

Approval of the Cabinet Committee on Parliamentary Affairs is solicited to the Government's stand in respect of Bills as indicated in column 5 of the statement at Appendix.

This Note has been seen and approved by the Minister of Parliamentary Affairs.

( )
SECRETARY

To all the members/special invitees of the
Cabinet Committee on Parliamentary Affairs(except MPA).

APPENDIX

Statement regarding Government's stand on Private Members' Bills in Lok Sabha/Rajya Sabha set down for consideration on __________.

Sl. No.	Title of the Bill Name of Member-in-charge	Purport	Ministry/ Department concerned	Stand proposed by the Ministry	Reasons for stand of the Ministry (relevant paras of the brief note indicated)
1	2	3	4	5	6
1.					
2.					

ANNEX VI-E

MINISTRY OF PARLIAMENTARY AFFAIRS
(LEGISLATIVE I SECTION)

Note for Cabinet Committee on Parliamentary Affairs

(Note No. ________ dated __________)

Subject: Approval of Government's Stand on Private Members' Resolutions in the Lok Sabha/Rajya Sabha.

LOK SABHA

A copy of the List of Private Members' Business (Resolutions) for the Lok Sabha for ________________, is at Annex 'A'. It contains ___ Resolutions on the following subjects:

RESOLUTIONS

(i)
(ii)
(iii)
(iv)

The Resolution mentioned at sl. nos. __ above has been discussed in part and has so far taken two hours against an allotment of two hours. The Government's stand on the Resolution mentioned at sl.no.__ above has already been approved by the Cabinet Committee on Parliamentary Affairs. Brief in respect of the Resolution mentioned at sl. no. __ has been received from the Ministry of _________. Brief in respect of the Resolution mentioned at sl. no. ____ has not yet been received from the Ministry of __________________.

RAJYA SABHA

A copy of the List of Private Members' Business (Resolutions) for the Rajya Sabha for ________________, is at Annex 'B'. It contains __ Resolutions on the following subjects:

RESOLUTIONS

(i)
(ii)
(iii)
(iv)

Brief in respect of the Resolution mentioned at sl. no. ___ has been received from the Ministry of ___________________. Briefs in respect of the Resolutions mentioned at sl.nos. ___ and ____ have not yet been received from the concerned Ministries.

A statement indicating the title of the Private Members' Resolutions, name of the Member-in-charge, purport of the Resolution, Ministry concerned, Government's stand and reasons therefor, in respect of the Resolution mentioned at Sl. No.___ in para _____in the Lok Sabha and at sl. no. ___ in para ___ in the Rajya Sabha, whose briefs have been received, is at Appendix.

Approval of the Cabinet Committee on Parliamentary Affairs is solicited to the Government's stand in respect of the Resolutions, as indicated in column __ of the statement at Appendix.

This Note has been seen and approved by the Minister of Parliamentary Affairs.

( )
SECRETARY

To all the members/special invitees of the Cabinet Committee on Parliamentary Affairs (except MPA).

APPENDIX

Statement regarding Government's Stand on Private Members' Resolutions set down for consideration in Lok Sabha/Rajya Sabha on ________.

Sl. No.	Text of the Resolution, and Member-in-charge	Purport	Ministry/ Department concerned	Stand proposed by the Ministry	Reasons for stand of the Ministry (relevant paras of the brief note indicated)
1	2	3	4	5	6

ANNEX VI-F

F.No. 44(L)/PR/75-PA
Government of India
Department of Parliamentary Affairs

90, Parliament House,
New Delhi.

Dated: 18.10.75

OFFICE MEMORANDUM

Subject: Procedure for advising President in cases requiring his Recommendation under article 117(1) and 117(3) of the Constitution for introduction and/or consideration of Private Members' Bills in either House of Parliament - consolidation of existing instructions.

As Ministry of Home Affairs etc. are aware, a large number of Bills are introduced by Private Members during the various sessions of Parliament. A majority of these legislative proposals involves expenditure from the Consolidated Fund of India when enacted and brought into operation and therefore require recommendation of the President under article 117(3) of the Constitution before they are taken up in either House of Parliament. Similarly some Bills sponsored by Private Members require the recommendation of the President under article 117(1) of the Constitution before they are introduced in the Lok Sabha. In response to queries made by the Ministries on the scope of granting or withholding of such recommendation, the question was considered in consultation with the Ministry of Law who opined as under:

> "The recommendation of the President is for the introduction or moving of the Bill. The grant of this recommendation is an executive act to be performed on the advice of the Ministry. The fact that the Ministry advise recommendation only means that it has no

> objection to the introduction or moving of the Bill. It does not preclude the Government from opposing the passing of the Bill into law. It may, therefore, oppose the Bill on merits at any stage after introduction."

Keeping the Law Ministry's advice in view, it was decided that the President's recommendation required under clause (1) and/or (3) of article 117 of the Constitution for introduction/ consideration of Private Members' Bills should ordinarily be granted unless very exceptional circumstances, specially warrant withholding of the President's recommendation. It was further decided that Ministries should make a reference to the Cabinet Committee on Parliamentary Affairs only in such cases where the recommendation of the President under article 117(1) and/or (3) of the Constitution is sought to be withheld owing to very exceptional circumstances. In that event, 30 copies of a brief explaining the exceptional circumstances necessitating the withholding of the recommendation should be supplied to the Department of Parliamentary Affairs for obtaining the approval of the Cabinet Committee.

This supersedes the previous instructions on the subject issued by this Department from time to time.

The receipt of this Office Memorandum may kindly be acknowledged.

Sd/-
(K.N. KRISHNAN)
DEPUTY SECRETARY

To

All Ministries/Deptts. of the Government of India.

ANNEX VI-G

CONFIDENTIAL

MINISTRY OF PARLIAMENTARY AFFAIRS
GOVERNMENT OF INDIA

87, Parliament House,
New Delhi - 110001.

OCTOBER 17, 2000

No.F. 44(2)/2000-Leg. I

To

All the Secretaries
to the Government of India,
New Delhi.

Subject: Recommendation of the President under article 117(3) of the Constitution of India

Sir,

With reference to the subject cited above, I am directed to state that article 117(3) of the Constitution of India provides as under:-

> "A Bill which, if enacted and brought into operation, would involve expenditure from the Consolidated Fund of India, shall not be passed by either House of Parliament unless the President has recommended to that House the consideration of the Bill."

As per the recommendation made by the Committee on Private Members' Bills and Resolutions of the Lok Sabha, Private Members' Bills awaiting recommendation of the President under article 117(3) of the Constitution of India can also be included in the List of

Business to be transacted by the House. In pursuance of this recommendation, such Bills are being included in the List of Business to be transacted by the Lok Sabha.

Recently a case has come to notice where the concerned Ministry could not complete the exercise of obtaining the President's recommendation for consideration of a Private Member's Bill for five months and the Bill was included in the List of Business to be transacted by the Lok Sabha. This led to a piquant situation where the concerned Ministry had to make frantic efforts to obtain the requisite recommendation of the President to stave off the embarrassment of the Bill coming up for consideration in the House without the President's recommendation.

In view of the constitutional provision and the recommendation of the Committee on Private Members' Bills and Resolutions of the Lok Sabha quoted above, you are requested kindly to ensure that the constitutional requirement of obtaining/withholding the recommendation of the President under article 117(3) in the case of a Private Member's Bill is obtained with due dispatch on receipt of the notice of such a Bill.

The receipt of this letter may kindly be acknowledged.

Yours faithfully,

Sd/-

(D.R. TIWARI)

JOINT SECRETARY TO THE GOVT. OF INDIA

TEL.NO. 3034734

ANNEX VI-H

MINISTRY OF PARLIAMENTARY AFFAIRS
(LEGISLATIVE-I SECTION)

F.No.__________-Leg.I Dated:_____

Subject: Prorogation of both the Houses of Parliament

Lok Sabha and Rajya Sabha are scheduled to adjourn *sine die* on __________. It is, therefore, proposed to prorogue both the Houses of Parliament after their adjournment *sine die* on __________.

Approval of the Cabinet Committee on Parliamentary Affairs to prorogue both the Houses of Parliament is solicited by circulation of papers.

This Note has been seen and approved by the Minister of Parliamentary Affairs.

(   )
SECRETARY

To all the members/special invitees of the Cabinet Committee on Parliamentary Affairs (except MPA).

ANNEX VI-I

CHECK LIST

1. To find out from the Parliamentary Bulletins of each House the date on which Private Members' Bills and Resolutions will be taken up in the two Houses during the session.
2. To find out from Parliamentary Bulletins the date on which the ballot will be held each for Private Members' Bills and Resolutions in the two Houses.
3. After the result of the ballot of Private Members' Bills in the Lok Sabha has been notified in the Parliamentary Bulletin, Ministries concerned may be requested at Secretary's level, to furnish the requisite number of copies of the Briefs on Bills which secure first ten positions in the ballot.
4. Obtaining advance copies of the Private Members' Bills and Resolutions from the two Parliamentary Secretariats and taking action to obtain copies of the Briefs from the such Ministries/Departments, which have not already furnished them. Scrutinising printed Lists of Business of Private Members' Bills and Resolutions in the two Houses for each Private Members' days and taking action in regard to obtaining copies of Briefs wherever they have not been received from the Ministries concerned.
5. Telephonically reminding the Ministries concerned from whom the Briefs are awaited.
6. Submission of Note for Cabinet Committee on Parliamentary Affairs on Thursday or one day before the day scheduled for the Private Members' Business, as the case may be, for approval of Government's stand on the Private Members' Bills and Resolutions by the Cabinet Committee on Parliamentary Affairs.

ANNEX VII-A

GUIDELINES FORMULATED IN APRIL, 1969 TO REGULATE THE CONSTITUTION AND FUNCTIONING OF THE CONSULTATIVE COMMITTEES FOR VARIOUS MINISTRIES AND DEPARTMENTS

1. The Informal Consultative Committees will henceforth be known as Consultative Committees. These committees are not, however, comparable to the Standing Committees of Parliament. The deliberations of these committees would remain informal and no reference to the discussions held in the meetings thereof would be made on the floor of the House.
2. Government will fix the strength of these committees in consultation with the Opposition parties with due regard to the respective strengths of various parties in Parliament. Each party may choose its own nominees to these committees.
3. The Minister concerned with each Ministry/Department shall preside over the meeting of the Consultative Committee attached to his Ministry. Whenever for exceptional reasons, this is not possible, the meeting will either be presided over by the Minister of State of the Ministry or the meeting will be postponed.
4. Notices etc. for Consultative Committee meeting will be issued to the regular Members of the committee. If any Member other than the members of the Consultative Committees suggests any points for discussion in the meeting of a particular committee, he may be invited for the meeting subject to the condition that he will not be entitled to any TA/DA for attending such meeting. A regular member will, however, be entitled to TA/DA for attending the meeting held during the intersession period as per prescribed administrative orders.
5. Meetings of the committees should be normally arranged during the session period. It has also been agreed to

hold one meeting of each committee during the intersession period and the date of that meeting may be decided, if possible, during the previous meeting. The duration of the meeting should be left to the Chairman depending on the business to be transacted.

6. These meetings would be attended by the senior officers of the Ministries who could assist the Minister in regard to information on specific items on the agenda and provide the Minister with facts and figures. The committees would not have the right to summon any witness, to send for or demand the production of any files, or to examine any official records. The Chairman of the committee may, however, furnish any additional information required by Members.

7. A brief record of the discussion in the meetings on specific matters for which adequate notice has been given, will be circulated to the members. Where there is unanimity of view in the committee, Government will normally accept the view subject to the following exceptions, viz.,

   (i) any view having financial implications;
   (ii) any view concerning Security, Defence, External Affairs and Atomic Energy; and
   (iii) any matter falling within the purview of an autonomous corporation.

   In case of non-acceptance, reason thereof will be given to the Committee.

8. These committees would be formed for all the Ministries/ Departments.

9. The reconstitution of the committees will normally be timed with the Budget Session.

10. Secretary of the Ministry of Parliamentary Affairs will notify the constitution of these committees.

11. At these committees, Members of Parliament are free to discuss any matter which can appropriately be discussed in Parliament. It would not, however, be desirable to refer on the floor of the House, to anything which might have taken place in the Consultative Committees. This will be binding on both the Government and the Members.

ANNEX VII-B(I)

D.O. No. F. 7-1/2004-CB

As you are aware, the Ministry of Parliamentary Affairs constitutes Consultative Committees of Members of Parliament attached to each Ministry of the Government of India. These committees function under a set of guidelines, a copy of which is enclosed as **Annex-I.** The maximum membership of a committee is 40.

It is proposed to nominate members on each of these committees in such a manner that the committee's composition reflects the relative strengths of parties in both Houses of Parliament. There are in all 38 Consultative Committees to be constituted as shown in **Annex-II.**

According to the strength of your party in the Lok Sabha/ Rajya Sabha, you may nominate a maximum of *_____ Members from the Lok Sabha and *_____from the Rajya Sabha on each of the 38 committees. This number has been worked out on the assumption that each committee may have an approximate strength of 19 MPs (total strength of MPs in LS/RS divided by the total number of Committees). There may be a slight increase or decrease in the membership of your party on each committee depending on the total membership of the committee.

I shall be grateful if you kindly suggest names of members of your party belonging to the Lok Sabha/Rajya Sabha for nomination on these committees subject to the limitation that a Member is to be nominated on one committee only, at an early date so that the committees could be Constituted and their meetings arranged at the earliest possible.

With kind regards,

Yours sincerely,

(Ghulam Nabi Azad)
Minister of Parliamentary Affairs

Leader of BJP, CPI(M), SP
in Lok Sabha/Rajya Sabha

* BJP
CPI(M)
SP

ANNEX VII-B(II)

D.O. No. F. 7-1/2004-CB

As you are aware, the Ministry of Parliamentary Affairs constitutes Consultative Committees of Members of Parliament attached to each Ministry of the Government of India. These committees function under a set of guidelines, a copy of which is enclosed as **Annex-I.** The maximum membership of a committee is 40.

It is proposed to constitute 38 Consultative Committees as shown in **Annex-II.** Keeping in view the strength of your Party, you are requested to suggest not more than one Member either of the Lok Sabha or Rajya Sabha for a Consultative Committee.

I shall be grateful if you kindly suggest names of members of your party belonging to the Lok Sabha/Rajya Sabha for nomination on these committees subject to the limitation that a member is to be nominated on one committee only, at an early date so that the committees could be Constituted and their meetings arranged at the earliest possible.

With kind regards,

Yours sincerely,

(Ghulam Nabi Azad)
Minister of Parliamentary Affairs

Leaders of Parties with membership
of 5 to 39 in both the Houses

ANNEX VII-B(III)

D. O. No. F. 7-1/2004-CB

As you are perhaps aware, the Ministry of Parliamentary Affairs constitutes Consultative Committees of Members of Parliament attached to each Ministry of the Government of India. These committees function under a set of guidelines, a copy of which is enclosed as **Annex-I.** The maximum membership of a committee is 40.

I am enclosing a list of 38 Consultative Committees to be constituted **(Annex-II).** The maximum membership of a committee is 40. A Member of Parliament can be nominated on one committee only.

I shall be grateful if you kindly indicate, in the proforma enclosed, any three committees in order of your preference for nomination and return the proforma to the Ministry of Parliamentary Affairs at the earliest. It will be our endeavour to nominate you on the committee of your first preference. In case it is not possible to do so for want of a vacancy on the committee, we shall nominate you on the committee of your second/third preference.

I request you kindly to return the proforma at the earliest so that the committees could be constituted and their meetings arranged at the earliest possible.

With regards,

Yours sincerely,

(Ghulam Nabi Azad)
Minister of Parliamentary Affairs

1. MPs of Indian National Congress (INC)
2. MPs of smaller parties with membership of less than 5 in both Houses
3. Nominated MPs; and
4. Independent MPs

ANNEXURS VII-C

NOMINATION ON CONSULTATIVE COMMITTEE

I may be nominated on one of the following Consultative Committees in order of preference:-

....

....

....

Signature

....

Name

....

(in capital letters)

Member : Lok Sabha/Rajya Sabha
Party Affiliation:
Telephone and Fax Number at

(a) Delhi Address ....

....

(b) Permanent Address

....

....

To

Under Secretary,
Ministry of Parliamentary Affairs,
90, Parliament House,
New Delhi.

Telephone No.: 011-23034274
Fax No. : 011-23792067
011-23017557

ANNEX VII-D

No..................
Government of India
Ministry of Parliamentary Affairs

8, Parliament House,
New Delhi.

Dated:

NOTIFICATION

Subject: Constitution of Consultative Committee for the Ministry of -----.

Government of India have decided to constitute the Consultative Committee of Members of Parliament for the Ministry of --------. The personnel of the Committee will be as under:-

Sh.------------, Minister of ----------------Chairman.

Sh. -----------, Minister of State in the Ministry of -----------------.

MEMBERS OF LOK SABHA

MEMBERS OF RAJYA SABHA

Minister of State in the Ministry of Parliamentary Affairs and Minister of State in the Ministry of Defence (*Ex Officio* Member)
Minister of State in the Ministry of Parliamentary Affairs and Minister of State in the Ministry of Personnel, Public Grievances and Pensions (*Ex Officio* Member)
Minister of State in the Ministry of Parliamentary Affairs and Minister of State in the Ministry of Rural Development (*Ex Officio* Member)

The Committee will meet as often as considered necessary.

( )

Secretary to the Government of India

To

Members of the Committee
(at both addresses)

Copy to:-

PS to Minister of --------------.
PS to Minister of State in the Ministry of -----------.
PS to Minister of Parliamentary Affairs
PSs to Ministers of State in the Ministry of Parliamentary Affairs.
PS to Secretary, Ministry of -------------.
PPS/PS/PA to Secretary/DS (L)/US (C), MPA.
PAO/PNO/MSandA Branch, Lok Sabha/Rajya Sabha Secretariate
Ministry of --------------- (Parliament Section).
All Party Offices in Parliament House, New Delhi.
General Section, Ministry of Parliamentary Affairs.

ANNEX VII-E

LIST OF CONSULTATIVE COMMITTEES EXISTING BEFORE DISSOLUTION OF XIII LOK SABHA

Ministry of Agriculture
Ministry of Chemicals and Fertilizers
Ministry of Civil Aviation
Ministry of Coal and Mines
Ministry of Commerce and Industries
Ministry of Communications and Information Technology
Ministry of Defence
Ministry of Environment and Forests
Ministry of External Affairs
Ministry of Finance and Company Affairs
Ministry of Food Processing Industries
Ministry of Health and Family Welfare
Ministry of Heavy Industries and Public Enterprises
Ministry of Home Affairs
Ministry of Human Resource Development
Ministry of Information and Broadcasting
Ministry of Labour
Ministry of Petroleum and Natural Gas
Ministry of Power
Ministry of Railways
Ministry of Road Transport and Highways
Ministry of Rural Development
Ministry of Science and Technology and
Deptt. of Ocean Development
Ministry of Social Justice and Empowerment
Ministry of Steel
Ministry of Textiles
Ministry of Tourism and Culture
Ministry of Urban Development and Poverty Alleviation
Ministry of Water Resources
Ministry of Youth Affairs and Sports

ANNEX VII-F

No.F. 12(26)/94-CB
Government of India
Ministry of Parliamentary Affairs

86-B, Parliament House,
New Delhi.

Dated 16-10-1995

OFFICE MEMORANDUM

Subject: Ban on holding meetings of the Consultative Committees outside Delhi-relaxation thereof.

The undersigned is directed to state that there has been a complete ban on holding the meetings of the Consultative Committees of various Ministries/Departments outside Delhi since July, 1981. The matter of relaxation of this ban was taken up with the Ministry of Finance and, with the approval of Minister of Finance, it has now been decided that Ministries/Departments may hold one meeting of their Consultative Committee in a year during an Inter-session period anywhere in India if the Chairman of the committee so desires. While conveying the approval, the Minister of Finance in his D.O. letter No. F.1(46)-E(Coord)/94 dated September, 1995 has hoped that the number of officers attending the meetings outside Delhi would be kept to the minimum.

The Ministry of Home Affairs etc. are requested to take note of the above decision for information and necessary action.

(Sd/)
J.B. GUPTA
Deputy Secretary to the Govt. of India
Tele.No. 3034844

To,

All Ministries/Departments of
Government of India (Parliament Section),
New Delhi.

Copy to:

MSandA Branch, Lok/Rajya Sabha Sectt. Parliament House Annexe, New Delhi.
PAO, Lok Sabha/Rajya Sabha Sectt.,Parliament House Annexe,New Delhi.

ANNEX VII-G

No.F.12 (26)/96-CB
Government of India
Ministry of Parliamentary Affairs

94-A, Parliament House,
New Delhi.

11 February, 1997

OFFICE MEMORANDUM

Subject: Holding of meetings of the Consultative Committees outside Delhi clarification regarding 'Year'

The undersigned is directed to refer to this Ministry's O.M. of even number dated 16 October, 1995 on the subject noted above and to state that a question has arisen as to whether 'year' in this regard is to be taken as calendar year or financial year.

It is herby clarified that 'year' in this regard shall be taken as 'calendar year'.

The Ministry of Home Affairs etc. are requested to take note of the above clarification for information and necessary action.

Sd/-
(K.K. Thakur)
Under Secretary to the Govt. of India
Tele. No. 3034274

To

All Ministries/Departments of
Government of India (Parliament Section)
New Delhi.

ANNEX VII-H

No.F.8-1/2000-CB
Government of India
Ministry of Parliamentary Affairs

86-B, Parliament House,
New Delhi-110001

Dated:

OFFICE MEMORANDUM

Subject: Meeting of the Consultative Committee of various Ministries during the Session period of Parliament.

As the Ministry of Home Affairs etc. are aware that one meeting of each Consultative Committee has to be held during the session period. The _____ Session of Parliament is scheduled to commence from _________ and is likely to conclude on ____________________. It is, therefore, requested that necessary action in this regard may kindly be taken and the date and time convenient to the Minister (Chairman of the Consusltative Committee) for holding the meeting of the committee be communicated to this Ministry early so that notices could be issued to the Members.

The Ministry will make every effort to arrange a committee room in the Parliament House/Parliament House Annexe for the meeting. If a committee room in these buildings is not available, the Ministry concerned will have to arrange the venue of the meeting themselves. In that case, they will have to make transport arrangements for the Members from Parliament House to the venue of the meeting and back to Parliament House on conclusion of the meeting.

It is noticed that most of the Ministries fix their meetings towards the end of the session period which results in overlapping of several meetings on the same date making it very difficult to get committee rooms in Parliament House/Parliament House Annexe. In view of this, Ministries are requested kindly to fix the date of the meeting of their Consultative Committees as much in advance as possible and intimate the same to this Ministry for booking committee rooms and issuing notices to the Members.

As for the time and duration of meetings, the Ministries may kindly note the following suggestions:

> In the morning, the meeting may commence any time between 9.00 a.m. and 9.30 a.m. but may be concluded before 11.00 a.m. to enable Members to reach Parliament House for the sitting of the House; and
>
> In the evening, the meeting may be held after 6.30 p.m.

The Ministries are reminded that the time schedule etc. for circulation of papers to Members through this Ministry for the meeting is as under:

Minutes of the last meeting Action taken report on the Minutes of the last meeting Agenda papers of the ensuing meeting.	At least ten working days before the date of meeting
Number of copies to be supplied to this Ministry	Number of Members plus ten

It may be noted that action on papers received after 4.00 p.m. in this Ministry will be taken only on the next working day. The Ministries are, therefore, requested to ensure that the papers are delivered in this Ministry before 4.00 p.m. positively if these are to be distributed to Members on the same day.

This may kindly be treated as **MOST IMMEDIATE.**

( )
Deputy Secretary to the Govt. of India
Telephone No.23034844

Ministries/Departments of
(Shri/Smt.)
New Delhi.

ANNEX VII-I

No.F.8-1/2000-CB
Government of India
Ministry of Parliamentary Affairs

86-B, Parliament House
New Delhi.

Dated:

OFFICE MEMORANDUM

Subject: Meeting of the Consultative Committee of various Ministries during the Inter-Session period

As the Ministry of Home Affairs etc. are aware that one meeting of each Consultative Committee has to be held during the inter-session period. The _____ Session of Parliament has concluded on ___________ and the next session is likely to commence sometime in ______________________________. It is, therefore, requested that the date and time convenient to the Minister (Chairman of the Consultative Committee) for holding the meeting of the committee be communicated to this Ministry early so that notices regarding the meeting could be issued to the Members.

The Ministry will make every effort to arrange a committee room in the Parliament House/Parliament House Annexe for the meeting. If a committee room in these buildings is not available, the Ministry concerned will have to arrange a committee room for holding the meeting themselves. In that case, they will have to make transport arrangements for the Members from Parliament House to the venue of the meeting and back to Parliament House on conclusion of the meeting.

It is noticed that most of the Ministries fix their meeting towards the end of the Inter-Session period which results in overlapping of several meetings on the same date making it very difficult for this Ministry to get committee rooms in Parliament House/Parliament House Annexe for the purpose. In view of this, Ministries are requested kindly to fix the date of meetings of their Consultative Committee as much in advance as possible and intimate the same to this Ministry for booking committee rooms and issuing notices to the Members.

It is also stated that Ministry/Department can hold one meeting of their Consultative Committee in a calendar year during an inter-session period outside Delhi anywhere in India if the Chairman of the committee so desires.

During the inter-session period, Members are normally away at their constituencies, and notices of the meetings, agenda papers etc. are, therefore, to be sent to them both at their Delhi and permanent addresses. The Ministries/Departments are, therefore, requested to keep this in view and give sufficient time to the Members to suggest items for discussion and/or study the agenda papers.

The Ministries are reminded that the time schedule etc. for circulation of papers to Members through this Ministry for the meeting is as under:

Minutes of the last meeting Action taken report on the minutes of the last meeting Agenda papers of the ensuing meeting.	At least, ten working days before the date of the next meeting.
Number of copies to be supplied to this Ministry	Double the number of Members plus ten

It may be noted that action on papers received after 4.00 p.m. in this Ministry will be taken only on the next working day. The Ministries are, therefore, requested to ensure that the papers are delivered in this Ministry before 4.00 p.m. positively if these are to be sent to Members on the same day.

This may kindly be treated as **IMMEDIATE.**

( )
DEPUTY SECRETARY TO THE GOVT. OF INDIA
TELE.NO.23034844

Ministry/Department of
(Shri/Smt.)
New Delhi.

To

All Ministries/Departments of Govt. of India,
(Parliament Section),
New Delhi.

ANNEX VII-J

TIME SCHEDULE FOR SUPPLY OF PAPERS TO MEMBERS OF CONSULTATIVE COMMITTEES

Papers to be supplied	Time Schedule	No. of copies to be supplied to this Ministry during session period meetings	No. of copies to be supplied to this Ministry during inter-session meetings
1. Minutes of the meeting	Ten working days before the date of meeting (Irrespective of whether the meetings are to be held during the session or in the inter-session period)	Number of Members of the Committee plus ten	Double the number of the Members of the Committee plus ten
2. Agenda	-do-	-do-	-do-
3. Action taken Report on the minutes of the last meeting	-do-	-do-	-do-

ANNEX VII-K

No.F. 7-1/74-CB
Government of India
Department of Parliamentary Affairs

87, Parliament House,
New Delhi.

July 17, 1974.

OFFICE MEMORANDUM

The undersigned is directed to state that at a meeting with the Leaders of Opposition parties held by the Minister of Parliamentary Affairs on 30.4.74 regarding briefing of the press about the deliberations of the Consultative Committees, the earlier decision of the Chief Whips/Whips circulated with office memorandum of even number dated 2 April, 1974 was reviewed and in lieu thereof it has been decided as follows:-

> "While it was agreed that in the Consultative Committees the discussions should be free and frank, it was also decided that any information which in the opinion of the Committee was of a classified and confidential nature, should not be reported to the press".

The Ministry of Home Affairs etc. are requested to kindly keep in view the above decision while dealing with the deliberations of the Consultative Committees.

Sd/-
R.M. Bhargava
Deputy Secretary to the Govt. of India

To

All the Ministries/Deptts.
(Shri----------------------------)
Ministry/Deptt. of ----------------
New Delhi.

ANNEX VII-L

GUIDELINES FOR SANCTION OF TA/DA TO MEMBERS OF PARLIAMENT IN CONNECTION WITH THE MEETINGS OF CONSULTATIVE COMMITTEES

(Prepared in consultation with the Ministry of Finance)

S. No.	Contingency	Entitlement of the Member
1.	Member reaches place of Meeting for attending the meeting. The meeting was cancelled/postponed earlier but the Member did not receive the intimation regarding postponement/cancellation before starting for the place of the meeting. Or, Member reaches the place of meeting and the meeting is cancelled on the day of the meeting or on the previous day.	Both TA and DA may be paid, with the approval of the Minister of Parliamentary Affairs
2.	Member reaches place of meeting late on the day of the meeting due to delayed arrival of plane or train, or due to breakdown of vehicle or due to any other reasons beyond his control;	Only TA may be approval of the Minister of Parliamentary Affairs
3.	Member reaches place of meeting but is unable to attend the meeting due to illness; and	

4.	Member reaches place of meeting for the meeting, but on the day of the meeting he receives message of somebody's death or serious illness or some similar emergent occurrence compelling him to leave Delhi immediately.	Only TA may be paid, with the approval of the Minister of Parliamentary Affairs.

[MPA F. No. 19 (1)/86-CB/Pt.II and Ministry of Finance (Department of Expenditure) D.O. No. 3(13)/MD-II/86 dated 15-5-87 and of 15-7-87]

ANNEX VII-M

No. F.6-8/98-CB
Government of India
Ministry of Parliamentary Affairs

86-B, Parliament House,
New Delhi

21st November, 1994

OFFICE MEMORANDUM

Subject: Constitution and functioning of Sub-Committees of Consultative Committees

1. Consultative Committees of Members of Parliament attached to the various Ministries function under a set of guidelines. While these guidelines do not speak of any sub-committee to be set up by the Consultative Committee, in the last few years, some Consultative Committees have constituted sub-committees to go into certain aspects of the working of their Ministries.

2. The matter relating to sub-committees of Consultative Committees has been reviewed in the Ministry of Parliamentary Affairs and it has been decided, with the approval of the Minister of Parliamentary Affairs, to issue the following instructions with regard to the constitution and functioning of sub-committees of the Consultative Committees:

   (i) Consultative Committees, being informal bodies, should not ordinarily, set up sub-committees;
   (ii) Instead of setting up sub-committees for a detailed enquiry they should get exhaustive information regarding any particular aspect of working of the Ministry. The Minister-in-charge who presides over the meetings of Consultative Committees can direct the officials to furnish the relevant information;

(iii) In rare cases, where the Members insist on constituting a sub-committee, it can be constituted with the approval of Minster-in-charge and in consultation with the Ministry of Parliamentary Affairs. *The term of a sub-committee shall in no case exceed three months. No request for any extension of tenure of a sub-committee beyond three months shall be entertained;*

(iv) The sub-committees may meet only at Delhi and in case they are required to visit places outside Delhi, the Members may kindly make the visit on the strength of their free railway/air passes.

3. All Ministries/Departments are requested to strictly follow the above instructions while processing the proposals for constituting the sub-committees.

4. The receipt of this O.M. may please be acknowledged.

Sd/
(G.V. Subrahmanyam)
Deputy Secretary to the Govt. of India
Tele.No. 3034732

To
All Ministries/Departments

ANNEX VII-N

CHECK LIST

1. The Consultative Committees may be constituted as soon as possible after the constitution of the new Lok Sabha.
2. The maximum limit of Membership on a Consultative Committee is 40 Members from both the Houses.
3. Consultative Committees are not constituted for a Ministry/Department if a minimum of 10 Members have not given their option for being nominated on that committee.
4. Members having special interest in subjects concerning a particular Ministry/Department can be nominated as Permanent Special Invitees on Consultative Committee attached with such Ministry/Department. A maximum of 4 Members can be nominated as Permanent Special Invitees on a Consultative Committee.
5. Leaders of allied parties, opposition parties/groups other than those having strength of less than 5 Members are requested by the Minister of Parliamentary Affairs to furnish preferences in respect of Members of their parties for nomination on Consultative Committees.
6. Members of the main ruling party and those opposition and allied parties having less than 5 Members as also nominated Members are individually requested by the Minister of Parliamentary Affairs to furnish their preferences for nomination on the three Consultative Committees in the order of their preferences.
7. Each Consultative Committee is expected to hold one meeting each during the session and inter-session period, the only exception being the Consultative Committee for the Ministry of Railways.
8. Ministries/Departments may hold one meeting each of their Consultative Committee, in a calendar year, during an inter-session period, anywhere in India, if the Chairman of the committee so desires.

9. During the session period, meetings of the Consultative Committees may be held preferably at 9.00 or 9.30 a.m. and after 6.30 p.m. to enable the Members to attend their respective Houses.
10. There is no requirement of quorum in the meetings of the Consultative Committees.
11. Any information which in the opinion of the committee is of a classified/confidential nature should not be reported to the press.

ANNEX VIII-A

F.No.1(__)/____ Leg.II
Government of India
Ministry of Parliamentary Affairs

90, Parliament House,
New Delhi.

Dated:

OFFICE MEMORANDUM

Subject: Matters raised under Rule 377 in the Lok Sabha

The undersigned is directed to state that under Rule 377 of the Rules of Procedure and Conduct of Business in the Lok Sabha, Members of the Lok Sabha are permitted by the Speaker to bring to the notice of the House important matters deserving Special Mention. Extracts from the proceedings of the House containing these points are forwarded to the concerned Ministries/ Departments by the Lok Sabha Secretariat.

With a view to enable the Parliament Sections of the various Ministries/Departments to watch the progress of the disposal of such matters, the Ministry of Parliamentary Affairs also sends a weekly statement of matters raised in the Lok Sabha. A statement indicating the matters raised during the week commencing______________________________ is sent herewith for favour of necessary action.

Parliament Section of the Ministry of Home Affairs etc., are requested to ensure that replies in respect of these matters are sent to the Members over the Signature of the Minister as expeditiously as possible, but within a month from the date of the matters being raised in the House.

It may invariably be ensured that all communications containing interim or final replies are endorsed to this Ministry and the concerned Parliament Secretariat without any loss of time to obviate avoidable criticism on the floor of the House for delayed action on the part of Ministries /Departments.

( )

Under Secretary to the Govt. of India
Telephone No.:

Ministry of____________________
Parliament Section
New Delhi.

ANNEX VIII-B

F.No.2(__)/____ Leg.II
Government of India
Ministry of Parliamentary Affairs

90, Parliament House,
New Delhi.

Dated:

OFFICE MEMORANDUM

Subject: Matters of urgent public importance in the Rajya Sabha-Special Mentions

The undersigned is directed to state that Chairman, Rajya Sabha, permits Members to mention matters of urgent public importance in the Rajya Sabha after the disposal of questions and Calling Attention. Extracts from the proceedings of the House containing these points are forwarded to the concerned Ministries/ Departments by the Rajya Sabha Secretariat.

With a view to enable the Parliament Sections of the various Ministries /Departments to watch the progress of the disposal of such matters, the Ministry of Parliamentary Affairs also sends a weekly statement of matters raised in Rajya Sabha. A statement indicating the matters raised during the week commencing .... is sent herewith for favour of necessary action.

Parliament Section of the Ministry of Home Affairs etc. are requested to ensure that replies in respect of these matters are sent to the Members over the signature of Minister as expeditiously as possible but within a period of one month from the date of the matters being raised in the House.

It may invariably be ensured that all communications containing interim or final replies are endorsed to this Ministry and the concerned Parliament Secretariat without any loss of time to obviate avoidable criticism on the floor of the House for delayed action on the part of Ministries/Departments.

( )
Under Secretary to the Govt. of India
Telephone No.

Ministry of____________________
Parliament Section
New Delhi.

ANNEX VIII-C

No.F.14(3)/89-Leg.II
Government of India
Ministry of Parliamentary Affairs

New Delhi.
Dated: 15th July ,1993

OFFICE MEMORANDUM

Subject: Matters raised under Rule 377 in Lok Sabha and by way of Special Mentions in Rajya Sabha - Procedure regarding

As Ministry of Home Affairs etc. are aware, Members of the Lok Sabha are permitted by the Speaker to raise matters of urgent public importance under Rule 377 of the Rules of Procedure and Conduct of Business in the Lok Sabha. Similarly in the Rajya Sabha, Members are allowed to raise such matters in the form of "Special Mentions". The Ministry of Parliamentary Affairs is the nodal Ministry for ensuring follow-up action by the Ministries on the matters raised under Rule 377 in the Lok Sabha and by way of Special Mentions in the Rajya Sabha. Ministries are supplied by the respective Parliament Secretariat extracts of the proceedings containing the above matters raised in the House. In addition , this Ministry sends to each Ministry a weekly list of such items raised in both Houses .

As regards the procedure to be followed for follow-up action on these matters , several circulars have been issued by this Ministry from time to time. For facility of ready reference all the instructions issued on the subject are consolidated hereunder:

1.	Immediate action on receipt of extracts of proceedings	On receipt of extracts of proceedings from the Lok Sabha/ Rajya Sabha Secretariat, the Ministries are expected to submit the same to their Minister for

information. On receipt of the weekly list of items from this Ministry, the Ministries should cross check the same with the extracts of proceedings and any discrepancy found between the two must immediately be brought to the notice of this Ministry.

2. Time limit for replies to be sent to Members	As per the decision of the Rules Committee of the Lok Sabha and Rajya Sabha, the Ministries should examine the matters and send replies to Members who raised them in the House, within a period of one month from the date the matters have been raised. In case it is not possible to stick to this time limit in respect of any matter for reasons such as having to collect information from several sources etc., an interim reply should be sent from the Minister to the Members concerned stating the reasons for the likely delay and the approximate time that may be taken for final disposal of the matters. Copies of the letter should be endorsed to this Ministry and also to the concerned Parliament Secretariat for information.

When a reply is sent to the Member a copy of the same should invariably be sent to this Ministry and to the Parliament Secretariat concerned so that the item can be deleted from the pending list.

3. Address for sending communications to the Members	All communications should be sent to Members of Parliament at their Delhi addresses when Parliament is in session. During the inter-session period, such communications should be sent to local as well as permanent addresses of the Members.
4. Transfer of matters	In case a Ministry finds that the subject matter of any item does not belong to them but to some other Ministry, they may take expeditious action for transferring the same to the Ministry concerned with the subject. But, while transferring the subject they should ask the transferee Ministry to accept the transfer and to intimate the acceptance of the transfer to this Ministry and also to the concerned Parliament Secretariat It should be noted in this connection that till such an intimation is received from the transferee Ministry, the item will continue to be shown as pending against the Ministry to whom it was originally sent. (In case there is any doubt as to which Ministry a particular subject pertains, procedure contained in Cabinet Secretary's D.O. letter No. 73/2/15/85-Estt. dated 25th April, 1985 should be followed.)
5. Signatory of the communications	Where a communication is addressed to a Minister , it will as far as practicable be replied to by the Minister himself. In other cases, a reply will normally be issued over the

	signature of an Officer not below the rank of Secretary.
6. Effect on matters of retirement of a Member	In case of matters under Rule 377 raised in the Lok Sabha by a Member who has subsequently resigned from the House or passed away, reply on the matters raised by him should be sent to the Lok Sabha Secretariat with a copy to this Ministry, so that the item can be deleted from the records. However, if the Member happens to be re-elected to the same Lok Sabha , the reply on the matter raised by him should be sent to him with copies to the Lok Sabha Secretariat and this Ministry. In case of Special Mentions made in the Rajya Sabha by a Member who has subsequently retired, resigned or has passed away, no reply need be sent to the Rajya Sabha Secretariat and this Ministry. However, if such a Member has been re-elected to the Rajya Sabha a reply on the Special Mention raised by him should be sent to him with a copy to the Rajya Sabha Secretariat and this Ministry. The difference in the procedure in regard to the matters raised under Rule 377 in the Lok Sabha and the Special Mentions made in the Rajya Sabha, as stated above, should be carefully noted.
7. The effect of dissolution of Lok Sabha	On the dissolution of the Lok Sabha just as Bills, Resolutions, Motions etc., the matters raised under Rule 377 will also lapse.

The importance of taking expeditious action on the matters raised by Hon'ble Members on the floor of the Lok Sabha/Rajya Sabha cannot be overemphasised. Any delay in taking action on such matters may lead to criticism by the Hon'ble Members on the floor of the House or in writing. It should be the effort of every Ministry to dispose of the matters raised by Members within the prescribed time limit, so as to avoid criticism on account of the delay.

The Ministry of Home Affairs, etc., are requested to kindly circulate the above instructions to all officers and sections in the Ministry and to ensure strict compliance with the same.

Sd/-
(G.V. SUBRAHMANYAM)
DEPUTY SECRETARY

To

All Ministries/Departments (Parliament Section)

ANNEX VIII-D

MINISTER OF PARLIAMENTARY AFFAIRS
GOVERNMENT OF INDIA

D.O.No. Dated:

This is regarding prompt disposal of matters raised by MPs under Rule 377 in the Lok Sabha and by way of Special Mentions in the Rajya Sabha.

Replies to such matters are required to be sent by the Ministries/ Departments under the signature of their Minister to the Members concerned within a period of one month from the date on which they are raised in the House.

A recent review undertaken of the pendency pertaining to your Ministry shows that .... items are pending as on ....I request you to expedite replies, on the basis of facts, in respect of all such matters pending in your Ministry, to the Members concerned, under intimation to the Ministry of Parliamentary Affairs and the Lok Sabha/Rajya Sabha Secretariat, as the case may be, at the earliest.

If any of the matters given in the list do not concern your Ministry/Department, you are requested kindly to get the transfer of the matter accepted by the concerned Ministry. The matter will continue to remain pending against your Ministry until its acceptance is received from the transferee Ministry. In case you have already sent replies to the Members to any of these matters, please arrange to send copies of those replies to the Ministry of Parliamentary Affairs so that the same can be deleted from the list of pending matters.

With regards,

Yours sincerely,

( )

Minister of Parliamentary Affairs

To

Ministers in-charge of the Ministries/Departments conccerned

ANNEX VIII-E

D.O.No. Dated:

During a recent review of the pending matters raised under Rule 377 in the Lok Sabha and Special Mention in the Rajya Sabha, and of the assurances given by the Ministers in both the Houses of Parliament, it has been found that a large number of cases are still pending with your Department (lists enclosed). As you are aware, the Department concerned is expected to take action on these matters within a stipulated timeframe and send suitable replies to the Members concerned/lay the copy of the Implementation Report on the Table of the concerned House in respect of assurances. The Chairman, Rajya Sabha, has also expressed concern over the long pending Special Mentions.

In order to expedite replies of pending matters under Rule 377 and Special Mentions, the Hon'ble Minister of Parliamentary Affairs and Health and Family Welfare has recently written to the Minister of Finance.

As desired by the Hon'ble Minister of Parliamentary Affairs and Health and Family Welfare, it has been decided to convene a meeting at .... on .... in room no. .... Parliament House to discuss these pending matters/assurances as per the lists enclosed.

I shall be grateful if you could please depute the concerned Joint Secretary/Secretaries to provide details of action taken/ proposed to be taken in order to reduce the pendency.

With regards,

Yours sincerely,

( )
SECRETARY

Shri ....
Secretary,
....
....
....

ANNEX VIII-F

CHECK LIST

1. Whether the Bulletin Part-I of the two Houses *inter alia* containing the gist of matters raised under Rule 377/ Special Mentions is being received daily.
2. Whether endorsement to communications addressed to various Ministries/Departments by the Parliament Secretariats were received in the Ministry along with relevant extracts from the proceedings on the following day on which these matters were raised in the two Houses.
3. Whether the number and subject of the extracts received from the two Secretariats for each sitting of the House correspond with the gist of such matters appearing in Parliamentary Bulletins Part - I of the two Houses for those dates.
4. Whether pendency of matters raised in the two Houses was reconciled with the position of pendency of these matters as obtaining in the two Secretariats periodically, particularly at the commencement of each Parliament session.
5. Whether review of pendency of these matters was undertaken during each inter-session period and, where necessary, the meetings either in Parliament House or in the room of the Secretary of the respective Ministries, as the case may be, were convened to ensure expeditious disposal of these matters.
6. Whether on retirement, resignation or expiry of Members, matters relating to such Members were deleted and Ministries concerned informed thereof.
7. Whether on dissolution of the Lok Sabha, a circular was sent to all the Ministries/Departments informing them that all the matters pending in the Lok Sabha have lapsed on dissolution of the Lok Sabha.

ANNEX IX-A

STANDARD LIST OF EXPRESSIONS CONSTITUTING ASSURANCES

1. The matter is under consideration.
2. I shall look into it.
3. Enquiries are being made.
4. I shall inform the Hon'ble Member.
5. This is primarily the concern of the State Government but I shall look into it.
6. I shall write to the State Governments.
7. I assure the House all suggestions by Hon'ble Member will be carefully considered.
8. I shall study the conditions on the spot during my tour.
9. I shall consider the matter.
10. I will consider it.
11. I will suggest to the State Government.
12. We will put the matter in the shape of a resolution.
13. I shall see what can be done about it.
14. I will look into the matter before I can say anything.
15. The suggestion will be taken into consideration.
16. The matter will be considered at the conference to be held on....
17. The matter is still under examination and if anything is required to be done it will certainly be done.
18. The matter will be taken up with the Government of.....
19. I have no information; but I am prepared to look into the matter.
20. Efforts are being made to collect the necessary data.
21. The suggestions made will be borne in mind while framing the rules.
22. If the Hon'ble Member so desires, I can issue further instructions.
23. Copy of the report, when finalised, will be placed in the Parliament Library.
24. I shall supply it to the Hon'ble Member.

25. I think it can be done.
26. If the Hon'ble Member's allegation is true, I shall certainly have the matter gone into.
27. We shall have to find that out.
28. I shall draw the attention of the.......Government who I hope will take adequate steps in this direction.
29. It is a suggestion for action which will be considered.
30. (Discussion of Railway Budget). All the points raised by various Members will be considered and the result will be communicated to each Member.
31. Information is being collected and will be laid on the Table of the Lok Sabha/Rajya Sabha.
32. I am reviewing the position.
33. Directions by the Speaker/Chairman, Deputy Speaker/Deputy Chairman or the Vice-Chairman involving action on the part of Ministers.
34. All specific points on which information is asked for and promised.

ANNEX IX-B

MINISTRY OF PARLIAMENTARY AFFAIRS

Revised instructions Regarding the Decentralisation of Powers in Respect of Disposal of Cases in Each Section of Ministry of Parliamentary Affairs

---

Implementation I and II Sections

1. Assurances may be culled out after approval of Under Secretary. However, assurances relating to MPs, Ministers and the assurances relating to the Ministry of Parliamentary Affairs may be culled out after approval of Secretary.
2. The cases of extension for implementation of assurances should normally be processed after approval of the Under Secretary. However, cases in which assurances were extracted with the approval of senior officers may be processed with the approval of Joint Secretary.
3. Cases relating to dropping of assurances may be processed after obtaining the approval of Joint Secretary.
4. Cases relating to scrutinising and laying the Implementation Reports in respect of assurances should normally be decided at the level of Under Secretary. However, Implementation Reports in respect of assurances relating to MPs, Ministers and any other important Implementation Report may be laid on the Table after approval of Secretary.
5. All cases of assurances pending five years or more should be put up to Joint Secretary.
6. Recommendations of a general nature made by the Committee on Government Assurances may be processed after having the approval of Secretary.
7. Intimation about the implementation of assurances may be sent at the level of Section Officer in respect of Ministries/Departments and at the level of Under Secretary in respect of Members of Parliament.

ANNEX IX-C

INSTRUCTIONS

An assurance is required to be fulfilled within a period of three months from the date of the assurance. This time-limit has to be strictly observed. If, however, there are any genuine and practical difficulties in fulfilling the assurance within this period, the Ministry/Department may make a reference with the approval of the Minister of State in charge of the concerned Ministry/ Department to the respective Committee on Government Assurances direct, with a copy to the Ministry of Parliamentary Affairs, giving specific reasons for the delay and the probable time required for fulfilling the assurance. Such requests should reach the respective Secretariats well before the expiry of the original stipulated period of three months or the expiry of any extension already sought/granted.

If the Ministry/Department feel that this does not constitute an assurance or it is not feasible to fulfil the same for any valid reasons they may write with the approval of the Minister/Minister of State in charge of the concerned Ministry/Department to the respective Committee on Government Assurances direct with a copy to the Ministry Parliamentary Affairs, requesting for the deletion of the assurance. Such requests should be based on cogent and convincing reasons.

The Implementation Report should be sent only to the Ministry of Parliamentary Affairs, addressed to the Under Secretary (Implementation) (and not to the Rajya Sabha/Lok Sabha Secretariat). No advance copies of the Implementation Reports are to be endorsed to the Rajya Sabha/Lok Sabha Secretariats.

The Implementation Report should strictly be in the 5-column Proforma enclosed herewith. The report should contain the headings shown on the top of the proforma and the matter given in columns 1 to 3 without any change whatsoever. In column 4, the Ministry may indicate how the assurance has been fulfilled, or enclose a self-contained statement for the purpose mentioning in column 4 that a statement is enclosed.

In case an assurance is not fulfilled within the stipulated time of three months, reasons for the delay should invariably be stated in column-5 (Remarks column) of the Implementation Report. Implementation Reports found deficient in this respect will be returned to the Ministry/Department concerned.

As for the number of copies, if the assurance was given to one Member, 15 copies of the report should be furnished to this Ministry. For each additional Member, one extra copy has to be added to this number.

As all papers to be laid on the Table of the House are required to be bilingual, the Implementation Reports should be sent to this Ministry in both English and Hindi versions simultaneously.

It should be ensured that there is no discrepancy in the facts and figures stated in the English and Hindi versions.

Utmost care should be taken in the preparation of the Implementation Reports as these are to be submitted to Parliament. The reports should be neat and very legible. There should be no over-writings/interpolations/cutting or too many corrections which may make the report look shabby.

The communication forwarding the Implementation Report to this Ministry should clearly state that the report has the approval of the Minister/Minister of State in charge of the concerned Ministry/Department.

In case the Ministry/Department envisage unduly long delay in collecting the information for full implementation of the assurance, they may furnish part-Implementation Reports in the same proforma containing the information collected form time to time.

All communications addressed to this Ministry should invariably carry the telephone numbers of the officers signing the same.

ANNEX IX-D

CHECK LIST FOR LAYING OF IMPLEMENTATION REPORTS ON ASSURANCES

The Implementation Reports of the assurances are laid on the Table of the Houses by Minister/Ministers of State of Parliamentary Affairs twice during a session—once in the first week and the other in the last week.

1. Implementation Reports received from the Ministries/ Departments are scrutinized for errors and corrections are carried out wherever necessary.
2. Implementation Reports are submitted for approval (Under Secretary/Deputy Secretary Level).
3. A note is submitted about 8 days prior to the proposed date of laying seeking convenience of Hon'ble Minister of State MOS(LS) or MOS (RS) as the case may be.
4. Session-wise/Year-wise/Ministry-wise sets of Implementation Reports are prepared and stitched. In case of Rajya Sabha assurances, a quarterly status-note detailing Ministry-wise pendency position of the assurances is also attached alongwith the sets.
5. After convenience of Minister of State is received, advance intimation for including the items in the list of business for that day is sent 4-5 days ahead of the date of laying to the Table Office of Lok Sabha/Rajya Sabha and our Legislative-I Section.
6. One set of Implementation Reports is submitted to MOS 4 days in advance of the date of laying for authentication.
7. The authenticated sets along with two other sets are sent to the Table Office of the Lok Sabha/Rajya Sabha 3 days in advance of the date of laying.
8. A brief detailing the year-wise position of pendency and number of Implementation Reports being laid etc. is prepared and sent to HMPA/MO/Secretary/MPA/ DS(A)/US(A) one day before the day of laying.

9. DS(A)/US(I)/SO(I-II) are present in the official gallery at the time of laying.
10. After the Implementation Reports are laid on the Table of the House, on the same day, two sets of the Implementation Reports are sent to the Secretariat of the Committee on Government Assurances (LS/RS).
11. A copy of the individual Implementation Reports in respect of the assurances are sent to the Members concerned after the laying.

After intimation is sent to the Members of Parliament, Ministries/Departments are informed about the laying of the Implementation Reports concerning them.

ANNEX X-A

STATEMENT SHOWING THE SALARY, ALLOWANCES AND OTHER FACILITIES ADMISSIBLE TO MEMBERS OF PARLIAMENT

(As on 9.01.2004)

S. No.	Item	Admissibility
1.	Salary	Rs. 12,000 per month
2.	Daily Allowances	Rs. 500. The MPs have to sign the register except on holidays.
3.	Other Allowances	Constituency Allowances @ Rs. 10,000 per month and Office Expense Allowances @ Rs. 14,000 per month, out of which Rs. 3000 should be for expenses on stationery items etc., Rs. 1000 p.m. for franking of letters and Lok Sabha/Rajya Sabha Secretariat may pay up to Rs. 10,000 per month to the person(s) engaged by the MP for obtaining secretarial assistance.
4.	Telephone	1,50,000 free calls per annum on all the three telephones at Delhi, constituency residence and for Internet connectivity purposes, pooled together. Trunk call bills adjusted within the monetary ceiling of 1,50,000 local calls per annum. Excess calls made over and above the quota allowed to be adjusted in the next year's quota. Members whose constituencies are 1000 km. away from Delhi have been allowed 20,000 additional free local calls. Members have also been provided Mobile

		phone with the provision that the calls made from it will be adjusted against 1,50,000 free local calls already available to them.
5.	Housing	Rent-free flats only (including hostel accommodation). If a Member is allotted bungalow at his request, he shall pay full normal rent if he is entitled to such accommodation. Rent free furniture up to the monetary ceiling of Rs. 24,000 for durable furniture and Rs.6,000 for non-durable furniture. Free washing of sofa covers and curtains every three months. Tiles in bathroom, kitchen wherever demanded by MP.
6.	Water and Electricity	50,000 units of electricity per annum, 25,000 units each on Light/Power meters or pooled together. Members who have no power meters installed are allowed 50,000 units per annum on light meter and 4,000 kilolitres of water per annum beginning January every year.
7.	Medical	As available to Grade-I Officers of the Central Government under CGHS.
8.	Conveyance Advance	Rs. 1,00,000 on interest @ as applicable to the Central Government employees recoverable within a maximum period of five years not extending beyond the tenure of MP.
9.	Travelling Allowances	*Rail* One 1st Class + One II Class fare. *Air:* One and one-fourth air fare in any airline. Also air fare for one companion in case of a blind/physically incapacitated MP.

	Steamer : One and 3/5th of the fare for the highest Class (without diet). *Road* : (i) Rs. 8 per km, (ii) Minimum 120 to/fro from Delhi airport and residence at Delhi, (iii) TA by rail or by road during session/committee meetings for to and fro journeys between usual place of duty to the nearest airport when the places are not connected by mail/express and superfast trains, (iv) TA for air journey(s) during the short interval between two sittings of a Department related Standing Committee during budget session recess, limited to one air fare + DA for the days of absence, (v) Spouse of member also entitled to eight single journeys in a year, (vi) Members residing within 300 km distance from Delhi may travel by road and claim road mileage @ Rs. 8 per km, and (vii) Members from North-Eastern States of Arunachal Pradesh, Assam, Manipur Meghalaya, Mizoram, Nagaland, Sikkim, and Tripura may travel by road from their residence in the constituency/State to the nearest airport.
10. Travelling facility	(i) Railway pass for MP for travelling in AC-I Class or Executive Class of any Indian Railway. Spouse can also travel with MP in the same class. If such journey or part thereof is undertaken by air from place other than usual place of residence of the Member to Delhi and back, an MP is entitled to an amount equal to the fare by air for such journey or part thereof or the amount equal to the journey performed by air from usual place of residence of the Member to Delhi and back whichever is less, (ii) Companion can also travel with MP in AC II tier, (iii) Member having no spouse can take one person with him in AC-I/Executive Class in addition to the companion allowed in

		AC-II tier, (iv) To and fro air travel for the MP from Ladakh for Member and spouse/ companion, (v) To and fro air travel facility for the Member and spouse/companion between the Island and the mainland, (vi) Blind or physically incapacitated Member can take an attendant in the air/ rail journey in which he himself travels in lieu of the companion in AC-II tier, (vii) Thirty two single air journeys in a year from any place to another place in India either alone or along with spouse or any number of companions or relatives within this ceiling, (viii) Spouse or companion of a Member may travel alone to join the Member eight times in a year against 32 air journeys available to the Member in a year, (ix) Steamer passes for highest class of steamer for MPs and spouse/ companion (without diet), and (x) To and fro air travel when the usual place of residence is inaccessible by rail, road or steamer, between the nearest place in his constituency where there is air service and the nearest place having rail service.
11.	Travelling facility to the Spouse of Member	The Spouse of a member has been allowed to and fro rail/air journeys once during each session of Parliament and twice during the Budget Session with the maximum limit of 8 such single journeys in a year.
12.	Miscellaneous	Newly elected/nominated Members of Lok Sabha and Rajya Sabha reaching Delhi prior to publication of notification by Election Commission will be entitled to TA and Transit accommodation.

ANNEX X-B

FACILITIES EXTENDED TO EX-MEMBERS OF PARLIAMENT

1.	Pension	(i) Minimum pension of Rs. 3,000 per month to every person who has served for any period, as Member of Provisional Parliament or either House of Parliament and Rs. 600 per month for every year of membership of Parliament in excess of five years without any maximum ceiling. (ii) Ex-MPs pension allowed irrespective of any other pension without any upper limit on the aggregate. (iii) A period of nine months or more is reckoned equivalent to a complete one year for the purpose of payment of additional pension.
2.	Family Pension	Family pension @ Rs. 1500 p.m. for a period of five years from the date of death of the MP, to the spouse/dependent, if any.
3.	Travelling Facility	(i) Ex-MPs along with a companion are entitled to free AC-II tier rail travel facility from one place to any other place in India, on the basis of an authorisation issued for this purpose by the concerned Secretariat of Parliament as the case may be. (ii) Entitled to travel alone in any train by any railway by AC I Class in lieu of two AC-II tier journeys.
4.	Medical Facilities	CGH Scheme is applicable to former Members of Parliament residing in cities covered by the CGH Scheme on payment of contribution at the same rate as they were

		paying as Members of Parliament. This facility can be obtained direct from the Director General (CGHS), Ministry of Health and Family Welfare, Nirman Bhawan, New Delhi.
5.	Facilities to Members of Prematurely dissolved Lok Sabha	(a) The Members of prematurely dissolved Lok Sabha are allowed to utilise the balance of unutilised (i) free 1,50,000 telephone calls, (ii) 50,000 units of electricity, and (iii) 4,000 kls. of water during the period from dissolution of the Lok Sabha till constitution of the new Lok Sabha . In case of excess consumption of such units, the same will be allowed to be adjusted in case the member is elected to the new Lok Sabha against the quota that will be available to him. (b) Residential accommodation can be retained for a maximum period of one month from the date of dissolution till the constitution of the next (new) Lok Sabha. (c) Ex-Members of a dissolved Lok Sabha are allowed to retain the general pool residential accommodation on payment of normal licence fee, provided that such ex-Members will vacate the accommodation within a period of 15 days from the date of constitution of the new Lok Sabha. In case any ex-Member does not vacate the general pool accommodation within 15 days from the date of constitution of the next Lok Sabha, he/she will be charged damages for the entire period of overstay beyond the normal concessional period of one month.

ANNEX XI-A

संसदीय कार्य मंत्रालय
MINISTRY OF PARLIAMENTARY AFFAIRS

प्रोटोकॉल एवं कल्याण अनुभाग
Protocol and Welfare Section

ADMISSION OF MPs TO HOSPITALS IN DELHI FOR TREATMENT

As on: 10.11.2003 Time: 11.15 A.M.

S. No.	Name of the Member	Date of Admi-ssion	Nature of illness	Nature of Hospital	Particulars of Ward, Room No. Doctor Incharge	Date of visit to the Hospital
1.	Sh. Kanshi Ram, MP (RS), BSP	16.9. 2003	Brain Stroke	Batra Hospital	New Building, Room No. 535 Dr. M.L. Sindhwani	*18.9.2003
2.	Sh. Mohamad Anwarul Haque, MP (LS), RJD (D)	21.10. 2003	Diabetes	AIIMS	Private Ward, No. 501 Prof. S.C. Tiwari	*24.10.2003
3.	Dr. Ram Lakhan Singh, MP(LS) BJP	22.10. 2003	Gallbla-dder problem	AIIMS	Private Ward, Room No. 301 Dr. S.K. Acharya	*24.10.2003

* Bouquet was presented on behalf of HMPA

SECTION OFFICER(P&W)

Copy for information to: PSs to HMPA/MOSs/Secretary/DS(R&C)/US(ME)/Concerned Parl. Party Office/NIC-MPA.

ANNEX XI-B

CHECK LIST

Transportation of Dead Body of Members of Parliament

1. Receive call from hospitals etc.
2. Carry money/exchange voucher/list of important telephone numbers.
3. Contact bereaved family members/party and find out their wishes about place of last rites, mode and time of travel etc.
4. Inform MPA/MOSs/Secretary/JS/DS(RandC).
5. Instructions to florist for wreath.
6. Arrange staff car (if possible) or alternatively Taxi.
7. Obtain Death Certificate and make copies.
8. Obtain No Objection Certificate from local Police and make copies.
9. Inform Undertaker for Coffin Box, Hearse Van etc. and tie up timing.
10. Inform Anatomy Department for Embalming.
11. (a) Accompany dead body for embalming;
    (b) carry death certificate/money;
    (c) receive embalmed body/obtain embalming certificate and make copies;
    (d) obtain cash memo of payment of embalming charges from hospital.
12. (a) Purchase Air/Rail Tickets for accompanying persons (only one);
    (b) ensure confirmation of reservation of ticket (also reservation for relatives) through Office of Minister of Civil Aviation/Railways;
    (c) Keep Airport Manager/Cargo Manager/Duty Officer/Station Master (Railways) alert.
13. (a) Ascertain timing of MPA/MOSs for paying homage to departed soul and keep the wreath ready;
    (b) Keep Secretary/JS/DS(RandC) informed about it.

14. Accompany dead body up to Airport/Railway Station and Meet Duty Officer.
15. Book the Coffin (carry cash/exchange voucher/ embalming certificate/NOC/ death certificate) and ensure loading of box.
16. Hand over papers (for releasing the box at destination) to accompanying persons.
17. Intimate DS(R&C)/JS/Secretary at the end of the operation.
18. Prepare a report.
19. Claim/adjust expenditure.
20. Pass and forward bill to A&P Section.

ANNEX XII-A

No.F.1-1/95-CB
Government of India
Ministry of Parliamentary Affairs

86-B, Parliament House,
New Delhi - 110 001

Dated: 9 November, 1995

OFFICE MEMORANDUM

Subject: Nomination of Members of Parliament on Committees, Councils, Boards, Commission etc. set up by the Government

As the Ministry of Home Affairs etc. are aware, the subject of 'Nomination of Members of Parliament on Committees and other bodies set up by the Government' is a subject allocated to the Ministry of Parliamentary Affairs under the Government of India (Allocation of Business) Rules made by the President under article 77(3) of the Constitution. By virtue of this, Members of Parliament are to be selected and nominated on all Government bodies by the Minister of Parliamentary Affairs only. This function has been entrusted specifically to the Minister of Parliamentary Affairs for the reasons (a) that there should be a single authority through which all nominations of Members of Parliament on various bodies set up by the Government are made, (b) the Minister of Parliamentary Affairs being the Government Chief Whip is eminently suited to discharge this function as he is in the know of the interest, aptitude, experience, suitability and availability of Members of Parliament in relation to the proposed assignments and (c) that certain uniform, fair and objective norms would be observed for equitable distribution of memberships of the various Government bodies among the Members belonging to different sections of both Houses of Parliament to avoid a situation where some Members come to be over burdened with assignments while others have none.

This Ministry has been advising the Ministries/Departments from time to time that they should not nominate Members of Parliament on Government bodies, but should leave the selection of Members and their nomination to the Minister of Parliamentary Affairs. It has been noticed of late that in spite of the above advice, some Ministries continue to nominate or select Members of Parliament and mention their names in the proposal itself which, it may be appreciated, causes embarrassment to all concerned in case these names are not found compatible with the requirements mentioned in para-1 above.

Considering all aspects of the matter, it has been decided, with the approval of the Minister of Parliamentary Affairs, to lay down clear cut guidelines on the subject, consolidating, and in supersession of, all instructions issued earlier. These GUIDELINES are stated below:

Guidelines

(1) No Ministry, except the Ministry of Parliamentary Affairs, shall nominate Members of Parliament on any Committees, Councils, Commissions, Boards, etc. (hereinafter called 'Government bodies') set up by the Government of India in any Ministry. (This does not include bodies on which Members of Parliament are to be nominated by the Speaker, Lok Sabha or Chairman, Rajya Sabha or to be elected by either House of Parliament by virtue of any statutory provisions).

(2) If the Ministry sponsoring the proposal consider any particular Member(s) of Parliament suitable for the assignment, this information with full supporting reasons, should be conveyed 'confidentially' at the Ministers' level or Secretaries' level. No names of Members of Parliament should be mentioned in the proposal. Care should be taken to ensure that the proposal is not leaked to the Members concerned before their names are approved by the Minister of Parliamentary Affairs.

(3) All proposals for nomination of MPs should be sent to the Ministry of Parliamentary Affairs, only in the proforma at Annex XII-B. Proposals sent otherwise than in this proforma will be returned to the Ministry concerned for compliance with these guidelines.

(4) The Minister of Parliamentary Affairs will select Members of Parliament for nomination. Thereafter, the Members and the

Ministry concerned will be informed about the nomination/re-nomination by this Ministry. Consent of the Members regarding their nomination is not called for. However, Members are requested to let this Ministry know, if for any reasons they find it difficult to serve on the body. Members are also informed that under the Parliament (Prevention of Disqualification) Act, 1959, they may draw only "compensatory allowance" and no other remuneration for attending the meeting of the body. "Compensatory allowance" according to the above Act means:

> "Any sum of money payable to the holder of an office by way of daily allowance, such allowance not exceeding the amount of daily allowance to which a Member of Parliament is entitled under the Salary, Allowances and Pension of Members of Parliament Act, 1954 (30 of 1954), any conveyance allowance, house rent allowance or travelling allowance for the purpose of enabling him to recoup any expenditure incurred by him in performing the functions of that office".

(5) On receipt of the communication regarding nomination of Members of Parliament, Ministries should proceed to notify their nomination and supply to them all necessary literature including the constitution, functions, programme of work, etc. of the Body under intimation to this Ministry. A copy of the Notification shall invariably be endorsed to the Ministry of Parliamentary Affairs.

(6) Proposal for nomination of Members of Parliament on a Government body should be sent to the Ministry of Parliamentary Affairs, only if the Ministry setting up the body is in a position to issue Notification regarding the nomination of the Member of Parliament soon after receipt of the communication from this Ministry. Where a Government body is to comprise representatives of any other interests, nomination of such representatives of other interests may be finalised and then only the proposal for nomination of Members of Parliament be sent to the Ministry of Parliamentary Affairs so that delay in issuing Notification by the concerned Ministry is obviated.

(7) If for any reason it is proposed not to constitute the Government body during any of the above stages, the fact should be communicated to the Ministry of Parliamentary Affairs with all the reasons for such decision.

(8) Where a Government body is proposed to be wound up or discontinued, it shall be brought to the notice of the Ministry of Parliamentary Affairs with reasons for the decision.

(9) If it is decided to curtail or extend the term of a Government body, the decision shall be communicated to the Ministry of Parliamentary Affairs, as it implies curtailment or extension of the term of the Members of Parliament nominated thereon.

(10) Even where a Member of Parliament is proposed to be nominated on a Government body in his individual capacity or as a representative of a particular class, trade, profession, institution, etc., the concurrence of the Minister of Parliamentary Affairs should be obtained.

(11) Whenever a person already serving on a Government body becomes a Member of Parliament and it is proposed to continue his membership of the body, a reference should be made to the Ministry of Parliamentary Affairs in the prescribed proforma (Annex XII-B), for approval of the Minister of Parliamentary Affairs.

(12) In cases where a Member of Parliament nominated on a Government body ceases to be a Member thereof by resignation, expiration of his term on the body or death, fresh proposals should be sent to the Ministry of Parliamentary Affairs in the prescribed proforma (Annex XII-B) for filling up the vacancy.

(13) On the dissolution of Lok Sabha, all Members of the House cease to be Members of the Government bodies on which they were nominated. In such cases, fresh proposals should be sent to the Ministry of Parliamentary Affairs for nominating Members of the new Lok Sabha in their place. The Members of the Rajya Sabha nominated on a Government body, however, continue to serve thereon till the expiration of their term on the body or the date of their retirement from the Rajya Sabha, whichever is earlier. If, however, the Ministry decides to reconstitute the body for a fresh term and communicates this decision to the Ministry of Parliamentary Affairs, nominations of Members of Lok Sabha and Rajya Sabha will be made on the body *de novo.*

(14) In the case of Rajya Sabha Members, as stated in the above guidelines, they cease to be Members of the Government bodies on their retirement from the House. In such cases also, fresh proposals are to be sent to the Ministry of Parliamentary Affairs in the prescribed proforma for filling up the vacancies.

All Ministries/Departments are requested to strictly observe the above guidelines.

Receipt of this O.M. may be acknowledged.

Sd./-
(J. B. GUPTA)
Deputy Secretary to the Government of India
Tele. No. 23034844

To

All Ministries/Departments of Government of India (Parliament Sections) - with the request that copy of this O.M.may please be circulated to all concerned

Copy to:

PSs to all Secretaries to the Government of India (for being placed before Secretaries)

ANNEX XII-B

PROFORMA

Form for seeking nomination of Members of Parliament on Committees, Councils, Boards, Commissions, etc. set up by the Government

1. Name of the Committee, Council Board, Commission, etc.
2. No. of Members of Parliament required to be nominated (ratio between Lok Sabha and Rajya Sabha, if any).
3. The source of authority under which the body is set up (namely statute, resolution, order, decision of the Government, etc.).
4. (i) Is the body being constituted for the first time or being reconstituted?
   (ii) In case of reconstitution please indicate
      (a) the name of all the MPs nominated earlier, and
      (b) how and when the vacancies have arisen.
5. The functions of the body in brief.
6. The date of expiry of the earlier term (in case of reconstitution of the body).
7. The present term of the body from ______________ to ______________
8. The term of the Members of Parliament to be now nominated on the body from ______________ to ______________

9. The entitlements of the Members of Parliament nominated on this body:

   (a) Honorarium,
   (b) Travelling Allowance,
   (c) Daily Allowance, and
   (d) Any other allowances, perquisites, facilities etc.

10. Who will preside over the meetings of the body?
11. Name and designation (with office address and telephone no.) of the Joint Secretary/Deputy Secretary concerned with this subject in the Ministry).

Signature ____________________

Designation ____________________

Telephone No. ____________________

Note: Notification regarding the nomination of the Members of Parliament on this body should be issued within a reasonable time and a copy thereof endorsed to the Ministry of Parliamentary Affairs.

ANNEX XII-C

No.F. ....
Government of India
Ministry of Parliamentary Affairs

86-B, Parliament House,
New Delhi - 110 001

(Date)

OFFICE MEMORANDUM

Subject: Nomination of Members of Parliament on ....

The undersigned is directed to refer to the Ministry of .... Office Memorandum No. .... dated .... on the subject noted above and to state that the Hon'ble Minister of Parliamentary Affairs has nominated/ re-nominated the following Members of Parliament on ....:

S.No.	Name of Member

The above Members are being informed about his/their nomination/re-nomination on this body. But no formal consent is being called from them. It is presumed that they are willing to accept the assignment.

In view of the above, Ministry of .... are requested not to wait for the consent of the Members, but to proceed to notify their nomination on this body and supply to them all the necessary literature including the constitution, function and programme of work etc. of this body under intimation to this Ministry.

Members of Parliament serving on the Committees, Councils

and Boards etc. set up by the Government are entitled to get TA/DA for attending the meetings of those bodies in accordance with the provisions of the Salary, Allowances and Pension of Members of Parliament Act, 1954 as amended from time to time and the rules made thereunder. The Ministry are, therefore, advised to make suitable provisions for the purpose.

( )
Deputy Secretary to the Government of India
Telephone No. 23034844

Ministry of __________________

____

____

ANNEX XII-D

No.F.
Government of India
Ministry of Parliamentary Affairs

86-B, Parliament House,
New Delhi - 110 001

(Date)

From :

____

Deputy Secretary

To

____

Member of Parliament
(Lok Sabha/Rajya Sabha)

Subject: Nomination of Members of Parliament on ....

Sir/Madam,

I am directed to inform you that the Hon'ble Minister of Parliamentary Affairs has nominated/re-nominated you as a member on the above mentioned Committee, etc. The Hon'ble Minister hopes that you will be able to spare some of your valuable time for this assignment.

Ministry of .... is being requested to issue a formal notification/resolution about your nomination/re-nomination and also to supply to you all necessary information about the constitution, functions and programme of the committee, etc.

If, however, for any reason you find it difficult to serve on this committee etc., please let us know at your earliest.

You may kindly note that under the Parliament (Prevention of Disqualification) Act, 1959 (18 of 1959) you may draw only "Compensatory allowance" and no other remuneration for attending the meeting of this Committee. "Compensatory allowance" according to the above Act means:

> **"Any sum of money payable to the holder of an office by way of daily allowance, such allowance not exceeding the amount of daily allowance to which a Member of Parliament is entitled under the Salary, Allowances and Pension of Members of Parliament Act, 1954 (30 of 1954), any conveyance allowance, house rent allowance or travelling allowance for the purpose of enabling him to recoup any expenditure incurred by him in performing the functions of that office".**

Yours faithfully,

( )

Deputy Secretary to the Government of India

Telephone No. 23034844

ANNEX XII-E

Santosh Gangwar

MINISTER OF STATE FOR PETROLEUM AND NATURAL GAS AND PARLIAMENTARY AFFAIRS GOVERNMENT OF INDIA SHASTRI BHAWAN, NEW DELHI-110001

D.O.No-2-29 (2)/2002-CB

Dated: 28.10.2002

Respected Shanta Kumar Ji,

Please refer to your D.O.No. Q-13018/2/2002-AI(RD) dated 9th September, 2002 addressed to the Minister of Parliamentary Affairs regarding nomination of Members of the Lok Sabha as Chairmen of the District Level Vigilance and Monitoring Committees of District Rural Development Agencies (DRDAs).

Minister of Parliamentary Affairs has approved the following guidelines for nomination of Members as Chairmen of the DRDAs:

1. Where there is only one Member of Lok Sabha in a district, he/she may be nominated as Chairman of the committee irrespective of the fact whether he/she is Speaker/Deputy Speaker, Lok Sabha or a Minister in the Union Council of Ministers.
2. Where there are more than one Member of the Lok Sabha in a district, Speaker, Deputy Speaker, Lok Sabha or a Minister in the Union Council of Ministers, if there is any one of these amongst Members, should be nominated as Chairman and other Member(s) may be nominated as Co-Chairman of the committee. If, however, all are Members, one who is representing maximum

geographical area of the district as a part of his/her constituency should be nominated as Chairman and the other Member(s) should be nominated as the Co-Chairman.

3. Where there is only one Member of the Lok Sabha in a district and he/she is representing more than one district, he/she may be nominated as Chairman of the committee in all districts which he/she is representing (Such situation is likely to be more in North-Eastern States where an MP is representing many districts).

I shall be grateful if the Members of the Lok Sabha are appointed as Chairmen of DRDAs as per the above guidelines.

With regards,

Yours sincerely,

Sd/-
(Santosh Gangwar)

Shri Shanta Kumar,
Minister of Rural Development,
Government of India,
New Delhi.

ANNEX XII-F

CHECK LIST

1. Whether the proposal has been received in the prescribed proforma with relevant details/copies of documents etc.
2. Availability of the Members, if any, earlier nominated on the body (in case of reconstitution/renomination).
3. To watch the Notification of the nomination of the Members of Parliament by the Ministry concerned.

ANNEX XIII-A

DATA RELATING TO ROOMS ALLOTTED TO THE MINISTERS

Ground Floor:	
Standard Room: 13	
(a) Equal to Standard Room:	6,7,13,27,35,36 (with wood panelling) 39, 40, 41, 42
(b) Slightly smaller than Standard Room:	37
(c) Much smaller than Standard Room:	38, 38A
First Floor:	
(a) Bigger than Standard Room:	64A
(b) Equal to Standard Room:	68B
(c)Slightly smaller than Standard Room:	48A, 48B, 68A
(d) Small cubicles:	69A, 69B, 69C, 69D
Note: There are common entries for Rooms No. 48A and 48B; 68A and 68B; 69A to 69D.	
Second Floor:	
Rooms No.102A and 102B are half the size of Standard Room.	
These have been newly partitioned and furnished.	
Third Floor:	
Standard Room:105A (Half the size of Room No.13 on Ground Floor)	
(a) Equal to Standard Room (105A)	105B, 115, 115A, 116, 116A, 117, 117A, 118, 118A, 118B
(b) Slightly bigger than Standard Room (105A):	112, 112A, 112B, 113, 113A

Rooms Already Allotted:

Ground Floor

9-12	:	PMO
14-15	:	MPA
43-44	:	Leaders of Opposition (LS and RS)
45B	:	MOS(BH)

First Floor:

56	:	MOS(SK)
64	:	MOS(SP)

ANNEX XIII-B

No.F.
Government of India
Ministry of Parliamentary Affairs

Parliament House,
New Delhi
Dated:

OFFICE MEMORANDUM

Subject: Allotment of Rooms in Parliament House to Ministers during the .... Session of .... the Lok Sabha and .... Session of the Rajya Sabha

The undersigned is directed to enclose a statement showing allotment of Rooms to Ministers in Parliament House for the .... Session of the .... Lok Sabha and .... Session of the Rajya Sabha.

Private Secretaries to Ministers concerned are requested to inspect the rooms and arrange furniture, telephone, draperies, etc., with the assistance of the Caretaker, Parliament House, and the Engineering Supervisor (Telephones), Parliament House. It is stressed that the primary responsibility for the safety of articles, instruments etc., kept in the Parliament House for the Minister's use lies with the Ministry/Department concerned. Personal staff of the Ministers may, therefore, ensure that as soon as their Ministers leave Parliament House, nothing is left unlocked in the room or the varandah adjacent thereto. Similarly the telephone, when it is not in use, may be removed from the varandah to prevent unauthorized calls being made.

In case any additions/alterations are desired to be made in the rooms allotted to the Ministers, the Ministry/Department concerned is requested to take up the matter directly with the Assistant Engineers I and III, Parliament Works Division No. I, C.P.W.D., Parliament House, New Delhi (Telephone No.23034765) for obtaining necessary estimates of expenditure involved, for issue of administrative approval and to sanction expenditure involved for execution of the additional/alteration work.

The Caretaker, Parliament House, and the Engineering Supervisor (Telephones) are being advised to arrange for furnishing of the rooms and installation of telephones etc. in consultation with Private Secretaries to Ministers or Ministries concerned.

( )
UNDER SECRETARY TO THE GOVT. OF INDIA
TELE.NO

To
All Private Secretaries to Ministers as given in the list.

Copy forwarded for necessary action to:

1. The Caretaker, Parliament House, for furnishing the rooms allotted to Ministers in consultation with the Private Secretaries to the Ministers concerned (5 copies);
2. Engineering Supervisor (Telephones), Parliament House for installation of telephones in the rooms of Ministers in consultation with the Private Secretaries of the concerned Ministers (5 copies);
3. Lok Sabha Secretariat;
4. Rajya Sabha Secretariat;
5. The President's Secretariat;
6. The Prime Minister's Office;
7. The Cabinet Secretariat;
8. P.S. to Minister/Ministers of State for Parliamentary Affairs;
9. Additional Secretary, Lok Sabha Secretariat;
10. Assistant Director (WG), Lok Sabha Secretariat;
11. Executive Engineer, P.W.D.-II, C.P.W.D., New Delhi;
12. The Assistant Engineers I and III, Parliament Works Division No I, Parliament House, New Delhi;
13. Executive Engineer(E), Parliament Air-Conditioning Division, CPWD, Vidyut Bhavan, New Delhi;
14. The Chief Watch and Ward Officer, Lok Sabha Secretariat;
15. The Reception Officer, Parliament House, Lok Sabha and Rajya Sabha Secretariats;
16. P.P.S. to Secretary/P.S. to Joint Secretary, Ministry of Parliamentary Affairs; and
17. All Deputy Secretaries, Under Secretary (Admn.), Ministry of Parliamentary Affairs.

( )
UNDER SECRETARY
Phone:

ANNEX XIII-C(I)

D.O.No.F.56(3)/2004-Leg.I Dated:

As you are aware, there is a convention that at least some Ministers are always present in the two Houses when Parliament is in session. To ensure this, all the Ministers are allotted roster duties in the two Houses, by rotation, during the session period. In the ensuing session of Parliament, you have been allotted the following roster duties:

Lok Sabha :

Rajya Sabha :

I am sure that by following the past conventions and practices, and by our exemplary behaviour and performance of our duty, we will succeed in obtaining the cooperation of our allies, supporting parties and even opposition parties in our endeavour to maintain proper decorum and dignity in the two Houses and help the Presiding Officers to conduct the business of the Houses efficiently and smoothly. I trust that I will be getting your full cooperation in this regard. I would also request you kindly to fix your programme on the days of the session keeping in view your roster duties mentioned above.

With kind regards,

Yours sincerely,

(Ghulam Nabi Azad)

All Cabinet Ministers who are allotted roster duties

ANNEX XIII-C(II)

D.O.No.F.56(3)/2004-Leg.I Dated:

As you are aware, there is a convention that at least some Ministers are always present in the two Houses when Parliament is in session. To ensure this, all the Ministers are allotted roster duties in the two Houses, by rotation, during the session period. In the ensuing session of Parliament, you have been allotted the following roster duties:

Lok Sabha :

Five minutes before the Lok Sabha is to reassemble after lunch to 3.30 p.m.

Or

From 1.30 p.m. to 3.30 p.m. in case there is no lunch.

I am sure that by following the past conventions and practices, and by our exemplary behaviour and performance of our duty, we will succeed in obtaining the cooperation of our allies, supporting parties and even opposition parties in our endeavour to maintain proper decorum and dignity in the two Houses and help the Presiding Officers to conduct the business of the Houses efficiently and smoothly. I trust that I will be getting your full cooperation in this regard. I would also request you kindly to fix your programme on the days of the session keeping in view your roster duties mentioned above.

With kind regards,

Yours sincerely,

(Ghulam Nabi Azad)

All Ministers of State who are assigned roster duties in Lok Sabha

ANNEX XIII-C(III)

D.O.No.F.56(3)/2004-Leg.I Dated:

As you are aware, there is a convention that at least some Ministers are always present in the two Houses when Parliament is in session. To ensure this, all the Ministers are allotted roster duties in the two Houses, by rotation, during the session period. In the ensuing session of Parliament, you have been allotted the following roster duties:

Rajya Sabha : 2.00 p.m. to 4.00 p.m.

Day(s)

I am sure that by following the past conventions and practices, and by our exemplary behaviour and performance of our duty, we will succeed in obtaining the cooperation of our allies, supporting parties and even opposition parties in our endeavour to maintain proper decorum and dignity in the two Houses and help the Presiding Officers to conduct the business of the Houses efficiently and smoothly. I trust that I will be getting your full cooperation in this regard. I would also request you kindly to fix your programme on the days of the session keeping in view your roster duties mentioned above.

With kind regards,

Yours sincerely,

(Ghulam Nabi Azad)

All Ministers of State assigned roster duties in Rajya Sabha

ANNEX XIII-D

No.F.
Government of India
Ministry of Parliamentary Affairs

Parliament House
New Delhi.

Dated:

OFFICE MEMORANDUM

Subject: Roster of Attendance of Ministers in Parliament during the .... Session of .... the Lok Sabha and .... Session of the Rajya Sabha

The undersigned is directed to forward, herewith, a copy of roster of attendance of Ministers in both the Houses of Parliament during the .... Session of the .... the Lok Sabha and .... Session of the Rajya Sabha for information and necessary action.

( )
Under Secretary to the Government of India
Tele.No.......................

To

1. P.S. to Hon'ble Chairman, Rajya Sabha;
2. P.S. to Hon'ble Speaker, Lok Sabha;
3. P.S. to Hon'ble Deputy Chairman, Rajya Sabha;
4. P.S. to Hon'ble Deputy Speaker, Lok Sabha;
5. P.S. to Minster of Parliamentary Affairs;
6. P.S. to Leader of the House in Lok Sabha/Rajya Sabha;
7. P.S. to all Cabinet Ministers/MOS(Independent Charge)/MOSs;
8. P.S. to MOS ( );

9. P.S. to MOS ( );
10. P.S. to MOS ( );
11. Shri ...., Under Secretary, Prime Minister's Office;
12. All Ministries/Departments of the Government of India (Parliament Section);
13. P.P.S. to Secretary/P.S. to Joint Secretary, Ministry of Parliamentary Affairs; and
14. P.As. to Deputy Secretary(Legislative)/Under Secretary(Legislative), Ministry of Parliamentary Affairs;

MOS - Minister of State
PPS - Principal Private Secretary
P.S. - Private Secretary
P.A. - Personal Assistant

ANNEX XIII-E

No.F……………..-Leg.II
Government of India
Ministry of Parliamentary Affairs

(Date)

OFFICE MEMORANDUM

Subject: Matters raised during Zero-Hour in Lok Sabha/Rajya Sabha

A matter concerning the Ministry of……………………………….... was raised by ……………………………………………….....during Zero-Hour in Lok Sabha/Rajya Sabha on ………………………..

Relevant extracts from the proceedings of the House are enclosed for appropriate action.

( )
Under Secretary

Ministry of ………………………….
(Parliament Section)
New Delhi.

Copy, with relevant extracts, forwarded to Private Secretary to Minister of ………………………….with the request that enclosed extracts of the proceedings of the House may be placed before the Hon'ble Minister.

( )
Under Secretary

ANNEX XIII-F

D.O.No.................................   Dated:

During Zero Hour in the Lok Sabha/Rajya Sabha today ...., Shri/Ms. ....raised the matter regarding .... Thereupon, I assured the House that I would convey it to the concerned Minister for necessary action.

Extracts of the proceedings are enclosed for information and such action as deemed fit.

With regards,

Yours sincerely,

(   )
Minister of Parliamentary Affairs

Shri ____________________
Minister of ____________
Government of India,
New Delhi.

ANNEX XIII-G

MOST IMMEDIATE

It has been observed that assurances given by the Leader of the House or by me on the floor of the Houses on matters raised by Members during zero hour have not been duly conveyed to the Ministers concerned as no officer has taken note of them.

I desire that at least one senior officer of the Ministry must be present in the official gallery of each House to take note of important developments in the Houses and bring the same to my notice with necessary follow up action. I may be informed of the arrangements made in this regard.

(Ghulam Nabi Azad)
Minister of Parliamentary Affairs
and Urban Development
9-7-2004

Secretary

ANNEX XIII-H

MINISTRY OF PARLIAMENTARY AFFAIRS (LEGISLATIVE-II SECTION)

No. F. 17(1)/2001-Leg.II July, 2004

Subject: Roster duties of Under Secretaries for attendance in Official Galleries of Lok Sabha/Rajya Sabha during Zero Hour

It has been decided to assign roster duties for attendance in Lok Sabha/Rajya Sabha Official Galleries during Zero hour (from 11.55 a.m. onwards) to the Under Secretaries as follows:

Day	Lok Sabha	Rajya Sabha
Monday	Under Secretary(A)	Under Secretary (C)
Tuesday	Under Secretary(RandC)	Under Secretary (L)
Wednesday	Under Secretary (C)	Under Secretary (ME)
Thursday	Under Secretary (ME)	Under Secretary (A)
Friday	Under Secretary (L)	Under Secretary (RandC)

In case an assurance is given by the Leader of the House or the Minister of Parliamentary Affairs/any other Minister/Minister of State or if there is any direction from the Presiding Officer to the Government, the Under Secretary attending in the Official Gallery may report the matter raised and the assurance/direction thereon to the Deputy Secretary (L) with copy to Addl. P.S. to HMPA for information and to Section Officer (L-II) for further necessary action. If there is no assurance, then also a report to that effect may be sent.

If any Under Secretary wishes to avail leave on the day of his duty, he/she may make his own arrangement with some other Under Secretary or Deputy Secretary, in advance and will inform the Deputy Secretary (L) about the same.

This is issued with the approval of Secretary.

Sd/-
(K.K. THAKUR)
DEPUTY SECRETARY(L)

US(A)/ US(RandC)/ US(ME)/ US(L)/US(C)

Copy to:-

Secretary/Joint Secretary/DS(A)/DS(RandC)/Addl. P.S. to HMPA/S.O.(L-II)

ANNEX XIII - I

Dated:

To

The Secretary-General,
Lok Sabha,
New Delhi.

Sir,

I give notice of my intention to move the following Motion during the current Session of the Lok Sabha:

> "That the members of this House do proceed to elect, in the manner required by sub-rule(1) of Rule 309 of the Rules of Procedure and Conduct of Business in Lok Sabha, fifteen members from among themselves to serve as members of the Committee on Public Accounts for the term ending on the 30th April, 2005".

> "That this House do recommend to Rajya Sabha that Rajya Sabha do agree to nominate seven members from Rajya Sabha for being associated with the Committee on Public Accounts of the House for the term ending on the 30th April, 2005 and do communicate to this House the names of the members so nominated by Rajya Sabha".

Yours faithfully,

(   )
Minister of Parliamentary Affairs

ANNEX XIII - J

Dated:

To

The Secretary-General,
Lok Sabha,
New Delhi.

Sir,

I give notice of my intention to move the following motion during the current Session of the Lok Sabha:

> "That the members of this House do proceed to elect, in the manner required by sub-rule(1) of Rule 311 of the Rules of Procedure and Conduct of Business in Lok Sabha, thirty members from among themselves to serve as members of the Committee on Estimates for the term ending on the 30th April, 2005".

Yours faithfully,

(   )
Minister of Parliamentary Affairs

ANNEX XIII-K

Dated:

To

The Secretary-General,
Lok Sabha,
New Delhi.

Sir,

I give notice of my intention to move the following Motion during the current Session of the Lok Sabha:

> "That the members of this House do proceed to elect, in the manner required by sub-rule (1) of Rule 312 B of the Rules of Procedure and Conduct of Business in Lok Sabha, fifteen members from among themselves to serve as members of the Committee on Public Undertakings for the term ending on the 30th April, 2005".

> "That this House do recommend to Rajya Sabha that Rajya Sabha do agree to nominate seven members from Rajya Sabha for being associated with the Committee on Public Undertakings of the House for the term ending on the 30th April, 2005 and do communicate to this House the names of the members so nominated by Rajya Sabha".

Yours faithfully,

( )
Minister of Parliamentary Affairs

ANNEX XIII-L

Dated:

To

The Secretary-General,
Lok Sabha,
New Delhi.

Sir,

I give notice of my intention to move the following Motion during the current Session of the Lok Sabha:

> "That the members of this House do proceed to elect, in the manner required by sub-rule (1) of Rule 331 B of the Rules of Procedure and Conduct of Business in Lok Sabha, twenty members from among themselves to serve as members of the Committee on the Welfare of Scheduled Castes and Scheduled Tribes for the term ending on the 30th April, 2005".
>
> "That this House do recommend to Rajya Sabha that Rajya Sabha do agree to nominate ten members from Rajya Sabha for being associated with the Committee on the Welfare of Scheduled Castes and Scheduled Tribes of the House for the term ending on the 30th April, 2005 and do communicate to this House the names of the members so nominated by Rajya Sabha".

Yours faithfully,

( )
Minister of Parliamentary Affairs

ANNEX XIII-M

Dated:

To

The Secretary-General,
Rajya Sabha,
New Delhi.

Sir,

I give notice of my intention to move the following Motion during the current Session of the Rajya Sabha:

> "That this House concurs in the recommendation of the Lok Sabha that the Rajya Sabha do agree to nominate seven Members from Rajya Sabha to associate with the Committee on Public Accounts of the Lok Sabha for the term ending on the 30th April, 2005, and do proceed to elect in such manner as the Chairman may direct, seven Members from among the Members of the House to serve on the said Committee".

Yours faithfully,

( )
Minister of State for Parliamentary Affairs

ANNEX XIII-N

Dated:

To

The Secretary-General,
Rajya Sabha,
New Delhi.

Sir,

I give notice of my intention to move the following Motion during the current Session of the Rajya Sabha:

> "That this House concurs in the recommendation of the Lok Sabha that the Rajya Sabha do agree to nominate seven Members from Rajya Sabha to associate with the Committee on Public Undertakings of the Lok Sabha for the term ending on the 30th April, 2005 and do proceed to elect in such manner as the Chairman may direct, seven Members from among the Members of the House to serve on the said Committee."

Yours faithfully,

( )
Minister of State for Parliamentary Affairs

ANNEX XIII-O

Dated:

To

The Secretary-General,
Rajya Sabha,
New Delhi.

Sir,

I give notice of my intention to move the following Motion during the current Session of the Rajya Sabha:

> "That this House resolves that the Rajya Sabha do join the Committee of both the Houses on the Welfare of Scheduled Castes and Scheduled Tribes for the term ending on the 30th April, 2005, and do proceed to elect, in accordance with the system of proportional representation by means of the single transferable vote, ten Members from among the Members of the House to serve on the said Committee."

Yours faithfully,

(   )
Minister of State for Parliamentary Affairs

ANNEX XIII-P

D.O.No.5(1)/2004-Leg.II Dated:

I enclose a list of issues likely to be raised during the forthcoming session of Parliament.

It is requested that a brief note on each one of them concerning your Ministry may be sent to the PMO, with endorsement to this Ministry, for use by hon'ble PM/hon'ble Minister of Parliamentary Affairs.

Yours sincerely,

( )
Secretary

Secretary,
Ministry of ....,
Government of India,
New Delhi.

ANNEX XIV-A

STATEMENT SHOWING THE DETAILS OF ALL INDIA WHIPS' CONFERENCES HELD BY THE MINISTRY OF PARLIAMENTARY AFFAIRS

Sl. No.	No. of AIWC	Place where held	Date and year of Conference	Remarks
1	First	Indore	13th September, 1952	Held under the auspices of the Congress Party in Parliament
2	Second	Mysore	15th and 16th January, 1955	Inaugurated by Shri K. Hanumanthayya, Chief Minister of Mysore
3	Third	Srinagar	24th and 25th September, 1956	Inaugurated by Shri G.M. Bakshi, Prime Minister of Kashmir
4	Fourth	The Council Hall, Bombay	24th and 25th October, 1962	Inaugurated by Shri Y.B. Chavan, Chief Minister of Maharashtra
5	Fifth	Vidhan Soudha, Bangalore	4th to 6th January, 1966	Inaugurated by Shri N. Nijalingappa, Chief Minister of Mysore
6	Sixth	Himachal Bhavan, Shimla	4th to 6th October, 1967	Inaugurated by Dr. Y.S. Parmar, Chief Minister of Himachal Pradesh
7	Seventh	Rajaji Hall, Madras	21st to 23rd September, 1969	Inaugurated by Shri M. Karunanidhi, Chief Minister of Tamil Nadu.
8	Eighth	Vidhan Sabha Bhavan, Bhopal	3rd and 4th November, 1972	Inaugurated by Shri S.N. Sinha, Governor, Madhya Pradesh.
9	Ninth	Legislative Assembly Hall, Shimla	27th and 28th October, 1983	Inaugurated by Shri Vir Bhadra Singh, Chief Minister of Himachal Pradesh.

Contd. .....

Sl. No.	No. of AIWC	Place where held	Date and year of Conference	Remarks
10.	Tenth	Main Committee Room Parliament House Annexe, New Delhi.	26th November, 1988	Inaugurated by Dr. M Thambi Durai, Deputy Speaker, Lok Sabha.
11	Eleventh	Banquet Hall, Vidhan Soudha, Bangalore.	17th to 19th January, 1994	Inaugurated by Shri M. Veerappa Moily, Chief Minister of Karnataka.
12	Twelfth	*S.K.I.C.C., Srinagar	21st and 22nd August, 1997	Inaugurated by Dr. Farooq Abdulla, Chief Minister of Jammu and Kashmir.

* Sher-I-Kashmir International Conference Centre, Srinagar

ANNEX XIV-B

RECOMMENDATIONS OF 12TH ALL INDIA WHIPS' CONFERENCE HELD ON 21ST AND 22ND AUGUST, 1997 AT SRINAGAR

Recommendation No.1

Status, Functions and Facilities for the Chief Whips/ Whips

The Chief Whips of recognised parties in Parliament and the State Legislatures should be provided secretarial assistance and facilities of telephones at office and residence and accommodation in the premises of legislatures, by giving them statutory recognition. (Secretarial assistance means one Stenographer Grade 'B'; one Peon; a Computer; a Fax Machine and postage facilities.)
The conference recommends that the Chief Whip of the party having more than 1/10th of strength of the House should be given the status of a Minister of State.

Recommendation No.2

Setting Up of Department of Parliamentary Affairs in the States/Union Territories

An independent Department of Parliamentary Affairs should be set up in the States/Union territories where it has not been set up so far. The conference recommends that all States/Union territory Governments should submit a report to the Ministry of Parliamentary Affairs in this regard within a period of six months.

Recommendation No.3

Introduction of Youth Parliament Scheme in Various States/Union territories

The State Governments/Union territory Administrations, which have not introduced the scheme of Youth Parliament Competitions in their States/Union territories, should take urgent steps to introduce this scheme on the pattern adopted by the Central Ministry of Parliamentary Affairs.

The Central Ministry of Parliamentary Affairs should provide all encouragement to the State Governments/Union territory Administrations for introducing implementing the scheme by offering free literature, training and financial assistance up to Rs.2 lakhs per annum on reimbursement basis.

Recommendation No.4

Periodical Consultation between Government and Leaders of Opposition Parties/Groups in Pariament

All State Governments/Union territory Administrations should follow the convention established at the Centre in holding frequent meetings with the Leaders of opposition parties/groups on important issues.

The Ministers of Parliamentary Affairs or the Government Chief Whips in all the States/Union territories, as the case may be, should convene meetings of Whips of all parties/groups from time to time to discuss matters pertaining to the items of business coming before the States/Union territory Legislatures. At least one meeting may be arranged before the commencement of every session.

The conference recommends that a "Committee of Whips" be formed in Parliament/State Legislatures for better floor management. This committee should meet at least twice every session.

Recommendation No.5

Constitution of a Minitoring Group to Watch the Progress of Implementation of Recommendations of the Twelfth All India Whips' Conference and the Views Expressed in the Plenary Sessions

A Monitoring Group to watch the progress of implementation of recommendations of the Twelfth All India Whips' Conference and the views expressed in its Plenary Sessions should be constituted. The Minister of Parliamentary Affairs will be the Chairman of the group. The group may consist of 15 members. The nominees from Parliament and State Legislatures should be adequately represented on the Group.

Recommendation No.6

Strengthening of Research Cell

The Conference recommends that the Research Cell in Parliament should be strengthened and every State Legislature should take steps to establish similar cells. State Legislatures including Assembly Libraries should be brought under the network of Internet.

Recommendation No.7

Provision of Computers

The practice of providing computers to Members of Parliament and by the Andhra Pradresh Government to MLAs should be followed by other States as it has considerably improved the efficiency and functioning of Legislators.

Recommendation No.8

Publication of All India Reporter

The Central Ministry of Parliamentary Affairs should start publishing an "All India Reporter" from time to time providing information on issues of common interest on Parliamentary Affairs and Constitutional matters.

Recommendation No.9

Appointment of Chief Whips

Chief Whips of political parties should be appointed by their respective Leaders in the House.

Recommendation No.10

Maintenance of Quorum in the House

Having noted that the recommendation made by the Eleventh All India Whips' Conference regarding maintenance of quorum is being implemented by most of the States including the National Capital territory of Delhi, and the Union Ministry of Parliamentary Affairs has also introduced a Bill in the Lok Sabha to provide for secretarial assistance and certain telephone facilities to the Leaders and Chief Whips of the recognised parties and groups in each House of Parliament. With a view to enabling the Leaders/Chief Whips and Whips to discharge their responsibilities including maintenance of quorum effectively, it is recommended that functional facilities should be provided to the Leaders, Chief Whips and Whips of recognised parties and groups including small groups in Parliament and State Legislatures by 31st December, 1997.

Recommendation No.11

Commencement/Duration and Sittings of the Legislatures - Role of Government

Commencement and duration of the Legislatures should be left to the discretion of the Government. Parliament should normally meet in three sessions of not less than 130 days and the State Legislatures should normally meet in three sessions of not less than 75 working days in a year in order to provide ample opportunity for Members' participation on all the issues brought before them.

Recommendation No.12

Planning and Coordination of Government Business through the Ministry of Parliamentary Affairs

Having noted that the practice of planning and coordination of Government Business through the Ministry of Parliamentary Affairs at the Centre has resulted in timely and smooth passage of Government Business in Parliament, the conference recommends that the same practice should be suitably adopted by the States/ Union territories. For successful accomplishment of this task, the States/Union territories may depute their officers to the Union Ministry of Parliamentary Affairs to receive practical training or they may invite officers from the Ministry to their States/ Union territories to impart training in this regard.

The conference further recommends that the entire cost of the training including payment of TA and DA to the officers of State Governments may be borne by the Union Ministry of Parliamentary Affairs.

Recommendation No.13

Code to Regulate Relationship between Members of Parliament/ State Legislatures with Government

The instructions regarding official dealing between the Administration and Members of Parliament and the State Legislatures issued by the Central Ministry of Personnel, Public Grievances and Pensions (Department of Personnel and Training) may be reiterated to all the Ministries/Departments of the Government of India and Chief Secretaries of all State Governments/Union territory Administrations. Instructions in this regard may also be made available to the Members of Parliament and State Legislatures.

Code of Conduct for the Members of Parliament and State Legislatures

The conference recommends that a committee may be constituted under the Chairmanship of the Union Minister of Parliamentary Affairs to prepare a draft code for the Members of the Legislatures for being enforced by their parties in and outside the House.

The committee may consist of not more than eleven members from various parties represented in Parliament and State Legislatures. The conference further recommends that the draft code, after preparation, may be sent to all the Chief Ministers of States/Union territories and Leaders of various parties and groups represented in Parliament and the State Legislatures.

Recommendation No.14

Status and Facilities to the Leader of Opposition in States

Having noted that most of the States/Union territories have already implemented the recommendation made by the Eleventh All India Whips' Conference regarding status and facility to the recognised Leader of the Opposition in their State/Union territory Legislature, this conference recommends that the States/Union territories, which have not so far implemented that recommendation, may take immediate steps to provide the salary, status and other facilities to the recognised Leader of the Opposition in their State/Union territory Legislatures as are available to their Cabinet Ministers by the 31st March, 1998.

Recommendation No.15

Drawal of Daily Allowance Contingent upon Signing of the Attendance Register

Having noted that Members of Parliament are not entitled to their daily allowance unless they sign the attendance register maintained for this purpose by the Lok Sabha/Rajya Sabha Secretariat, the conference recommends that similar provision for drawal of daily allowance by the Members of the State/Union territory Legislatures may be adopted by the States/Union territory Administrations.

Recommendation No.16

Constitution and Functioning of the Consultative Committees

The conference reiterates the view held by the Eleventh All India Whips' Conference that the institution of Consultative Committees attached to the various Ministries serves a very useful purpose of consultation between the Government and the Members of

Parliament on programmes, policies and actions of the Government and therefore this institution needs to be further strengthened and recommends that Consultative Committees should be set up in the States/Union territories, where these have not been set up so far, on the Central pattern and these committees should hold meetings in the districts, if possible, even in remote villages so as to establish healthy contact with the people at the grassroots level. The conference further recommends that the Consultative Committees be made more effective, meetings of the Consultative Committees should be held regularly ..... at least four meetings in a year ...., and that the suggestions given by the Members at these meetings be implemented fully and effectively.

Recommendation No.17

Implementation of Assurances

The conference reiterates the recommendations made by the Tenth and Eleventh All India Whips' Conferences and urges upon all States/Union territories who have not yet implemented the recommendation to take early steps to set up a mechanism and evolve appropriate procedures as at the Centre for culling out from the daily proceedings the legislative assurances given by Ministers and ensure their early implementation within a stipulated time limit.

The conference, having taken note of the fact that a very long time is taken by the Government to implement the assurances given in the House, recommends that if the assurances are not implemented within a year and no satisfactory reply is received by the Committee on Government Assurances during this period, the matters should be taken note of seriously.

Recommendation No.18

Role of Central Ministry of Parliamentary Affairs in Implementation of the Recommendations of Parliamentary/ House Committees

The conference reiterates the recommendation made by the earlier Whips' Conference that the Ministry of Parliamentary Affairs at the Centre has been functioning as a nodal agency to ensure that the recommendations of some of the Parliamentary Committees are acted upon by the Ministries concerned. The Conference feels that this is a healthy practice which may be adopted by the States/ Union territories also to ensure that the recommendations of as many of their House Committees as possible are implemented by the Executive, with the Department of Parliamentary Affairs playing the vital role of coordinating agency.

Recommendation No.19

Nomination of Members of Parliament on Committees/ Commissions etc. set up by the Government

The Conference reiterates the recommendations made by the Tenth and Eleventh All India Whips' Conferences and stresses the need for associating the legislators in the States/Union territories with Government bodies at various levels, namely, State, Local Bodies etc., and recommends to the States/Union territories to take early steps to implement the recommendations.

This conference further recommends that Government while nominating Members to serve on various committees/commissions evolve objective parameters for such appointments. One of the parameters is that adequate representation should be given to Members of Parliament/State Legislatures/Local Bodies, etc.

Recommendation No.20

Follow-up Action on Matters Raised Under Rule 377 of the Lok Sabha and by Way of Specoial Mention in the Rajya Sabha

The Conference reiterates the following recommendation made by the Eleventh All India Whips' Conference:

Noting that apart from ventilating views through the devices provided under the Rules of the House, Members also sometimes raise points of urgent public importance with the permission of the Chair, the conference is of the view that Governments in the States and Administrations of Union territories should take follow up action on such points also and inform the Members concerned about the action taken thereon within a timeframe. The Central Ministry of Parliamentary Affairs has evolved a mechanism and procedure for this purpose and a time limit has been laid down for follow up action on matters raised under Rule 377 (Lok Sabha) and Special Mentions (Rajya Sabha). The conference recommends to the States/Union territories who have not so far adopted a similar mechanism and procedure to adopt the same early.

The conference recommends that reply on matters raised under Rule 377 should be sent to Members within one month.

Recommendation No.21

Follow up Action on Matters of Urgent Public Importance During Zero Hour

The conference while reiterating the recommendation made by the Eleventh All India Whips' Conference recommends that it should be ensured that Zero Hour is kept to the absolute minimum and Members should fully cooperate with any system evolved for regulating the items to be raised during this period.

This conference also considers that the Zero Hour is very important and useful for parliamentary practice in a democracy. At the same time, it has been observed that there is no proper utilisation of the Zero Hour as the matters raised during this hour go unanswered. This conference recommends that a Working Group should be set up which may consider the working of Zero Hour in Parliament/ State Legislatures and it may suggest in what way the Zero Hour should be effectively utilised and whether it requires any amendment of the Rules of Procedure.

Recommendation No.22

Periodic Training Programmes in the Legislature's Procedures for Officers Dealing with Parliamentary Work

The conference notes with satisfaction that the Ministry of Parliamentary Affairs organises training programmes on parliamentary procedures and practices for the officers of the State Governments/Union territory Administrations and stresses that such training programmes are of great help in exchange of knowledge and information about the procedures and practices prevalent at the Centre and in the various States/Union territories and will lead to standardization of procedures and better performance of officials. The committee recommends that such training programmes may continue to be organised periodically.

Recommendation No.23

Setting up of Welfare Cell to Render Assistance to State Legislators

The conference reiterates that recommendation made by the Eleventh All India Whips' Conference that a Welfare Cell be set up in the Department of Parliamentary Affairs in States/Union territories to look after the welfare of Legislators on the pattern of a similar section functioning in the Central Ministry of Parliamentary Affairs. At the Centre, the Minister of Parliamentary Affairs personally meets a Member of Parliament admitted in hospitals and enquires about his condition and medical facilities provided to him. In case a Member requires treatment abroad, or wants to undertake study tours abroad, the Ministry of Parliamentary Affairs co-ordinates with the concerned Ministries to render necessary assistance to such Members. Thus, the Welfare Section of the Ministry of Parliamentary Affairs helps Members discharge their duties effectively. The Welfare Cells to be set up in the Departments of Parliamentary Affairs in the States/Union territories may also undertake similar duties in respect of the Legislators.

The conference further recommends that there should be a Group Insurance Scheme for Members. If any Member becomes invalid, he should be given pension for the rest of his term and other welfare steps should be taken, if possible.

Recommendation No.24

Study Camps, Seminar for Legislators including Study Tours to National Projects

The conference reiterates the following recommendations made by the Eleventh All India Whips' Conference:

(a) After noting the various services rendered to Members of Parliament by the Ministry of Parliamentary Affairs, this conference recommends that more frequent study tours of Members of Parliament to various Public Sector Undertakings, National Projects and other institutions should be organised for groups of Members interested in the related subjects. Members should be treated as State Guests throughout the visit and they should be allowed to draw allowances as per their entitlements under the Salary, Allowances and Pension of Members of Parliament Act. This Conference further recommends that Members of State Legislatures should also be included for the visits to various National Projects.

(b) The Conference attaches the highest importance to promoting knowledge and expertise among Members of Parliament and State Legislators on various subjects such as Agriculture, Rural Development, Science and Technology etc. and recommends that the Central Ministry of Parliamentary Affairs should organise from time to time Workshops and Seminars for Members of Parliament and State Legislators interested in the subjects. For this purpose, co-operation of organisations/institutions dealing with the subject may also be enlisted.

ANNEX XIV-C

UPDATED LIST OF THE MEMBERS OF THE MONITORING GROUP CONSTITUTED TO WATCH THE PROGRESS OF IMPLEMENTATION OF THE RECOMMENDATIONS MADE BY THE 12TH ALL INDIA WHIPS' CONFERENCE

1.	Smt. Sushma Swaraj, Minister of Health and Family Welfare and Parliamentary Affairs	—	Chairperson
2.	Shri Santosh Kumar Gangwar, Minister of State for Labour and Parliamentary Affairs	—	Vice-Chairman
3.	Shri O. Rajagopal, Minister of State for Defence and Parliamentary Affairs	—	Vice-Chairman
4.	Smt. Bhavnaben Chikhalia, Minister of State for Parliamentary Affairs and Tourism and Culture.	—	Vice-Chairman

Members:

1.	Shri P.R. Dasmunshi, Member of Parliament (Lok Sabha)	—	INC
2.	Dr. M. Jagannath, Member of Parliament (Lok Sabha)	—	TDP
3.	Shri Shivaji Mane, Member of Parliament (Lok Sabha)	—	Shiv Sena
4.	Shri Ram Sajivan, Member of Parliament (Lok Sabha)	—	BSP
5.	Shri S.S. Ahluwalia, Member of Parliament (Rajya Sabha)	—	BJP
6.	Shri Nilotpal Basu, Member of Parliament (Rajya Sabha)	—	CPI(M)
7.	Prof. Vijay Kumar Malhotra, Member of Parliament (Lok Sabha)	—	BJP

8. Shri Pranab Mukherjee, Member of Parliament (Rajya Sabha) — INC
9. Shri Rupchand Pal, Member of Parliament (Lok Sabha) — CPI(M)
10. Kunwar Akhilesh Singh, Member of Parliament (Lok Sabha) — Samajwadi Party
11. Dr.(Smt.) V. Saroja, Member of Parliament (Lok Sabha) — AIADMK
12. Shri S.S. Palanimanickam, Member of Parliament (Lok Sabha) — DMK
13. Shri Braja Kishore Tripathy, Minister of State for Steel — BJD
14. Smt. Vanga Geetha, Member of Parliament (Rajya Sabha) — TDP

ANNEX XIV-D

UPDATED LIST OF THE MEMBERS OF TWO SUB-COMMITTEES OF THE MONITORING GROUP CONSTITUTED TO WATCH THE PROGRESS OF IMPLEMENTATION OF THE RECOMMENDATIONS MADE BY THE 12TH ALL INDIA WHIPS' CONFERENCE

Members of Sub-committee "A": (To cover Andhra Pradesh, Haryana, Himachal Pradesh, Karnataka, Kerala, Madhya Pradesh, Punjab, Rajasthan, Tamil Nadu, Uttar Pradesh, Chhattisgarh, Uttaranchal, Delhi and Pondicherry)

1. Shri P.R. Dasmunshi, Member of Parliament (Lok Sabha) — Convenor
2. Dr. M. Jagannath, Member of Parliament (Lok Sabha) — Joint Convenor
3. Shri Shivaji Mane, Member of Parliament (Lok Sabha) — Member
4. Shri Ram Sajivan, Member of Parliament (Lok Sabha) — do -
5. Shri S.S. Ahluwalia, Member of Parliament (Rajya Sabha) — do -
6. Shri Nilotpal Basu, Member of Parliament (Rajya Sabha) — do -

Members of Sub-committee "B": (To cover Assam, Arunachal Pradesh, Bihar, Goa, Gujarat, Jammu and Kashmir, Maharashtra, Meghalaya, Manipur, Mizoram, Nagaland, Orissa, Sikkim, Tripura, West Bengal and Jharkhand)

1. Prof. Vijay Kumar Malhotra, Member of Parliament (Lok Sabha) — Convenor
2. Shri Pranab Mukherjee, Member of Parliament (Rajya Sabha) — INC

3.	Shri Rupchand Pal, Member of Parliament (Lok Sabha)	—	CPI(M)
4.	Kunwar Akhilesh Singh, Member of Parliament (Lok Sabha)	—	Samajwadi Party
5.	Dr.(Smt.) V. Saroja, Member of Parliament (Lok Sabha)	-	AIADMK
6.	Shri S.S. Palanimanickam, Member of Parliament (Lok Sabha)	-	DMK
7.	Shri Braja Kishore Tripathy, Minister of State for Steel	-	BJD
8.	Smt. Vanga Geetha, Member of Parliament (Rajya Sabha)	-	TDP

ANNEX XIV-E

CHECK LIST FOR ARRANGING ALL INDIA WHIPS' CONFERENCE

1. D.O. letter to the hosting state to make necessary arrangements.
2. Depute an officer of the Ministry to the hosting state to discuss and finalise the programme of the conference.
3. D.O. letters to the Chief Ministers of all the States to furnish the names and addresses of the Chief Whips of the ruling party and the Chief Whips of the opposition parties in their Legislatures so that they may be invited to participate in the conference. They may also be advised to request the delegates to send items of agenda to this Ministry.
4. D.O. letters to the Leaders of the Opposition in the Lok Sabha/Rajya Sabha to furnish the names and addresses of the Whips of their parties. They may be requested to advise the delegates to send items of agenda to this Ministry.
5. Selection of Whips/regional Whips from the ruling party at the Centre. They may also be requested to send items for the agenda.
6. Preparation of notes on agenda items.
7. Request the hosting state to supply relevant material and literature on the place of the conference and other adjoining towns for distribution to the delegates. (Letter to the Department of Tourism).
8. The State Government should be requested to provide maps showing the venue of the conference and the approach roads.
9. Asking for messages from dignitaries for the success of the conference.
10. Issue of invitations to delegates both at the Centre and in the States.
11. Prepare a press note.
12. Publicity and press coverage for the conference - write a D.O. letter to Ministry of Information and Broadcasting.

13. Write a letter to Secretary, Ministry of Information and Broadcasting, requesting him to place the services of the Information Officer attached to this Ministry, during the conference.
14. Prepare a tentative programme of the conference.
15. Prepare a detailed note on the working of each section in the Ministry.
16. Send note to Administration Section to sanction advance.
17. Note to Administration Section for arrangement of reporters/typewriters.
18. Arrangements of banners, cards, badges and ribbons etc.
19. Letter to Railway Board for reservation of seats.
20. Note to supply latest printed lists of Members of Parliament of both Houses and of Railway Time Table.
21. Note to Administration Section to supply service stamps.
22. Note to Administration Section regarding preparation of two indicators of each of the three committees (A, B and C).
23. Note to Administration Section to supply the stationery and other materials.
24. Tentative list of the subjects to be discussed at the conference and its committees.
25. Printing work:

    (a) Presidential address;
    (b) Inaugural address;
    (c) Invitation cards for the inaugural ceremony of the conference; and
    (d) Invitation cards for the Minister's dinner.

26. Note to the Administration Section for supply of wooden stands for fixing the name plates of the delegates.
27. Formation of committees of the staff in the Ministry for organising the Whips' Conference.
28. List of items of work to be done by the advance party/other committees.
29. Reservations for return journey.
30. Preparation of proforma for the acceptance of invitations.
31. Papers etc. to be distributed to the delegates.

32. Statements to be submitted for the Secretary's persual.
33. Articles to be taken to conference - preparing list of.
34. Files to be taken to conference - preparing list of.
35. Note to the A&P Section for supply of the following

    (i) Boxes and trunks;
    (ii) Copies of Who's Who of the two Houses of Parliament;
    (iii) Stationery items; and
    (iv) Gifts for delegates.

36. Messages - compilations of.
37. List of invitees.
38. Preparation of the final programme of the conference.
39. Programme and other circulars of the conference to be issued both in Hindi and English.

ANNEX XIV-F

D.O.No. September, 2004

As may be aware, the Union Ministry of Parliamentary Affairs has been holding All India Whips' Conference since 1952. Twelve such Conferences have been held so far. The Thirteenth All India Whips' Conference is scheduled to be held in Bangalore on 4 and 5 November, 2004. An optional sightseeing visit will be organized on 6 November. Ministers of Parliamentary Affairs/Legislative Affairs, Chief Whips of major political parties, ruling as well as opposition, in the Parliament and the State Legislature attend this Conference.

The Conference provides an opportunity to discuss all important issues relating to the functioning of Parliament and State Legislatures. I, therefore, request you to kindly depute the Minister of Parliamentary Affairs/Legislative Affairs, or any other Minister dealing with Legislative Affairs in your State, to participate in the Conference on behalf of your government. You may also kindly request the Chief Whips of all recognized political parties in the Legislative Assembly and Legislative Council, as the case may be, of your State/U.T. in consultation with their leaders, if necessary, to attend the Conference. The names and addresses (including telephone, fax and cell-phone numbers) of the proposed participants may please be forwarded to us at an early date (Fax No. 011-23017726).

The TA and DA for the delegates so deputed will have to borne by the concerned State Government. A tentative programme, along with details of nodal officers dealing with the Conference, is enclosed.

I shall be grateful if you could also kindly let me have your Message for this Conference.

I shall be thankful for an early reply.

With kind regards,

Yours sincerely,

( )
MINISTER

Chief Ministers of All States/Union Territories

Copy to:-

Chief Secretaries of States/UTs and Secretaries, Department of Parliamentary Affairs as per list attached.

SECRETARY TO THE GOVT. OF INDIAANNEX

ANNEX XIV-G

D.O. No. September, 2004

The Thirteenth All India Whips' Conference is scheduled to be held in Bangalore on 4 and 5 November, 2004. An optional sightseeing visit will be organised on 6 November. The Chief Whips of all major political parties/groups in the Parliament as well in the State Legislatures would be attending the Conference.

As in the past, the Conference would be a forum for exchange of views and discussions on the functioning of the Legislatures, both at the Centre and the States. As vital functionaries of the parliamentary system, the Whips of various parties at the Centre as well as the States are expected to put forward important suggestions/recommendations for further improving the working of the Legislatures in the country.

I would like to invite the Chief Whip of your party/group in the Lok Sabha/Rajya Sabha to this Conference. I shall be grateful if you could kindly let me know immediately the name (along with telephone/cell-phone and fax numbers) of either the Chief Whip, or, in his absence, any other Whip who would represent your party/group at the Conference.

A tentative programme along with details of the nodal officers dealing with the Conference is enclosed.

The travelling and daily allowances for attending the Conference will be paid by the Ministry of Parliamentary Affairs, as per rules.

The Government of Karnataka would be hosting the Conference and will provide necessary hospitality to the delegates.

With kind regards,

Yours sincerely,

( )

MINISTER

Leaders of recognized Parties/Groups in Lok/Rajya Sabha

ANNEX XIV-H

D.O.No.F September, 2004

The Ministry of Parliamentary Affairs has been holding, from time to time, All India Whips' Conferences, which are generally attended by Chief Whips/Whips of all major political parties in the Parliament and the State Legislatures. The Conference discusses important matters concerning the working of the parliamentary system and makes valuable recommendations. So far twelve Whips' Conferences have been held. The last Conference was held in Srinagar in 1997.

The recommendations of the Conference are forwarded to the Chief Ministers of all the State Governments/Union territories and Presiding officers of Parliament and State Legislatures for implementation.

The Thirteenth All India Whips' Conference is scheduled to be held in Bangalore on 4 and 5 November, 2004.

I shall be very grateful if you could kindly honour us with a message from you to guide the deliberations of the Conference.

With kind regards,

Yours sincerely,

( )
MINISTER

As per list enclosed:

1. President of India.
   President House, New Delhi.
2. Vice-President of India.
   6, Maulana Azad Road, New Delhi.
3. Prime Minister of India.
   7, Race Course Road, New Delhi.
4. Speaker, Lok Sabha.
5. Deputy Speaker, Lok Sabha.
6. Deputy Chairman, Rajya Sabha.

ANNEX XIV-I

D.O.No. September, 2004

As you are aware the Chief Minister of Karnataka, *vide* his letter No.CN.626OSD.2004 dated 28.9.2004 addressed to the Minister of Parliamentary Affairs has kindly agreed to host the 13th All India Whips' Conference from 4-6 November, 2004 in Bangalore. We are grateful that the Government of Karnataka has agreed to host this Conference. In this connection the Government of Karnataka will have to provide the following facilities:

(i) Venue of the Conference and rooms for the meetings of 3-4 Sub-committees;
(ii) Secretarial Assistance for the Conference, including a Conference Secretariat;
(iii) Accommodation for the stay of Delegates and Officers/staff of Ministry of Parliamentary Affairs;
(iv) Lunch, Dinner and refreshments for the participants;
(v) Security arrangements;
(vi) Transport arrangements for the Delegates and Officers;
(vii) Reception and Protocol arrangements;
(viii) Sightseeing and cultural programmes; and
(ix) Arrangements for a media centre at the place of conference.

As you may be aware, the Government of Karnataka had earlier hosted the Eleventh All India Whips' Conference in the year 1994. The Government of Karnataka communication number DPAR.148.HGG.93 refers in this regard.

I shall be grateful if you could issue necessary instructions in this regard and also nominate a senior officer to act as a nodal officer.

I, along with one officer, would like to meet you and your

officers in Bangalore for a detailed discussion on the arrangements for the conference at your earliest convenience.

Soliciting an early reply.

Yours sincerely,

(   )
Secretary, Ministry of Parliamentary Affairs

Chief Secretary

ANNEX XV-A

SCHEME OF YOUTH PARLIAMENT COMPETITION FOR RECOGNISED EDUCATIONAL INSTITUTIONS IN THE NATIONAL CAPITAL TERRITORY OF DELHI

Object of the Youth Parliament - With a view to strengthen the roots of democracy, inculcate healthy habits of discipline, tolerance of views of others and to enable the student community to know something about the working of the Parliament, the Ministry of Parliamentary Affairs have decided in pursuance of a recommendation of the All India Whips' Conference, to hold annually a Competition of Youth Parliament of such of the recognised educational institutions in Delhi as may like to take part in it.

Eligibility for entry into the Competition - All recognised Senior Secondary Girls as well as Boys schools including Adult Educational Institutions in the N.C. Territory of Delhi run by the Government, the Municipal and Local authorities or by Trusts and private Charities can take part in the competition. They are required to send intimation to this effect through the Director of Education or direct to the Ministry of Parliamentary Affairs, by a date which would be specified every year.

Period during which the Competition of Youth Parliament will be held - The competition of Youth Parliament will be held every year, The detailed programme shall be drawn up by the Ministry of Parliamentary Affairs and circulated to the institutions taking part in the competition well before its commencement.

Number of participants in the Youth Parliament - While the number of persons constituting the Youth Parliament is not limited, it would appear desirable that there should be a limit in regard to the participation in a sitting. This would naturally mean that many of the other participants may only have sitting roles and may not be required to speak.

Duration of the Youth Parliament Session - The duration of the Youth Parliament sitting should be not more than 45 minutes. Of this, about 10 to 12 minutes may be devoted to questions.

Subject for discussion at the Youth Parliament- It is not proposed to prescribe any particular subjects for questions and answers or for other discussion. It would, however, be desirable that the matters raised in the Youth Parliament relate to subjects of welfare activity, defence of the country, social justice, social reforms, economic development, communal harmony, health, student discipline, etc. Each institution should be free to select its own subject intimation about which may be conveyed to the Ministry of Parliamentary Affairs before the commencement of the competition. It is suggested that particular stress may be placed on the concept of human rights and at least one item of business on this subject may invariably be included.

Language - The participants can speak in Hindi or English as they like.

Venue of the Youth Parliament - Each institution shall hold the Youth Parliament sitting in its own building or such other place of its choice as it may like. The competing institutions shall be required to intimate the venue of their sitting along with the intimation regarding subjects for discussion ten days before the date of the competition.

Prizes - There will be the following prizes:

(i) Shield (parliamentary Shield).

(ii) One Trophy for the Educational District performance of which turns out to be the best on the basis of marks obtained by the schools under that district.

(iii) Trophies for the institutions for meritorious performance in the competition, on the basis of the order of merit.

(iv) One Trophy for the institution which wins first place from among the new entrants to the competition.

(v) Individual merit prizes in the shape of medals/cups/books for some selected participants from each institution.

The shield will be a running shield to be kept for a period of one year by the institution which is placed first in the competition. However, if a particular institution wins the shield for three consecutive years it will be retained permanently by that institution.

A certificate as in Annex XV-A(I) will be awarded to all the students who win individual merit prizes in the competition.

Committee of Judges - A Committee of Judges shall be constituted by the Ministry of Parliamentary Affairs consisting of ordinarily a Member of Parliament or an ex-Member of Parliament, an officer of the Ministry of Parliamentary Affairs and an officer of the Directorate of Education, Government of the National Capital Territory of Delhi.

Consideration for drawing up the merit list - The Committee of Judges shall keep in view the following points while assessing the performance of the institutions:

		Marks
(i)	Discipline and Decorum	10
(ii)	Observance of Parliamentary Procedure	20
(iii)	Selection of subjects for questions and supplementaries and quality of answers thereto	20
(iv)	Selection of subjects for debates	10
(v)	Delivery or quality of speeches delivered, standard of debates	30
(vi)	General assessment of the performance as a whole.	10
	Total	100

Repeat Performance - The institution winning first place may be required to give a repeat performance in a Prize Distribution Function to be held at a venue to be decided by the Ministry of Parliamentary Affairs. To this performance may be invited guests and the public. The programme for this performance will be drawn up by the Ministry of Parliamentary Affairs and intimated to the institution well in advance.

Distribution of Prizes - The Ministry of Parliamentary Affairs shall fix a date, time and venue for the occasion. The prizes shall be distributed by a high dignitary. Invitations to the prize winners, participating institutions and such of the other institutions, etc., as are considered necessary, will be sent by the Ministry of Parliamentary Affairs.

ANNEX XV-A (I)

GOVERNMENT OF INDIA
MINISTRY OF PARLIAMENTARY AFFAIRS

'YOUTH PARLIAMENT COPETITION'

This is to certify that .... Student of .... Class................................ New Delhi/Delhi, was awarded a merit prize for his/her meritorious performance in the .... "Youth Parliament Competition" held in the year ....

Secretary

( )
Ministry of Parliamentary Affairs

New Delhi-110001

Dated:

ANNEX XV-B

CHECK LIST FOR ORGANISING YOUTH PARLIAMENT COMPETITION IN RECOGNISED EDUCATIONAL INSTITUTIONS IN THE NATIONAL CAPITAL TERRITORY OF DELHI

A Youth Parliament Competition is held annually by the Ministry of Parliamentary Affairs in coordination with the Directorate of Education, Govt. of NCT of Delhi in the recognised educational institutions in Delhi.

Meeting

First of all a meeting with the officers of the Directorate of Education, Govt. of NCT of Delhi and NDMC is held to finalise the modalities of holding the competition. The following decisions are taken in the meeting:

(i) Date and venue of the Orientation Course for the benefit of the teachers-in-charge of Youth Parliament activity in the participating schools;

(ii) Chalking out of programme for evaluation of the final Youth Parliament Competition; and

(iii) Fixing date of the Prize Distribution Function.

After holding the meeting the minutes thereon are circulated to all concerned. After receiving the name of the participating schools from the Directorate of Education, literature on Youth Parliament is sent to all participating schools.

Orientation Course

To acquaint teachers-in-charge of the Youth Parliament in the participating schools with the concept and background of the scheme, the Ministry of Parliamentary Affairs, in cooperation with the Directorate of Education and NDMC organises an Orientation Course.

Action to be taken for conducting the Orientation Course is as under:

(i) Preparation of note for drawal of advance to meet the estimated expenditure in connection with organisation of the Orientation Course for teachers-in-charge of the participating vidyalayas.
(ii) Approval of Secretary/IFD for the estimated expenditure.
(iii) Intimating the date and venue of the Orientation Courses to the participating vidyalayas.
(iv) Send letters to the Principals of participating schools requesting names of teachers-in-charge of Youth Parliament activity.
(v) Preparation of programme of the Orientation Course.
(vi) Arrangements for refreshment etc.
(vii) Preparation of banners.
(viii) Holding the Orientation Course as scheduled.
(ix) Distribution of certificates to the teachers-in-charge attending the Orientation Course.
(x) Submission of report on the Orientation Course.

The following items are distributed at the venue:

1. Material on Youth Parliament;
2. Cassettes/CD on Youth Parliament;
3. Bags, pens and writing pads; and
4. Attendance sheet (address and signature of participants).

Competition

After organising the Orientation Course, the competition is organised as per the time schedule. Detailed programme of the Youth Parliament Competition is drawn up by the Ministry of Parliamentary Affairs and circulated to the schools participating in the competition well before its commencement. According to the programme performances of participating schools are evaluated.

Committee of Judges for evaluation of Competition

A Committee of Judges is constituted by the Ministry of Parliamentary Affairs consisting of ordinarily a Member of Parliament or an ex-Member of Parliament, an officer of the Ministry of Parliamentary Affairs and an officer of the Directorate of Education, Government of National Capital Territory of Delhi.

MPs/ex-MPs who are associated with the team of judges are paid DA as per details given below:

Legislators	Amount of DA
1. M.P.	Rs. 500
2. Ex-MP	Rs. 300

Results of the Competition

After completing the competition, results, on the basis of the performances of the participating vidyalayas, of the whole competition are declared by this Ministry and circulated to all concerned.

Prize Distribution Function

After completion of the whole competition, a Prize Distribution Function is organised to distribute the prizes, certificates and trophies to the participants at a suitable place - normally at Mavlankar Auditorium, New Delhi.

Following actions are taken to organise the Prize Distribution Function:

1. Approval of advance from competent authority.
2. Drawal of advance and upkeep of its accounts.
3. Letter to Lok Sabha Secretariat for allotment of Mavlankar Auditorium.
4. Letter to Deputy Commissioner of Police requesting NOC for holding the function in Mavlankar Auditorium.
5. Letter to Executive Engineer, Mavlankar Auditorium, Air Conditioning unit etc. for necessary arrangements.
6. Preparation, checking and stamping of certificates.
7. Purchasing of bouquets for VIPs.

8. Arrangements for earthen flower pots in front of main and VIP gate of Mavlankar Auditorium..
9. Intimation to Principals of participating schools, zonal education officers etc. regarding time and date of the function.
10. Finalisation of programme of the function.
11. Printing of invitation cards.
12. Finalisation of the list of invitees.
13. Ensuring presence of prize winners three hours before the function.
14. Prizes-Shields, Trophies and Prize-books, their purchase, presentation of prize packets for individual prize-winners. All work connected therewith.
15. Catering for VIPs - All work connected therewith including finalisation of menu, placing of order and payment of bill etc.
16. Arrangements of furniture and refreshment for the invitees.
17. Constitution of committee to select prizes/shields etc.
18. Calling for quotations from the manufacturers.
19. Calling meeting of the committee for purchasing prizes/shields.
20. Letters to manufacturers.
21. Preparation of placards, sign boards and banners etc.
22. Despatch of invitation cards.
23. Preparation of draft speeches for
    (i) The Minister who will inaugurate the function;
    (ii) Inaugural speech by Secretary; and
    (iii) Vote of Thanks by DS(R&C).
24. Contacting the Principal of the school declared first in order of merit to keep the teacher and students ready for repeat performance.
25. Visit to school for the rehearsals of Youth Parliament in order to impart on the spot guidance and assistance to students.
26. All necessary arrangements in the hall and at the dias for holding function.
27. Arrangements at the dias of the tables, chairs, carpets, mikes and make-up of the children.

28. Allotment of duties to the members of staff on the day of the function.
29. Letter to Delhi Police for security/traffic arrangements.
30. Installation of telephone at Mavlankar Auditorium on the day of the function.
31. Arrangements for announcer/compere.
32. Arrangements for photographer.
33. Arrangements for bouquets for VIPs.
34. Letters to MPs/ex-MPs who acted as judges for inviting them for the function.
35. Preparation of Press Note.
36. Preparation of banners.
37. Preparation of folders for the Minister/Secretary/ officers of Ministry and Directorate of Education containing the following papers:

    (i) Copy of the programme,
    (ii) List of Business,
    (iii) Question List,
    (iv) Copies of Speeches,
    (v) Result,
    (vi) Press Note, and
    (vii) Scheme.

ANNEX XV-C

NATIONAL YOUTH PARLIAMENT COMPETITION SCHEME FOR KENDRIYA VIDYALAYAS

1. Objective of the Youth Parliament Scheme

With a view to strengthening the roots of democracy, inculcate healthy habits of discipline, tolerance of the views of others and enable the student community to know something about the working of Parliament, the Ministry of Parliamentary Affairs have decided in consultation with the Kendriya Vidyalaya Sangathan to introduce a scheme of National Youth Parliament Competition in the Kendriya Vidyalayas throughout the country and to hold annual competitions of "Youth Parliament' among the Kendriya Vidyalayas.

2. Eligibility for entry into the Competition

The scheme will be applicable to all the Kendriya Vidyalayas in the country. The selection of participating vidyalayas will be done by the Kendriya Vidyalayas Sangathan and intimated to Ministry of Parliamentary Affairs. The number of schools for participation during each year will be decided in consultation with the Ministry of Parliamentary Affairs.

3. Period during which the competition will be held

The competition would be held every year during a period considered to be convenient to the sangathan and the Ministry of Parliamentary Affairs.

4. Duration of Youth Parliament sitting

Duration of the sitting of the 'Youth Parliament' should not exceed one hour. Out of this 10-12 minutes may be devoted to

Questions and the remaining time be utilised for discussion on Bills, Motions or Resolutions etc.

5. Subjects for discussion at the Youth Parliament

It would be desirable that the matters raised in the Youth Parliament may relate to the subjects of welfare activities, defence of the country, social justice, social reforms, economic development, communal harmony, health, student discipline etc. No direct or indirect remarks may be made in the speeches so as to cast aspersions on political parties or leaders/persons etc.

6. Language

The participants may speak in English and/or Hindi.

7. Venue

The Competitons will be held in two phases - first at the Regional level and then at the Zonal level.

8. Outline of the Scheme

The competitions at the regional level will be held among such vidyalayas of the respective regions as are sponsored for the competition by the Kendriya Vidyalayas Sangathan from that region. These would be conducted under the supervision of Kendriya Vidyalaya Sangathan authorities. The competition at the zonal level will be held among the Kendriya Vidyalayas which obtain first place in their respective regions in the regional level competitions.

Based on the evaluation conducted by a team of judges consisting of an MP/ex-MP, officer of the Kendriya Vidyalaya Sangathan and Ministry of Parliamentary Affairs at the zonal level a merit list to declare zonal and national winners would be drawn.

For the purpose of the competition the regions will be the same as constituted by K.V.S. from time to time. There will be 6 zones each comprising of 3 regions as indicated below.

Bhopal	Calcutta	Delhi	Hyderabad	Jaipur	Lucknow
Jabalpur	Guwahati	Jammu	Bangalore	Bombay	Patna
Bhuban-eshwar	Silchar	Chandigarh	Madras	Ahmedabad	Dehradun

9. Orientation Course

To acquaint teachers-in-charge of organising the Youth Parliament in the participating vidyalayas with the concept and background of the scheme, the Ministry of Parliamentary Affairs in co-operation with the Kendriya Vidyalaya Sangathan shall organise an orientation course in New Delhi during the period convenient to Kendriya Vidyalayas.

10. Committee of Judges

The competitions at regional and zonal levels will be evaluated by a three member Committee of Judges.

The Committee of Judges for evaluation of performance of the competing vidyalayas at the regional level shall be constituted by the Assistant Commissioner, K.V.S. of the respective regions and shall consist of :

1. M.P./ex-MP/M.L.A./ex-M.L.A./M.L.C/ex-M.L.C.;
2. An officer of the Kendriya Vidyalaya Sangathan of the respective regions; and
3. Principal of non-participating vidyalaya of the region or some local prominent educationist.

The Committee of Judges for evaluation of the competition at the zonal level shall be constituted by the Ministry of Parliamentary Affairs and shall consist of:

1. Member of Parliament/ex-Member of Parliament;
2. An officer of the Ministry of Parliamentary Affairs; and
3. An officer of the Kendriya Vidyalaya Sangathan(Hqr.)

11. T.A. /DA

Members/ex-Members of Parliament associated with the evaluation of these competitions shall be paid DA for the day they are associated as one of the judges. The expenditure in this regard shall be borne by the Ministry of Parliamentary Affairs in accordance with the rules and regulations applicable to them.

Other officers concerned with the activity will draw their T.A./ D.A. from their own organisations as per their entitlement.

12. Consideration for drawing up the merit list

The Committee of Judges shall keep in view the following points while assessing the performance of the institutions-

		Marks
(i)	Discipline and decorum	10
(ii)	Observance of parliamentary procedure	20
(iii)	Selection of subjects for questions and supplementaries and quality of answers thereto	20
(iv)	Selection of subjects for debates	10
(v)	Delivery or quality of speeches delivered, standard of debates	30
(vi)	General assessment of the performance as a whole	10
	Total	100

13. Prizes

The following Prizes will be awarded:

(a) ***Running Shield***

'Nehru Running Shield' will be awarded to the Kendriya Vidyalaya declared first at the National Level Competition. If a particular vidyalaya wins the shield for three consecutive years, it will be retained permanently by that vidyalaya.

(b) ***Trophies***

(i) The vidyalaya declared first in the competition will also be awarded another merit trophy.

(ii) One Trophy each will be awarded to the vidyalaya which wins first place at zonal level in the respective zone (except the zone to which the vidyalaya declared first in the competition belongs).

(iii) One Trophy each will be awarded to the vidyalaya which is declared first in their respective regions at the regional level competition.

The trophies will be retained by the winning vidyalayas.

(c) *Medals/Cups*

Four students in every vidyalaya who give meritorious performances at the regional level will be awarded medals/books/cups. The number of prizes for students whose performance is adjudged meritorious is left to the discretion of the team of judges. (Students whose names appear for prizes both at regional and zonal/national level will be awarded prizes for their performance at zonal/national level only.

14. Certificates

(i) A Certificate shall be issued by the Ministry of Parliamentary Affairs to each vidyalaya for winning first place in the competition at the national level/for standing first at the regional level/for participation in the competition, depending upon the position of each participating vidyalaya in the competition.

(ii) A certificate shall also be issued to teacher-in-in charge of organising the "Youth Parliament Sitting' in each vidyalaya participating in the competition and to each of the prize winning students at regional and zonal level competitions.

(iii) Besides the prizes, the prize winning students will also be awarded certificates indicating their level of participation and position in the competitions.

15. Repeat Performance and Distribution of Prizes

The Kendriya Vidyalaya, adjudged best in the competition will give a repeat performance of their sitting of the Youth Parliament before a select audience in a Prize Distribution Function to be organised by the Ministry of Parliamentary Affairs in New Delhi. The Running Shield Trophies to the vidyalayas winning at the national/zonal/regional Level, will be awarded by the Ministry of Parliamentary Affairs to such vidyalayas in the function. Besides, prize winning students of vidyalyas declared first at national/Zonal level will also be awarded medals/ certificates in this function.

The Central Ministry of Parliamentary Affairs will fix a date and venue for other functions. The prizes shall be distributed by a high dignitary. Invitations to VIPs and others for attending this function will be issued by the Central Ministry of Parliamentary Affairs which shall bear the entire expenditure on this function, such as :

Expenditure:

(a) Rent of the hall/shamiana;
(b) Lighting and seating arrangements;
(c) Printing of invitation cards;
(d) Postage and stationery;
(e) Refreshment; and
(f) Other contingencies.

16. Assistance by Kendriya Vidyalaya Sangathan

Kendriya Vidyalaya Sangathan will give necessary assistance such as:

(i) Helping to find suitable auditorium etc. for holding the orientation course and arranging for board and lodging of participants;
(ii) All possible assistance for organising the function; and
(iii) Arranging board/Lodging/transport etc. for MPs/ex-MPs/officers who visit for adjudging performance and giving away prizes.

ANNEX XV-D

CHECK LIST FOR ORGANISING NATIONAL YOUTH PARLIAMENT COMPETITION FOR KENDRIYA VIDYALAYAS

This scheme is applicable to all the Kendriya Vidyalayas in the country. The Kendriya Vidyalaya Sangathan selects the participating vidyalayas and intimates the selection to the Ministry. The number of schools for participation during the year is decided in consultation with Ministry of Parliamentary Affairs.

Meeting

A meeting with the officers of the Kendriya Vidyalaya Sangathan is convened by this Ministry to finalise the modalities of holding the competition. The following decisions are taken in the meeting:

(i) Dates and venues of the Orientation Courses for benefit of the teachers-in-charge of Youth Parliament activity in the participating vidyalayas.

(ii) Finalisation of last date for sending results of the regional level competition to this Ministry.

(iii) Chalking out of programme for evaluation of the national level competition.

(iv) Fixing date of the Prize Distribution Function.

After holding the meeting the minutes thereon are circulated to all concerned. After receiving the name of the participating Vidyalayas from KVS, literature on Youth Parliament is sent to all participating Vidyalayas.

Orientation Course

To acquaint teachers-in-charge of the 'Youth Parliament' in the participating vidyalayas with the concept and background of the scheme, the Ministry of Parliamentary Affairs, in cooperation with the Kendriya Vidyalaya Sangathan, organises Orientation Courses.

Action to be taken for conducting the Orientation Courses is as under:

1. Preparation of note for drawal of advance to meet the estimated expenditure of the courses.
2. Approval of the competent authority for the estimated expenditure.
3. Deputing officers/officials of the Ministry for conducting Orientation Courses.
4. Intimating the date and venue of the Orientation Courses to the participating vidyalayas and seeking the names of teachers-in-charge who would attend the courses.
5. Preparation of programmes of the Orientation Courses.
6. Distribution of certificates to the teachers-in-charge attending the Orientation Courses.

Following items are distributed at the venues

i. Material on Youth Parliament;
ii. Cassettes on Youth Parliament;
iii. Bags, pens and writing pads;
iv. Banners;
v. Attendance sheet; and
vi. Receipts of payment of honorarium for lecturers.

Competition

After organising the Orientation Courses, the competition is organised as per the time schedule. The Competition is held at two levels - first at the regional level and then at the zonal level.

The competitions at the regional level are held among such Vidyalayas of the respective regions as are sponsored for the competition by the Kendriya Vidyalaya Sangathan from that region. This would be conducted under the supervision of Kendriya Vidyalaya Sangathan authorities. The competition at zonal level is held among the Kendriya Vidyalayas which are declared first in their respective regions.

Committee of Judges for Evaluation of Competition

For Regional Level Competition:

The Committee of Judges for evaluation of performance of the competing vidyalayas at the regional level is constituted by the Assistant Commissioner, K.V.S. of the respective regions and consists of:

1. An M.P./ex-M.P./M.L.A./ex-M.L.A./M.L.C./ex-M.L.C;
2. An Officer of the Kendriya Vidyalaya of the region; and
3. Principal of non-participating vidyalaya of the region or some prominent local educationist.

For Zonal Level Competition:

The Committee of Judges for evaluation of competition at zonal level is constituted by the Ministry of Parliamentary Affairs and consists of:

1. Member of Parliament/ex-Member of Parliament;
2. An officer of the Ministry of Parliamentary Affairs; and
3. An officer of the Kendriya Vidyalaya Sangathan (Hqrs.).

MPs/ex-MPs who are associated with the team of judges are paid DA as per details given below:

	Legislators	Amount of DA
1.	M.P.	Rs.500
2.	Ex-MP	Rs.300
3.	MLA/ex-MLA/ MLC/ex-MLC	NIL

For the purpose of the competition, regions remain the same as constituted by KVS from time to time. Generally, there are six zones each comprising of 3 regions as indicated below:

Bhopal	Kolkata	Delhi	Hyderabad	Jaipur	Lucknow
Bhopal	Kolkata	Delhi	Hyderabad	Jaipur	Lucknow
Jabalpur	Guwahati	Jammu	Bangalore	Mumbai	Patna
Bhuba-neswar	Silchar	Chandigarh	Chennai	Ahmedabad	Dehradun

Result of the competition

After completing the competition, results of the whole competition are declared by this Ministry. In respect of the result of the competition the following actions are taken:

1. The Assistant Commissioners of the respective regions of Kendriya Vidyalayas (regional offices) forward the regional level results to this Ministry.
2. After receiving the regional level result from the respective regions, this Ministry chalks out the programme for evaluation of the zonal/national level competition.
3. Results worked out on the basis of the performances of the participating vidyalayas and circulated to all concerned.

Prize Distribution Function

1. Approval of advance from competent authority.
2. Drawal of advance and upkeep of its accounts.
3. Letter to Lok Sabha Secretariat for allotment of the Mavlankar Auditorium.
4. Letter to Deputy Commissioner of Police requesting for NOC for holding the function in Mavlankar Auditorium.
5. Letter to Executive Engineer, Mavlankar Auditorium, Air Conditioning unit etc. for necessary arrangements.
6. Preparation, checking and stamping of certificates.
7. Letter to Horticulture for flowers.
8. Intimation to Principals of participating schools and officers of KVS regarding time and date of the function.
9. Finalisation of programme of the function.
10. Printing of invitation cards.
11. Finalisation of the list of invitees.
12. Ensuring presence of prize winners three hours before the function.
13. Prizes-Shields, Trophies and Prize books, their purchase, presentation of prize packets for individual prize winners. All work connected therewith.
14. Catering for VIPs - All work connected therewith including finalisation of menu, placing of order and payment of bill etc. etc.
15. Arrangements of furniture and refreshment for the invitees.
16. Constitution of committee to select prizes/shields etc.

17. Calling quotations from the manufacturers.
18. Calling meeting of the committee for purchasing prizes/ shields.
19. Letters to manufacturers.
20. Preparation of placards, sign boards and banners etc.
21. Dispatch of invitation cards.
22. Preparation of draft speeches for

    (i) The Minister who inaugurates the function
    (ii) Inaugural speech by Secretary
    (iii) Vote of Thanks by DS(R&C)

23. Contacting the Principal of the school standing first in order of merit to keep the teacher and students ready for repeat performance.
24. Visit to school for the rehearsals of Youth Parliament in order to impart on the spot guidance and assistance to students.
25. All necessary arrangements in the hall and at the dias for holding function.
26. Arrangements at the dias of the tables, chairs, carpets, mikes and make-up of the children.
27. Allotment of duties to the members of staff on the day of function.
28. Letter to Delhi Police for security/traffic arrangements.
29. Installation of telephone at Mavlankar Auditorium on the day of function.
30. Arrangements for announcer /compere.
31. Arrangements for photographer.
32. Arrangements for bouquets for VIPs.
33. Letter to MPs/ex-MPs who acted as judges inviting them for the function.
34. Preparation of Press Note.
35. Folders to be prepared for the Minister/Secretary/ officers of Ministry and KVS containing the following papers:

    (i) Copy of the programme,
    (ii) List of Business,
    (iii) Question List,
    (iv) Copies of speeches,
    (v) Result,
    (vi) Press Note, and
    (vii) Scheme.

ANNEX XV-E

NATIONAL YOUTH PARLIAMENT COMPETITIONS SCHEME FOR NAVODAYA VIDYALAYAS

1. Objective of the Youth Parliament Scheme

With a view to strengthening the roots of democracy, inculcate healthy habits of discipline, tolerance of the views of others and to enable the student community to know something about the working of Parliament, the Ministry of Parliamentary Affairs have decided in consultation with the Navodaya Vidyalaya Samiti to introduce a scheme of National Youth Parliament competition in Navodaya Vidyalayas throughout the country and to hold annual competitions of 'Youth Parliament' among the Navodaya Vidyalayas.

2. Eligibility for entry into the Competition

The scheme will be applicable to all the Navodya Vidyalayas in the country. The selection of participating vidyalayas will be done by the Navodya Vidyalayas Samiti and intimated to the Ministry of Parliamentary Affairs. The number of schools for participation during each year will be decided in consultation with the Ministry of Parliamentary Affairs.

3. Period during which the Competition will be held

The competition will be held every year during a period considered to be convenient to the Samiti and the Ministry of Parliamentary Affairs.

4. *Duration of Youth Parliament sitting*

The duration of the sitting of the 'Youth Parliament' should not exceed 45 minutes. Out of this 10-12 minutes may be devoted to Questions and the remaining time be utilised for discussion on Bills, Motions or Resolutions , etc.

5. Subjects for discussion at the Youth Parliament

It would be desirable that the matters raised in the Youth Parliament may relate to the subjects of welfare activities, defence of the country, social justice, social reforms, economic development, communal harmony, health, student discipline, etc. No direct or indirect remarks may be made in the speeches so as to cast as persons on the political parties or leaders/persons etc. It is suggested that particular stress may be given on the concept of human rights and at least one item of business on this subject may invariably be included.

6. Language

The participants may speak in English and/or Hindi.

7. Venue

Each institution shall ordinarily hold the Youth Parliament sitting in its own premises.

8. Outline of the Scheme

The competitions will be held in two phases - first at the regional level and then at the national level.

The competitions at regional level will be held among such vidyalayas of the respective regions as are sponsored for the competition by the Navodaya Vidyalaya Samiti from that region. This will be conducted under the supervision of the Navodaya Vidyalaya Samiti authorities. The competition at the national level will be held among the Navodaya Vidyalayas which stand first in their respective regions in the regional level competitions.

Based on the evaluation conducted by a team of judges consisting of an MP/ex-MP, officer of the Navodaya Vidyalaya Samiti and Ministry of Parliamentary Affairs at the national level a merit list to declare national winners would be drawn.

9. Orientation Course

To acquaint teachers-in-charge of organising 'Youth Parliament in the participating vidyalyas with the concept and background of the scheme, the Ministry of Parliamentary Affairs in co-operation with the Navodaya Vidyalaya Samiti shall organise an orientation course in New Delhi during the period convenient to Navodaya Vidyalayas.

10. Committee of Judges

The competition at regional and national levels will be evaluated by a three member Committee of Judges.

The Committee of Judges for evaluation of performance of the competing vidyalyas at the regional level shall be constituted by the Assistant Director, N.V.S. or the respective regions and shall consist of:

1. MP/ex-MP/MLA//ex-MLA/MLC/ex-MLC;
2. An officer of the Navodaya Vidyalaya Samiti of the respective region; and
3. The Principal of a non-participating vidyalaya of the region or some local prominent educationist.

The Committee of Judges for evaluation of the competition at the national level shall be constituted by the Ministry of Parliamentary Affairs and shall consist of :

1. Member of Parliament/ex-Member of Parliament;
2. An officer of the Ministry of Parliamentary Affairs; and
3. An officer of the Navodaya Vidyalya Samiti(Hqrs.).

11. TA /DA

Members/ex-Members of Parliament associated with the evaluation of these competitions shall be paid DA for the day they are associated as one of the judges. The expenditure in this regard shall be borne by the Ministry of Parliamentary Affairs in accordance with the rules and regulations applicable to them.

Other officers concerned with the activity will draw their T.A./ D.A. from their own organisations as per their entitlement.

12. Consideration for drawing up the Merit List

The Committee of Judges shall keep in view the following points while assessing the performance of the institutions-

		Marks
(i)	Discipline and decorum	10
(ii)	Observance of parliamentary procedure	20
(iii)	Selection of subjects for questions and supplementaries and quality of answers thereto	20
(iv)	Selection of subjects for debates	10
(v)	Delivery or quality of speeches delivered, standard of debates	30
(vi)	General assessment of the performance as a whole.	10
		Total 100

13. Prizes

The following Prizes will be awarded:

(a) Running Shield

The 'Nehru Running Shield' will be awarded to the Navodaya Vidyalaya declared first at the national level Completion. If a particular vidyalaya wins the shield for three consecutive years, it will be retained permanently by that vidyalaya.

(b) Trophies

(i) The vidyalaya declared first in the competition will also be awarded another merit trophy.

(ii) One Trophy each will be awarded to the vidyalayas which are declared first in their respective regions at the regional level competition.

The trophies will be retained by the winning vidyalayas

(c) Medals/Cups

Four students in every vidyalaya who give meritorious performances at the regional level will be awarded medals/books/cups. The number of prizes for students whose performance is adjudged meritorious is left to the discretion of the team of judges. (Students whose names appear for prizes both at regional and zonal/

national level will be awarded prizes for their performance at zonal/ national level only.)

14. Certificates

(i) A Certificate shall be issued by the Ministry of Parliamentary Affairs to each vidyalaya for standing first in the competition at national level/for standing first at regional level/for participation in the competition, depending upon the position of each participating vidyalaya in the competition.

(ii) A certificate shall also be issued to the teacher-in-charge of organising the 'Youth Parliament Sitting' in each vidyalaya participating in the competition and to each of the prize winning students at regional and zonal level competitions.

(iii) Besides the prizes, the prize winning students will also be awarded certificates indicating their level of participation and position in the competitions.

15. Repeat Performance and Distribution of Prizes

The Navodaya Vidyalaya, adjudged best in the competition will give a repeat performance of their sitting of the Youth Parliament before a select audience at a Prize Distribution Function to be organised by the Ministry of Parliamentary Affairs in New Delhi. The Running Shield/Trophies to the Vidyalayas declared first at the National/Zonal/Regional Level, will be awarded by the Minisitry of Parliamentary Affairs to such vidyalayas in the function. Besides, prize winning students of vidyalayas standing first at national/zonal level will also be awarded medals/ certificates at this function.

The Central Ministry of Parliamentary Affairs will fix a date and venue for the other function. The prizes shall be distributed by a high dignitary. Invitations to VIPs and others for attending this function will be issued by the Central Ministry of Parliamentary Affairs which shall bear the entire expenditure on this function, such as :

(a) Rent of the hall/shamiana;
(b) Lighting and seating arrangements;
(c) Printing of invitation cards;
(d) Postage and stationery;
(e) Refreshment; and
(f) Other contingencies.

16. Assistance by NavodayaVidyalaya Samiti

The Navodaya Vidyalaya Samiti will give necessary assistance such as :

(i) Helping to find suitable auditorium etc. for holding the orientation course and arranging for board and lodging of participants;
(ii) All possible assistance for organising the function; and
(iii) Arranging board/lodging/transport etc. for MPs/ex-MPs/officers who visit for adjudging the performance and giving guidance to the participants.

17. Financial Assistance to Navodaya Vidyalaya Samiti by Ministry of Parliamentary Affairs

The Ministry of Parliamentary Affairs will extend the following financial assistance to the Navodaya Vidyalaya Samiti for conducting the National Youth Parliament Competition in the Jawahar Navodaya Vidyalayas:

(i) Reimbursement of expenses up to a sum of Rs. 5000 to each Jawahar Navodaya Vidyalaya participating in the competition to meet expenditure towards organising the competition subject to production of receipts of expenses incurred.
(ii) Reimbursement of transportation expenditure up to a maximum of Rs. 30,000 to the First Prize winning vidyalaya in the Competition attending the Prize Distribution Function to stage their repeat performance.

The participating vidyalayas will submit a statement of expenditure incurred along with relevant vouchers and rout the same through the Navodaya Vidyalaya Samiti (Headquarters) who would submit a consolidated statement of expenditure at the conclusion of the competition to the Ministry of Parliamentary Affairs.

ANNEX XV-F

CHECK LIST FOR ORGANISING NATIONAL YOUTH PARLIAMENT COMPETITION FOR JAWAHAR NAVODAYA VIDYALAYAS

The scheme would be applicable to all the Navodaya Vidyalayas in the country. The Navodaya Vidyalaya Samiti selects the participating vidyalayas and intimates the selection to the Ministry of Parliamentary Affairs. The number of vidyalayas for participation during the year is decided in consultation with the Ministry of Parliamentary Affairs.

Meeting

A meeting with the officers of the Navodaya Vidyalaya Samiti is convened by this Ministry to finalise the modalities of organising the

- (i) dates and venues of the Orientation Courses for the benefit of the teachers-in-charge of Youth Parliament activity in the participating vidyalayas;
- (ii) finalisation of the last date for sending results of the regional level competition to this Ministry;
- (iii) chalking out of programme for evaluation of the national level competition; and
- (iv) fixing date of the Prize Distribution Function.

After holding the meeting the minutes thereon are circulated to all concerned. After receiving the names of the participating vidyalayas from NVS, literature on the Youth Parliament is sent to all participating vidyalayas.

Orientation Course

To acquaint teachers-in-charge of the 'Youth Parliament' in the participating vidyalayas with the concept and background of the scheme, the Ministry of Parliamentary Affairs, in cooperation with the Navodaya Vidyalaya Samiti, organises Orientation Courses.

Action to be taken for conducting the Orientation Courses is as under:

1. Preparation of note for drawal of advance to meet the estimated expenditure of the courses.
2. Approval of the competent authority for the estimated expenditure.
3. Deputing officers/officials of the Ministry for conducting Orientation Course.
4. Intimating the date and venue of the Orientation Courses to the participating vidyalayas and seeking the names of teachers-in-charge who would attend the courses.
5. Preparation of programmes of the Orientation Courses.
6. Distribution of certificates to the teachers-in-charge attending the Orientation Courses.

The following items are distributed at the venues :

a. Material on Youth Parliament,
b. Cassettes on Youth Parliament,
c. Bags, pens and writing pads,
d. Banners,
e. Attendance sheet, and
f. Receipts of payment of honorarium for lecturers.

Competition

After organising the Orientation Courses, the competition is organised as per the time schedule. The competition is held at two levels - first at the regional level and then at the national level.

The competitions at the regional level are held among such vidyalayas of the respective regions as are sponsored for the competition by the Navodaya Vidyalaya Samiti from that region. These will be conducted under the supervision of the Navodaya Vidyalaya Samiti authorities. The competition at the national level is held among the vidyalayas which are adjudged first in their respective regions.

Committee of Judges for evaluation of Competition

For Regional Level Competition:

The Committee of Judges for evaluation of performance of the competing vidyalayas at the regional level is constituted by the

Assistant Director, N.V.S. of the respective regions and consists of:

1. M.P./ex-M.P./M.L.A./ex-M.L.A./M.L.C./ex-M.L.C.;
2. An officer of the Navodaya Vidyalaya Samiti of the respective region; and
3. Principal of non-participating vidyalaya of the region or some local prominent educationist.

For Zonal Level Competition:

The Committee of Judges for evaluation of competition at the national level is constituted by the Ministry of Parliamentary Affairs and consists of:

1. Member of Parliament/ex-Member of Parliament;
2. An officer of the Ministry of Parliamentary Affairs; and
3. An officer of the Navodaya Vidyalaya Samiti (Hqrs.).

MPs/ex-MPs who are associated with the team of judges are paid DA as per details given below-

Legislators	Amount of DA
1. M.P.	Rs.500
2. ex-MP	Rs.300
3. MLA/ex-MLA/ MLC/ex-MLC	NIL

Results of the Competition

After completing the competition, the results of the whole competition are declared by this Ministry. The following actions are then taken:

1. The Deputy Directors of the respective regions of the Navodaya Vidyalaya Samiti (regional offices) forward the regional level results to this Ministry.
2. After receiving the regional level results from the respective regions this Ministry chalks out the programme for evaluation of the national level competition.

3. Results worked out on the basis of the performances of the participating vidyalayas are circulated to all concerned.

Prize Distribution Function

After completion of the whole competition, a Prize Distribution Function is organised to distribute the prizes, certificates and trophies to the participants at a suitable place - normally at Mavlankar Auditorium, New Delhi.

The following actions are taken to organise the Prize Distribution Function:

1. Approval of advance from competent authority.
2. Drawal of advance and upkeep of its accounts.
3. Letter to Lok Sabha Secretariat for allotment of Mavlankar Auditorium.
4. Letter to Deputy Commissioner of Police requesting NOC for holding the function in Mavlankar Auditorium.
5. Letter to Executive Engineer, Mavlankar Auditorium, Air Conditioning unit etc. for necessary arrangements.
6. Preparation, checking and stamping of certificates.
7. Letter to Horticulture for flowers.
8. Intimation to Principals of participating schools and officers of KVS regarding time and date of the function.
9. Finalisation of programme of the function.
10. Printing of invitation cards.
11. Finalisation of the list of invitees.
12. Ensuring presence of prize winners three hours before the function.
13. Prizes-Shields, Trophies and Prize books, their purchase, presentation of prize packets for individual prize winners. All work connected therewith.
14. Catering for VIPs - All work connected therewith including finalisation of menu, placing of order and payment of bill etc. etc.
15. Arrangements of furniture and refreshment for the invitees.
16. Constitution of committee to select prizes/shields etc.
17. Calling for quotations from the manufacturers.
18. Calling meeting of the committee for purchasing prizes/ shields.

19. Letters to manufacturers.
20. Preparation of placards, sign boards and banners etc.
21. Despatch of invitation cards.
22. Preparation of draft speeches for
    i. The Minister who inaugurates the function,
    ii. Inaugural speech by Secretary, and
    iii. Vote of Thanks by DS(R&C).
23. Contacting the Principal of the School securing first place in order of merit to keep the teacher and students ready for repeat performance.
24. Visit to the school for the rehearsals of the Youth Parliament in order to impart on the spot guidance and assistance to students.
25. All necessary arrangements in the hall and at the dias for holding the function.
26. Arrangements at the dias of the tables, chairs, carpets, mikes and make-up of the children.
27. Allotment of duties to the members of staff on the day of function.
28. Letter to Delhi Police for security/traffic arrangements.
29. Installation of telephone at Mavlankar Auditorium on the day of function.
30. Arrangements for announcer /compere.
31. Arrangements for photographer.
32. Arrangements for bouquets for VIPs.
33. Letter to MPs/ex-MPs who acted as judges inviting them for the function.
34. Preparation of Press Note.
35. Folders to be prepared for the Minister/Secretary/ Officers of Ministry and NVS containing the following papers:

    i. Copy of the programme,
    ii. List of Business,
    iii. Question List,
    iv. Copies of speeches,
    v. Result,
    vi. Press Note, and
    vii. Scheme.

ANNEX XV-G

SCHEME OF NATIONAL YOUTH PARLIAMENT COMPETITION FOR UNIVERSITIES/COLLEGES

1. Objectives of the Youth Parliament Scheme

With a view to strengthening the roots of democracy, inculcate healthy habits of discipline, tolerance of the views of others and to enable the student community to understand the working of our parliamentary institutions, the Ministry of Parliamentary Affairs has introduced the Scheme of National Youth Parliament Competition in universities/colleges throughout the country. These competitions are conducted on an annual basis in each academic year.

2. Eligibility for entry in the Competition

All the universities/colleges who sponsor their nominees for attending the orientation course conducted by the Ministry of Parliamentary Affairs prior to the start of the competition would be eligible for participation. The Ministry of Parliamentary Affairs may add any additional institution for participation in the competition.

3. Format and period of the Competition

The competition would normally be held in two stages depending on the number of participating institutions - the first stage at the group level where the institutions will be divided into various groups and secondly at the national level between the winners of the various groups. The schedule of the group and national level competitions will be finalised by the Ministry of Parliamentary Affairs and the entire competition will be conducted within the same academic year. Each participating institution will prepare a single team of students who will participate as a team representing the institution.(For the purpose of organising the group-level competitions, the Ministry of Parliamentary Affairs may nominate a co-ordinator from amongst the participating institutions to conduct and co-ordinate the competition in respect of that group and submit a report thereon to the Ministry).

4. Duration of the Youth Parliament Sitting

The duration of the sitting of the' Youth Parliament' should not exceed 60 to 75 minutes. Out of this, nearly 20 minutes may be devoted to Questions and the remaining time be utilised for discussion on Bills, Motions, Resolutions etc. as indicated in the literature on the subject which would be made available during the Orientation Course conducted by the Ministry of Parliamentary Affairs prior to the commencement of each competition.

5. Subjects for Discussion in the 'Youth Parliament Session'

The matters raised in the 'Youth Parliament Session' may relate to welfare activities, defence of the country, social justice, social reforms, economic development, communal harmony, public health, student discipline etc. Special emphasis may be laid on issues relating to human rights. A list of suggested topics on which items may be presented is at **Annex XV-G(I).**

No direct or indirect remarks may be made in the speeches which may cast aspersions on political parties or leaders/persons etc. and controversial topics based on actual events of recent occurrence should be avoided. It would be desirable to take up issues based on hypothetical events for expounding upon the basic principles proposed to the debated. A list of 'Do's and Dont's' elucidating the various points to be kept in mind during the conduct of the 'Youth Parliament Session' is given at **Annex XV-G(II).**

6. Language

The participants may speak in English and/or Hindi.

7. Venue

Each institution shall ordinarily hold their 'Youth Parliament Session' in its own premises with the help of available facilities. Needless expenditure should be avoided.

8. Evaluation of the Competition at the National Level

At the national level competition the performances of each team would be evaluated by a panel of judges consisting of:

(i) MP/ex-MP/MLA/ex-MLA/MLC/ex-MLC;
(ii) An officer of the Ministry of Parliamentary Affairs; and
(iii) An academician of repute from a non-participating institution.

Based on this evaluation a merit list will be drawn to select the 'National Winner'. Individual performances will also be evaluated and prizes awarded to the selected team members on the basis of their meritorious performance.

The institutions participating at the national level would be selected on the basis of group-level competitions among the various institutions.

[The group-level competitions would be evaluated by a team consisting of:
(i) An MP/ex-MP/MLA/ex-MLA/MLC/ex-MLC;
(ii) A coordinator to be appointed from among the institutions participating in that group (for evaluating the performance of the coordinator's own institution another nominee from amongst the other participating institutions of that group would sit on the evaluation panel instead of the coordinator.)
(iii) An academician of repute from a non-participating institution.]

9. Shields, Trophies, Prizes etc.

At the national level the following will be awarded:

(a) Running Shield

A running shield will be awarded to the institution declared as first at the national level competition. If a particular institution wins the shield for three consecutive years, the shield will be retained permanently by that institution.

(b) Trophies

(i) The institution declared as first in the national level competition will be awarded another trophy.
(ii) One trophy each will be awarded to the other institutions participating in the national level by virtue of their

having secured first position in their respective groups in the first stage (group-level) of the competition.

(The trophies at (i) and (ii) above will be retained by the respective institutions).

(c) Prizes and certificates

(i) Prizes and Certificates will be awarded to the students selected by the evaluating panel for their meritorious performances at the national level competition. (If any of these students have won prizes at the group-level competitions also, they would be awarded only the national level prizes and certificates.)

(ii) Certificates will be awarded to the teacher-in-charge of the team. (In addition, each student who is a member of the team of the institution which has stood first at the national level will be awarded a certificate and a prize.)

(iii) At the group-level, prizes and certificates will be awarded to students of each of the participating institutions selected by the evaluating panel for their meritorious performance. At the group-level six students will be selected by the evaluating panel for the prizes and certificates.

10. Prize Distribution Function

The Prize Distribution Function will be organised by the Ministry of Parliamentary Affairs at a suitable date and venue after the competition is completed. At the function, the running shield, trophies to the institutions and prizes and certificates to the students at the national level will be awarded.

The institution which stands first at the national level will be required to give a repeat performance of their 'Youth Parliament Session' before a selected audience at the Prize Distribution Function. The duration of this 'Youth Parliament Session' should not exceed 55 minutes.

The Ministry of Parliamentary Affairs will fix a date and venue for the function. The prizes shall be distributed by a high dignitary. Invitations to VIPs and others for attending this function will be issued by the Ministry of Parliamentary Affairs which shall bear the entire expenditure on this function such as :

Expenditure on:

(a) Rent of the hall/shamiana;
(b) Lighting and seating arrangements;
(c) Printing of invitation cards;
(d) Postage and stationery;
(e) Refreshment; and
(f) Other contingencies.

The Prize Distribution Function will be attended by the prize winning students and the respective teachers-in-charge of the institutions which participated at the national level. The Ministry of Parliamentary Affairs will reimburse TA to the students restricted to ordinary second class/sleeper class railway fare. One escort teacher accompanying the students would be reimbursed TA restricted to the rail fare to his/her entitled class. The TA reimbursement for both the escort and the students would be from their usual place of residence to Delhi and back.

11. Financial Assistance

(i) The Ministry of Parliamentary Affairs will reimburse expenses incurred by each institution for organising the Youth Parliament session up to Rupees five thousand for the first stage (group-level) competitions. Those institutions which qualify and participate in the second stage (national level) of the competitions would be reimbursed an additional amount up to Rupees five thousand. The reimbursement of expenditure in either case will be made on receipt of statements of expenditure and the relevant vouchers.

(ii) The Ministry of Parliamentary Affairs would also reimburse, within permissible limits, actual TA/DA expenses incurred in connection with journeys undertaken by the co-coordinators nominated for conducting/coordinating the group-level competitions in respect of each group during the paragraph 3 of this scheme. The Group co-ordinators may submit their claims in the standard formats of TA/DA claims prescribed in their individual institutions and forward the same to the Ministry for reimbursement.

ANNEX XV-G (I)

CERTAIN SUGGESTED SUBJECTS FOR DISCUSSION IN YOUTH PARLIAMENT COMPETITION FOR UNIVERSITIES/COLLEGES IN ADDITION TO THOSE MENTIONED IN THE RULES AND REGULATIONS OF THE ADOPTED SCHEME BASED ON THE SUGGESTIONS RECEIVED AND THE SUBJECTS DEBATED IN VARIOUS YOUTH PARLIAMENT SESSIONS AND DURING ORIENTATION COURSES

1. Should Parliament have unfettered powers of legislation?
2. Implementation of the Members of Parliament Local Area Development Scheme - how should the allocations be made/execution of works be monitored?
3. Human Rights with focus on right to life enshrined in articles 21 and 22 of the Constitution.
4. Reservation for women in legislative bodies and in services.
5. Need to prescribe some minimum education and experience in public service for legislators.
6. National integration with focus on growth of ethnicity.
7. Matters regarding population control and policy with focus on legislation to provide incentives/disincentives.
8. Electoral reforms with focus on corruption.
9. Right of legislators to decide their own perks. How else to decide?
10. Ways to provide a competent and stable Government in the event of a hung Parliament.
11. Privileges and Code of Conduct for legislators.
12. Ways to check corruption and inefficiency in public sector.
13. Caretaker Government - Status and Functioning.
14. Presidential Form of Government.
15. Proportional representation/list system.
16. People's rights to good governance.
17. Representation of sports-persons, beauty queens and cine-stars in legislative bodies.

ANNEX XV-G (II)

DO'S AND DONT'S FOR THE PARTICIPANTS IN THE YOUTH PARLIAMENT COMPETITIONS

1. The institutions and students participating in the Youth Parliament Competitions should bear in mind that this scheme is a unique one. It is aimed to make these Youth Parliaments as the nurseries of future parliamentarians. If rightly implemented and its organisers are imbued with a sense of duty and dedication, it is likely to pay rich dividends in the shape of all round improvement in our national character and outlook. This aspect should always be kept in view while the institutions volunteer themselves for participation in these competitions.

2. It should not be forgotten that democracy offers political methods by which every citizen has the opportunity of participating through discussion and debates in an attempt to reach a voluntary agreement as to what should be done for the good of the community as a whole. It precludes the method of arriving at a decision on social policy in the streets as these are the ways of mobocracy and not of democracy. Thus the scheme of Youth Parliament would help to start a movement amongst students to channel their energy into healthy and constructive activities so that they may become useful citizens of tomorrow.

3. The subjects to be selected for discussion in these Youth Parliaments should be as far as possible non-controversial. They should largely deal with the problems confronting educational institutions and their day-to-day problems. The subject should relate to welfare activities, defence of the country, social justice and social reforms, economic development, communal harmony, discipline, health of the students, human rights, etc.

4. Two most important parts of the List of Business of a 'Youth Parliament' are the 'Questions' and the 'Debate' or 'Discussion'. During Question Hour, the judges are likely to be impressed by the quality of questions asked and the quality of replies given by the Ministers. During the debate or discussions, they particularly look for the standard of the debate and the quality of expression.

5. The participants should scrupulously avoid mention of the existing political parties and political personalities in the country. They should give imaginary or fictitious names to their parties and personalities. They should not give any impression that they have any leanings or bias for or against any political party or philosophy.

6. It would be in the interest of the participating institutions if they were to have their own "Permanent Youth Parliaments" which should serve as the "Debating societies" for promoting debating talents in their students. Thus, at the time of selecting the names of participants they can draw upon the talent from these "Parliaments".

7. The participants should show utmost respect to the Chair. They should abide by the decisions of the Chair and should have faith in his impartiality and judgement.

8. Every member while coming to the House for its sitting should bow to the Chair and also while leaving the chamber.

9. The members should not say or do anything on the floor of the House that is not warranted by the rules or procedures or by the ruling or precedence or by the accepted and established customs and conventions of the House.

10. There should be no discussion on sensitive policy matters affecting the relations of our country with foreign friendly Governments or which will prove embarrassing for the country and its present day Government.

11. A member should never cross the floor while the House is sitting i.e. he should never pass between the Chair and any member who is speaking. Violation of this rule is regarded as a breach of parliamentary etiquette.

12. Members should not sit with their backs to the Chair. When a member wants to speak he should raise hand to attract the attention of the Chair. No member should speak unless he or she has 'caught' the eye of the Speaker and has been permitted by the Chair by name or by a sign, to speak.

13. Every member should resume his seat as the Speaker rises to speak or calls out "order" and also when any other member is in possession of the floor. Two or more members should not keep standing at the same time.

14. No member should rise or leave the House when the Speaker is addressing the House. 'The Speaker is always to be heard in silence.'

15. No member should read out a written speech. However, a member may feel free to consult his notes whenever he loses track of his prepared speech or text.

16. Personal references by way of imputations or questions against the bonafides of any member should not be resorted to. A member must not address individual members of the House. He should always address the Chair and make all remarks to other members through the Chair.

17. Members should not distribute within the precincts of the House or inside the legislature questionnaires or pamphlets not connected with the business of the House.

18. Members during participation in the discussion can use either English or Hindi. However, if a member wants to speak in any other language, he is suppose to do so with the permission of the Speaker, but before speaking he is supposed to furnish in advance a copy of the translation of this speech.

19. In short all participants in these Youth Parliaments should so conduct themselves as to inspire respect for Parliament and Parliamentary Institutions.

ANNEX XV-H

CHECK LIST FOR ORGANISING NATIONAL YOUTH PARLIAMENT COMPETITION IN UNIVERSITIES

Orientation Course

Prior to holding a competition, an Orientation Course is conducted by this Ministry to acquaint coordinators organising the 'Youth Parliament' in the participating institutions with the concept and background of the scheme.

The following actions are taken for organising the Orientation Course:

1. Issuing of letters to all the universities to sponsor their nominees called coordinators for the Orientation Course.
2. Giving advertisements also in national dailies throughout the country for the above purpose.
3. Scrutinizing the details of the applications received and preparing the list of eligible nominees/coordinators.
4. Selecting a suitable place for holding the Orientation Course after due consultation with the concerned authorities.
5. Making necessary arrangements for transport, board and lodging of the participants at the venue of the course.
6. Preparation of note for drawal of advance to meet the estimated expenditure.
7. Approval of Secretary/IFD for the estimated expenditure.
8. Deputing officers/officials of the Ministry for conducting Orientation Course.
9. Intimating the date and venue of the Orientation Course to the participants.
10. Preparing of programme of the Orientation Course.
11. Distribution of certificates to the coordinators attending the Orientation Course.

12. Dividing the institutions into various groups for conducting group level competitions.
13. Nominating a Group Coordinator for each group for evaluating/coordinating group level competitions.
14. Providing TA to the coordinators.

The following items are distributed/taken at the venues:

1. Material on Youth Parliament,
2. Cassettes on Youth Parliament,
3. Bags, pens and writing pads,
4. Big bags for carrying material,
5. Banners,
6. Attendance sheet (address and signature of participants), and
7. Receipt of payment of honorarium for lecturers.

Orientation Course is conducted as per the specimen programme **(Annex XVI-H(I)).**

Expectation of the Ministry

We expect the UGC to take over this work.

Competition

After holding the Orientation Course as per the schedule, the competition is organised. The competition is held at two levels - first at group level and then at national level.

The competition at group level is held among the institutions in each group. This is conducted under the supervision of Group Coordinators. The competition at national level is held among the institutions which stand first in their respective groups.

Following actions are taken to organise the competition:

1. Issuing of letters to all the participating institutions for conducting the group level competitions as per the schedule.
2. Scrutinising the group level results received from different group coordinators to select the group winning institutions for participation at the national level.

3. Contacting institutions to fix up the dates and times of national level competitions.
4. Evaluating the national level competitions.
5. Declaring results of the whole competition.
6. Sending the results to all the participating institutions.

Committee of Judges for evaluation of Competitions

For Group Level Competition

(i) An MP/ex-MP/MLA/ex-MLA/MLC/ex-MLC;
(ii) A coordinator to be appointed from among the institutions participating in that group (for evaluating the performance of the coordinator's own institution another nominee from amongst the other participating institutions of that group would sit on the evaluation panel instead of the coordinator); and
(iii) An academician of repute from a non-participating institution.

For National Level Competition

(i) An MP/ex-MP/MLA/ex-MLA/MLC/ex-MLC;
(ii) An officer of the Ministry of Parliamentary Affairs; and
(iii) An academician of repute from a non-participating institution.

MPs/ex-MPs who are associated with the team of judges are paid DA as per details given below:

	Legislators	**Amount of DA**
1.	M.P.	Rs.500
2.	Ex-MP	Rs.300
3.	MLA/ex-MLA/ MLC/ex-MLC	NIL

Financial Assistance

The following financial assistance is provided by this Ministry for holding the Youth Parliament Competitions:

To Institutions

An Institution is provided financial assistance for holding group level competition up to Rs.5,000 on production of a statement of expenditure supported by original vouchers. The institution participating in the national level competition would be eligible again for such financial assistance.

To Group coordinators

A group coordinator is provided TA/DA on production of his TA claim in the proforma prescribed in his institution. The TA is restricted up to the fare of AC-II tier by train.

Expectation of the Ministry

Competitions at the Group Level are organised through group coordinators. The competitions at the national level are evaluated by the Committee of Judges including an officer of this Ministry. Presently, this Ministry is consolidating the results of the group level as well as national level competitions. We expect the UGC to organise the competition at both the levels and compile the results themselves and inform the Ministry about the particulars of the institutions securing the first position at the group level as well as the national level for organising the Prize Distribution Function.

The Committee of Judges for evaluation of the Youth Parliament Competitions can be re-constituted suitably as per the suggestions of the UGC.

Prize Distribution Function

After completion of the whole competition, a Prize Distribution Function is organised to distribute the prizes, certificates and trophies to the participants at suitable place - normally at Mavalankar Auditorium, New Delhi.

The following actions are taken to organise the Prize Distribution Function:

1. Approval of advance from competent authority.
2. Drawal of advance and upkeep of its accounts.
3. Arrangements for board and lodging for the students and escort professors.

4. Letter to Lok Sabha Secretariat for allotment of the Mavlankar Auditorium.
5. Letter to Deputy Commissioner of Police requesting NOC for holding the function in Mavlankar Auditorium.
6. Letter to Executive Engineer, Mavlankar Auditorium, Air Conditioning unit etc. for necessary arrangements.
7. Finalisation of programme of the function.
8. Printing of invitation cards.
9. Finalisation of the list of invitees.
10. Preparation, checking and stamping of certificates.
11. Letter to Horticulture for flowers.
12. Invitation to Vice Chancellors/Registrars etc. of the Group Level First institutions for attending the Function.
13. Ensuring presence of prize winners three hours before the function.
14. Purchase of prizes, shields, trophies etc. for distribution to the prize winners. All work connected therewith.
15. Catering for VIPs - All work connected therewith including finalisation of menu, placing of order and payment of bill etc.
16. Arrangement of furniture and refreshments for the invitees.
17. Constitution of committee to select prizes/shields etc.
18. Calling for quotations from the manufacturers.
19. Calling meeting of the committee for purchasing prizes/shields.
20. Letters to manufacturers.
21. Preparation of placards, sign boards and banners etc.
22. Despatch of invitation cards.
23. Preparation of draft speeches for

    a. The Minister who is the Chief Guest at the function;
    b. Inaugural speech by Secretary; and
    c. Vote of Thanks by DS(R&C).

24. Contacting the coordinators of the institution standing first in the competition to keep the students ready for repeat performance.
25. Visit to institution for the rehearsals of Youth Parliament in order to guide them for the repeat performance.

26. All necessary arrangements in the Hall and at the dias for holding function.
27. Arrangements at the dias of the tables, chairs, carpets, mikes and make-up of the children.
28. Allotment of duties to the members of staff on the day of function.
29. Letter to Delhi Police for security/traffic arrangements.
30. Installation of telephone at Mavlankar Auditorium on the day of function.
31. Arrangements for announcer /compere.
32. Arrangements for photographer.
33. Arrangements for bouquets for VIPs.
34. Invitation to MPs/ex-MPs who acted as judges for evaluating the Youth Parliament Competition.
35. Preparation of Press Note.
36. Folders to be prepared for the Minister/Secretary/ Officers of Ministry and containing the following papers:

    i. Copy of the programme,
    ii. List of Business,
    iii. Questions List,
    iv. Copies of Speeches,
    v. Result,
    vi. Press Note, and
    vii. Scheme.

37. Arrangements for local sight seeing.

Travelling Allowance

(A) Travelling allowance up to 2nd AC of train to the coordinators and sleeper class to the prize winning students of the institutions participating at the national level other than the institution which stood first in the competition are provided.

(B) Transportation expenses up to Rs.30,000 are provided to the institution which is declared first in the competition and gives a repeat performance at the function.

ANNEX XV-H(I)

ORIENTATION COURSE FOR THE 7TH NATIONAL LEVEL YOUTH PARLIAMENT COMPETITION FOR UNIVERSITIES/COLLEGES

Programme

VENUE: Kodaikanal Christian College, Kodaikanal, Tamil Nadu

MONDAY, THE 17TH +MAY, 2004	
9.15 a.m. to 10.00 a.m.	Participants to assemble, register their presence and collect the material for Orientation Course.
10.00 a.m. to 10.05 a.m.	Welcome address by Dr. P. Chellathurai, Dean, College Development Council, Madurai Kamraj University, Madurai
10.05 a.m. to 10.30 a.m.	Inauguration of the Orientation Course by Dr. V.K. Agnihotri, Secretary, Ministry of Parliamentary Affairs, Government of India, New Delhi
10.30 a.m. to 10.55 a.m	Presidential Address by Vice Chancellor Madurai Kamraj University, Madurai
10.55 a.m. to 11.00 a.m.	Felicitation Address by Syndicate Member, Prof. Kailash Paliwal, Madurai Kamraj Univesity, Madurai
11.00 a.m. to 11.05 a.m.	Felicitation Address by Shri Sam Abraham, Chairman, Kodaikanal, Christian College, Kodaikanal
11.05 a.m. to 11.10 a.m.	Vote of Thanks by Shri Dhani Ram, Deputy Secretary, Ministry of Parliamentary Affairs, Government of India, New Delhi.

11.10 a.m. to 11.30 a.m.	**TEA BREAK**
SESSION – I	
11.30 a.m. to 12.30 p.m.	Speech on "Parliamentary System and its functioning" by Guest Speaker
12.30 p.m. to 2.00 p.m.	**LUNCH BREAK**
SESSION – II	
2.00 p.m. to 3.00 p.m.	Lecture on "Conducting Youth Parliament – Procedural aspects" by Shri Bhoj Raj, Under Secretary, Ministry of Parliamentary Affairs, Government of India, New Delhi.
3.00 p.m. to 3.20 p.m.	**TEA BREAK**
SESSION – III	
3.20 p.m. to 4.20 p.m.	Lecture on "Conducting Youth Parliament – Procedural aspects" by Shri Dhani Ram, Deputy Secretary, Ministry of Parliamentary Affairs, Government of India, New Delhi.
SESSION – IV	
4.20 p.m.to 5.20 p.m.	Lecture on "Conducting Youth Parliament – Procedural aspects" by Shri Bhoj Raj, Under Secretary, Ministry of Parliamentary Affairs, Government of India, New Delhi.
TUESDAY, THE 18TH MAY, 2004	
VENUE: Kodaikanal Christian College, Kodaikanal, Tamil Nadu	
SESSION - V	
9.15 a.m. to 10.15 a.m.	Lecture on "Conducting Youth Parliament – Procedural aspects" by

	Shri Dhani Ram, Deputy Secretary, Ministry of Parliamentary Affairs, Government of India, New Delhi.
SESSION – VI	
10.15 a.m. to 10.45 a.m.	Discussion by participants
SESSION – VII	
10.15 a.m. to 11.45 a.m.	Demonstration of 'Youth Parliament Session" by the participants
11.45 a.m. to 12.00 noon	**TEA BREAK**
SESSION – VIII	
12.00 noon to 12.45 p.m.	Question-answer session to be handled by the Officers of Ministry of Parliamentary Affairs, Government of India, New Delhi.
12.45 p.m. to 2.00 p.m.	**LUNCH BREAK**
2.00 p.m. to 3.00 p.m.	Valedictory Function 1. Report of the participants on the Orientation Course 2. Distribution of Certificates 3. Vote of thanks by participants
SIGHT SEEING	

ANNEX XV-I

SCHEME OF FINANCIAL ASSISTANCE TO STATE GOVERNMENTS/ UNION TERRITORIES FOR ARRANGING 'YOUTH PARLIAMENT COMPETITIONS' IN RECOGNISED HIGH/ HIGHER SECONDARY SCHOOLS IN THE STATES/UNION TERRITORIES

Introduction

The idea of organising "Youth Parliaments' in educational institutions was conceived by the Fourth All India Whips' Conference held at Bombay in 1962 which made, *inter alia,* the following recommendation:

> "This committee recommends that Government should encourage holding of Mock Parliament in educational institutions and through Panchayats in rural areas."

The above recommendation was reiterated by the Fifth All India Whips' Conference held at Bangalore in 1966 in the following terms:

> "The conference observes that the Fourth All India Whips' Conference held at Bombay had recommended holding of Mock Parliaments in village Panchayats for prompting awareness of the role of representative institutions. The recommendation has not been implemented in some of the States. The conference reiterates that the State Governments concerned should be persuaded to reconsider their decisions."

In pursuance of the above recommendations, the Ministry of Parliamentary Affairs drew up a detailed scheme of Mock Parliament (now "Youth Parliament") Competitions and decided to introduce it on an experimental basis in the Higher Secondary Schools of Delhi. The Sixth and Seventh All India Whips' Conferences held at Shimla in 1967 and at Madras in 1969 respectively made the following recommendations:

> "While appreciating the work done by the Ministry of Parliamentary Affairs with regard to promotion of 'Youth Parliament' in schools in Delhi, the conference recommends very strongly that the States should also arrange to introduce the scheme in their respective States (6th AIWC),"
>
> "Keeping in view the successful execution of the 'Mock Parliament' scheme in Delhi schools, the wider appreciation it received from leading Parliamentarians, the Press and Educationists and with a view to build a strong Parliamentary System in the country, the conference strongly recommends that:
>
> (a) All the States/Union territories should take steps to implement the scheme in their respective States/ Union territories on the pattern adopted by the Central Ministry of Parliamentary Affairs;
>
> (b) The Central Ministry of Parliamentary Affairs should provide all encouragement to the States/ Union territories for introducing the scheme by offering financial assistance, if necessary; and
>
> (c) The Central Ministry of Parliamentary Affairs should also organise inter-State competitions of the States/Union territories which have started implementation of the scheme (7th AIWC)."

In pursuance of part (b) of the above recommendation, made by the 7th All India Whips' Conference, the Ministry of Parliamentary Affairs, Government of India, have drawn this scheme of financial assistance to State Governments/Union territories for arranging Youth Parliament Competitions in recognised Higher Secondary Schools in the States/Union Territories.

Objective of the Scheme: With a view to strengthen the roots of democracy, inculcate healthy habits of discipline, tolerance of views of others and to enable the student community to know something about the working of Parliament, the Ministry of Parliamentary Affairs, Government of India, have been holding annually a competition of "Youth Parliament" of such of the recognized educational institutions in Delhi as may like to take part in it and are sponsored by the Directorate of Education, Government of NCT of Delhi, Delhi. The objective of the scheme is to give financial assistance to the State Governments/Governments of Union territories to organize similar competitions in their recognized schools.

Operation of the Scheme: The scheme will be operated by the Department of Parliamentary Affairs of the States/Uts' Governments concerned in collaboration with the Director of Education/Public Institution of the State/Union territory concerned. In a State/Union territory, where there is no Department of Parliamentary Affairs, the scheme will be operated by the Directorate of Education/Public Institutions.

Eligibility for Entry into the Competition: All recognized Higher Secondary (Girls as well as Boys) educational institutions/ High Schools in the State/Ut concerned can take part in the competition. The list of participating schools will be finalized by the Ministry of Parliamentary Affairs or the Directorate of Education/Public Institutions concerned as the case may be, by the 31st of March every year.

Period during which the Competition of Youth Parliament will be held: The competition of Youth Parliament will be held every year. The detailed programme shall be drawn up by the Ministry of Parliamentary Affairs/Directorate of Education/Public Institutions of the State/Ut concerned and circulated to the institutions taking part in the annual competition, under intimation to the Central Ministry of Parliamentary Affairs, New Delhi.

Number of Participants in the Youth Parliament: The number of persons constituting the Youth Parliament is not limited. However, it would appear desirable that there should be a limit in regard to the duration of a sitting. This would naturally mean that many of the participants may only have nominal sitting roles and may not be required to speak.

Duration of the Youth Parliament Session: The duration of the Youth Parliament sitting should not be more than an hour and out of this about 20 minutes may be devoted to the questions.

Subjects for Discussion at the Youth Parliament: It is not proposed to prescribe any particular subjects for questions and answers or other discussion. It would, however, be desirable that the matters raised in the Youth Parliament relate to subjects of welfare activity, defence of the country, social justice, social reforms, economic development, communal harmony, health, student discipline, etc. Each institution should be free to select its own subject, intimation about which may be conveyed to the Ministry of Parliamentary Affairs/Directorate of Education/Public Institutions of the State/Ut concerned before the commencement of the competition.

Language: The participants can speak in Hindi or English or the regional language to be specified by the Department of Parliamentary Affairs/Directorate of Education/Public Institutions of the State/Ut concerned.

Venue of the Youth Parliament: Each institution shall hold the Youth Parliament sitting in its own building or such other place of its choice as it may like. The competing institutions shall be required to intimate the venue of their sittings along with the information regarding subjects for discussion ten days before the date of the competition to the Ministry of Parliamentary Affairs/Directorate of Education/Public Institutions of the State/Ut concerned.

Prizes: There will be the following prizes :

(i) Shield (Parliamentary Shield);
(ii) Trophies for five institutions for meritorious performance in the competition, on the basis of the order of merit;
(iii) Individual merit prizes in the shape of Medals/Cups/Books for some selected participants from each institution. The total number of prizes should not exceed 80; and
(iv) Miscellaneous expenditure.

Note: The Department of Parliamentary Affairs/Directorate of Education/Public Institutions of the State/Ut concerned may vary the expenditure on each of the above four items to suit local conditions. The amount reimbursable annually will, however, not exceed Rs.1,00,000 (Rupees one lakh only).

The shield will be a running shield to be kept for a period of one year by the institution which stands first in the competition. However, if a particular institution wins the shield for three consecutive years, it will permanently retain the shield.

A certificate as in **Annex XV-E(I)** may be issued to all the institutions who take part in the competition.

A certificate as in **Annex XV-E(I)** may be issued to all the students who win individual merit prizes in the competition.

Committee of Judges: A Committee of Judges shall be constituted by the Ministry of Parliamentary Affairs/Directorate of Education/ Public Institutions of the State/Ut concerned consisting of educationists/Members of Legislative Assembly/Council and others connected with the running of Parliamentary Institutions. The Directorate of Education/Public Institution shall be an *ex-officio* member of the committee.

Considerations for Drawing up the Merit List : The Committee of Judges shall keep in view the following points while assessing the performance of the institutions:

		Marks
(i)	Discipline and decorum	10
(ii)	Observance of parliamentary procedures	20
(iii)	Selection of subjects for questions; for supplementaries and quality of answers thereto	20
(iv)	Selection of subjects for the debates	10
(v)	Delivery and quality of speeches delivered and standard of debates.	30
(vi)	General assessment of the performance as a whole	10
		Total: 100

Repeat Performance: The institutions declared first may be required to give a repeat performance at a venue and date to be decided by the Department of Parliamentary Affairs/Directorate of Education/Public Institutions of the State/Ut concerned at the time of Prize Distribution.

Report: The Department of Parliamentary Affairs/Directorate of Education/Public Institutions of the State/Ut concerned will send on conclusion of the competition a report indicating the number of schools which participated including the first five on the basis of the order of merit, number of individual merit prizes etc.

The details of expenditure incurred on the competition and Prize Distribution Function should be sent to the Ministry of Parliamentary Affairs, Government of India, New Delhi. The report will clearly and separately indicate the amount reimbursable to the State/Ut Governmenst by the Ministry of Parliamentary Affairs, Government of India. The report will be signed by a representative of the Ministry/Department in-charge of the scheme in the State/Ut concerned, not below the rank of Deputy Secretary. Full instructions about the payment in whose favour the cheque is to be drawn and the Head of Account etc. may be clear.

Limit of Reimbursement of Expenditure: The actual expenditure incurred by the State/Ut will be reimbursed by the Ministry of Parliamentary Affairs, Government of India, on the basis of the report and statement of expenditure up to the ceiling of Rs.1,00,000 (Rupees one lakh only).

ANNEX XV-I(I)

GOVERNMENT OF INDIA
MINISTRY OF PARLIAMENTARY AFFAIRS

"YOUTH PARLIAMENT COMPETITION"

This is to certify that .... participated in the 'Youth Parliament' Competition held in the year ....

SECRETARY
MINISTRY OF PARLIAMENTARY AFFAIRS

GOVERNMENT OF INDIA
MINISTRY OF PARLIAMENTARY AFFAIRS

"YOUTH PARLIAMENT COMPETITION"

This is to certify that ....student of ....Class of ....School, ...was awarded ....Prize for his/her meritorious performance in the .... 'Youth Parliament' Competition held in the year ....

SECRETARY
MINISTRY OF PARLIAMENTARY AFFAIRS

ANNEX XVI-A

F.No......................Leg.II
Government of India
Ministry of Parliamentary Affairs

90, Parliament House,
New Delhi.

Dated:

Subject: Orientation Course in Parliamentary Procedure and Practices for Under Secretaries/Section Officers/ Parliament Assistants/Assistants in various Ministries/Departments.

The undersigned is directed to state that this Ministry proposes to conduct the next Orientation Course in Parliamentary Procedure and Practices for Under Secretaries/Section Officers/Parliament Assistants/Assistants (not necessarily working in Parliament Unit) in various Ministries/Departments from...................... (Dates)......................(Time)....... in Parliament House, New Delhi. The objective of the training course is to acquaint the officers with the latest developments in Parliamentary Procedures and Practices and also to afford them an opportunity to come up with their difficulties in handling parliamentary work. The lectures on the various subjects (list enclosed) will be delivered by the officers of this Ministry dealing with the relevant subjects.

The Ministry of Home Affairs etc. are requested kindly to nominate Under Secretaries/Section Officers/Parliament Assistants/Assistants (not necessarily working in Parliament Units), for participation in the above course, indicating inter alia their designation, office address, telephone number etc. by..................... at the latest.

No allowances of any kind will be paid by the Ministry of Parliamentary Affairs to the officer deputed for the proposed course.

For any enquiry, the undersigned or Shri ....Section Officer (Telephone No.23034773) may be contacted.

( )
UNDER SECRETARY TO THE GOVT. OF INDIA
Tele. No.

To

All Ministries/Departments of the Govt. of India
(Establishment Sections),
New Delhi.

Encl: as above.

Copy to the Parliament Sections of Ministries/Departments.

Subjects to be Discussed during the Orientation Course

1. Legislative Business in Parliament
2. Parliament Questions
3. Matters raised under Rule 377/by way of Special Mentions and during Zero Hour
4. Powers, privileges, amenities and immunities of Members of Parliament
5. Government Assurances
6. Non-Legislative Business
   (Statements by Ministers in Parliament, Laying of Papers)
7. Parliamentary Committees
8. Subordinate Legislation
9. Private Members' Bills and Resolutions
10. Functioning of Consultative Committees, Nomination of Members of Parliament on Committees/Boards
11. Evolution of Parliamentary System and Constitutional provisions relating thereto

ANNEX XVI-B (I)

MINISTRY OF PARLIAMENTARY AFFAIRS
LEGISLATIVE-II SECTION

No.______________________ Date:

Subject: _______Orientation Course for Section Officers/ Parliament Assistants/Assistants in Parliamentary Procedure and Practices.

Venue: ____.

Dates: from __________________ to __________________.

Time: ____.

Day 1 (Time)	**Subject of discussion**
from________to________	Inauguration by Secretary/Joint Secretary, Ministry of Parliamentary Affairs, Group Photograph.
from________to________	"Government Legislative and Non-Legislative Business": *__________
from________to________	Visit to Chambers of Lok Sabha, Rajya Sabha and Central Hall.
from________to________	Lunch
from________to________	"Statements by Ministers in Paliament and laying of papers": *__________
from________to________	Interaction among participants Tea/Coffee.
from________to________	"Evolution of Parliamentary System and constitutional provisions relating thereto": *__________

* Name and designation of the officer concerned.

Day 2

from________to________ "Matters raised under Rule 377/ Special Mentions/Zero Hour" : *____________

from________to________ Tea/Coffee

from________to________ "Parliament Questions": *________

from________to________ Lunch

from________to________ "Financial Business, Private Members' Bills and Resolutions": *____________

from________to________ Interaction among participants/ Tea/Coffee

from________to________ "Subordinate Legislation": *____________

Day 3

from________to________ "Parliamentary Committees": *___________

from________to________ Tea/Coffee

from________to________ "Consultative Committees" : *____________

from________to________ Lunch

from________to________ "Power, privileges, amenities and immunities of Members of Parliament": * ____________

from________to________ "Implementation of Assurances" : *___________

from________to________ Objective type Test

from________ onwards Question-answer session, Valedictory, award of certificates.

( )
UNDER SECRETARY
Tele.No.

All officers concerned as per programme above/PPS to Secretary

Copy for information to all the officers of the level of Under Secretary and above with the request that they may kindly make it convenient to attend the concluding session of the course.

---

* Name and designation of the officer concerned

ANNEX XVI-B(II)

MINISTRY OF PARLIAMENTARY AFFAIRS
LEGISLATIVE-II SECTION

F.No.________________________ Date:

Programme

ORIENTATION COURSE IN PARLIAMENTARY PROCEDURE AND PRACTICES FOR OFFICERS OF STATE GOVERNMENTS/ LEGISLATURES.

Duration: ________to __________

Day 1 (Time)	**Subject of discussion**
from________to________	1. Introduction/meeting with Secretary, Ministry of Parliamentary Affairs
from________to________	2. "Origin, growth and functioning of Central Ministry of Parliamentary Affairs" : *______
from________to________	3. "Meeting with Leaders of Opposition Parties/Groups in Parliament and welfare of Members of Parliament": *____________
from________to________	4. Visit to Lok Sabha, Rajya Sabha Chambers, Central Hall, Parliament House, Parliament Library
Day 2	
from________to________	1. "Parliament Questions, Statements by Ministers. Laying of Papers": *___________
from________to________	2. "Government Assurances" : *_____________
from________to________	3. Visit to Assurances' Sections

Day 3

from_______to_______ 1. "All India Whips' Conference, Youth Paliament Competitions": *___________

from_______to_______ 2. "Matters raised under Rule 377/ Special Mentions/Zero Hour" : *___________

from_______to_______ 3. Visit to Leg.I and II Sections

Day 4

from_______to_______ 1. "Parliamentary Committees with Special reference to Committee on Subordinate Legislation": *___________

from_______to_______ 2. "Consultative Committees, nomination of Members of Parliament on Government Bodies etc.": *___________

from_______to_______ 3. Visit to R&C and ME Sections

Day 5

from_______to_______ 1. "Financial and Non-Legislative Business": *___________

from_______to_______ 2. "Legislative Business": *_______

from________onwards 3. Question-answers session, Valedictory, award of Certificates.

( )
UNDER SECRETARY TO THE GOVT. OF INDIA
PHONE:

All officers concerned as per programme above/PPS to Secretary.

Copy for information to all the officers of the level of Under Secretary and above with the request that they may kindly make it convenient to attend the concluding session of the course.

---

* Name and designation of the officer concerned

ANNEX XVI-C

संसदीय पद्धति एवम् प्रक्रिया पाठ्यक्रम

COURSE IN PARLIAMENTARY PROCEDURES AND PRACTICES

भारत सरकार
GOVERNMENT OF INDIA
संसदीय कार्य मंत्रालय
MINISTRY OF PARLIAMENTARY AFFAIRS

प्रमाणित किया जाता है कि ....ने ....से .... तक, संसदीय मंत्रालय द्वारा आयोजित संसदीय पद्धति एवं प्रक्रिया में अभिविन्यास पाठ्यक्रम में भाग लिया।

नई दिल्ली
दिनांक

सचिव

This is to certify

that ....participated in the Orientation Course in Parlimentary Procedure and Practices conducted by the Ministry of Parliamentary Affaris from .... to ....

New Delhi
Date

Secretary

ANNEX XVI-D

Ministry of Parliamentary Affairs
(Legislative-II Section)

ORIENTATION COURSE IN PARLIAMENTARY PROCEDURE AND PRACTICES FROM...

APPRECIATION SHEET

What in your view should be the duration of the Course ?

State whether you are satisfied with the lectures

How would you rate the Course conducted ?

- Excellent
- Very good
- Good
- Satisfactory

(Strike off whichever is not applicable)

Any suggestions for improvement ?

Signature

Name in Capital Letters
Ministry/Department ________

Telephone No.

New Delhi.

Dated: ________________

ANNEX XVI-E

ORIENTATION COURSE IN PARLIAMENTARY PROCEDURE AND PRACTICES

OBJECTIVE TEST

1. The period of Notice of a Motion for leave to introduce a Private Member's Bill:

   a) 7 days
   b) 15 days
   c) one month

2. One copy of the document proposed to be laid on the Table of the House by a Ministry must be authenticated by the concerned Minister:

   a) True
   b) False

3. When the Lok Sabha is not in session, all Notifications issued during the inter-session period should be laid within 7 days of the commencement of the next session:

   a) True
   b) False

4. When a Minister finds that incorrect information has been given to the House in reply to a Question or during a discussion, he may make a statement or lay it on the Table of the House:

   a) True
   b) False

5. Whenever a Bill seeking to replace an Ordinance is introduced, a statement should be laid explaining the circumstances which had necessitated immediate legislation by Ordinance:

   a) True
   b) False

6. Who can Chair the meetings of the Consultative Committees?

   a) Minister-in-charge
   b) Minister of Parliamentary Affairs
   c) Minister of State of the concerned Ministry

7. What is the number of meetings of the Consultative Committee, a Ministry is required to hold ?

   a) Six times in a year
   b) Thrice in a year
   c) One each during session and inter-session period.

8. How many meetings of a Consultative Committee can be held outside Delhi in a calender year ?

   a) Two meetings
   b) One meeting
   c) No meeting

9. What is the time schedule for circulation of papers such as Agenda/Minutes/Action Taken Report in connection with the meetings ?

   a) 10 days before the meeting
   b) One week before the meeting
   c) No time limit

10. What is the normal ratio of Members of the Lok Sabha and Rajya Sabha for nomination on any Government Body ?

a) 3:1
b) 2:1
c) 1:1

11. What constitutes an assurance?

a) Information is not available
b) Information has been called for
c) The matter is being looked into
d) The matter is subjudice
e) An undertaking or indication to give further information, report back reg. action taken, outcome of examination, consideration, investigation, etc.

12. What should be done when the required information is not forthcoming from States/Union territories for a long time :

a) Wait until complete information is available
b) Send part Implementation Report (I.R.) giving available information
c) Give available information and mention the factual position in respect of defaulting States/Union territories in the Implementation Report.

13. i. Whose approval is necessary to the I.R.; and
ii. do you have to indicate it anywhere :

i) a. Secretary
b. Minister
c. Minister of State concerned

ii) a. No
b. In the I.R.
c. In the forwarding letter

14. In what circumstances can you make a request for dropping of an assurance :

a) Never

b) When voluminous information is to be collected and the efforts involved are not commensurate with the result to be achieved.
c) When policy decision is to be taken and there is lot of uncertainty/circumstances are changing.
d) When the matter cannot be dealt with within some prescribed time-frame.
e) When the Ministry feel that the reply was complete and should not be treated as assurance for specified reasons.

15. An I.R. should contain :

a) All the available information on the subject.
b) Only in accordance to the promise made with reference to the Question/subject matter.
c) Least possible.

16. A copy of the reply sent to the Member of Parliament must also be endorsed to the concerned Parliament Secretariat and the Ministry of Parliamentary Affairs: (Matter under Rule 377/Special Mention)

a) True
b) False

17. If matter addressed to a Ministry is transferred to another Ministry but not yet accepted by the latter, it will continue to pend against the former:

a) True
b) False

18. Matters under Rule 377 in Lok Sabha which are awaiting replies to the concerned Members of Parliament lapse on the dissolution of the Lok Sabha:

a) True
b) False

19. Special Mentions raised in Rajya Sabha, which are pending in the Ministry, will lapse if the Members who had raised these, have expired/retired:

    a) True
    b) False

20. Prior recommendation of the President is required for introduction of certain Bills in Parliament. Name the article under which such a recommendation is necessary.
21. A Money Bill shall not be introduced in the Council of States. State the relevant article of Constitution in this regard.
22. The quorum to constitute a meeting of either House of Parliament has been specified in the Constitution. Tick (Ö) the relevant article:

    i) Article 98
    ii) Article 94
    iii) Article 101
    iv) Article 100

23. Under the Constitution, no amount can be withdrawn from the Consolidated Fund of India without the enactment of such a law by Parliament. Tick (Ö) the relevant article:

    i) Article 112
    ii) Article 113
    iii) Article 114
    iv) Article 115

24. Every Proclamation issued by the President in terms of article 356 of the Constitution shall, except where it is a proclamation revoking a previous Proclamation, cease to operate at the expiry of a specified time unless before the expiration of that period it has been approved by resolutions of both Houses of Parliament where the Lok Sabha has not been dissolved. Specify the period laid down in the Constitution.

ANNEX XVI-F

D.O.No.......................Leg.II

JOINT SECRETARY

Dated:

Dear

As you are aware, Ministry of Parliamentary Affairs has been conducting Orientation Courses in Parliamentary Procedure and Practices for officers of Ministries/Departments with the approval of Department of Personnel and Training since 1985.

_________Orientation Course in Parliamentary Procedure and Practices for Under Secretaries/Section Officers/Parliament Assistants/Assistants of various Ministries/Departments was conducted by the Ministry in Parliament House, New Delhi from _____________to_________. _______ officials from various Ministries/Departments attended the course. Asked about their views on the usefulness of the course, all the participants expressed complete satisfaction with the course.

As per the periodicity being followed for these courses, the next course will be held during the inter-session period following the _______session _______.

With kind regards,

Yours sincerely,

( )

Shri ....
Joint Secretary (Trg.)
Department of Personnel and Training,
Old JNU Campus,
New Mehrouli Road,
New Delhi.

ANNEX XVI-G

MINISTRY OF PARLIAMENTARY AFFAIRS

SECRETARY

8, PARLIAMENT HOUSE,
NEW DELHI-110001

Dated:

D.O.No.________________

The X All India Whips' Conference held in New Delhi in November, 1988 had *inter alia* recommended that the Ministry of Parliamentary Affairs should draw a regular scheme of Training in the functioning of this Ministry for the benefit of personnel from the States/Union territories [Annex XVI-G(i)]. This recommendation was reiterated by the XI All India Whips' Conference held in Bangalore in January, 1994.

In pursuance of the above recommendations, eleven training courses for officers of various States have been organized. It has been decided to conduct the next training course in Parliamentary Procedure and Practices for the officers of the States Governments/ Union territory Administrations of approximately one week duration during ______________________in Parliament House, New Delhi. The exact date and duration of the course will be intimated in due course.

A list of subjects on which the training will be imparted to the officers is enclosed at [Annex XVI-G(ii)]. The lectures on various subjects and practical training in regard to day-to-day working of the Ministry will be imparted by the officers of this Ministry.

The expenses on TA/DA of officers deputed for the course will be borne by this Ministry. However, they will have to make their own board and lodging arrangements in Delhi, preferably in their respective State Bhavans.

As part of this training course the trainee officers will also be taken to the two Houses of Parliament to enable them to witness the proceedings of the Lok Sabha/Rajya Sabha live.

In case you have any topic/subject concerning the working of Parliament for inclusion in the programme, you may feel free to send your suggestion by________________________.

I request you to nominate two officers of the level of Under Secretary/Deputy Secretary from your State preferably from the Department of Parliamentary Affairs/Legislative Affairs, if any, for the proposed training course latest by ________________________, along with the bio-data of the officers, their residential/official addresses, telephone numbers etc. in the proforma enclosed at [Annex XVI-G(iii)]. You may please fax the information to this Ministry at Fax No.________________________.

With kind regards,

Yours sincerely,

(   )

Copy to: Resident Commissioners concerned

ANNEX XVI-G(I)

RECOMMENDATIONS OF TENTH ALL INDIA WHIPS' CONFERENCE

"The Central Ministry of Parliamentary Affairs should draw a regular scheme of training in the functioning of that Ministry for the benefit of personnel from the States/Union territories. Advantage should be taken by the States/Union territories by deputing their selected personnel to such training programmes to facilitate the setting up of an independent Department of Parliamentary Affairs to acquire understanding of the working of the Ministry at the Centre."

RECOMMENDATION OF ELEVENTH ALL INDIA WHIPS' CONFERENCE

Periodic Training Programmes in Legislature's Procedures for Officers dealing with Parliamentary Work

"Having been informed that the training programmes for officers of State Governments/Union territories Administrations in Parliamentary Procedure and Practices could not be conducted owing to reasons of economy, the conference is of the view that the Central Ministry of Parliamentary Affairs should seek necessary relaxation from the Ministry of Finance/Department of Personnel and Training to hold at least two training programmes per year considering the fact that such training programmes are of great help in exchange of knowledge and information about the procedures and practices prevelant at the Centre and in the various States/ Union territories and will lead to standardization of procedures and better performances of officials.

The trainers for such programmes may be drawn to the extent possible from sitting or ex-Members of Parliament, Members of Legislative Assemblies etc. "

ANNEX XVI-G(II)

LIST OF SUBJECTS TO BE TAKEN UP DURING THE TRAINING COURSE

1. Legislative Business.
2. Parliament Questions, Statements made by Ministers, Laying of Papers.
3. Matters raised under Rule 377/Special Mentions/Zero Hour.
4. Assurances.
5. Powers, Privileges and Immunities of Members of Parliament.
6. Financial and Non-Legislative Business.
7. Parliamentary Committees with Special reference to Committee on Subordinate Legislation.
8. Functioning of Consultative Committees - Nomination of Members of Parliament on Committees/Boards.
9. All India Whips' Conference, Youth Parliament Competitions, Welfare of Members of Parliament.
10. Origin, Growth and Functioning of Central Ministry of Parliamentary Affairs.
11. Evolution of Parliamentary Form of Government in India.

ANNEX XVI-G(III)

PROFORMA

Name :

Designation :

Present Scale of Pay :

Present Pay :

Entitlement for travel on official tour :
(Officer(s) nominated for the course will be paid T.A. by this Ministry as per their entitlement only)

Date of Birth :

Educational Qualification :

Office Address and Telephone No. :

Residential Address and Telephone No. :

Signature :

Counter Signature of the appropriate Administrative/ Sponsoring Authority

The officers nominated for the Orientation Course may be advised to familiarise themselves with the practice and procedures of their own State Legislature in regard to subjects mentioned in the enclosed list which are likely to be taken up for discussion during the proposed Orientation Course, to make it more interactive, interesting and informative. They may also be advised to bring with them, a statement showing briefly, the salary, allowances, facilities, pension, etc. admissible to the Members, Leaders of the Opposition, Chief Whips and Leaders of other recognized parties/ groups etc. of the Legislative Assembly/Council/former Members, for use in this Ministry.

ANNEX XVI-H

CHECK LIST

1. Whether required number of copies of training material and certificates are available or, if sent for printing, whether printed copies have been received.
2. Whether approval of Internal Finance Division has been received.
3. Whether the stationery asked for from Accounts and Purchase Section has been received.
4. Whether confirmation of booking of committee room has been received.
5. Whether letters sent to Caretaker/Reception Officer/Deputy Director, Parliament House Security (for arrangement/entry passes/show round)/Railway Catering Unit, Parliament House have been received by them and necessary arrangements are confirmed.
6. Whether the photographer will be reaching at appointed time.
7. Whether Attendance Sheets/Feedback Forms are ready.
8. Whether copies of the Objective Type Test paper are ready (for training programme for central Ministries).
9. Whether folders, containing the following are ready for participants and have been sent to the Secretary, Joint Secretary and other officers concerned:

   (i) Programme,
   (ii) List of Participants, and
   (iii) List of publications/material etc. being supplied to the participants.

ANNEX XVII-A

CHECK LIST
FOR GOVERNMENT SPONSORED GOODWILL DELEGATIONS TO BE SENT ABROAD

1. Invitation received from foreign countries (through Ministry of External Affairs) has been approved by the Minister of Parliamentary Affairs.
2. Period/duration of the visit is finalised.
3. Composition of delegation is to be decided by the Minister of Parliamentary Affairs in consultation with the Leaders/Chief Whips of concerned political parties.
4. Political clearance for the delegation is obtained from the Ministry of External Affairs.
5. Approval of Screening Committee/Finance Ministry and the Prime Minister are obtained for the concerned delegates.
6. Issue of financial sanction in respect of the expenditure to be incurred on the delegation. (local transport, gifts, brief cases, refreshments at briefing meeting/ceremonial lounges etc. to be taken into account. It does not include expenditure on bar, laundry etc.)
7. Itinerary of the delegation is finalised (Cooperation may be obtained from ITDC/Air India).
8. Meetings of the delegation with foreign dignitaries in the countries of visit have been fixed up and included in the programme of the delegation.
9. Letters to members of the delegation are sent by way of preliminary information seeking their willingness to join the delegation.
10. Collection of passports/photographs of the members of the delegation and other information, such as their dietary habits, blood group, etc.
11. To obtain Visa Note from the Ministry of External Affairs. (To complete necessary formalities for obtaining visa and visa fee from the respective Embassies.)

12. To collect Speeches and Talking Points for Minister (Leader of delegation) from the Ministry of External Affairs.
13. To collect Country Note/Facts Sheet from MEA regarding the countries to be visited.
14. To prepare bio-data of the Leader of the delegation and other delegates and send them to our Missions abroad.
15. Reservation/blocking of seats in Airlines on all routes including layover etc. (Ticketing/supply of diet-list/ passport numbers etc. to travel agent.)
16. Inform Members of the Delegation about the weather, clothing and other do's and don'ts (liquor, tobacco, laundry, long distance calls, pay TV etc.)
17. Distribution of Country Note, Facts Sheets, detailed programme along with telephone numbers of Hotels and Missions abroad to the members of the delegation.
18. To issue press release, if any.
19. To purchase Gifts for being presented in the countries of visit. (MEA/Missions concerned may be consulted about the kind and number of gifts.)
20. To arrange Airport passes for the staff on duty from the Office of Directorate General of Civil Aviation Security.
21. To issue letters to Airport Director, Customs, Immigration and Airport Police for extending necessary courtesy. (Arrangements to be made for ceremonial lounges, VIP parking, refreshment etc.)
22. Arrangements of transport for picking up of Members and tea/snacks at Airport Restaurant through ITDC.
23. Briefing meeting of Minister (Leader of the Delegation) with Delegates. (Officers of MEA to brief; arrange ITDC agent for foreign exchange; luggage tags for delegation; Immunisation for Yellow Fever, if required.)
24. Secretary to the delegation has to take the items of stationery i.e. letter-heads, papers, stapler, cello tape, James clips/nylon rope, scissors, etc.
25. DA to Members/staff to be paid before departure.
26. Tips at Hotels/Airport etc.
27. Missions to be alerted about Departure Tax in certain countries.
28. Our Missions to be advised about the number of vehicles/

coaches to be brought to the airport for taking the delegates/luggage. (Missions to be advised whether the luggage and delegates should be taken to Hotels in separate vehicles or together.)

29. To arrange for photographers through our Missions abroad.
30. Depute staff to see off (floral sending) and receive the delegation at airport.
31. Prepare and send report to (i) PMO; and (ii) MEA about the visit of Delegation on return.
32. Payment of bills received from Airlines, our Missions abroad etc.

ANNEX XVII-B

CHECK LIST FOR RECEIVING A FOREIGN DELEGATION IN INDIA

1. Approval of the proposal by HMPA (period/duration/ number of delegates/leader/preferences of meeting dignitaries/ places of visit).
2. Sending invitation to the country concerned through Ministry of External Affairs.
3. To draw draft itinerary, keeping in view their preferences etc.
4. To send confirmation of hosting through MEA. (Indicate prohibition on liquor, laundry, tobacco and long distance calls.)
5. To prepare approximate budget and obtain approval of expenditure/services.
6. To draw advance cash for meeting contingencies.
7. To prepare list of delegates/programmes.
8. To collect bio-data of delegates, Country Note, Fact Sheet, Talking Points with assistance from MEA.
9. To make arrangements for Hotel and transport (through government agencies).
10. To request the Joint Secretary (Security), Ministry of Home Affairs for making security arrangements round the clock, Pilot vehicles. Pilot vehicles provided should be better and speedier in quality.
11. To arrange transport (staff car/taxi) for staff on duty (prior approval of competent authority to be obtained).
12. Preparation of list of addresses/telephone numbers of important persons/offices concerned.
13. To obtain confirmation for calling on meetings with HMPA, MOSs (Parliamentary Affairs), Speaker (LS), Chairman (RS), Minister of External Affairs etc. as desired by the delegation. Limited number of delegates should call on dignitaries in case of big delegation.
14. Arrange lunch/dinner by HMPA/MOSs etc. (Prepare

list of invitees/booking of Hotels/Banquet Hall, ascertain menu, printing of Invitation Cards, issue of Invitation Cards).

15. To request the other dignitaries on whom the delegation would be calling, to host lunch/dinner to the delegation. Ministry of External Affairs should be consulted in case of any change initiated by the visiting side in appointment with dignitaries.
16. To arrange flight tickets (domestic)/railway tickets wherever necessary.
17. To request the Airport Director/Customs/Immigration/ Airport Security/ Ceremonial Lounge for extending necessary courtesies and ITDC Airport Restaurant for necessary refreshments.
18. To arrange Airport passes for staff on duty through the Bureau of Civil Aviation Security.
19. Arrange entry passes for Parliament House/other Government buildings (if necessary - Distinguished Visitor's Gallery passes, car passes, through Joint Secretary (Security), Lok Sabha Secretariat).
20. Letter to Rajghat Samadhi Samiti for making arrangements to offer floral tribute by the delegation to the Father of the Nation.
21. Letter to Archaeological Survey of India for making arrangements for visit of the delegation to historical monuments.
22. Letters to Chief Secretaries of concerned States, which the delegation would be visiting, for extending appropriate courtesies.
23. Letters to concerned District Magistrates of the cities to be visited for making necessary arrangements.
24. Arrangement for hiring battery coaches for visiting Taj Mahal at Agra and also for engaging host Guide for sight seeing of places of historical importance.
25. To send the bio-data of Minister/Ministers of State for Parliamentary Affairs, Government of India, to the concerned Embassy.
26. (a) Preparation of sufficient number of sets of papers/ material for distribution to delegates (e.g. list of delegates, programme, telephone list, bio-data of dignitaries to be

called on, bio-data of delegates, Talking Points, Fact Sheet, Country Note etc.).

(b) To provide bags, pens, note pads, programme, tourism material (if any) to the delegates.

27. To purchase gifts/momentoes (to be presented by HMPA/MOSs at the meeting or at dinner/lunch). The items of gifts to be presented should be decided sufficiently in advance.
28. To propose dinner Speech for HMPA/MOSs with assistance from the MEA.
29. To purchase bouquets (for welcome), Rose petals (for paying Homage at Rajghat)/and bouquet roses (for Send Off).
30. To prepare car/coach banners.
31. Arrangement of National flags of India and of visiting countries along with suitable stand.
32. Deployment of officers/staff of Ministry for work relating to delegation.
33. To arrange for a photographer.
34. Reception of delegation at Airport (Contact Airport Manager/Immigration Officer/Airline Staff/Customs and Carry bouquets/airport passes).
35. Press Note to Press Information Bureau/Web-site.
36. Farewell to delegates at Airport (meet Airport Manager/Immigration Officer/Customs Officer/Airport Police, booking of luggage/tags for Handbags with Security Check stamp, ask Ashok Airport Restaurant for Tea/Coffee/Snacks).
37. Adjustment of advance drawn.
38. Processing of bills received.
39. Letters of thanks to all concerned.
40. Prepare report about the visit of delegation and update the office records.

ANNEX XVIII-A

SECRET

Copy No.
Most Immediate
By Special Messenger

No.F.70(2)/2004-Leg.I
Government of India
Ministry of Parliamentary Affairs

8, Parliament House,
New Delhi.
Dated:

Subject: Meeting of the Cabinet Committee on Parliamentary Affairs

A meeting of the Cabinet Committee on Parliamentary Affairs will be held at .... a.m./p.m. on ....(day), ...the (date) in Room No. .... Parliament House, New Delhi to consider the following:

"Subject of the items included in the Agenda to be indicated here"

A copy of the Note on the Agenda is enclosed.

You are requested kindly to make it convenient to attend.

( )
SECRETARY
Tel.No.23034644

To

I -All the Members of the Committee

II -Copy forwarded to the Special Invitees with a request to attend the meeting

( )
SECRETARY

Copy forwarded for information to the Cabinet Secretariat (Shri ...., Deputy Secretary).

( )
DEPUTY SECERETARY

ANNEX XVIII-B

SECRET

Ministry of Parliamentary Affairs
(Sansadiya Karya Mantralaya)

Meeting of the Cabinet Committee on Parliamentary Affairs held at .... hours on ....in Room No.... Parliament House, New Delhi.

Present

(Names of the members of the Committee along with their portfolios to be mentioned here)

Also Present

(Names of the Ministers who are not members of the Committee but have been requested to attend the meeting as special invitees to be mentioned here along with their portfolios)

Also Present

(Names of the Ministers who have been nominated to the Committee as Special Invitees to be mentioned here along with their portfolios)

In Attendance

(Names of officers from various Ministries who attend the meeting to be mentioned here along with their designation)

Secretariat

Shri ...., Secretary, Ministry of Parliamentary Affairs; and

Shri ...., Joint Secretary, Ministry of Parliamentary Affairs.

Draft Minutes are submitted for approval.

( )
SECRETARY

Minister of Parliamentary Affairs and Urban Development

Minister of Defence

Secret

Subject: Prorogation of both Houses of Parliament

The Committee considered the note dated .... from the Ministry of Parliamentary Affairs (Sansidiya Karya Mantaralaya) and approved the proposal contained in paragraph .... thereof.

Secret

ANNEX XVIII-C

LIST OF PARLIAMENTARY SECRETARIES

1.	Shri Satish Chandra	w.e.f. 11.6.1951
2.	Shri S. N. Mishra	w.e.f. 11.6.1951
3.	Shri K.D. Malavyer	w.e.f. 5.6.1952
4.	Shri M.V. Krishnappa	w.e.f. 12.7.1952
5.	Shri Sadath Ali Khan	w.e.f. 17.11.1953
6.	Shri Mono Mohan Dass	w.e.f. 18.12.1953
7.	Shri G. Rajgopalan	w.e.f 18.12.1953
8.	Dr. K. L. Shrimali	w.e.f 18.12.1953
9.	Shri Kakshmi N. Menon	w.e.f 11.8.1952
10.	Shri Jogendra Nath Hazarika	w.e.f 11.8.1952
11.	Shri Shah Nawaz Khan	w.e.f 11.8.1952
12.	Shri B.R. Bhagat	w.e.f 11.8.1952
13.	Shri Sadath Ali Khan	w.e.f 18.7.1961 to 31.3.1962
14.	Shri Jogendra Nath Hazarika	w.e.f 18.7.1961 to 31.3.1962
15.	Shri Fateh Singh Rao Pratap Singhrao Gaekwad	w.e.f 18.7.1961 to 31.3.1962
16.	Shri Anand Chandra Joshi	w.e.f 18.7.1961 to 31.3.1962
17.	Shri Gajendra Prasad Sinha	w.e.f 18.7.1961 to 31.3.1962
18.	Shri Shyam Dhar Mishra	w.e.f 18.7.1961 to 31.3.1962
19.	Shri Anna Saheb Shinde	w.e.f 12.5.1962
20.	Shri D. Erring	w.e.f 12.5.1962
21.	Shri S.C. Jamir	w.e.f 12.5.1962
22.	Shri S. Ahmad Mehdi	w.e.f 12.5.1962
23.	Shri Dadder Thimmaiah	w.e.f 12.5.1962
24.	Shri M. R. Krishna	w.e.f 12.5.1962
25.	Shri Lalit Sen	w.e.f 6.9.1964
26.	Shri Annasahib Shinde	w.e.f. 15.1.1966
27.	Shri Lalit Sen	w.e.f. 15.1.1966
28.	Shri S.C. Jamir	w.e.f. 15.1.1966
29.	Shri Arun Singh	w.e.f. 12.11.1984 to 24.9.1985
30.	Shri Oscar Fernandes	w.e.f. 12.11.1984 to 24.9.1985
31.	Shri Ahmed Patel	w.e.f. 12.11.1984 to 24.9.1985
32.	Shri Nakul Naik	w.e.f. 24.11.1990 to 21.6.1991

N.B. From 1967 to 11.11.1984, no Parliamentary Secretary was appointed)

ANNEX XVIII-D

F.No. 26(1)/95-Welfare
MINISTRY OF PARLIAMENTARY AFFAIRS
GOVERNEMENT OF INDIA

Subject : Dinner arrangement for Members of Parliament and Staff etc. when Lok Sabha/Rajya Sabha sits late

Minutes of the meeting held on the above subject at 12.00 noon on Monday, 18th September, 1995 in Room No. 87, Parliament House, New Delhi.

Shri D.R. Tiwari, Joint Secretary, Ministry of Parliamentary Affairs, presided over the meeting.

The following officers from the various organisations were present:

Organisations	**Name of the officers**
Lok Sabha Secretariat	Sh. D.R. Kalra, U.S.
Rajya Sabha Secretariat	Sh. S.K. Ganguly, U.S.
C.P.W.D.	Sh. N.K. Sinha, E.E.
	Sh. A.K. Jain, E.E (Elec.)
	Sh. O.P. Bansal, E.E.(E)
	Sh. L. Dung, A.E.E.(Civil)
	Sh. S.K. Yadav, A.E.(Civil)
	Sh.A.P.S. Shishodia, JE(E)
Watch and Ward	Sh. M.M. Sharma, D.D. (G)
D.T.C.	Sh. A.K. Sharma, Dy. Gen. Manager
C.G.H.S.(First Aid Post)	Dr. (Smt.) B.S. Bais
Tea Board	Sh. Mahinder Singh, Regional Manager
Coffee Board	Sh. B.R. Natesh, Liaison Officer
M.T.N.L.	Sh.T.R. Sharma, SDO
D.M.S.	Sh. Ram Swaroop, Manager
	Miss R. Kapur, Assistant Manager

N. Railway Catering	Mrs T.R. Boaz, Dy. Commercial Manager Sh. Vivek Angra, Senior Commercial Manager Sh. Unny C. Mohan, Circle Inspector (Catering)
Parliamentary Affairs	Sh. I.D. Sharma, D.S. Sh. Vijay Khanna, U.S. Sh. Dharam Pal, S.O.

Joint Secretary, Ministry of Parliamentary Affairs, invited suggestions after explaining the difficulties in making proper arrangements for the dinner in the event of Houses sitting late. In the light of discussion following decisions were taken:

1. Food packets will be served to the staff and officers up to the rank of Under Secretary.
2. Food packets for staff will be delivered to designated officers of particular Department who shall make arrangement to collect and distribute them among officers and staff.
3. Proper Security arrangements would be made by Watch and Ward staff/officer at the Central Hall/Room No. 70 and at the venue of the distribution of food packets.
4. Only members of the Press and officers of the rank of Deputy Secretary and above will be allowed to take their meals with Members of Parliament.

With a view to make proper arrangements, it was decided that all Department heads concerned with late sitting of the Houses would send the actual number of persons required to be served dinner, snacks within a week.

They will also intimate the names of the officers who would be responsible for making arrangements for collection of the coupons/food packets for distribution among their staff.

The meeting ended with a vote of thanks to the Chair.

ANNEX XVIII-E

CHECK LIST REGARDING ARRANGEMENTS FOR DINNER/REFRESHMENT AND TRANSPORTATION WHEN THE HOUSE(S) SITS LATE

1. Obtain orders for dinner arrangement from the office of HMPA followed by confirmation in writing. Ascertain whether both Houses have to sit late or only one of them.
2. Alert Northern Railway Catering, Parliament House, telephonically. Discuss the menu with the Office of HMPA and Senior Commercial Officer, Northern Railway Catering.
3. Decide the number of invitees i.e. MPs, press personnel and officers of the rank of Under Secretary and above and other staff on duty in consultation with the office of Minister of Parliamentary Affairs, Lok Sabha/Rajya Sabha Secretariats and the senior officers of the Ministry.
4. Prepare draft order to be sent to Northern Railway Catering indicating number of invitees i.e. MPs. press personnel and officers of the rank of Under Secretary and above and other staff on duty.
5. Prepare draft letter to be sent to Delhi Transport Corporation (DTC) for arrangement of buses on special hire, if the House is anticipated to sit beyond 2200 hours. Normally, 4 buses are hired to ply in different directions.
6. Obtain administrative approval of the competent authority to the estimated expenditure on 4 and 5 above.
7. Place order with the Northern Railway Catering, Parliament House.
8. Place order with Delhi Transport Corporation (DTC) for transport with endorsement to ATI, DTC in Parliament House.
9. Write to Watch and Ward for security deployment at venues of dinner for control and coordination.
10. Confirm the time of serving dinner from Railway Catering.

Intimate HMPA's office for announcement in the House through the Chair.

11. Prepare numbered coupons to be provided to the staff on duty.
12. Distribute coupons to various agencies against written requisition.
13. Supervise dinner arrangement/distribution at two venues (i.e. one for MPs and senior officers, and the other for staff members). Ensure due courtesy to Members of Parliament.
14. If the House(s) adjourn(s) before serving of dinner, cancellation order may be immediately given to the Railway Catering - first informally followed by formal cancellation order as soon as possible. Charges of perishable items etc. are, however, to be paid by the Ministry as per Railway Catering Rules.
15. Seek ex-post-facto approval of the expenditure from IFD.
16. Enter data in the relevant register maintained for the purpose in the Section.
17. Process the bills received from Northern Railway Catering, Delhi Transport Corporation and forward to A&P Section for payment.

परिशिष्ट 19क

हिन्दी अनुभाग

हिन्दी में मूल टिप्पण और आलेखन के प्रयोग को बढ़ावा देने के लिए नकद पुरस्कार योजना

(1) योजना का क्षेत्र और पात्रता

(क) संसदीय कार्य मंत्रालय के वे सभी अधिकारी और कर्मचारी इस योजना में भाग ले सकते हैं जो सरकारी काम पूर्णतः या कुछ हद तक मूल रूप से हिन्दी में करते हैं।

(ख) आशुलिपिक/टाईपिस्ट, जो सरकारी काम काज में हिन्दी के प्रयोग को बढ़ावा देने संबंधी किसी अन्य योजना के अंतर्गत आते हैं, इस योजना में भाग लेने के पात्र नहीं होंगे।

(ग) हिन्दी अधिकारी और हिन्दी अनुवादक जो सामान्यतः अपना काम हिन्दी में करते हैं वे इस योजना में भाग लेने के पात्र नहीं होंगे।

(घ) केवल वही अधिकारी/कर्मचारी पुरस्कार के पात्र होंगे जो वर्ष में कम से कम 20 हजार शब्द हिन्दी में लिखें। इसमें हिन्दी में मूल टिप्पण, प्रारूप तथा रजिस्टरों में इन्दराज शामिल होंगे।

(2) योजना की अवधि

यह योजना 1 अप्रैल, 2003 से 31 मार्च, 2004 तक की अवधि के लिए होगी। इस अवधि के दौरान किए गए काम के आधार पर ही पुरस्कारों का निर्धारण किया जाएगा।

(3) पुरस्कार

भाग लेने वाले कर्मचारी को इस वर्ष के दौरान उनके द्वारा हिन्दी में किए गए कार्य के आधार पर निम्नलिखित पुरस्कार किए जाएंगे:

प्रथम पुरस्कार (2 पुरस्कार)	प्रत्येक रुपये 100
द्वितीय पुरस्कार (3 पुरस्कार)	प्रत्येक रुपये 600
त तीय पुरस्कार (5 पुरस्कार)	प्रत्येक रुपये 300

परिशिष्ट 19ख

हिन्दी के प्रगामी प्रयोग की तिमाही प्रगति रिपोर्ट

अनुभाग का नाम ....
मार्च/जून/सितंबर/दिसंबर .... को समाप्त तिमाही के लिए निम्नलिखित जानकारी .... से संबंधित है।

यह जानकारी पूरी तरह सही है।

हस्ताक्षर ....
अनुभाग अधिकारी
तारीख ....

भाग 1. सभी अनुभागों द्वारा निम्नलिखित जानकारी दी जाएगी (यह जानकारी प्रत्येक तिमाही में दी जाए)

(1) राजभाषा अधिनियम, 1963 की धारा 3 (3) के अंतर्गत विनिर्दिष्ट कागजात जो इस तिमाही में जारी किए गए:

(1) कुल संख्या
(2) द्विभाषी
(3) केवल अंग्रेजी में
(4) केवल हिन्दी में

नोटः (1) धारा 3 (3) के अंतर्गत सामान्य आदेश, ज्ञापन, संकल्प, अधिसूचनाएं, नियम, करार, संविदा, टेंडर नोटिस, संसदीय रिपोर्ट, संसदीय प्रश्न आदि शामिल हैं।
(2) यह सूचना अनुभाग में उपलब्ध रिकार्ड तथा फाईलों से दी जाए।

विभाग के सभी अनुभाग अधिकारी, प्रोफोर्मा/फाईल पर प्रतिहस्ताक्षर करते समय इस बात को सुनिश्चित करें कि प्रतियोगी द्वारा अपने टिप्पण और आलेखन में अनावश्यक रूप में शब्दों का उपयोग करके यदि शब्दों की संख्या बढ़ाने की कोशिश की गई हो वहाँ वे अगर आवश्यक समझें तो शब्दों की गणना में उपयुक्त कमी कर दें। प्रतियोगियों द्वारा फाईल आदि पर की गई टिप्पणियों तथा आलेख (पत्रों की आफिस कॉपी आदि) को नष्ट न किया जाए ताकि आवश्यकता पड़ने पर उसकी जांच की जा सके।

प्रपत्र

श्री/श्रीमती/कुमारी .... की .... को समाप्त होने वाले सप्ताह में हिन्दी के मूल काम की साप्ताहिक विवरणी

क्रम.स.	तिथि	कुल फाइलों, रजिस्टरों आदि की संख्या जिनमें हिन्दी में काम किया गया	हिन्दी में लिखे गए टिप्पणी और आलेखन के शब्दों की संख्या	हिन्दी में किये गए और काम		उच्च अधिकारी के हस्ताक्षर (सप्ताह में एक बार)
				संक्षिप्त ब्यौरा	शब्दों की संख्या	
1	2	3	4	5	6	7

परिशिष्ट 19ख

हिन्दी के प्रगामी प्रयोग की तिमाही प्रगति रिपोर्ट

अनुभाग का नाम ....
मार्च/जून/सितंबर/दिसंबर .... को समाप्त तिमाही के लिए निम्नलिखित जानकारी .... से संबंधित है।

यह जानकारी पूरी तरह सही है।

हस्ताक्षर ....
अनुभाग अधिकारी
तारीख ....

भाग 1. सभी अनुभागों द्वारा निम्नलिखित जानकारी दी जाएगी (यह जानकारी प्रत्येक तिमाही में दी जाए)

(1) राजभाषा अधिनियम, 1963 की धारा 3 (3) के अंतर्गत विनिर्दिष्ट कागजात जो इस तिमाही में जारी किए गए:

(1) कुल संख्या
(2) द्विभाषी
(3) केवल अंग्रेजी में
(4) केवल हिन्दी में

नोटः (1) धारा 3 (3) के अंतर्गत सामान्य आदेश, ज्ञापन, संकल्प, अधिसूचनाएं, नियम, करार, संविदा, टेंडर नोटिस, संसदीय रिपोर्ट, संसदीय प्रश्न आदि शामिल हैं।
(2) यह सूचना अनुभाग में उपलब्ध रिकार्ड तथा फाईलों से दी जाए।

(2) हिन्दी में प्राप्त पत्रों की स्थिति

(राजभाषा नियम-5)

(क) अनुभाग में कार्यालय पद्धति मैनुअल के अध्याय 4, पैरा 12 (1) के अनुसार निर्धारित डायरी रजिस्टर के अनुसार हिन्दी में प्राप्त कुल पत्र ....

(ख) इनमें से कितनों के उत्तर अंग्रेजी में दिए गए ....

(3) अनुभाग द्वारा भेजे गए कुल पत्रों का ब्यौरा:-

प्रतिशत	हिन्दी में	अंग्रेजी में	भेजे गए पत्रों से पिछली तिमाही में	हिन्दी पत्रों का इस तिमाही में
	1	2	3	4
"क" क्षेत्र को				
"ख" क्षेत्र को				
"ग"क्षेत्र को				

नोटः (1) इस पत्राचार के साथ तार, टेलैक्स, फैक्स और मद संख्या 2 में दिखाए गए उत्तरस्वरूप हिन्दी/अंग्रेजी में प्रेषित की संख्या भी शामिल कर ली जाए।

(2) "ग" क्षेत्र को जो पत्र द्विभाषी भेजे गए हों उन्हें उक्त कालम 1 में शामिल करें। यदि पत्र मूल रूप से हिन्दी में तैयार किया गया हो और अपेक्षानुसार उसका अंग्रेजी रूपांतर किया गया हो।

(3) "ग" क्षेत्र में स्थित राज्य सरकारों/उनके कार्यालयों/व्यक्तियों/ को भेजे गए पत्रों की संख्या इस मद में शामिल न करें।

(4) अनुभाग में किए गए टंकण कार्य का विवरण

	हिन्दी में	अंग्रेजी में	हिन्दी में किए गए कार्य का विवरण
तिमाही के दौरान किए गए टंकण के कार्य का ब्यौरा			

(5) कंप्यूटर पर किए कार्य का ब्यौरा

	हिन्दी में	अंग्रेजी में	हिन्दी में किए गए कार्य का विवरण
तिमाही के दौरान किए गए कंप्यूटर के कार्य का ब्यौरा			

(6) फाइलों पर हिन्दी में कार्य

(क) तिमाही के अंत तक कुल कितनी फाइलें खोली गईं ....

(ख) इनमें से कितनी फाइलों पर हिन्दी में टिप्पणियां लिखी जा रही हैं ....

(7) शीर्षस्थ प्रशासनिक बैठकें

(क) तिमाही के दौरान हुई शीर्षस्थ प्रशासनिक बैठकों की संख्या ....

(ख) ऐसी कितनी बैठकों में वार्तालाप/ कार्रवाईयां पूरी तरह हिन्दी में की गई ....

परिशिष्ट 19एफ

संसदीय कार्य मंत्रालय

(हिन्दी अनुभाग)

विषयः हिन्दी के प्रगामी प्रयोग के लिए संसदीय कार्य मंत्रालय का वर्ष 2003-2004 के लिए वार्षिक कार्यक्रम।

भाग 1: मंत्रालय के सभी अधिकारियों और सभी अनुभागों के लिए

1.1 मंत्रालय द्वारा मूल पत्राचार में हिन्दी का प्रयोग (तार-बेतार, टेलेक्स, फैक्स, आरेख आदि सहित)

(राजभाषा विभाग द्वारा जारी कार्यक्रम के लिए निर्धारित लक्ष्य की मद संख्या 1)

(क)	मंत्रालय द्वारा "क" और "ख" क्षेत्र में स्थित केन्द्रीय सरकार के कार्यालयों को भेजे जाने वाले सभी पत्रादि केवल हिन्दी में होने चाहिए	लक्ष्यः 100%
(ख)	मंत्रालय द्वारा "क" और "ख" क्षेत्रों के राज्यों/संघ राज्य क्षेत्रों की सरकारों और उनके कार्यालयों को तथा उनमें व्यक्तियों को पत्र केवल हिन्दी में भेजे जाएं।	लक्ष्यः 100%
(ग)	मंत्रालय द्वारा "ग" क्षेत्र में स्थित केन्द्रीय सरकार के कार्यालयों को भेजे जाने वाले पत्रादि।	लक्ष्यः 100%

(घ) हिन्दी में प्राप्त पत्रों, हिन्दी के आवेदन या हिन्दी में हस्ताक्षर वाले आवेदन के उत्तर अनिवार्य रूप से हिन्दी में दिए जाएं। जिस अधिकारी के हस्ताक्षर से कोई पत्रादि जारी होता है स्वयं उसकी यह जिम्मेदारी है कि यदि पत्रादि हिन्दी में प्राप्त है तो उसका उत्तर हिन्दी में दिया जाए।

(ङ) मंत्रालय द्वारा भारत सरकार के अन्य मंत्रालयों/विभागों को भेजे जाने वाले पत्र आदि यथासंभव हिन्दी में भेजे जाएं।

(च) सामान्य जिम्मेदारी

राजभाषा अधिनियम की धारा 3 (3) के अंतर्गत संकल्प, सामान्य

आदेश, नियम अधिसूचना, करार, प्रशासनिक या अन्य प्रतिवेदन या प्रैस विज्ञप्ति आदि द्विभाषी रूप में ही जारी की जाए। किसी प्रकार के उल्लंघन के लिए हस्ताक्षर करने वाले अधिकारी को जिम्मेदार ठहराया जाएगा।

(राजभाषा विभाग द्वारा जारी नीति संबंधी प्रमुख निर्देश की मद संख्या 1)

(छ) अनुपालन के लिए प्रशासनिक प्रधान का उत्तरदायित्व

राजभाषा अधिनियम, 1976 के प्रावधान के अनुसार, सरकार के प्रशासनिक प्रधान का उत्तरदायित्व है कि वह यह सुनिश्चित करे कि राजभाषा अधिनियम और नियमों के उपबंधों और केन्द्रीय सरकार द्वारा इस बारे में जारी किए गए निर्देशों का समुचित रूप से अनुपालन हो रहा है। उसकी यह भी जिम्मेदारी है कि वह इस प्रयोजना के लिए उपयुक्त और प्रभावकारी जांच के वास्ते उपाय करें।

1.2 हिन्दी में टिप्पण

(राजभाषा विभाग द्वारा जारी कार्यक्रम के लिए निर्धारित लक्ष्य की मद संख्या 2)

मंत्रालय में कार्यरत सभी अधिकारी/कर्मचारी वर्ष के दौरान उन द्वारा लिखी जाने वाली कुल टिप्पणियों में से 50 प्रतिशत टिप्पणियां हिन्दी में लिखेंगे।

(लक्ष्य : 50%)

1.3 हिन्दी पुस्तकों आदि की खरीद पर पुस्तकालय के लिए उपलब्ध कुल अनुदान का % खर्च, जर्नल और मानक संदर्भ ग्रंथों को छोड़कर

(राजभाषा विभाग द्वारा जारी कार्यक्रम के लिए निर्धारित लक्ष्य की मद संख्या 6)

सभी अनुभाग अपने विषयों पर हिन्दी में उपलब्ध पुस्तकें खरीदने के लिए पुस्तकों की मांग लेखा और खरीद अनुभाग को भेजेंगे।

पुस्तकालयों के लिए उपलब्ध अनुदान की कम से कम 50 प्रतिशत राशि हिन्दी में उपलब्ध शब्दकोशों, शब्दावलियों, सहायक तथा संदर्भ साहित्य और अन्य हिन्दी पुस्तकों पर खर्च की जाएं।

(लक्ष्यः 50%)

1.4 मंत्रालय के अनुभागों में हिन्दी में कार्य-निष्पादन

सभी अनुभाग अधिकारी यह सुनिश्चित करें कि उनके अनुभाग में विनिर्दिष्ट (जैसा कि नीचे दर्शाया गया है) की गई मात्रा में हिन्दी में कार्य हो।

सामान्य, हिन्दी, कार्यान्वयन-1, कार्यान्वयन-2, विधायी-2, प्रशासन 100%

अनुसंधान एवं सम्मेलन, प्रोटोकॉल और कल्याण, विधायी-1

सांसद परिलब्धियां, लेखा और क्रय समिति 50%

1.5 द्विभाषी वैबसाईट तैयार करना

(राजभाषा विभाग द्वारा जारी कार्यक्रम के लिए निर्धारित लक्ष्य की मद संख्या 8)

मंत्रालय के सभी अनुभाग यह सुनिश्चित करें कि वैबसाईट में उनके अनुभाग से संबंधित जो जानकारी भरी गई है अथवा भरी जानी है वह द्विभाषी (हिन्दी और अंग्रेजी) में हो। जिन अनुभागों ने अभी तक केवल अंग्रेजी में जानकारी भरी है वह उसका हिन्दी रूपांतर भी वैबसाईट में भरें।

(लक्ष्यः 100%)

1.6 कोड, मैनुअल, फार्म, प्रक्रिया साहित्य का हिन्दी अनुवाद

(राजभाषा विभाग द्वारा जारी कर्यक्रम के लिए निर्धारित लक्ष्य की मद संख्या 11)

सभी अनुभाग यह सुनिश्चित करें कि अनुभाग में प्रयोग होने वाले सभी प्रकार के कोड, मैनुअल, फार्म एवं प्रक्रिया साहित्य आदि का हिन्दी अनुवाद करवा लिया गया है। वर्ष के दौरान इसका लक्ष्य 100% रखा गया है।

(लक्ष्यः 100%)

1.7 राजभाषा हिन्दी के कार्यान्वयन में हुई प्रगति की समीक्षा मंत्रालय के प्रशासनिक प्रधानों द्वारा जी जाने वाली बैठक में करना

सरकार की राजभाषा नीति के प्रति अधिकारियों/कर्मचारियों को सुग्राही बनाने की द ष्टि से यह आवश्यक है कि सरकारी कामकाज में राजभाषा हिन्दी के कार्यान्वयन में हुई प्रगति की समीक्षा को मात्र राजभाषा कार्यान्वयन समिति की बैठकों तक ही सीमित न रखा जाए। इस संबंध में मानीटरिंग को और अधिक प्रभावी और कारगर बनाने के लिए यह जरूरी है कि मंत्रालयों/विभागों/कार्यालयों के प्रशासनिक प्रधानों द्वारा ली जाने वाली प्रत्येक बैठक में इस पर नियमित रुप से विस्त त चर्चा की जाए और इसे कार्यव त्त के एक स्थायी मद के रूप में शामिल किया जाए।

(राजभाषा विभाग द्वारा जारी नीति संबंधी प्रमुख निर्देशों की मद संख्या 12)

भाग-2 विभिन्न अनुभागों के लिए

2.1 हिन्दी अनुभाग के लिए

(क) हिन्दी प्रशिक्षण

(राजभाषा विभाग द्वारा जारी कार्यक्रम के लिए निर्धारित लक्ष्य की मद संख्या 5)

मंत्रालय में कार्यरत सभी अधिकारियों/कर्मचारियों/को हिन्दी में प्रशिक्षित होना चाहिए। प्रशिक्षण के लिए शेष कर्मचारियों को प्रशिक्षण के लिए नामित किया जाए और वे पूरी तत्परता से प्रशिक्षण प्राप्त करें।

(लक्ष्यः 100%)

(ख) हिन्दी कार्यशाला का आयोजन

मंत्रालय में प्रत्येक वित्तीय वर्ष के दौरान तीन हिन्दी कार्यशालाओं का आयोजन किया जाएगा।

(ग) हिन्दी पखवाड़ा/दिवस का आयोजन

सरकारी कामकाज में राजभाषा के रुप में हिन्दी के प्रति जागरूकता तथा उसके प्रयोग में गति लाने के लिए मंत्रालय में हिन्दी पखवाड़ा/दिवस का आयोजन हर वर्ष किया जाएगा।

(घ) मंत्रालय के अनुभागों का निरीक्षण

[राजभाषा विभाग द्वारा जारी कार्यक्रम के लिए निर्धारित लक्ष्य की मद संख्या 9 (2)]

वर्ष में अनुभागों का एक बार निरीक्षण तिमाही-बद्ध कार्यक्रम द्वारा किया जाएगा।

(लक्ष्यः 25%न्यूनतम)

(ङ) हिन्दी सलाहकार समिति की बैठकें

[राजभाषा विभाग द्वारा जारी कार्यक्रम के लिए निर्धारित लक्ष्य की मद संख्या 10(क)]

हिन्दी सलाहकार समिति की वर्ष में कम से कम तीन बैठकें आयोजित की जाएं।

[लक्ष्यः वर्ष में 3 बैठकें (न्यूनतम)]

(च) राजभाषा कार्यान्वयन समिति की बैठकें

[राजभाषा विभाग द्वारा जारी कार्यक्रम के लिए निधारित लक्ष्य की मद संख्या 10 (ग)]

राजभाषा कार्यान्वयन समिति की वर्ष में चार बैठकें अर्थात प्रत्येक तिमाही में एक बैठक आयोजित की जाएं जिसमें हिन्दी के कार्यान्वयन में हुई प्रगति पर नियमित रूप से विस्त त चर्चा की जाए।

[लक्ष्यः वर्ष में 4 बैठकें (प्रति तिमाही एक बैठक)]

(छ) मंत्रालय/विभाग के ऐसे अनुभाग जहाँ सारा कार्य हिन्दी में हो

(राजभाषा विभाग द्वारा जारी कार्यक्रम के लिए निर्धारित लक्ष्य की मद संख्या 12)

हिन्दी अनुभाग वर्ष के अन्त तक कम से कम 7 अनुभागों में 100 प्रतिशत कार्य हिन्दी में करवाने के लिए कार्रवाई करे।

(लक्ष्यः न्यूनतम 7 अनुभाग)

(ज) अनुवादकों के लिए शब्दकोश उपलब्ध करना

लेखा और क्रय अनुभाग अनुवादाकों को मानक शब्दकोश (अंग्रेजी–हिन्दी व हिन्दी–अंग्रेजी) तथा अन्य तकनीकी शब्दावलियां उपलब्ध कराना सुनिश्चित करे ताकि वे अनुवाद कार्य में इनका उपयोग कर सकें।

(राजभाषा विभाग द्वारा जारी राजभाषा नीति संबंधी प्रमुख निर्देशों की मद संख्या 15)

2.2 सामान्य अनुभाग के लिए

(क) निर्धारित कागजातों को हिन्दी अथवा द्विभाषी रूप में भेजना

सामान्य अनुभाग में जांच बिन्दु स्थापित किया गया है जो यह सुनिश्चित करेगा कि राजभाषा अधिनियम, 1963 की धारा 3(3) में उल्लिखित सभी दस्तावेज आदि हिन्दी तथा अंग्रेजी दोनों भाषाओं में जारी होने चाहिए। इसके लिए सामान्य अनुभाग, जहाँ ऐसे दस्तावेज साइक्लोस्टाइल किए जाते हैं, में जांच बिन्दु बनाया गया है और ऐसे दस्तावेज तभी साइक्लोस्टाइल किए जाएं जब उनका हिन्दी रूपांतर भी साथ भेजा गया हो। साथ ही सामान्य अनुभाग जो इन दस्तावेजों के प्रेषण का काम करता है, वह यह सुनिश्चित करें कि सभी प्रकार के दस्तावेज साथ–साथ हिन्दी में भी जारी हो रहे हैं। जारी करते समय यह ध्यान रखा जाए कि हिन्दी रूपांतर अंग्रेजी रूपांतर के ऊपर/पहले रहे।

सामान्य अनुभाग जिसे जांच बिन्दु बनाया गया है, वह अनुभाग यह सुनिश्चित करे कि "क" तथा "ख" क्षेत्रों की राज्य सरकारों को जाने वाले पत्रादि आदि को प्रेषण के लिए तभी स्वीकार करें जब ये हिन्दी में हों या उनका हिन्दी अनुवाद साथ हो।

यदि ऐसा कोई पत्र केवल अंग्रेजी में जारी करने के लिए प्राप्त होता है तो उसे हिन्दी रूपांतर के बिना जारी न किया जाए। यदि कोई पत्र अंग्रेजी में जारी करना अति आवश्यक हो जाए तो उसके लिए राजभाषा अधिकारी (संयुक्त सचिव) के लिखित आदेश ले लिए जाएं। जारी करते समय वह अनुभाग यह ध्यान रखे कि हिन्दी रूपांतर अंग्रेजी रूपांतर के ऊपर/पहले रहे।

(ख) लिफाफों पर हिन्दी में पते लिखना

सामान्य अनुभाग यह सुनिश्चित करे कि "क" और "ख" क्षेत्र को जाने वाले पत्रों के लिफाफों पर पता देवनागरी लिपि में हो।

(ग) देवनागरी टाईपराईटर की खरीद

(राजभाषा विभाग द्वारा जारी कार्यक्रम के लिए निर्धारित लक्ष्य की मद संख्या 4)

सामान्य अनुभाग यह सुनिश्चित करे कि मंत्रालय में केवल अंग्रेजी के की-बोर्ड (कुंजी-पटल) का कोई भी टाईपराईटर न हो। अंग्रेजी की-बोर्ड के जो टाईपराईटर इस समय मंत्रालय में उपलब्ध हैं उनका कुंजी-पटल बदलवा कर देवनागरी हिन्दी में करवा लिया जाए ताकि वर्ष 2003–2004 तक सभी टाईपराईटर देवनागरी के अथवा द्विभाषी हो जाएं। मंत्रालय में 100 प्रतिशत टाईपराईटर हिन्दी के होने चाहिए। सामान्य अनुभाग यह सुनिश्चित करे कि मंत्रालय के प्रत्येक अनुभाग में कम से कम एक हिन्दी टाईपराईटर होना चाहिए।

(लक्ष्यः 100%)

(घ) कोड, मैनुअल, फार्म, प्रक्रिया साहित्य का हिन्दी अनुवाद

सामान्य अनुभाग कोड, मैनुअल, फार्म, प्रक्रिया साहित्य का द्विभाषी प्रकाशन सुनिश्चित करे।

(लक्ष्यः 100%)

2.3 लेखा और क्रय अनुभाग के लिए

(क) अनुवादकों को मानक शब्दकोश उपलब्ध कराना

लेखा और क्रय अनुभाग अनुवादकों को मानक शब्दकोष (अंग्रेजी–हिन्दी व हिन्दी–अंग्रेजी) तथा अन्य तकनीकी शब्दावलियां उपलब्ध कराना सुनिश्चित करे ताकि वे अनुवाद कार्य में इनका उपयोग कर सकें।

(राजभाषा विभाग द्वारा जारी नीति संबंधी प्रमुख निर्देशों की मद संख्या 15)

(ख) मंत्रालय में हिन्दी टाईपराईटरों की खरीद

(राजभाषा विभाग द्वारा जारी कार्यक्रम के लिए निर्धारित लक्ष्य की मद संख्या 4)

वार्षिक कार्यक्रम के अनुसार मंत्रालय में हिन्दी टाईपराईटरों का लक्ष्य 100 प्रतिशत रखा गया है। लेखा और क्रय अनुभाग यह सुनिश्चित करे कि भविष्य

में खरीदे जाने वाले टाईपराईटर देवनागरी अर्थात हिन्दी की-बोर्ड (कुंजी-पटल) के हों अथवा द्विभाषी हों।

(लक्ष्य 100%)

(ग) पत्र-शीर्ष, स्टेशनरी, लिफाफे, नाम-पट्ट, रबड़ की मोहरें, सूचना पट्ट, मोहर, सील, रजिस्टर, साईन बोर्ड, आमंत्रण-पत्र आदि द्विभाषी छपवाना

लेखा और क्रय अनुभाग इन सभी को भी द्विभागी रूप में छपवाएं/बनवाएं।

(घ) सभी प्रकार के इलैकट्रोनिक उपकरणों की द्विभाषी रूप में खरीद

(राजभाषा विभाग द्वारा जारी कार्यक्रम के लिए निर्धारित लक्ष्य की मद संख्या 7)

लेखा और क्रय अनुभाग यह सुनिश्चित करे कि यांत्रिक सुविधाएं जैसे कि इलैक्ट्रोनिक टाईपराईटर आदि खरीदते समय राजभाषा विभाग द्वारा इनके केवल द्विभाषी खरीदने के बारे में जारी आदेश का पूर्णतः पालन हो। इलैक्ट्रानिक टाईपराईटर शत् प्रतिशत द्विभाषी खरीदे जाएं।

(लक्ष्यः 100%)

(ङ) हिन्दी पुस्तकों आदि की खरीद पर पुस्तकालय के लिए उपलब्ध कुल अनुदान का खर्च, जर्नल और मानक संदर्भ ग्रंथों को छोड़कर

(राजभाषा विभाग द्वारा जारी कार्यक्रम के लिए निर्धारित लक्ष्य की मद संख्या 6)

लेखा और क्रय अनुभाग यह सुनिश्चित करें कि पुस्तकालयों के लिए उपलब्ध अनुदान की कम से कम 50 प्रतिशत राशि हिन्दी में उपलब्ध शब्दकोशों, शब्दावलियों, सहायक तथा संदर्भ साहित्य और अन्य हिन्दी पुस्तकों की खरीद करने हेतु खर्च की जाए।

(लक्ष्यः 50%)

2.4 प्रशासन अनुभाग के लिए

(क) हिन्दी टंकक, आशुलिपिक की भर्ती

राजभाषा विभाग द्वारा जारी कार्यक्रम के लिए निर्धारित लक्ष्य की मद संख्या प्रशासन अनुभाग कर्मचारियों की भर्ती करते समय यह सुनिश्चित करें कि हिन्दी टंककों और हिन्दी आशुलिपिकों की ही नियुक्ति की जाए।

(राजभाषा विभाग द्वारा जारी नीति संबंधी प्रमुख निर्देशों की मद संख्या 5)

(लक्ष्यः 100%)

(ख) सेवा-पुस्तिका (सर्विस बुक)/रजिस्टरों में प्रविष्टियां

प्रशासन अनुभाग यह सुनिश्चित करें कि मंत्रालय के अधिकारियों एवं कर्मचारियों की सेवा-पुस्तिका/रजिस्टरों में प्रविष्टियां हिन्दी में की जाएं।

(ग) सभी प्रकार के टेलीप्रिन्टर/कम्पयूटर इत्यादि मंत्रों में द्विभाषी सुविधा उपलब्ध हो

(घ) कार्यालय में बैठने के लिए समुचित स्थान

प्रशासन अनुभाग प्रशिक्षण और कार्यशालाओं सहित हिन्दी में कार्य कर रहे अधिकारियों/कर्मचारियों को भी कार्यालय में बैठने के लिए अच्छा और समुचित स्थान उपलब्ध करवाएं ताकि वे अपने कर्तव्यों का निर्वाह ठीक तरह से कर सकें।

(राजभाषा विभाग द्वारा जारी नीति संबंधी निर्देशों की मद संख्या 13)

(ङ) भारतीय प्रशासनिक सेवा/अन्य अखिल भारतीय सेवा के अधिकारियों को हिन्दी भाषा का प्रशिक्षण दिलाना

भारतीय प्रशासनिक सेवा और अन्य अखिल भारतीय सेवा के अधिकारियों के लिए लाल बहादुर शास्त्री प्रशासनिक अकादमी, मसूरी में प्रशिक्षण के दौरान हिन्दी भाषा का प्रशिक्षण अनिवार्य रूप से दिया जाता है ताकि सरकारी कामकाज में वह इसका प्रयोग कर सकें। परन्तु अधिकांश अधिकारी सेवा में आने के पश्चात् सरकारी काम काज में हिन्दी का प्रयोग नहीं करते। इससे उनके अधीन कार्य कर रहे अधिकारियों/कर्मचारियों में सही संदेश नहीं जाता। परिणामस्वरूप, सरकारी कामकाज में हिन्दी का प्रयोग अपेक्षित मात्रा में नहीं हो पाता। मंत्रालयों/विभागों/कार्यालयों/ उपक्रमों आदि के वरिष्ठ अधिकारियों का यह संवैधानिक दायित्व है कि वह अपने सरकारी कामकाज में अधिक से अधिक हिन्दी का प्रयोग करें। इससे उनके अधीन कार्य कर रहे अधिकारियों/कर्मचारियों को प्रेरणा मिलेगी तथा राजभाषा नीति के अनुपालन को गति मिलेगी।

(राजभाषा विभाग द्वारा जारी नीति संबंधी निर्देशों की मद संख्या 9)

2.5 अनुसंधान और सम्मेलन अनुभाग के लिए

(क) युवा संसद के आयोजन के लिए साहित्य आदि हिन्दी में उपलब्ध कराया जाए।

(ख) युवा संसद में संबंधित अभिविन्यास पाठ्यक्रम के लिए साहित्य/सामग्री हिन्दी में भी उपलब्ध कराई जाए।

(राजभाषा विभाग द्वारा जारी नीति संबंधी प्रमुख निर्देशों की मद संख्या 4)

2.6 विधायी-2 अनुभाग के लिए

संसदीय कार्य में लगे अधिकारियों एवं विभिन्न केन्द्रीय और राज्य मंत्रालयों/विभागों के अधिकारियों के लिए अल्पावधि प्रशिक्षण पाठ्यक्रम का साहित्य हिन्दी में भी उपलब्ध कराया जाए।

(राजभाषा विभाग द्वारा जारी नीति संबंधी निर्देशों की मद संख्या 4)

वार्षिक कार्यक्रम के संबंध में सामान्य सूचना

1. सामान्य आदेश की परिभाषा

सामान्य आदेश में निम्नलिखित सम्मिलित हैं:

(क) ऐसे सभी आदेश, निर्णय या अनुदेश, परिपत्र जो विभागीय प्रयोग के लिए हों और स्थायी प्रकार के हों, तथा

(ख) ऐसे सभी आदेश, अनुदेश, पत्र, ज्ञापन, नोटिस, परिपत्र आदि जो सरकारी कर्मचारियों के समूह के संबंध में या उनके लिए हों।

2. हिन्दी में प्रवीणता की परिभाषा

किसी कर्मचारी के बारे में यह समझा जाएगा कि उसने हिन्दी में प्रवीणता प्राप्त कर ली है, यदि उसने:

(क) मैट्रिक परीक्षा या उसके समतुल्य या उससे ऊंची कोई परीक्षा हिन्दी के माध्यम से उत्तीर्ण कर ली है, या

(ख) स्नातक परीक्षा में अथवा स्नातक परीक्षा के बराबर या उससे ऊंची किसी परीक्षा में हिन्दी को एक वैकल्पिक विषय के रूप में लिया था, या

(ग) वह राजभाषा नियम में संलग्न प्रारूप में यह घोषणा करता है कि उसे हिन्दी में प्रवीणता प्राप्त है।

3. पत्र व्यवहार के लिए देश में "क", "ख" तथा "ग" क्षेत्रों का विवरण

"क" क्षेत्र में: बिहार, हरियाणा, हिमाचल प्रदेश, मध्य प्रदेश, दिल्ली, राजस्थान, उत्तर प्रदेश राज्य तथा अण्डमान और निकोबार द्वीप समूह संघ राज्य क्षेत्र;

"ख" क्षेत्र में: गुजरात, महाराष्ट्र, पंजाब राज्य तथा चण्डीगढ़ संघ राज्य क्षेत्र; और

"ग" क्षेत्र में: बाकी सभी राज्य और संघ राज्य क्षेत्र।

INDEX

अनुक्रमणिका